LINUX
IN A NUTSHELL

A Desktop Quick Reference

LINUX

IN A NUTSHELL

A Desktop Quick Reference

Jessica Perry Hekman

O'REILLY™

Cambridge · Köln · Paris · Sebastopol · Tokyo

Linux in a Nutshell

by Jessica Perry Hekman

Copyright © 1997 O'Reilly & Associates, Inc. All rights reserved.
Printed in the United States of America.

Published by O'Reilly & Associates, Inc., 101 Morris Street, Sebastopol, CA 95472.

Editor: Andy Oram

Production Editor: Jane Ellin

Printing History:

January 1997:   First Edition.

November 1997:   Minor corrections.

This book is printed on acid-free paper with 85% recycled content, 15% post-consumer
waste. O'Reilly & Associates is committed to using paper with the highest recycled
content available consistent with high quality.

ISBN: 1-56592-167-4

Table of Contents

Preface

This is a book about Linux, a freely available clone of the UNIX operating system for personal computers. Linux has been developed primarily by Linus Torvalds, who built the first Linux kernel, and a host of other programmers and hackers all over the world, all connected through the Internet. Beyond the kernel code, Linux includes utilities and commands from the Free Software Foundation's GNU project, Berkeley UNIX (BSD), and a complete port of the X Window System (XFree86) from the X Consortium, in addition to many features written specifically for Linux.

This book is a quick reference for the basic commands and features of the Linux operating system. As with other books in O'Reilly's "in a Nutshell" series, this book is geared toward users who know what they want to do and have some idea how to do it, but just can't remember the correct command or option. We hope this guide will become an invaluable desktop reference for the Linux user.

Other Resources

This book will not tell you how to install and maintain a Linux system. For that, you will need *Running Linux*, by Matt Welsh and Lar Kaufman. For networking information, check out *Linux Network Administrator's Guide* by Olaf Kirch. In addition to O'Reilly's Linux titles, our wide range of UNIX and X titles may also be of interest to the Linux user.

The Net is also full of information about Linux. One of the best resources is the Linux Documentation Project at *http://sunsite.unc.edu/mdw*. For online information about the GNU utilities covered in this book, FTP to *prep.ai.mit.edu* in the *pub/gnu* directory, or look on the Web at *http://www.delorie.com/gnu*.

Conventions

The desktop quick reference follows certain typographic conventions, outlined below:

Bold   is used for commands, programs, and options. All terms shown in bold are typed literally.

Italic   is used to show arguments, options, and variables that should be replaced with user-supplied values. Italic is also used to indicate filenames and directories, and to highlight comments in examples.

`Constant Width` is used to show the contents of files or the output from commands.

`Constant Bold`   is used in examples and tables to show commands or other text that should be typed literally by the user.

`Constant Italic` is used in examples and tables to show text which should be replaced with user-supplied values.

%, $ are used in some examples as the C shell prompt (%) and as the Bourne shell prompt ($).

[ ]   surround optional elements in a description of syntax. (The brackets themselves should never be typed.) Note that many commands show the argument [*files*]. If a filename is omitted, standard input (e.g., the keyboard) is assumed. End with an end-of-file character.

EOF   indicates the end-of-file character (normally **CTRL-D**).

| is used in syntax descriptions to separate items for which only one alternative may be chosen at a time.

→   is used at the bottom of a right-hand page to show that the current entry continues on the next page. The continuation is marked by a ←.

A final word about syntax. In many cases, the space between an option and its argument can be omitted. In other cases, the spacing (or lack of spacing) must be followed strictly. For example, **-w***n* (no intervening space) might be interpreted differently from **-w** *n*. It's important to notice the spacing used in option syntax.

Contact O'Reilly & Associates

We have tested and verified all of the information in this book to the best of our ability, but you may find that features have changed (or even that we have made mistakes!). Please let us know about any errors you find, as well as your suggestions for future editions, by writing:

O'Reilly & Associates, Inc.
101 Morris Street
Sebastopol, CA 95472
1-800-998-9938 (in the US or Canada)
1-707-829-0515 (international/local)
1-707-829-0104 (FAX)

You can also send us messages electronically. To be put on the mailing list or request a catalog, send email to:

info@oreilly.com   (via the Internet)

To ask technical questions or comment on the book, send email to:

bookquestions@oreilly.com (via the Internet)

Acknowledgments

I'd like to thank all my friends at O'Reilly for helping with this book—my editors, Andy Oram and Robert Denn; the production editor, Jane Ellin; Stephen Spainhour, who finished it when my RSI wouldn't let me do the work myself; Seth Maislin, who provided (as always) an excellent index; David Futato, who did the early production work; Madeleine Newell and Kismet McDonough-Chan, who also helped with production; Clairemarie Fisher O'Leary and Sheryl Avruch for quality control; everybody in the tools group (especially Lenny Muellner, who did most of the tools work for this book, but also Erik Ray and Ellen Siever); and Edie Freedman, who created the cover. Norm Walsh and Tanya Herlick, my various managers, were gracious enough to provide me with time to work on this project (even when I was supposed to be working for Norm full time). Special thanks go to Stephen Figgins in O'Reilly technical support for testing large numbers of commands, and even rewriting many to fit the facts. Thanks also to Greg Hankins of the Linux Documentation Project for his technical review. Finally, this book owes a great debt to all the O'Reilly books which I consulted extensively (that's a polite phrase for copied). It was built on a solid foundation.

The actual months I spent writing Linux Nut are fading into very hazy memories, but I well remember those people who got me through that summer: Dave Vernal, JD Paul, Paul Berger, Elizabeth Haynes, Kevin Lyda, Neil Laughlin, my mother, and my brother. Adam, I hadn't met you yet, but I like to pretend that you have retrospective influence. And, of course, much love to my cat, who shed on the monitor and let me know when I'd been working too long.

CHAPTER 1

Introduction

Linux is a freely available clone of the UNIX operating system. You may find yourself working with it for many reasons. Perhaps you have to obtain a personal system for some project and hang it off a network consisting of UNIX systems at your job—and since you're interacting with UNIX systems, you want something compatible on your own machine. Perhaps you're a new computer user who wants to do something for which UNIX has traditionally been suited, like running a Web server; because Linux is free and runs with surprisingly little memory, it provides the most cost-effective solution available today. Perhaps you just bought a personal computer and want to have Linux on it at home, because you use UNIX systems at work. Or maybe you're just fed up with other computer systems that decide what's good for you and keep you from doing things you want to do—then you're ripe for Linux.

If you haven't obtained Linux yet, or have it but don't know exactly how to get started using it, buy the O'Reilly & Associates book *Running Linux*, by Matt Welsh and Lar Kaufman. This will give you everything you need in order to install your Linux system, configure it, and start becoming productive. The book you're looking at now will then prove useful.

The Excitement of Linux

Linux revives the grand creativity and the community of sharing that UNIX was long known for. The unprecedented flexibility and openness of UNIX—which newcomers usually found confusing and frustrating, but which they eventually found they couldn't live without—continually inspired extensions, new tools like Perl, and experiments in computer science that sometimes ended up in mainstream commercial computer systems.

Many fondly remember the days when AT&T gave UNIX away free to universities, and the University of Berkeley started distributing its version in any manner that allowed people to get it. For these older hackers, Linux can bring back the spirit of working together—all the more so because the Internet is now widespread.

1

And for the many who are too young to remember the first round of open systems (such as the hordes of students attracted to Linux) or whose prior experience has been woefully constricted by proprietary operating systems, now is the time to discover the wonders of freely distributable source code and infinitely adaptable interfaces.

The Linux kernel itself was originally designed by Linus Torvalds at the University of Helsinki in Finland, and later developed through collaboration with many volunteers worldwide. By "kernel" we mean the core of the operating system itself—not the applications (such as the compiler, shells, and so forth) that run on it. Today, the term "Linux" is often used to mean the kernel as well as the applications and complete system environment.

Most Linux systems cannot be technically referred to as a "version of UNIX," as they have not been submitted to the required tests and licensed properly. However, at least one Linux distribution has in fact been branded as POSIX.1. Linux offers all the common programming interfaces as standard UNIX systems, and as you can see from this book, all the common UNIX utilities have been ported to Linux. It is a powerful, robust, fully usable system for those who like UNIX.

The economic power behind Linux's popularity is its support for an enormous range of hardware used with IBM-compatible personal computers. People who are accustomed to MS-DOS and Microsoft Windows are often amazed at how much faster their hardware appears to work with Linux—it makes efficient use of its resources. And now it is appearing on a number of other hardware systems, notably the PowerPC and the Digital Alpha, one of the fastest workstations on the market. Ports for the Sparc, m68k, and others are under way.

Commands on Linux

Linux commands are not the same as standard UNIX ones. They're better! This is because most of them are provided by the GNU project run by the Free Software Foundation (FSF). Benefitting from years of experience with standard UNIX utilities and advances in computer science, programmers on the GNU project have managed to create versions of standard tools that have more features, run faster and more efficiently, and lack the bugs or inconsistencies that persist in the original standard versions.

While GNU provided the programming utilities and standard commands like *grep*, most of the system and network administration tools on Linux came from the Berkeley Software Distribution (BSD). In addition, some people wrote tools specifically for Linux to deal with special issues such as filesystems that only Linux supports. This book documents all the standard UNIX commands that are commonly available on most Linux distributions.

The third major source of Linux software is the X Consortium, which developed the X Window System, and the XFree86 project that ported that windowing system to standard Intel chips. This book does not discuss the X Window System; O'Reilly offers other books for that.

---

*Before an O/S can be called "UNIX," it must be branded by X/Open.

What This Book Offers

Many years ago, one of the early books published by O'Reilly & Associates was *UNIX in a Nutshell*, a quick reference that soon turned up on the desks of busy users everywhere. Many people turn to *UNIX in a Nutshell* instead of the supposedly more authoritative and more complete manual pages for their system. Some say that this is the book they refer to most often, of all their computer books.

UNIX in a Nutshell doesn't teach you UNIX—it is, after all, a quick reference—but novices as well as highly experienced users find it of great value. When you have some idea what command you want but aren't sure exactly how it works or what combinations of options give you the exact output required, this book is the place to turn. It is also an eye-opener: it can make you aware of options that you never knew about before.

With *Linux in a Nutshell*, we have thoroughly updated and adapted *UNIX in a Nutshell* for Linux. Not only that, we've produced a book that many other UNIX users will want too, because for the first time this reference work covers the tools produced by the FSF for the GNU project. GNU tools are popular on a lot of UNIX systems, so you may be using them even if you don't run Linux.

Like computer systems from the age in which UNIX was born (the early 1970s), Linux is mostly a command-driven system. The trend in modern systems, since the Xerox STAR (a commercial failure) and the Apple Macintosh (successful and therefore better known), is to provide graphical interfaces for system functions. While some versions of Linux provide a few graphical tools, that's not what you're getting Linux for. The more interesting things you can do involve commands. When you get used to the UNIX command interpreter (called the shell) and a handful of the most useful commands on Linux, you'll find you can work much faster than you can on a graphical interface. Moreover, you'll find the system much more adaptable. Repeating commands is easy, and with a little practice so is the automation of functions you carry out regularly.

Of course, Linux offers a windowing system—a very rich and flexible one, as befits a rich and flexible operating system. But a lot of the time you'll just open a simulated VT100 terminal (the *xterm* program) and enter commands into that. You'll find yourself moving back and forth between graphical programs and the commands listed in this book.

So the first thing you've got to do, once you're over the hurdle of installing Linux, is to get used to the most common commands. These are described in Chapter 2, *Linux User Commands*. If you know absolutely nothing about UNIX, we recommend you read a basic guide (there's an introductory chapter in *Running Linux* that can get you started). But if you know a few commands already and have an idea where to look, Chapter 2 will provide a wealth of information.

All commands are interpreted by the shell. The shell is simply a program that accepts commands from the user and executes them. Different shells sometimes use slightly different syntax to mean the same thing. Under Linux, two popular shells are **bash** and **tcsh**, and they differ in subtle ways (one of the nice things about Linux, and other UNIX systems, is that you have a variety to choose from, each with strengths and weaknesses). We offer several chapters on shells. You may decide to read these after you've used Linux for a while, because they mostly cover powerful, advanced features that you'll want when you're a steady user.

Before then, you'll have to learn some big, comprehensive utilities, so you can get real work done: an editor, a compiler or scripting tool, and so on. Two major editors are used on Linux: vi and Emacs. Both have chapters in this book. We also have a separate book about each one (as we do about each of the major utilities in this book) which you may want, because neither is completely intuitive upon first use. (Emacs does have an excellent built-in tutorial, though; to invoke it, press the **Escape** key followed by **x**, and then enter `help-with-tutorial` and press the **Return** key.)

Programming utilities are covered in Chapter 12, *Programming Overview and Commands*. The UNIX programming environment has become something of a model for other systems, and it rewards a little study with great support for building programs, using source control, and so forth.

System and network administration are major topics that are covered in Chapter 13, *System and Network Administration Overview*, and Chapter 14, *System and Network Administration Commands*. A few books you may want to buy, in order to get the background necessary to understand these complicated tasks, are *Essential System Administration*, Second Edition, by Æleen Frisch, *Linux Network Administrator's Guide*, by Olaf Kirch, and *TCP/IP Network Administration*, by Craig Hunt. Your Linux distribution (such as the one sold by O'Reilly) provides graphical interfaces for some functions. But commands are necessary for many functions, and these commands are all in this book.

Every distribution of Linux is slightly different, but you'll find that the commands we document are what you use most of the time, and that they work the same on all distributions. Basic commands, programming utilities, system administration, and network administration are all covered here. But some areas were so big that we had to leave them out. TEX (a text-processing tool used extensively in academia and by Linux users in general) didn't make the cut, nor did Tcl/Tk (the Tool Command Language and its graphical toolkit) or Perl, a text-processing language. Furthermore, this book does not discuss the X Window System. These subjects would stretch the book out of its binding, and they deserve a more detailed look. For information on these subjects, we recommend the following O'Reilly books:

- *Making TEX Work*, by Norm Walsh

- *Tcl/Tk Tools*, by Mark Harrison, due Spring 1997

- *Programming Perl*, Second Edition, by Larry Wall, Tom Christiansen, and Randal L. Schwartz

- The X Window System series, in particular *Volume 3: The X Window System User's Guide*, by Valerie Quercia and Tim O'Reilly

Our goal in producing this book is to provide convenience, and that means keeping it small. It certainly doesn't have everything the manual pages have. But you'll find that it has what you need 95% of the time.

Sources and Licenses

When you get Linux, you also get the source code. The same goes for all the utilities on Linux (unless your vendor offered a commercial application or library as a special enhancement). You may never bother looking at the source code, but it's key to Linux's strength. The source code has to be provided by the vendor, under the Linux license, and it permits those who are competent at such things to fix bugs, provide advice about the system's functioning, and submit improvements that benefit all of us. The license is the well-known General Public License, also known as the GPL or "copyleft," invented and popularized by the FSF.

The FSF, founded by Richard Stallman, is a phenomenon that many people would believe to be impossible if it did not exist. (The same thing goes for Linux too, in fact—five years ago, who would imagine a robust operating system developed by collaborators over the Internet and distributed for free?) One of the most popular editors on UNIX, GNU Emacs, comes from the FSF. So do *gcc* and *g++* (C and C++ compilers), which for a while used to set the standard for optimization and fast code.

Dedicated to the sharing of software, the FSF provides all its code and documentation on the Internet and allows anyone with a whim for enhancements to alter the source code. It is working on a project that resembles Linux, but is broader: a complete clone of UNIX that will be available free. GNU (which means "GNU's not UNIX"—you can't get the first word of the phrase to mean anything) is the name of the whole project, and HURD is the name of the operating system under development.

In order to prevent hoarding, the FSF requires that the source code for all enhancements be distributed under the same GPL that it uses. This encourages individuals or companies to make improvements and share them with others. The only thing someone cannot do is add enhancements and then try to sell the product as commercial software—that is, to withhold the source code. That would be taking advantage of the FSF and the users.

As we said earlier, many tools on Linux come from BSD instead of GNU. BSD is also free software. The license is significantly different, but that doesn't have to concern you as a user. The effect of the difference is that the people who created BSD keep control over further development.

Commands

CHAPTER 2

Linux
User Commands

This section presents the user-level Linux commands (as opposed to the programming-level or system-administration–level commands). Each entry is labeled with the command name on the outer edge of the page. The syntax line is followed by a brief description and a list of all available options. Many commands come with examples at the end of the entry. If you need only a quick reminder or suggestion about a command, you can skip directly to the examples.

Typographic conventions for describing command syntax are listed in the Preface. For additional help in locating commands, see the index at the back of this book.

If you can't find a command in this section, it may be listed as a programming-level or administration-level command. See the alphabetical listings in those sections. Applications using the X Window System are not covered in this book.

---

apropos [*options*] *keyword*   **apropos**

Search man pages for occurrences of *keyword*. The search is limited to the short descriptions at the beginning of each man page.

Options

   -m *system*[, ...], --**systems**=*system*[, ...]
            Also search man pages on *system*. Separate list of systems with commas.

   -M *path*, --**manpath**=*path*
            Search through *path* instead of the normal path in which you would expect to find man pages (specified in $MANPATH). Directories should be separated by colons.

→

apropos
←
	-r, --regex
	    Enable regular expression parsing on *keyword*.
	-w, --wildcard
	    Expect shell style wildcards in *keyword*.

arch	**arch** Print machine architecture type.
at	**at** [*options*] *time* Execute commands entered on standard input at a specified *time* and optional *date*. (See also **batch**.) End input with *EOF*. *time* can be formed either as a numeric hour (with optional minutes and modifiers) or as a keyword. It can contain an optional *date*, formed as a month and date, a day of the week, or a special keyword (*today* or *tomorrow*). An increment can also be specified. Details are given in the following entries.

Options

    -b   Same as **batch**.

    -d   Same as **atrm**.

    -f *file*   Read job from *file*, not standard input.

    -l [*job_id*]

            Report all jobs that are scheduled for the invoking user, or, if *job_id* is specified, report only for those. Same as **atq**.

    -m   Mail user when job has completed, regardless of whether output was created.

    -q *letter* Place job in queue denoted by *letter*, where *letter* is any single letter from a–z. Default queue is c. (The batch queue defaults to b.) Run higher-lettered queues at a lower priority. Submit upper-case lettered queues to batch.

Time

    hh:*mm* [*modifiers*]

            Hours can have one digit or two (a 24-hour clock is assumed by default); optional minutes can be given as one or two digits; the colon can be omitted if the format is *h*, *hh*, or *hhmm*; e.g., valid times are 5, 5:30, 0530, 19:45. If modifier **am** or **pm** is added, *time* is based on a 12-hour clock. If the keyword **zulu** is added, times correspond to Greenwich Mean Time.

    midnight | **noon** | **teatime** | **now**

            Use any one of these keywords in place of a numeric time. **teatime** translates to 4 p.m.; **now** must be followed by an *increment*.

Date

> *month num[, year]*
>
> > *month* is one of the 12 months, spelled out or abbreviated to its first three letters; *num* is the calendar date of the month; *year* is the four-digit year. If the given *month* occurs before the current month, **at** schedules that month next year.
>
> *day*   One of the seven days of the week, spelled out or abbreviated to its first three letters.
>
> today | tomorrow
>
> > Indicate the current day or the next day. If *date* is omitted, **at** schedules **today** when the specified *time* occurs later than the current time; otherwise, **at** schedules **tomorrow**.

Increment

> Supply a numeric increment if you want to specify an execution time or day *relative* to the current time. The number should precede any of the keywords **minute, hour, day, week, month,** or **year** (or their plural forms). The keyword **next** can be used as a synonym of **+ 1**.

Examples

> Note that the first two commands are equivalent:

```
at 1945 pm December 9
at 7:45pm Dec 9
at 3 am Saturday
at now + 5 hours
at noon next day
```

---

atq [*options*] [*job–id*]

List the user's pending jobs, unless the user is a privileged user; in that case, everybody's jobs are listed. If *job-id* is specified, report on only those jobs. Same as **at-l**.

Options

> -q *queue*   Query only the specified queue and ignore all other queues.
>
> -v   Show jobs that have completed, but not yet been deleted.

---

atrm *job* [*job . . .*]

Delete a job that has been queued for future execution. Same as **at -d**.

banner	**banner** [*option*] [*characters*]
	Print *characters* as a poster on the standard output. Each word supplied must contain ten or fewer characters. If no *characters* are supplied, read from standard input.
	Option
	-w *width* Set width to *width* characters. Default is 132. Note that if your banner is in all lowercase, it will be narrower than *width* characters.
batch	**batch** [*options*] [*time*]
	Execute commands entered on standard input. If time is omitted, execute them when the system load permits (when the load average falls below 0.5). Very similar to **at**, but does not insist that the execution time be entered on the command line. See **at** for details.
	Options
	-f *file* Read job from *file*, not standard input.
	-m Mail user when job has completed, regardless of whether output was created.
bash	**bash** [*options*] [*file* [*arguments*]] **sh** [*options*] [*file* [*arguments*]]
	Standard Linux shell, a command interpreter into which all other commands are entered. For more information, see Chapter 4, *bash: The Bourne Again Shell*.
bc	**bc** [*options*] [*files*]
	bc is a language (and compiler) whose syntax resembles that of C, but with unlimited-precision arithmetic. **bc** consists of identifiers, keywords, and symbols, which are briefly described in the following entries. Examples are given at the end.
	Interactively perform arbitrary-precision arithmetic or convert numbers from one base to another. Input can be taken from *files* or read from the standard input. To exit, type **quit** or **EOF**.
	Options
	-l Make functions from the math library available.
	-s Ignore all extensions, and process exactly as in POSIX.
	-w When extensions to POSIX **bc** are used, print a warning.

Identifiers

An identifier is a series of one or more characters. They must begin with a lowercase letter, but then may also contain digits and underscores. No uppercase letters are allowed. Identifiers are used as names for variables, arrays, and functions. Variables normally store arbitrary-precision numbers. Within the same program you may name a variable, an array, and a function using the same letter. The following identifiers would not conflict:

x Variable x.

$x[i]$ Element i of array x. i can range from 0 to 2047 and can also be an expression.

$x(y,z)$ Call function x with parameters y and z.

Input-output keywords

ibase, **obase**, **scale**, and **last** store a value. Typing them on a line by themselves displays their current value. You can also change their values through assignment. The letters A–F are treated as digits whose values are 10–15.

ibase = n Numbers that are input (e.g., typed) are read as base n (default is 10).

obase = n Numbers that are displayed are in base n (default is 10). Note: Once **ibase** has been changed from 10, use the digit A to restore **ibase** or **obase** to decimal.

scale = n Display computations using n decimal places (default is 0, meaning that results are truncated to integers). **scale** is normally used only for base-10 computations.

last   Value of last printed number.

Statement keywords

A semicolon or a newline separates one statement from another. Curly braces are needed when grouping multiple statements.

if (*rel -expr*) {*statements*} [**else** {*statements*}]

Do one or more *statements* if relational expression *rel-expr* is true. Otherwise, do nothing, or, if *else* (an extension) is specified, do alternative *statements*. For example:

```
if(x==y) {i = i + 1} else {i = i - 1}
```

while (*rel -expr*) {*statements*}

Repeat one or more *statements* while *rel-expr* is true; for example:

```
while(i>0) {p = p*n; q = a/b; i = i-1}
```

$\rightarrow$

for (*expr1*; *rel-expr*; *expr2*) {*statements*}

Similar to **while**; for example, to print the first 10 multiples of 5, you could type:

```
for(i=1; i<=10; i++) i*5
```

GNU bc does not require three arguments to **for**. A missing argument 1 or 3 means that those expressions will never be evaluated. A missing argument 2 evaluates to the value 1.

break Terminate a **while** or **for** statement.

print *list*

GNU extension; it provides an alternate means of output. *list* consists of a series of comma-separated strings and expressions; **print** displays these entities in the order of the list. It does not print a newline when it terminates. Expressions are evaluated, printed, and assigned to the special variable *last*. Strings (which may contain special characters, i.e., characters beginning with \) are simply printed. Special characters can be:

a   Alert or bell
b   Backspace
f   Form feed
n   Newline
r   Carriage return
q   Double quote
t   Tab
\   Backslash (\)

continue

GNU extension. When within a **for** statement, jump to the next iteration.

halt GNU extension. Cause the **bc** processor to quit.

limits GNU extension. Print the limits enforced by the local version of **bc**.

Function keywords

define *j* (*args*) {

Begin the definition of function *j* having the arguments *args*. The arguments are separated by commas. Statements follow on successive lines. End with a }.

auto *x*, *y*

Set up *x* and *y* as variables local to a function definition, initialized to 0 and meaningless outside the function. Must appear first.

return(*expr*)

Pass the value of expression *expr* back to the program. Return 0 if (*expr*) is left off. Used in function definitions.

sqrt(*expr*)
> Compute the square root of expression *expr*.

length(*expr*)
> Compute how many significant digits are in *expr*.

scale(*expr*)
> Same as **length**, but count only digits to the right of the decimal point.

read( ) GNU extension. Read a number from standard input. Return value is the number read, converted via the value of **ibase**.

Math library functions

These are available when **bc** is invoked with –l. Library functions set **scale** to 20.

s(*angle*)   Compute the sine of *angle*, a constant or expression in radians.

c(*angle*)   Compute the cosine of *angle*, a constant or expression in radians.

a(*n*)   Compute the arctangent of *n*, returning an angle in radians.

e(*expr*)   Compute **e** to the power of *expr*.

l(*expr*)   Compute the natural log of *expr*.

j(*n*, *x*)   Compute the Bessel function of integer order *n*.

Operators

These consist of operators and other symbols. Operators can be arithmetic, unary, assignment, or relational:

arithmetic	+ – * / % ^
unary	– ++ ––
assignment	=+ =– =* =/ =% =^ =
relational	< <= > >= == !=

Other symbols

/* */ Enclose comments.

( )   Control the evaluation of expressions (change precedence). Can also be used around assignment statements to force the result to print.

{ }   Use to group statements.

[ ]   Indicate array index.

"*text*" Use as a statement to print *text*.

Examples

Note below that when you type some quantity (a number or expression), it is evaluated and printed, but assignment statements produce no display.

```
ibase = 8        Octal input
20               Evaluate this octal number
```

→

```
16                   Terminal displays decimal value
obase = 2            Display output in base 2 instead of base 10
20                   Octal input
10000                Terminal now displays binary value
ibase = A            Restore base 10 input
scale = 3            Truncate results to 3 decimal places
8/7                  Evaluate a division
1.001001000          Oops!  Forgot to reset output base to 10
obase=10             Input is decimal now, so A isn't needed
8/7
1.142                Terminal displays result (truncated)
```

The following lines show the use of functions:

```
define p(r,n){       Function p uses two arguments
   auto v            v is a local variable
   v = r^n           r raised to the n power
   return(v)}        Value returned

scale=5
x=p(2.5,2)           x = 2.5 ^ 2
x                    Print value of x
6.25
length(x)            Number of digits
3
scale(x)             Number of places right of decimal point
2
```

biff

biff [*arguments*]

Notify user of mail arrival and sender's name. **biff** operates asynchronously. Mail notification works only if your system is running **sendmail** or **smail**. The command **biff y** enables notification, and the command **biff n** disables notification. By default, it reports **biff**'s current status.

cal

cal [*-jy*] [[*month*] *year*]

Print a 12-month calendar (beginning with January) for the given *year* or a one-month calendar of the given *month* and *year*. *month* ranges from 1 to 12. *year* ranges from 1 to 9999. With no arguments, print a calendar for the previous month, current month, and next month.

Options

-j   Display Julian dates (days numbered 1 to 365, starting from January 1).

-y   Display entire current year.

Examples

```
cal 12 1995
cal 1994 > year_file
```

cat [*options*] [*files*]

Read one or more *files* and print them on standard output. Read standard input if no *files* are specified or if – is specified as one of the files; end input with *EOF*. You can use the > operator to combine several files into a new file; use >> to append files to an existing file.

Options

-e   Print a $ to mark the end of each line.

-n, --number
      Print the number of the output line to the line's left; start with 1.

-s, --squeeze-blank
      Squeeze out extra blank lines.

-t   Print each tab as ^I and each form feed as ^L.

-u   Ignored; retained for UNIX compatibility.

-v, --show-nonprinting
      Display control and nonprinting characters, with the exception of LFD and TAB.

-A, --show-all
      Same as –vET: print control characters, nonprinting characters, tabs, and end-of-lines.

-E, --show-ends
      Print '$' at the end of each line.

-T, --show-tabs
      Print TAB characters as ^I.

Examples

`cat ch1`	*Display a file*
`cat ch1 ch2 ch3 > all`	*Combine files*
`cat note5 >> notes`	*Append to a file*
`cat > temp1`	*Create file at terminal; end with EOF*
`cat > temp2 << STOP`	*Create file at terminal; end with STOP*

chattr [*options*] *mode files*

Modify file attributes. Specific to Linux Second Extended File Systems. Behaves similarly to symbolic **chmod**, using +, –, and =; *mode* is in the form *opcode attribute*.

Options

-R   Modify directories and their contents recursively.

-V   Print modes of attributes after changing them.

-v *version*
      Set the file's version.

→

chattr ←	*Opcodes*
	
	    + Add attribute.
	    - Remove attribute.
	    = Assign attributes (removing unspecified attributes).
	
	Attributes
	
	    a Append only
	    c Compressed
	    d No dump
	    i Immutable
	    s Secure deletion
	    u Undeletable
	    S Synchronous updates

chfn	**chfn** [*options*] [*username*]
	
	NFS/NIS command—change the information that is stored in */etc/passwd* and displayed when a user is fingered. Without *options*, **chfn** will enter interactive mode and prompt for changes. To make a field blank, enter the keyword **none**.
	
	Options
	
	    -f, --full-name
	           Specify new full name.
	    -h, --home-phone
	           Specify new home phone number.
	    -o, --office
	           Specify new office.
	    -p, --office-phone
	           Specify new office phone number.

chgrp	**chgrp** *newgroup files*
	
	Change the group of one or more *files* to *newgroup*. *newgroup* is either a group ID number or a group name located in */etc/group*. Only the owner of a file or a privileged user may change its group.
	
	Options
	
	    -c, --changes
	           Print information about those files that are affected.
	    -f, --silent, --quiet
	           Do not print error messages about files that cannot be affected.
	    -R, --recursive
	           Traverse subdirectories recursively, applying changes.

chmod [*options*] *mode files*

Change the access *mode* (permissions) of one or more *files*. Only the owner of a file or a privileged user may change its mode. *mode* can be numeric or an expression in the form of *who opcode permission*. *who* is optional (if omitted, default is **a**); choose only one *opcode*. Multiple modes may be specified, separated by commas.

Options

   -c, --changes

        Print information about files that are affected.

   -f, --silent, --quiet

        Do not notify user of files that **chmod** cannot change.

   -v, --verbose

        Print information about each file, whether changed or not.

   -R, --recursive

        Traverse subdirectories recursively, applying changes.

Who

u	User
g	Group
o	Other
a	All (default)

Opcode

+	Add permission
-	Remove permission
=	Assign permission (and remove permission of the unspecified fields)

Permission

r	Read
w	Write
x	Execute
s	Set user (or group) ID
t	Sticky bit; save text (file) mode or prevent removal of files by nonowners (directory)
u	User's present permission
g	Group's present permission
o	Other's present permission
l	Mandatory locking

Alternatively, specify permissions by a three-digit octal number. The first digit designates owner permission; the second, group

→

chmod	permission; and the third, other's permission. Permissions are calculated by adding the following octal values:
←	

4   Read

2   Write

1   Execute

Note: A fourth digit may precede this sequence. This digit assigns the following modes:

4   Set user ID on execution

2   Set group ID on execution or set mandatory locking

1   Set sticky bit

Examples

Add execute-by-user permission to *file*:

```
chmod u+x file
```

Either of the following will assign read-write-execute permission by owner (7), read-execute permission by group (5), and execute-only permission by others (1) to *file*:

```
chmod 751 file
chmod u=rwx,g=rx,o=x file
```

Any one of the following will assign read-only permission to *file* for everyone:

```
chmod =r file
chmod 444 file
chmod a-wx,a+r file
```

Set the user ID, assign read-write-execute permission by owner, and assign read-execute permission by group and others:

```
chmod 4755 file
```

---

chown

chown *newowner files*

Change the ownership of one or more *files* to *newowner*. *newowner* is either a user ID number or a login name located in */etc/passwd*. **chown** also accepts users in the form *newowner:newgroup*. Only the current owner of a file, or a privileged user, may change its owner.

Options

-c, --changes

> Print information about those files that are affected.

-f, --silent, --quiet

> Do not print error messages about files that cannot be affected.

-v, --verbose

> Print information about all files that **chown** attempts to change, whether or not they are actually affected.

-R, --recursive

> Traverse subdirectories recursively, applying changes.

---

chsh [*options*] [*username*]

Change your login shell, interactively or on the command line. Warn if *shell* does not exist in */etc/shells*.

Options

-l, --list-shells

> Print valid shells, as listed in */etc/shells*, and exit.

-s, --shell

> Specify new login shell.

---

cksum [*file*]

Compute a cyclic redundancy check (CRC) for all *files* to check for corruption. Read from standard input if the character – or no files are given. Display the result of the check, the number of bytes in the file, and (unless reading from standard input) the filename.

---

clear

Clear the terminal display.

---

cmp [*options*] *file1 file2*

Compare *file1* with *file2*. Use standard input if *file1* is - or missing. See also **comm** and **diff**.

Options

-c, --print-chars

> Print differing bytes as characters.

-i *num*, --ignore-initial=*num*

> Ignore the first *num* bytes of input.

-l, --verbose

> Print offsets and codes of all differing bytes.

-s, --quiet, --silent

> Work silently; print nothing, but return exit codes:
> 0   Files are identical
> 1   Files are different
> 2   Files are inaccessible

$\rightarrow$

cmp ←	*Example* Print a message if two files are the same (exit code is 0): `cmp -s old new && echo 'no changes'`
colcrt	**colcrt** [*options*] [*file*] A postprocessing filter that handles reverse linefeeds and escape characters, allowing output from *tbl* (or *nroff*) to appear in reasonable form on a terminal. - Do not underline. -2 Double space by printing all half lines.
colrm	**colrm** [*start* [*stop*]] Remove specified columns from a file, where a column is a single character in a line. Read from standard input and write to standard output. Columns are numbered starting with 1; begin deleting columns at (including) the *start* column, and stop at (including) the *stop* column. Entering a tab increments the column count to the next multiple of either the start or stop column; entering a backspace decrements it by 1.

column	**column** [*options*] [*file*]
	
	Format input into columns, filling rows first. Read from standard input if *file* is not specified.
	
	Options
	-c *num*
	    Format output into *num* columns.
	-s *char*
	    Delimit table columns with *char*. Meaningful only with **-t**.
	-t Format input into a table. Delimit with whitespace, unless an alternate delimiter has been provided with **-s**.
	-x Fill columns before filling rows.

comm	**comm** [*options*] *file1 file2* Compare lines common to the sorted files *file1* and *file2*. Three-column output is produced: lines unique to *file1*, lines unique to *file2*, and lines common to both files. **comm** is similar to **diff** in that both commands compare two files. But **comm** can also be used like **uniq**; that is, **comm** selects duplicate or unique lines between *two* sorted files, whereas **uniq** selects duplicate or unique lines within the *same* sorted file.

-     Read the standard input.
- *-num* Suppress printing of column **num**. Multiple columns may be specified and should not be space-separated.

Examples

Compare two lists of top-ten movies, and display items that appear in both lists:

```
comm -12 siskel_top10 ebert_top10
```

---

cp [*options*] *file1 file2*

cp [*options*] *files directory*

cp

Copy *file1* to *file2*, or copy one or more *files* to the same names under *directory*. If the destination is an existing file, the file is overwritten; if the destination is an existing directory, the file is copied into the directory (the directory is *not* overwritten).

Options

-a, --archive
> Preserve attributes of original files where possible. Same as **-dpR**.

-b, --backup
> Back up files that would otherwise be overwritten.

-d, --no-dereference
> Do not dereference symbolic links; preserve hard link relationships between source and copy.

-f, --force
> Remove existing files in the destination.

-i, --interactive
> Prompt before overwriting destination files.

-l, --link
> Make hard links, not copies, of nondirectories.

-p, --preserve
> Preserve all information, including owner, group, permissions, and time stamps.

-r   Copy directories recursively.

-s, --symbolic-link
> Make symbolic links instead of copying. Source filenames must be absolute.

-u, --update
> Do not copy a nondirectory that has an existing destination with the same or newer modification time.

-v, --verbose
> Before copying, print the name of each file.

$\rightarrow$

cp
←
	-x, --one-file-system
	    Ignore subdirectories on other filesystems.
	-P, --parents
	    Preserve intermediate directories in source. The last argument must be the name of an existing directory. For example, the command **cp --parents jphek-man/book/ch1 newdir** copies the file *jphek-man/book/ch1* to *newdir/jphekman/book/ch1*, creating intermediate directories as necessary.
	-R, --recursive
	    Recursively copy directories.
	-S, --suffix backup-suffix
	    Set suffix to be appended to backup files. This may also be set with the SIMPLE_BACKUP_SUFFIX environment variable. The default is ˜.
	-V, --version-control {numbered | existing | simple}
	    Set the type of backups made. You may also use the VERSION_CONTROL environment variable. The default is **existing**. Valid arguments are:

t, numbered	Always make numbered backups.
nil, existing	Make numbered backups of files that already have them; otherwise, make simple backups.
never, simple	Always make simple backups.

cpio	**cpio** *flags* [*options*]
	
	Copy file archives in from or out to tape or disk, or to another location on the local machine. Each of the three flags **-i**, **-o**, or **-p** accepts different options:
	
	-i [*options*] [*patterns*]
	    Copy in (extract) files whose names match selected *patterns*. Each pattern can include filename metacharacters from the Bourne shell. (Patterns should be quoted or escaped so they are interpreted by **cpio**, not by the shell.) If no pattern is used, all files are copied in. During extraction, existing files are not overwritten by older versions in the archive (unless **-u** is specified).
	
	-o [*options*]
	    Copy out a list of files whose names are given on the standard input.
	
	-p [*options*] *directory*
	    Copy files to another directory on the same system. Destination pathnames are interpreted relative to the named *directory*.

Options available to the `-i`, `-o`, and `-p` flags are shown respectively in the first, second, and third row below. (The `-` is omitted for clarity.)

```
i: 0a c        vABL VC HM O F
o:  bcdf mnrtsuv B SVCEHMR IF
p: 0a  d lm    uv  L V    R
```

Options

-0, --null

> Expect list of filenames to be terminated with null, not newline. This allows files with a newline in their names to be included.

-a, --reset-access-time

> Set access times of input files to now.

-A, --append

> Append files to an existing archive, which must be a disk file. Specify this archive with **-O** or **-F**.

-b, --swap

> Swap bytes and half-words.

-B

> Block input or output using 5120 bytes per record (default is 512 bytes per record).

-c

> Read or write header information as ASCII characters; useful when source and destination machines are of differing types.

-C *n*, **--io-size=***n*

> Like **-B**, but block size can be any positive integer *n*.

-d, --make-directories

> Create directories as needed.

-E *file*, **--pattern-file=***file*

> Extract filenames listed in *file* from the archives.

-f, --nonmatching

> Reverse the sense of copying; copy all files *except* those that match *patterns*.

-F, --file=*file*

> Use *file* as archive, not **stdin** or **stdout**. *file* can exist on another machine, if given in the form *user@hostname:file*.

--force-local

> Do not assume that *file* (provided by **-F**, **-I**, or **-O**) exists on remote machine, even if it contains a @.

-H *type*, **--format=***type*

> Use *type* format. Default in copy-out is **bin**. Valid formats (all caps also accepted):

> | | |
> |---|---|
> | **bin** | Binary |
> | **odc** | Old (POSIX.1) portable format |
> | **newc** | New (SVR4) portable format |
> | **crc** | New (SVR4) portable format with checksum added |

→

cpio
←

tar	Tar
ustar	POSIX.1 tar (also recognizes GNU tar archives)
hpbin	HP-UX's binary (obsolete)
hpodc	HP-UX's portable format

−I *file* Read *file* as an input archive. May be on a remote machine (see −**F**).

−**k** Ignored. For backwards compatibility.

−l, −−link
Link files instead of copying.

−L, −−dereference
Follow symbolic links.

−m, −−preserve-modification-time
Retain previous file modification time.

−M *msg*, −−message=*msg*
Print *msg* when switching media, as a prompt before switching to new media. Use variable %d in the message as a numeric ID for the next medium. −**M** is valid only with −**I** or −**O**.

−n, −−numeric-uid-gid
When verbosely listing contents, show user ID and group ID numerically.

−−no-preserve-owner
Make all copied files owned by yourself, instead of the owner of the original. Useful only if you are a privileged user.

−O *file* Direct the output to *file*. May be a file on another machine (see −**F**).

−**r** Rename files interactively.

−R [*user*][:.][*group*], −−owner [*user*][:.][*group*]
Reassign file ownership and group information to the user's login ID (privileged users only).

−s, −−swap-bytes
Swap bytes.

−S, −−swap-half-words
Swap half-words.

−t, −−list
Print a table of contents of the input (create no files). When used with the −**v** option, resembles output of ls −l.

−u, −−unconditional
Unconditional copy; old files can overwrite new ones.

−**v** Print a list of filenames.

−V, −−dot
Print a dot for each file read or written (this shows **cpio** at work without cluttering the screen).

Examples

Generate a list of old files using **find**; use list as input to cpio:

```
find . -name "*.old" -print | cpio -ocBv\
    > /dev/rst8
```

Restore from a tape drive all files whose names contain **save** (subdirectories are created if needed):

```
cpio -icdv "save" < /dev/rst8
```

Move a directory tree:

```
find . -depth -print | cpio -padm /mydir
```

---

csh [*options*] [*file* [*arguments*]]   csh

C shell, a command interpreter into which all other commands are entered. For more information, see Chapter 5, *csh and tcsh*.

---

csplit [*options*] *file arguments*   csplit

Separate *file* into sections and place sections in files named **xx00** through **xx**n ($n < 100$), breaking *file* at each pattern specified in *arguments*. See also **split**.

Options

-        Read from standard input.

-b, --suffix-format=*suffix*
        Append *suffix* to output filename. *suffix* must specify how to convert the binary integer to readable form by including exactly one of the following: **%d**, **%i**, **%u**, **%o**, **%x**, or **%X**. The value of *suffix* determines the format for numbers as follows:

%d   Signed decimal

%i   Same as **%d**

%u   Unsigned decimal

%o   Octal

%x   Hexadecimal

%X   Same as **%x**. This option causes **-n** to be ignored.

-f *prefix*, --prefix=*prefix*
        Name new files *prefix*00 through *prefix*n (default is **xx00** through **xx**n).

-k, --keep-files
        Keep newly created files, even when an error occurs (which would normally remove these files). This is

$\rightarrow$

useful when you need to specify an arbitrarily large
repeat argument, {*n*}, and you don't want an out
of range error to cause removal of the new files.

-n, --digits=*num*
> Use output filenames with numbers *num* digits long.
> The default is 2.

-s, -q, --silent, --quiet
> Suppress all character counts.

-z, --elide-empty-files
> Do not create empty output files. However, number
> as if those files had been created.

Arguments

Any one or a combination of the following expressions.
Arguments containing blanks or other special characters
should be surrounded by single quotes.

/*expr*/ [*offset*]
> Create file from the current line up to the line con-
> taining the regular expression *expr*. *offset* should be
> of the form +*n* or -*n*, where *n* is the number of lines
> below or above *expr*.

%*expr*% [*offset*]
> Same as /*expr*/ except no file is created for lines
> previous to line containing *expr*.

num   Create file from current line up to line number *num*.
> When followed by a repeat count (number inside {}),
> put the next *num* lines of input into another output
> file.

{*n*}   Repeat argument *n* times. May follow any of the
> above arguments. Files will split at instances of *expr*
> or in blocks of *num* lines. If * is given instead of *n*,
> repeat argument until input is exhausted.

Examples

Create up to 20 chapter files from the file **novel**:

```
csplit -k -f chap. novel '%CHAPTER%' '{20}'
```

Create up to 100 address files (**xx00** through **xx99**), each
four lines long, from a database named **address_list**:

```
csplit -k address_list 4 {99}
```

---

cut

cut *options* [*files*]

Cut out selected columns or fields from one or more *files*. In the
following options, *list* is a sequence of integers. Use a comma
between separate values and a hyphen to specify a range (e.g.,
1-10,15,20, or 50-). See also **paste**, **join**, and **newform**.

Options

-b, --**bytes** *list*

> Specify *list* of positions: only bytes in these positions will be printed.

-c, --**characters** *list*

> Cut the column positions identified in *list*.

-d, --**delimiter** *c*

> Use with -f to specify field delimiter as character *c* (default is tab); special characters (e.g., a space) must be quoted.

-f, --**fields** *list*

> Cut the fields identified in *list*.

-s, --**only-delimited**

> Use with -f to suppress lines without delimiters.

Examples

Extract usernames and real names from **/etc/passwd**:

```
cut -d: -f1,5 /etc/passwd
```

Find out who is logged on, but list only login names:

```
who | cut -d" " -f1
```

Cut characters in the fourth column of *file*, and paste them back as the first column in the same file:

```
cut -c4 file | paste - file
```

---

date [*options*] [*+format*] [*date*]

date

Print the current date and time. You may specify a display *format*. *format* can consist of literal text strings (blanks must be quoted) as well as field descriptors, whose values will appear as described in the following entries (the listing shows some logical groupings).

Options

+format

> Display current date in a non-standard format. For example:
>
> ```
> % date +"%A E %j %n%k %p"
> Tuesday 248
> 15 PM
> ```
>
> The default is %a %b %e %T %Z %Y—e.g., Tue Sep 5 14:59:37 EDT 1995.

-d *date*, --**date** *date*

> Print *date*, which may be in the format *d* **days** or *m* **months** *d* **days** to print a date in the future. Specify **ago** to print a date in the past. You may include formatting (see the "Format" section that follows).

→

date	-s *date*, --set *date*
←	Set the date.

-u, --universal
> Set the date to Greenwich Mean Time, not local time.

Format

%	Literal %.
-	Do not pad fields (default: pad fields with zeroes).
_	Pad fields with space (default: zeroes).
%a	Abbreviated weekday.
%b	Abbreviated month name.
%c	Country-specific date and time format.
%h	Same as %b.
%j	Julian day of year (001–366).
%k	Hour in 24-hour format, without leading zeroes (0–23).
%l	Hour in 12-hour format, without leading zeroes (1–12).
%m	Month of year (01–12).
%n	Insert a newline.
%p	String to indicate a.m. or p.m. (default is AM or PM).
%r	Time in %I:%M:%S %p (12-hour) format.
%s	Seconds since "The Epoch," 1970-01-01 00:00:00 UTC (a nonstandard extension).
%t	Insert a tab.
%w	Day of week (Sunday = 0).
%x	Country-specific date format.
%y	Last two digits of year (00–99).
%A	Full weekday.
%B	Full month name.
%D	Date in %m/%d/%y format.
%H	Hour in 24-hour format (00–23).
%I	Hour in 12-hour format (01–12).
%M	Minutes (00–59).
%S	Seconds (00–59).
%T	Time in %H:%M:%S format.
%U	Day of month (01–31).
%W	Week number in year (00–53); start week on Monday.
%X	Country-specific time format.
%Y	Four-digit year (e.g., 1996).
%Z	Time zone name.

Strings for setting date

Strings for setting the date may be numeric or nonnumeric. Numeric strings consist of time, day, and year in the format *MMddhhmmyy*, with an optional *.ss* appended. Non-numeric strings may include month strings, time zones, a.m., and p.m.

time A two-digit hour and two-digit minute (*HHMM*); *HH* uses 24-hour format.

day A two-digit month and two-digit day of month (*mmdd*); default is current day and month.

year The year specified as either the full four digits or just the last two digits; default is current year.

Examples

Set the date to July 1 (0701), 4 a.m. (0400), 1995 (95):

```
date 0701040095
```

The command:

```
date +"Hello%t Date is %D %n%t Time is %T"
```

produces a formatted date as follows:

```
Hello       Date is 05/09/93
            Time is 17:53:39
```

---

df [*options*] [*name*]

Report the amount of free disk space available on all mounted file systems or on the given *name*. (Cannot report on unmounted filesystems.) Disk space is shown in 1K blocks (default) or 512-byte blocks (if the variable POSIXLY_CORRECT is set). *name* can be a device name (e.g., */dev/hd**), the directory name of a mounting point (e.g., */usr*), or a directory name (in which case **df** reports on the entire filesystem in which that directory is mounted).

Options

-a, --all   Include empty filesystems (those with 0 blocks).

-i, --inodes
:   Report free, used, and percent-used inodes.

-k, --kilobytes
:   Print sizes in kilobytes, not 512 bytes.

-t, --type=*type*
:   Show only *type* filesystems.

-x, --exclude-type=*type*
:   Show only filesystems that are not of type *type*.

-P, --portability
:   Use POSIX output format, i.e., print information about each filesystem on exactly one line.

-T, --print-type
:   Display a type for each filesystem, for use as an argument to -t or -x.

diff

diff [*options*] [*diroptions*] *file1 file2*

Compare two text files. **diff** reports lines that differ between *file1* and *file2*. Output consists of lines of context from each file, with *file1* text flagged by a < symbol and *file2* text by a > symbol. Context lines are preceded by the **ed** command (**a**, **c**, or **d**) that would be used to convert *file1* to *file2*. If one of the files is -, standard input is read. If one of the files is a directory, **diff** locates the filename in that directory corresponding to the other argument (e.g., **diff my_dir junk** is the same as **diff my_dir/junk junk**). If both arguments are directories, **diff** reports lines that differ between all pairs of files having equivalent names (e.g., *olddir/program* and *newdir/program*); in addition, **diff** lists filenames unique to one directory, as well as subdirectories common to both. See also **cmp**.

Options

   -b, --ignore-space-change
        Ignore repeating blanks and end-of-line blanks; treat successive blanks as one.

   -e, --ed
        Produce a script of commands (**a**, **c**, **d**) to recreate *file2* from *file1* using the **ed** editor.

   -H   Speed output of large files by scanning for scattered small changes; long stretches with many changes may not show up.

   -i, --ignore-case
        Ignore case in text comparison. Upper- and lower-case are considered the same.

   -w, --ignore-all-space
        Ignore all white space in files for comparisons.

   -B, --ignore-blank-lines
        Ignore blank lines in files.

   -I *regexp*, --ignore-matching-lines=*regexp*
        Ignore lines in files that match the regular expression *regexp*.

   -a, --text
        Treat all files as text files. Useful for checking to see if binary files are identical.

   -c   Context **diff**: print 3 lines surrounding each changed lines.

   -u   Unified **diff**: print old and new versions of lines in a single block.

   -q, --brief
        Output only whether files differ.

   -n, --rcs
        Produce output in RCS diff format.

-y, --side-by-side
> Produce two-column output.

-w *n* For two-column output (-y), produce columns with
> *n* characters of maximum width. Default is 130.

--left-column
> For two-column output (-y), show only left column
> of common lines.

--suppress-common-lines
> For two-column output (-y), do not show common
> lines.

-l, --paginate
> Paginate output by passing it to **pr**.

-t, --expand-tabs
> Produce output with tabs expanded to spaces.

-T, --initial-tab
> Insert initial tabs into output to line up tabs prop-
> erly.

-r, --recursive
> Compare subdirectories recursively.

-N, --new-file
> Treat nonexistent files as empty.

-s, --report-identical-files
> Indicate when files do not differ.

-x *regexp*, --exclude=*regexp*
> Do not compare files in a directory whose names
> match *regexp*.

-X *filename*, --exclude-from=*filename*
> Do not compare files in a directory whose names
> match patterns described in the file *filename*.

-S *filename*
> For directory comparisons, begin with the file
> *filename*.

-d, --minimal
> To speed up comparison, ignore segments of
> numerous changes and output a smaller set of
> changes.

---

diff3 [*options*] *file1 file2 file3*

Compare three files and report the differences with the following codes:

====   All three files differ.
====1 *file1* is different.
====2 *file2* is different.
====3 *file3* is different.

→

diff3
←

diff3 is also designed to merge changes in two differing files from a common ancestor file, i.e., when two people have made their own set of changes to the same file. **diff3** can find changes between the ancestor and one of the newer files, and generate output that adds those differences to the other new file. Unmerged changes are places where both of the newer files differ from each other, and at least one of them from the ancestor. Changes from the ancestor that are the same in both of the newer files are called merged changes. If all three files differ in the same place, it is called an overlapping change.

This scheme is used on the command line with the ancestor being *file2*, the second filename. Comparison is made between *file2* and *file3*, with those differences then applied to *file1*.

Options

- -3
  Create an **ed** script to incorporate into *file1* unmerged, nonoverlapping differences between *file1* and *file3*.

- -a, --text
  Treat files as text.

- -A, --show-all
  Create an **ed** script to incorporate all changes, showing conflicts in bracketed format.

- -e, --ed
  Create an **ed** script to incorporate into *file1* all unmerged differences between *file2* and *file3*.

- -E, --show-overlap
  Create an **ed** script to incorporate unmerged changes, showing conflicts in bracketed format.

- -x, --overlap-only
  Create an **ed** script to incorporate into *file1* all differences where all three files differ (overlapping changes).

- -X
  Same as -**x**, only show conflicts in overlapping the changes in bracketed format.

- -m, --merge
  Create file with changes merged (not an **ed** script).

- -L *label*, --label=*label*
  Use *label* to replace filename in output.

- -i
  Append the **w** (save) and **q** (quit) commands to **ed** script output.

- -T, --initial-tab
  Begin lines with a tab instead of two spaces in output to line tabs up properly.

du [*options*] [*directories*]

Print disk usage, i.e., the number of 1K blocks used by each named directory and its subdirectories (default is current directory).

Options

-a, --all
> Print usage for all files, not just subdirectories.

-b, --bytes
> Print sizes in bytes.

-c, --total
> In addition to normal output, print grand total of all arguments.

-k, --kilobytes
> Print sizes in kilobytes (this is the default).

-l, --count-links
> Count the size of all files, whether or not they have already appeared (i.e., via a hard link).

-r
> Print cannot open message if a file or directory is inaccessible.

-s, --summarize
> Print only the grand total for each named directory.

-x, --one-file-system
> Display usage of files in current filesystem only.

-D, --dereference-args
> Follow symbolic links, but only if they are command-line arguments.

-L, --dereference
> Follow symbolic links.

-S, --separate-dirs
> Do not include the sizes of subdirectories when totaling the size of parent directories.

dumpkeys [*options*]

Print information about the keyboard driver's translation tables to standard output. Further information is available in the manual pages under *keytables*.

Options

-c*charset*, --charset=*charset*
> Specify character set with which to interpret character code values. Valid character sets are **iso-8859-1** (default), **iso-8859-2**, **iso-8859-3**, **iso-8859-4**, and **iso-8859-8**.

--compose-only
> Print compose key combinations only.

$\rightarrow$

dumpkeys ←	**-f, --full-table** Output in canonical, not short, form: for each key, print a row with modifier combinations divided into columns. **--funcs-only** Print function key string definitions only; do not print key bindings or string definitions. **-i, --short-info** Print in short-info format, including information about acceptable keycode keywords in the keytable files; the number of actions that can be bound to a key; a list of the ranges of action codes (the values to the right of a key definition); and the number of function keys that the kernel supports. **--keys-only** Print key bindings only; do not print string definitions. **-l, --long-info** Print the same information as in **--short-info**, plus a list of the supported action symbols and their numeric values. **-n, --numeric** Print action code values in hexadecimal notation; do not attempt to convert them to symbolic notation.
echo	**echo** [-n] [*string*] This is the **/bin/echo** command. **echo** also exists as a command built into the C shell and Bourne shell. The following character sequences have special meanings. *Options* \a Alert (bell) \b Backspace \c Suppress trailing newline \f Form feed \n Newline \r Carriage return \t Horizontal tab \v Vertical tab \\ Literal backslash *nnn* The octal character whose ASCII code is *nnn*.

-e	Enable character sequences with special meaning. (In some versions, this option is not required in order to make the sequences work.)
-n	Suppress printing of newline after text.

Examples

```
echo "testing printer" | lp
echo "TITLE\nTITLE" > file ; cat doc1 doc2 >> file
echo "Warning: ringing bell \07"
```

---

egrep [*options*] [*regexp*] [*files*]

Search one or more *files* for lines that match a regular expression *regexp*. egrep doesn't support the regular expressions \(, \), \n, \<, \>, \{, or \}, but does support the other expressions, as well as the extended set +, ?, |, and ( ). Remember to enclose these characters in quotes. Regular expressions are described in Chapter 6, *Pattern Matching*. Exit status is 0 if any lines match, 1 if none match, and 2 for errors. See also **grep** and **fgrep**. **egrep** typically runs faster than those commands.

Options

-*num*	Print *num* leading and trailing lines of context, but never print any given line more than once.
-b	Precede each line with its block number.
-c	Print only a count of matched lines.
-e *regexp*	Search for the pattern *regexp*. The -e flag is useful in protecting patterns beginning with a -.
-f *file*	Take expression from *file*.
-i	Ignore uppercase and lowercase distinctions.
-l	List filenames but not matched lines.
-h	List matched lines but not filenames.
-n	Print lines and their line numbers.
-q	Suppress normal output.
-s	Do not print error messages about files that do not exist or cannot be read.
-w	Match on whole words only. Words are divided by characters that are not letters, digits, or underscores.
-x	Match on entire lines only.
-v	Print all lines that *don't* match *regexp*.
-A *num*	Print *num* lines of trailing context.
-B *num*	Print *num* lines of leading context.
-C	Print two lines of leading and trailing context.
-L	List files that contain no matching lines.

→

egrep ←	**Examples** Search for occurrences of *Victor* or *Victoria* in *file*: ``` egrep 'Victor(ia)*' file egrep '(Victor|Victoria)' file ``` Find and print strings such as *old.doc1* or *new.doc2* in *files*, and include their line numbers: ``` egrep -n '(old|new)\.doc?' files ```
emacs	**emacs** [*options*] [*files*] A text editor and all-purpose work environment. For more information, see Chapter 7, *The Emacs Editor*.

env	**env** [*option*] [*variable=value* ...] [*command*]
	
	Display the current environment or, if an environment *variable* is specified, set it to a new *value* and display the modified environment. If *command* is specified, execute it under the modified environment.
	
	Options
	
	-, -i, --ignore-environment
	    Ignore current environment entirely.
	
	-u *name*, **--unset** *name*
	    Unset the specified variable.

ex	**ex** [*options*] *file* An interactive command-based editor. For more information, see Chapter 9, *The ex Editor*.

expand	**expand** [*options*] *files*
	
	Convert tabs in given files (or standard input, if the file is named –) to appropriate number of spaces; write results to standard output.
	
	Options
	
	-, -t, --tabs *tabs*
	        tabs is a comma-separated list of integers that specify the placement of tab stops. If exactly one integer is provided, the tab stops are set to every *integer* spaces. By default, tab stops are 8 spaces apart. With **-t** and **--tabs**, the list may be separated by whitespace instead of commas.
	
	-i, --initial
	        Convert tabs only at the beginning of lines.

expr *arg1 operator arg2* [*operator arg3* ...]

Evaluate arguments as expressions and print the result. Arguments and operators must be separated by spaces. In most cases, an argument is an integer, typed literally or represented by a shell variable. There are three types of operators: arithmetic, relational, and logical. Exit status for **expr** is **0** (expression is nonzero and nonnull), **1** (expression is 0 or null), or **2** (expression is invalid).

Arithmetic operators

Use these to produce mathematical expressions whose results are printed.

+   Add *arg2* to *arg1*.
−   Subtract *arg2* from *arg1*.
*   Multiply the arguments.
/   Divide *arg1* by *arg2*.
%   Take the remainder when *arg1* is divided by *arg2*.

Addition and subtraction are evaluated last, unless they are grouped inside parentheses. The symbols *, (, and) have meaning to the shell, so they must be escaped (preceded by a backslash or enclosed in single quotes).

Relational operators

Use these to compare two arguments. Arguments can also be words, in which case comparisons are defined by the locale. If the comparison statement is true, the result is 1; if false, the result is 0. Symbols > and < must be escaped.

=, ==   Are the arguments equal?
!=   Are the arguments different?
>   Is *arg1* greater than *arg2*?
>=   Is *arg1* greater than or equal to *arg2*?
<   Is *arg1* less than *arg2*?
<=   Is *arg1* less than or equal to *arg2*?

Logical operators

Use these to compare two arguments. Depending on the values, the result can be *arg1* (or some portion of it), *arg2*, or 0. Symbols | and & must be escaped.

| Logical OR; if *arg1* has a nonzero (and nonnull) value, the result is *arg1*; otherwise, the result is *arg2*.
&   Logical AND; if both *arg1* and *arg2* have a nonzero (and nonnull) value, the result is *arg1*; otherwise, the result is 0.
:   Like **grep**; *arg2* is a pattern to search for in *arg1*. *arg2* must be a regular expression. If part of the *arg2* pattern is enclosed in \(\), the result is the

→

portion of *arg1* that matches; otherwise, the result is simply the number of characters that match. By default, a pattern match always applies to the beginning of the first argument (the search string implicitly begins with a ^). Start the search string with .* to match other parts of the string.

match *string* **regex**

Same as *string : regex*.

substr *string start length*

Return a section of *string*, beginning with *start*, with a maximum length of *length* characters. Return null when given a negative or nonnumeric *start* or *length*.

index *string character-list*

Return the first position in *string* that matches the first possible character in *character-list*. Continue through *character-list* until a match is found, or return 0.

length *string*

Return the length of *string*.

Examples

Division happens first; result is 10:

```
expr 5 + 10 / 2
```

Addition happens first; result is 7 (truncated from 7.5):

```
expr \( 5 + 10 \) / 2
```

Add 1 to variable i. This is how variables are incremented in shell scripts:

```
i=`expr $i + 1`
```

Print 1 (true) if variable **a** is the string "hello":

```
expr $a = hello
```

Print 1 (true) if **b** plus 5 equals 10 or more:

```
expr $b + 5 \>= 10
```

In the examples that follow, variable **p** is the string "version.100". This command prints the number of characters in **p**:

```
expr $p : '.*'          Result is 11
```

Match all characters and print them:

```
expr $p : '\(.*\)'      Result is "version.100"
```

Print the number of lowercase letters at the beginning of **p**:

```
expr $p : '[a-z]*'        Result is 7
```

Match the lowercase letters at the beginning of **p**:

```
expr $p : '\([a-z]*\)'  Result is "version"
```

Truncate **$x** if it contains five or more characters; if not, just print **$x**. (Logical OR uses the second argument when the first one is 0 or null; i.e., when the match fails.)

```
expr $x : '\(.....\)' \| $x
```

In a shell script, rename files to their first five letters:

```
mv $x `expr $x : '\(.....\)' \| $x`
```

(To avoid overwriting files with similar names, use **mv -i**.)

false	**false**

A null command that returns an unsuccessful (nonzero) exit status. Normally used in Bourne shell scripts. See also **true**.

fdformat [*options*] *device*	**fdformat**

Low-level format of a floppy disk. The device for a standard format is usually **/dev/fd0** or **/dev/fd1**.

Option

-n   Do not verify format after completion.

fgrep [*options*] [*pattern*] [*files*]	**fgrep**

Search one or more *files* for lines that match a literal, text-string *pattern*. Exit status is 0 if any lines match, 1 if not, and 2 for errors. See also **egrep** and **grep**.

Options

-b   Precede each line with its block number.

-c   Print only a count of matched lines.

-e *pat*   Search for pattern *pat*. Same as specifying a pattern as an argument, but useful in protecting patterns beginning with –.

-f *file* Take a list of patterns from *file*.

-h   Print matched lines but not filenames (inverse of –l).

-i   Ignore uppercase and lowercase distinctions.

-l   List filenames but not matched lines.

-n   Print lines and their line numbers.

-*num*   Print *num* lines of leading and trailing text.

→

fgrep		
←	**-v**	Print all lines that *don't* match *pattern*.
	-w	Match on whole words only. Words are divided by characters that are not letters, digits, or underscores.
	-x	Print lines only if *pattern* matches the entire line.
	-A *num*	
		Print *num* lines of text that occur before the matching line.
	-B *num*	
		Print *num* lines of text that occur after the matching line.
	-C	Print two lines of leading and trailing content.
	-L	List files that contain no matching lines.

Examples

Print lines in *file* that don't contain any spaces:

```
fgrep -v ' ' file
```

Print lines in *file* that contain the words in **spell_list**:

```
fgrep -f spell_list file
```

file	**file** [*options*] *files*

Classify the named *files* according to the type of data they contain. **file** checks the magic file (usually */etc/magic*, but sometimes */usr/lib/magic*) to identify some file types.

Options

	-c	Check the format of the magic file (*files* argument is invalid with **-c**).
	-f *list*	Run **file** on the filenames in *list*.
	-m *file*	
		Search for file types in *file* instead of */etc/magic*.
	-z	Attempt checking of compressed files.
	-L	Follow symbolic links. By default, symbolic links are not followed.

Many file types are understood. Output lists each filename, followed by a brief classification such as:

```
ascii text
c program text
c-shell commands
data
empty
iAPX 386 executable
directory
[nt]roff, tbl, or eqn input text
shell commands
symbolic link to ../usr/etc/arp
```

Example

List all files that are deemed to be troff/nroff input:

```
file * | grep roff
```

find [*pathnames*] [*conditions*]   find

An extremely useful command for finding particular groups of files (numerous examples follow this description). **find** descends the directory tree beginning at each *pathname* and locates files that meet the specified *conditions*. The default pathname is the current directory. The most useful conditions include -**print** (which is the default if no other expression is given), -**name** and -**type** (for general use), -**exec** and -**size** (for advanced users), and -**mtime** and -**user** (for administrators).

Conditions may be grouped by enclosing them in \(\) (escaped parentheses), negated with ! (use \! in the C shell), given as alternatives by separating them with -**o**, or repeated (adding restrictions to the match; usually only for -**name**, -**type**, -**perm**). Modification refers to editing of a file's contents. Change refers to modification, permission or ownership changes, etc.; therefore, for example, -**ctime** is more inclusive than -**atime** or -**mtime**.

Conditions and actions

-atime +*n* | -*n* | *n*

> Find files that were last accessed more than *n* (+*n*), less than *n* (-*n*), or exactly *n* days ago. Note that **find** changes the access time of directories supplied as *pathnames*.

-ctime +*n* | -*n* | *n*

> Find files that were changed more than *n* (+*n*), less than *n* (-*n*), or exactly *n* days ago. A change is anything that changes the directory entry for the file, such as a **chmod**.

-depth

> Descend the directory tree, skipping directories and working on actual files first (and *then* the parent directories). Useful when files reside in unwritable directories (e.g., when using **find** with **cpio**).

-exec *command* { } \;

> Run the UNIX *command*, from the starting directory on each file matched by **find** (provided *command* executes successfully on that file; i.e., returns a 0 exit status). When *command* runs, the argument { } substitutes the current file. Follow the entire sequence with an escaped semicolon (\;).

→

-follow

> Follow symbolic links and track the directories visited (don't use this with -type l).

-group *gname*

> Find files belonging to group *gname*. *gname* can be a group name or a group ID number.

-inum *n*

> Find files whose inode number is *n*.

-links *n*

> Find files having *n* links.

-mount, -xdev

> Search for files that reside only on the same filesystem as *pathname*.

-mtime +*n* | -*n* | *n*

> Find files that were last modified more than *n* (+*n*), less than *n* (-*n*), or exactly *n*, days ago. A modification is a change to a file's data, reflected in an ls -l listing.

-name *pattern*

> Find files whose names match *pattern*. Filename metacharacters may be used, but should be escaped or quoted.

-newer *file*

> Find files that have been modified more recently than *file*; similar to -mtime. Affected by –follow only if it occurs after –follow on the command line.

-ok *command* { } \;

> Same as -exec, but prompts user to respond with y before *command* is executed.

-perm *nnn*

> Find files whose permission flags (e.g., rwx) match octal number *nnn* exactly (e.g., 664 matches -rw-rw-r--). Use a minus sign before *nnn* to make a "wildcard" match of any unspecified octal digit (e.g., -perm -600 matches -rw-******, where * can be any mode).

-print Print the matching files and directories, using their full pathnames. Return true.

-size *n*[c]

> Find files containing *n* blocks, or if c is specified, *n* characters long.

-type *c*

> Find files whose type is *c*. *c* can be b (block special file), c (character special file), d (directory), p (fifo or named pipe), l (symbolic link), s (socket), or f (plain file).

-user *user*

Find files belonging to *user* (name or ID).

-daystart

Calculate times from the start of the day today, not 24 hours ago.

-maxdepth *num*

Do not descend more than *num* levels of directories.

-mindepth *num*

Begin applying tests and actions only at levels deeper than *num* levels.

-noleaf

Normally, **find** assumes that each directory has at least two hard links that should be ignored (a hard link for its name and one for ".")—i.e., two fewer "real" directories than its hard link count indicates. -noleaf turns off this assumption, a useful practice when **find** runs on non-UNIX filesystems. This forces **find** to examine all entries, assuming that some might prove to be directories into which it must descend (a time-waster on UNIX).

-amin +*n* | -*n* | *n*

Find files last accessed more than *n* (+*n*), less than *n* (-*n*), or exactly *n*, minutes ago.

-anewer *file*

Find files that were accessed after they were last modified. Affected by **-follow** when after **-follow** on the command line.

-cmin +*n* | -*n* | *n*

Find files last changed more than *n* (+*n*), less than *n* (-*n*), or exactly *n* minutes ago.

-cnewer *file*

Find files that were changed after they were last modified. Affected by **-follow** when after **-follow** on the command line.

-empty

Continue if file is empty. Applies to regular files and directories.

-false   Return false value for each file encountered.

-fstype *type*

Match files only on *type* filesystems. Acceptable types are **ufs**, **4.2**, **4.3**, **nfs**, **tmp**, **mfs**, **S51K**, **S52K**.

-gid *num*

Find files with numeric group ID of *num*.

-ilname *pattern*

A case-insensitive version of **-lname**.

-iname *pattern*

A case-insensitive version of **-name**.

→

-ipath *pattern*
> A case-insensitive version of -**path**.

-iregex *pattern*
> A case-insensitive version of -**regex**.

-lname *pattern*
> Search for files that are symbolic links, pointing to files named *pattern*. *pattern* can include shell meta-characters, and does not treat / or . specially. The match is case-insensitive.

-mmin +*n* | -*n* | *n*
> Find files last modified more than *n* (+*n*), less than *n* (-*n*), or exactly *n* minutes ago.

-nouser
> The file's user ID does not correspond to any user.

-nogroup
> The file's group ID does not correspond to any group.

-path *pattern*
> Find files whose names match *pattern*. Expect absolute pathnames: i.e., do not treat / or . specially.

Examples

List all files (and subdirectories) in your home directory:

```
find $HOME -print
```

List all files named *chapter1* in the */work* directory:

```
find /work -name chapter1 -print
```

List all files beginning with *memo* owned by *ann*:

```
find /work /usr -name 'memo*' -user ann -print
```

Search the filesystem (begin at root) for manpage directories:

```
find / -type d -name 'man*' -print
```

Search the current directory, look for filenames that *don't* begin with a capital letter, and send them to the printer:

```
find . \! -name '[A-Z]*' -exec lp {} \;
```

Find and compress files whose names *don't* end with .**gz**:

```
gzip `find . \! -name '*.gz' -print`
```

Remove all empty files on the system (prompting first):

```
find / -size 0 -ok rm {} \;
```

Search the system for files that were modified within the last two days (good candidates for backing up):

```
find / -mtime -2 -print
```

Recursively **grep** for a pattern down a directory tree:

```
find /book -print | xargs grep '[Nn]utshell'
```

---

finger [*options*] *users*

Display data about one or more *users*, including information listed in the files **.plan** and **.project** in each *user*'s home directory. You can specify each *user* either as a login name (exact match) or as a first or last name (display information on all matching names). Networked environments recognize arguments of the form *user@host* and *@host*.

Options

  -l   Force long format (default): everything included by the **-s** option, and home directory, home phone, login shell, mail status, **.plan**, **.project**, and **.forward**.

  -m   Suppress matching of users' "real" names.

  -p   Omit **.plan** and **.project** file from display.

  -s   Show short format: login name, real name, terminal name, write status, idle time, office location, and office phone number.

---

fmt [*options*] [*files*]

Convert text to specified width by filling lines and removing newlines. Concatenate files on the command line, or text from standard input. By default, preserve blank lines, spacing, indentation. **fmt** attempts to break lines at the end of sentences, and to avoid breaking lines after a sentence's first word or before its last.

Options

  -c, --**crown-margin**
        Crown margin mode. Do not change each paragraph's first two lines' indentation. Use the second line's indentation as the default for subsequent lines.

  -p *prefix*, --**prefix**=*prefix*
        Format only lines beginning with *prefix*.

  -s, --**split-only**
        Suppress line-joining.

  -t, --**tagged-paragraph**
        Tagged paragraph mode. Same as crown mode when the indentation of the first and second lines differs. If the indentation is the same, treat the first line as its own separate paragraph.

$\rightarrow$

fmt ←	**-u, --uniform-spacing**
	    Print exactly one space between words, and two between sentences.
	-width *width*, **-w** *width*, **--width=***width*
	    Set column width to *width*. The default is 75.

fold	**fold** [*option*] [*files*]
	
	Break the lines of the named *files* so that they are no wider than the specified width (default 80). **fold** breaks lines exactly at the specified width, even in the middle of a word. Reads from standard input when given - as a file.
	
	Options
	-b, --bytes
	    Count bytes, not columns; i.e., consider tabs, backspaces, and carriage returns to be one column.
	-s, --spaces
	    Break at spaces only, if possible.
	-w, --width *width*
	    Set the maximum line width to *width*. Default is 80.

formail	**formail** [*options*]
	
	Filter standard input into mailbox format. If no sender is apparent, provide the sender *foo@bar*. By default, escape bogus **From:** lines with >.
	
	Options
	+*skip*** **Do not split first *skip* messages.
	-*total*** **Stop after splitting *total* messages.
	-a *headerfield*
	    Append *headerfield* to header, unless it already exists. If *headerfield* is Message-ID or Resent-Message-ID with no contents, generate a unique message ID.
	-b Do not escape bogus **From** lines.
	-c When header fields are more than one line long, concatenate the lines.
	-d Do not assume that input must be in strict mailbox format.
	-e Allow messages to begin one immediately after the other; do not require empty space between them.
	-f Do not edit non-mailbox-format lines. By default, formail prepends **From** to such lines.
	-i *headerfield*
	    Append *headerfield* whether or not it already exists. Rename each existing *headerfield* to **Old-***headerfield*, unless they are empty.

-k   For use only with **-r**. Keep the body as well as the fields specified by **-r**.

-m *minfields*
        Require at least *minfields* before recognizing the beginning of a new message. Default is 2.

-n   Allow simultaneous **formail** processes to run.

-p *prefix*
        Escape lines with *prefix* instead of **>**.

-q   Do not display write errors, duplicate messages, and mismatched **Content-Length** fields. This is the default; use **-q-** to turn it off.

-r   Throw away all existing fields, retaining only **X-Loop**, and generate auto-reply header instead. You can preserve particular fields with the **-i** option.

-s   Must be the last option; everything following it will be assumed to be its arguments. Divide input to separate mail messages, and pipe them to the program specified, or concatenate them to standard output (by default).

-t   Assume sender's return address to be valid. (By default, **formail** favors machine-generated addresses.)

-u *headerfield*
        Delete all but the first occurrence of *headerfield*.

-x *headerfield*
        Display the contents of *headerfield* on a single line.

-z   When necessary, add a space between field names and contents. Remove ("zap") empty fields.

-A *headerfield*
        Append *headerfield* whether or not it already exists.

-B   Assume that input is in BABYL **rmail** format.

-D *maxlen idcache*
        Remember old message IDs (in *idcache*, which will grow no larger than approximately *maxlen*). When splitting, refuse to output duplicate messages. Otherwise, return true on discovering a duplicate. With **-r**, look at the sender's mail address instead of the message ID.

-I *headerfield*
        Append *headerfield* whether or not it already exists. Remove existing fields.

-R *oldfield newfield*
        Change all fields named *oldfield* to *newfield*.

-U *headerfield*
        Delete all but the last occurrence of *headerfield*.

→

formail ←	−Y Format in traditional Berkeley style; i.e., ignore **Content-Length**: fields. −X *headerfield* Display the field name and contents of *headerfield* on a single line.

free	**free**
	
	Display statistics about memory usage: total free, used, physical, swap, shared, and buffers used by the kernel.
	
	Options
	   −b Calculate memory in bytes.
	   −k Default. Calculate memory in kilobytes.
	  −m Calculate memory in megabytes.
	   −o Do not display "buffer adjusted" line. The −o switch disables the display "−/+ buffers" line.
	  −s *time*
	      Check memory usage every *time* seconds.
	   −t Display all totals on one line at the bottom of output.

ftp	**ftp** [*options*] [*hostname*]
	
	Transfer files to and from remote network site *hostname*. ftp prompts the user for a command. The commands are listed below, following the options. Some of the commands are toggles, meaning they turn on a feature when it is off, and vice versa.
	
	Options
	   −d Enable debugging.
	   −g Disable filename globbing.
	   −i Turn off interactive prompting.
	   −n No auto-login upon initial connection.
	   −v Verbose. Show all responses from remote server.
	
	Commands
	![*command* [*args*]]
	      Invoke an interactive shell on the local machine. If arguments are given, the first is taken as a command to execute directly, with the rest of the arguments as that command's arguments.
	
	$ *macro-name* [*args*]
	      Execute the macro *macro-name* that was defined with the **macdef** command. Arguments are passed to the macro unglobbed.

account [*passwd*]

    Supply a supplemental password that will be required by a remote system for access to resources once a login has been successfully completed. If no argument is given, the user will be prompted for an account password in a non-echoing mode.

append *local-file* [*remote-file*]

    Append a local file to a file on the remote machine. If *remote-file* is not given, the local filename is used after being altered by any **ntrans** or **nmap** setting. File transfer uses the current settings for *type, format, mode,* and *structure.*

ascii   Set the file transfer type to network ASCII (default).

bell   Sound a bell after each file transfer command is completed.

binary   Set file transfer type to support binary image transfer.

bye   Terminate FTP session and exit **ftp**.

case   Toggle remote computer filename case mapping during **mget**. The default is **off**. When **case** is **on**, files on the remote machine with all-uppercase names will be copied to the local machine with all-lower-case names.

cd *remote-directory*

    Change working directory on remote machine to *remote-directory.*

cdup   Change working directory of remote machine to its parent directory.

chmod [*mode*] [*remote-file*]

    Change file permissions of *remote-file.* If options are omitted, the command prompts for them.

close   Terminate FTP session and return to command interpreter.

cr   Toggle carriage return stripping during ASCII-type file retrieval.

delete *remote-file*

    Delete file *remote-file* on remote machine.

debug [*debug-value*]

    Toggle debugging mode. If *debug-value* is specified, it is used to set the debugging level.

dir [*remote-directory*] [*local-file*]

    Print a listing of the contents in the directory *remote-directory,* and, optionally, place the output in *local-file.* If no directory is specified, the current working directory on the remote machine is used. If no local file is specified, or – is given instead of the filename, output comes to the terminal.

$\rightarrow$

disconnect
> Synonym for **close**.

form *format*
> Set the file transfer form to *format*. Default format is *file*.

get *remote-file* [*local-file*]
> Retrieve the *remote-file* and store it on the local machine. If the local filename is not specified, it is given the same name it has on the remote machine, subject to alteration by the current **case**, **ntrans**, and **nmap** settings. If local file is –, output comes to the terminal.

glob
> Toggle filename expansion for **mdelete**, **mget**, and **mput**. If globbing is turned off, the filename arguments are taken literally and not expanded.

hash
> Toggle hash-sign (#) printing for each data block transferred.

help [*command*]
> Print help information for *command*. With no argument, **ftp** prints a list of commands.

idle [*seconds*]
> Get/set idle timer on remote machine. *seconds* specifies the length of the idle timer; if omitted, the current idle timer is displayed.

image
> Same as **binary**.

lcd [*directory*]
> Change working directory on local machine. If *directory* is not specified, the user's home directory is used.

ls [*remote-directory*] [*local-file*]
> Print listing of contents of directory on remote machine, in a format chosen by the remote machine. If *remote-directory* is not specified, current working directory is used.

macdef *macro-name*
> Define a macro. Subsequent lines are stored as the macro *macro-name*; a null line terminates macro input mode. When **$i** is included in the macro, loop through arguments, substituting the current argument for **$i** on each pass. Escape $ with \.

mdelete *remote-files*
> Delete the *remote-files* on the remote machine.

mdir *remote-files local-file*
> Like **dir**, except multiple remote files may be specified.

mget *remote-files*

>   Expand the wildcard expression *remote-files* on the remote machine and do a **get** for each filename thus produced.

mkdir *directory-name*

>   Make a directory on the remote machine.

mls *remote-files local-file*

>   Like **nlist**, except multiple remote files may be specified, and the local file must be specified.

mode [*mode-name*]

>   Set file transfer mode to *mode-name*. Default mode is stream mode.

modtime [*file-name*]

>   Show last modification time of the file on the remote machine.

mput [*local-files*]

>   Expand wildcards in *local-files* given as arguments and do a **put** for each file in the resulting list.

newer *remote-file* [*local-file*]

>   Get file if remote file is newer than local file.

nlist [*remote-directory*] [*local-file*]

>   Print list of files of a directory on the remote machine to *local-file* (or the screen if *local-file* is not specified). If *remote-directory* is unspecified, the current working directory is used.

nmap [*inpattern outpattern*]

>   Set or unset the filename mapping mechanism. The mapping follows the pattern set by *inpattern*, a template for incoming filenames, and *outpattern*, which determines the resulting mapped filename. The sequences $1 through $9 are treated as variables: for example, the *inpattern* **$1.$2**, along with the input file **readme.txt**, would set $1 to **readme** and $2 to **txt**. An *outpattern* of **$1.data** would result in an output file of **readme.data**. $0 corresponds to the complete filename. [**string1**, **string2**] is replaced by *string1*, unless that string is null, in which case it's replaced by *string2*.

ntrans [*inchars* [*outchars*]]

>   Set or unset the filename character translation mechanism. Characters in a filename matching a character in *inchars* are replaced with the corresponding character in *outchars*. If no arguments are specified, the filename mapping mechanism is unset. If arguments are specified:

>   • Characters in remote filenames are translated during **mput** and **put** commands issued without a specified remote target filename.

$\rightarrow$

- Characters in local filenames are translated during **mget** and **get** commands issued without a specified local target filename.

open *host* [*port*]

Establish a connection to the specified *host* FTP server. An optional *port* number may be supplied, in which case **ftp** will attempt to contact an FTP server at that port.

prompt

Toggle interactive prompting.

proxy *ftp-command*

Execute an FTP command on a secondary control connection—i.e., send commands to two separate remote hosts simultaneously.

put *local-file* [*remote-file*]

Store a local file on the remote machine. If *remote-file* is left unspecified, the local filename is used after processing according to any **ntrans** or **nmap** settings in naming the remote file. File transfer uses the current settings for *type*, *file*, *structure*, and *transfer mode*.

pwd   Print name of the current working directory on the remote machine.

quit   Synonym for **bye**.

quote *arg1 arg2*...

Send the arguments specified, verbatim, to the remote FTP server.

recv *remote-file* [*local-file*]

Synonym for **get**.

reget *remote-file* [*local-file*]

Retrieve a file (like **get**), except it restarts at the end of *local-file*. Useful for restarting a dropped transfer.

remotehelp [*command-name*]

Request help from the remote FTP server. If *command-name* is specified, remote help for that command is returned.

remotestatus [*file-name*]

Show status of the remote machine, or, if *file-name* specified, *file-name* on remote machine.

rename [*from*] [*to*]

Rename file *from* on remote machine to *to*.

reset   Clear reply queue.

restart *marker*

Restart the transfer of a file from a particular byte count.

rmdir [*directory-name*]
> Delete a directory on the remote machine.

runique
> Toggle storing of files on the local system with unique filenames. When this option is on, rename files as .1 or .2, etc., as appropriate, to preserve unique filenames, and report each such action. Default value is off.

send *local-file* [*remote-file*]
> Synonym for **put**.

sendport
> Toggle the use of **PORT** commands.

site [*command*]
> Get/set site-specific information from/on remote machine.

size *file-name*
> Return size of *file-name* on remote machine.

status   Show current status of **ftp**.

struct [*struct-name*]
> Set the file transfer structure to *struct-name*. By default, **stream** structure is used.

sunique
> Toggle storing of files on remote machine under unique filenames.

system   Show type of operating system running on remote machine.

tenex   Set file transfer type to that needed to talk to TENEX machines.

trace   Toggle packet tracing.

type [*type-name*]
> Set file transfer **type** to *type-name*. If no type is specified, the current type is printed. The default type is network ASCII.

umask [*mask*]
> Set user file-creation mode mask on the remote site. If mask is omitted, the current value of the mask is printed.

user *username* [*password*] [*account*]
> Identify yourself to the remote FTP server. **ftp** will prompt the user for the password, if not specified and the server requires it, and the account field.

verbose
> Toggle verbose mode.

? [*command*]
> Same as **help**.

fuser	**fuser** [*options*] *filename* ... [−]
	Display the process IDs of all processes that are using particular files or filesystems. The information given can be interpreted in the following way:
	c Current directory
	e Executable
	f Open file; omitted in default display mode
	r Root directory
	m **mmap**'ed file or shared library
	Options
	− Reset options to defaults.
	−*signal* Send *signal* to process. (Default signal is SIGKILL.) **fuser** recognizes signals by name (as listed in **fuser −l**) and number.
	−a Show all specified files, not just those that are being accessed by at least one process.
	−k Terminate all processes accessing the file.
	−l Print a list of signal names.
	−m Expect *filename* to refer to a mounted file system or block device, and list processes on this filesystem.
	−s Search silently—i.e., ignore −a, −u, and −v.
	−u Print names of process owners.
	−v Verbose: print process ID, user, command, and access fields.
gawk	**gawk** [*options*] '*script*' *var=value* ... *files* **gawk** [*options*] −f *scriptfile var=value* ... *files*
	The GNU version of **awk**, a program that does pattern matching, record processing, and other forms of text manipulation. For more information, see Chapter 11, *The gawk Scripting Language*.
getkeycodes	**getkeycodes**
	Print the kernel's scancode-to-keycode mapping table.
grep	**grep** [*options*] *regexp* [*files*]
	Search one or more *files* for lines that match a regular expression *regexp*. Regular expressions are described in Chapter 6, *Pattern Matching*. Exit status is 0 if any lines match, 1 if none match, and 2 for errors. See also **egrep** and **fgrep**.

-*num*** Print *num* leading and trailing lines of context, but never print any given line more than once.

-b   Precede each line with its block number.

-c   Print only a count of matched lines.

-e *regexp*
Search for the pattern *regexp*. The **-e** option is useful in protecting patterns beginning with a **–**.

-f *file* Take expression from *file*.

-h   Print matched lines but not filenames (inverse of **-l**).

-i   Ignore uppercase and lowercase distinctions.

-l   List filenames but not matched lines.

-n   Print lines and their line numbers.

-s   Suppress error messages for nonexistent or unreadable files.

-v   Print all lines that *don't* match *regexp*.

-A *num*
Print *num* lines of trailing context.

-B *num*
Print *num* lines of leading context.

-C   Print two lines of leading and trailing context.

-G   Default. Parse pattern as regular expression; i.e., do not extend special meaning to the characters ?, +, {, |, (, and), unless they are escaped with a \.

-E   Parse pattern as extended regular expression. Similar to **egrep**. Treat ?, +, {, |, (, and) as special characters, even when they are not escaped.

-F   Same as **fgrep**.

-L   List files that contain no matching lines.

-q   Suppress normal output.

-w   Match on whole words only. Words are divided by characters that are not letters, digits, or underscores.

-x   Match on entire lines only.

Examples

List the number of users who use the C shell:

```
grep -c /bin/csh /etc/passwd
```

List header files that have at least one **#include** directive:

```
grep -l '^#include' /usr/include/*
```

List files that don't contain *pattern*:

```
grep -c pattern files | grep :0
```

gzexe	**gzexe** [*options*] [*file*]

Compress executables. When run, these files will automatically uncompress, thus trading time for space. **gzexe** creates backup files (*filename~*) which should be removed after testing the original.

Option

   -d   Decompress files. |
| **gzip** | **gzip** [*options*] [*files*]
gunzip [*options*] [*files*]

Compress specified files (or read from standard input) with Lempel-Ziv coding (LZ77). Rename compressed file to *filename.gz*; keep ownership modes and access/modification times. Ignore symbolic links. Uncompress with **gunzip**, which takes all of **gzip**'s options, except those specified. Files compressed with the **compress** command can be decompressed using these commands.

Options

  -*num*, --fast, --best
       Control compression speed. *num* runs from 1 to 9, with 1 being fastest and 9 being best. Slower compression compresses more.

  -c, --stdout, --to-stdout
       Print output to standard output, and do not change input files.

  -d, --decompress, --uncompress
       Same as **gunzip**.

  -f, --force
       Force compression. **gzip** would normally prompt for permission to continue when the file has multiple links, its .gz version already exists, or it is reading compressed data to or from a terminal.

  -l, --list
       Expects to be given compressed files as arguments. Files may be compressed by any of the following methods: **gzip**, **deflate**, **compress**, **lzh**, and **pack**. For each file, list uncompressed and compressed sizes (the latter being always -1 for files compressed by programs other than **gzip**), compression ratio, and uncompressed name. With -v, also print compression method, the 32-bit CRC of the uncompressed data, and the time stamp. With -N, look inside the file for the uncompressed name and time stamp.

  -q, --quiet
       Print no warnings. |

-r, --recursive
> When given a directory as an argument, recursively compress or decompress files within it.

-S *suffix*, --suffix *suffix*
> Append *.suffix*. Default is **gz**. A null suffix while decompressing causes **gunzip** to attempt to decompress all specified files, regardless of suffix.

-t, --test
> Test compressed file integrity.

-v, --verbose
> Print name and percent size reduction for each file.

-N, --name
> Default. Save original name and time stamp. With **gunzip** or **gzip -d**, restore original name and time stamp.

---

head [*options*] [*files*]

Print the first few lines (default is 10) of one or more *files*. With no *files* defined or a − for *files*, read from standard input. With more than one file, print a header for each file.

Options

-c *num*, --bytes *num*
> Print first *num* bytes, or, if *num* is followed by **k** or **m**, first *num* kilobytes or megabytes.

-l, -n *num*, --lines *num*
> Print first *num* lines. Default is 10.

-v, --verbose
> Print filename headers, even for only one file.

Examples
> Display the first 20 lines of **phone_list**:

```
head -20 phone_list
```

> Display the first ten phone numbers having a 202 area code:

```
grep '(202)' phone_list | head
```

---

host [*options*] *host* [*server*]
host [*options*] *zone* [*server*]

Print information about specified hosts or zones in DNS. Hosts may be IP addresses or hostnames; **host** converts IP addresses to hostnames by default, and appends the local domain to hosts without a trailing dot. Default servers are determined in */etc/resolv.conf*. For more information about hosts and zones, try Chapters 1 and 2 of *DNS and BIND*, by Paul Albitz and Cricket Liu, published by O'Reilly & Associates.

→

host	**Options**	
←	`-a`	Same as **-t ANY**.

`-c` *class*

Search for specified resource record class (IN, INTERNET, CS, CSNET, CH, CHAOS, HS, HESIOD, ANY, or *). Default is IN.

`-d`   Debugging mode. **-dd** is a more verbose version.

`-e`   Do not print information about domains outside of specified zone. For hostname queries, do not print "additional information" or "authoritative nameserver".

`-f` *file*   Output to *file* as well as standard out.

`-i`   Given an IP address, return the corresponding *in-addr.arpa* address, class (always PTR), and hostname.

`-l` *zone*

List all machines in *zone*.

`-m`   Print only MR, MG, and MB records; recursively expand MR (renamed mail box) and MG (mail group) records to MB (mail box) records.

`-o`   Do not print output to standard out.

`-p` [*server*]

For use with **-l**. Query only the zone's primary nameserver (or *server*) for zone transfers, instead of those authoritative servers that respond. Useful for testing unregistered zones.

`-q`   Quiet. Suppress warning, but not error, messages.

`-r`   Do not ask contacted server to query other servers, but require only the information that it has cached.

`-t` *type* Look for *type* entries in the resource record. *type* may be A, NS, PTR, ANY, or * (all).

`-u`   Use TCP, not UDP.

`-v`   Verbose. Include all fields from resource record, even time-to-live and class, as well as "additional information" and "authoritative nameservers" (provided by the remote nameserver).

`-vv`   Very verbose. Include information about *host*'s defaults.

`-w`   Never give up on queried server.

`-x`   Allow multiple hosts or zones to be specified. If a server is also specified, the argument must be preceeded by **-X**.

`-A`   For hostnames, look up the associated IP address, and then reverse look up the hostname, to see if a match occurs. For IP addresses, look up the associated hostname, and determine whether the host recognizes that address as its own. For zones, check

IP addresses for all hosts. Exit silently if no incongruities are discovered.

-C Similar to -I, but also checks to see if the zone's nameservers are really authoritative. The zone's SOA (start of authority) records specify authoritative nameservers (in NS fields). Those servers are queried; if they do not have SOA records, host reports a lame delegation. Other checks are made as well.

-D Similar to -H, but includes the names of hosts with more than one address per defined name.

-E Similar to -H, but does not treat extra-zone hosts as errors. Extra-zone hosts are hosts in an undefined subdomain.

-H *zone*
Print the number of unique hosts within *zone*. Do not include aliases. Also list all errors found (extra-zone names, duplicate hosts).

-F *file* Redirect standard out to *file*, and print extra resource record output only on standard out.

-G *zone*
Similar to -H, but includes the names of gateway hosts.

-I *chars*
Do not print warnings about domain names containing illegal characters *chars*, such as _.

-L *level*
For use with -I. List all delegated zones within this zone, up to *level* deep, recursively.

-P *servers*
For use with -I. *servers* should be a comma-separated list. Specify preferred hosts for secondary servers to use when copying over zone data. Highest priority is given to those servers that match the most domain components in a given part of *servers*.

-R Treat non-fully-qualified host names as BIND does, searching each component of the local domain.

-S For use with -I. Print all hosts within the zone to standard out. Do not print hosts within subzones. Include class and IP address. Print warning messages (illegal names, lame delegations, missing records, etc.) to standard error.

-T Print time-to-live values (how long information about each host will remain cached before the nameserver refreshes it).

→

host ←	-X *server* Specify a server to query, and allow multiple hosts or zones to be specified. -Z When printing recource records, include trailing dot in domain names, and print time-to-live value and class name.

hostname	**hostname** [*option*] [*nameofhost*]
	
	Set or print name of current host system. A privileged user can set the hostname with *nameofhost* argument.
	
	Option
	  -d, --domain
	      Print DNS domain name.
	  -f, --fqdn, --long
	      Print fully qualified domain name.
	  -s, --short
	      Trim domain information from the printed name.
	  -F *file*, --file *file*
	      Consult *file* for hostname.

id	**id** [*options*] [*username*]
	
	Display information about yourself, or another user: user ID, group ID, effective user ID and group ID if relevant, and additional group IDs.
	
	Options
	  -g, --group
	      Print group ID only.
	  -n, --name
	      With **-u**, **-g**, or **-G**, print user or group name, not number.
	  -r, --real
	      With **-u**, **-g**, or **-G**, print real, not effective, user ID or group ID.
	  -u, --user
	      Print user ID only.
	  -G, --groups
	      Print supplementary groups only.

info	**info** [*options*] *topics* GNU hypertext reader: displays online documentation previously built from texinfo input. Info files are arranged in a hierarchy and can contain menus for subtopics. When entered without options, the command displays the top-level info file (usually */usr/local/info/dir*). When *topics* are specified, finds a subtopic

by choosing the first *topic* from the menu in the top-level info file, the next *topic* from the new file specified by the first *topic*, and so on. The initial display can also be controlled by the -f and -n options.

Options

-d *directories*, --**directory** *directories*
> Search *directories*, a colon-separated list, for info files. If this option is not specified, use INFOPATH environment variable or default (usually */usr/local/info*).

--**dribble** *file*
> Store each keystroke in *file*, which can be used in a future session with the --**restore** option to return to this place in info.

-f *file*, --**file** *file*
> Display specified info file.

-n *node*, --**node** *node*
> Display specified node in the info file.

-o *file*, --**output** *file*
> Copy output to *file* instead of displaying it at the screen.

--**help** Display brief help.

--**restore** *file*
> When starting, execute keystrokes in *file*.

--**subnodes**
> Display subtopics.

--**version**
> Display version.

---

ispell [*options*] [*files*]

Compare the words of one or more named *files* with the system dictionary. Display unrecognized words on the top of the screen, accompanied by possible correct spellings, and allow editing, via a series of commands.

Options

-b   Back up original file in *filename*.**bak**.

-d *file* Search *file* instead of standard dictionary file.

-m   Suggest different root/affix combinations.

-n   Expect nroff or troff input file.

-p *file* Search *file* instead of personal dictionary file.

-t   Expect TEX or LATEX input file.

-w *chars*
> Consider *chars* to be legal, in addition to a–z and A–Z.

→

ispell	-x	Do not back up original file.
←	-B	Search for missing blanks (resulting in concatenated words) in addition to ordinary misspellings.
	-C	Do not produce error messages in response to concatenated words.

-L *number*
    Show *number* lines of context.

-M   List interactive commands at bottom of screen.

-N   Suppress printing of interactive commands.

-P   Do not attempt to suggest more root/affix combinations.

-S   Sort suggested replacements by likelihood that each is correct.

-T *type*
    Expect all files to be formatted by *type*.

-W *n*   Never consider words that are *n* characters or less to be misspelled.

-V   Use hat notation (^L) to display control characters, and **M-** to display characters with the high bit set.

Interactive Commands

number
    Replace with suggestion number *number*.

!*command*
    Invoke shell and execute *command* in it. Prompt before exiting.

a   Consider word to be correctly spelled, but do not add it to personal dictionary.

i   Add word to personal dictionary.

l   Search system dictionary for words.

q   Exit without saving.

r   Replace word.

u   Add all-lowercase version of word to personal dictionary.

x   Skip to the next file, saving changes.

---

kbd_mode   **kbd_mode** [*option*]

Print current keyboard mode, which may be RAW, MEDIUM-RAW, or XLATE.

Options

-a   Set mode to XLATE (ASCII mode).

-k   Set mode to MEDIUMRAW (keycode mode).

-s   Set mode to RAW (scancode mode).

-u   Set mode to UNICODE (UTF-8 mode).

kill [*option*] *IDs*

Send a signal to terminate one or more process *IDs*. You must own the process or be a privileged user. This command is similar to the **kill** command that is built into the Bourne, Korn, and C shells. A minus sign before an *ID* specifies a process group ID. (The built-in version doesn't allow process group IDs, but it does allow job IDs that begin with %.)

Options

-l   List all signals.

-*signal*   The signal number (from **ps -f**) or name (from **kill** -l). With a signal number of 9, the kill cannot be caught. The default is TERM.

killall [*options*] [*name*]

Kill processes by name. If more than one process is running the specified command, kill all of them. Treat command names that contain a / as files: kill all processes that are executing that file.

Options

-*signal*   Send *signal* to process (default is TERM). *signal* may be a name or number.

-i   Prompt for confirmation before killing processes.

-l   List possible signal names.

-v   Verbose: after killing process, report success and process ID.

killall5

The System V equivalent of **killall**, this command kills all processes except those on which it depends.

less [*options*] [*filename*]

less is a program for paging through files or other output. It was written in reaction to the perceived primitiveness of **more** (hence its name). Some commands may be preceded by a number.

Options

-[z]*num*
>   Set number of lines to scroll to *num*. Default is one screenful. A negative *num* sets the number to *num* lines less than the current number.

+[+]*command*
>   Run *command* on startup. If *command* is a number, jump to that line. The option ++ applies this command to each file in the command-line list.

→

less
←

-?	Print help screen. Ignore all other options; do not page through file.
-a	When searching, begin after last line displayed. (Default is to search from second line displayed.)

-b*buffers*
> Use *buffers* buffers for each file (default is 10). Buffers are 1 kilobyte in size.

-c	Redraw screen from top, not bottom.
-d	Suppress dumb-terminal error messages.
-e	Automatically exit after reaching *EOF* twice.
-f	Force opening of directories and devices; do not print warning when opening binaries.
-g	Highlight only string found by past search command, not all matching strings.

-h*num*
> Never scroll backward more than *num* lines at once.

-i	Make searches case-insensitive, unless the search string contains uppercase letters.
-j*num*	Position "target" line on *num*th line of screen. "Target" line can be the result of a search or a jump. Count lines beginning from 1 (top line). A negative *num* is counted back from bottom of screen.
-k*file*	Read *file* to define special key bindings.
-m	Display **more**-like prompt, including percent of file read.
-n	Do not calculate line numbers. Affects **-m** and **-M** options, and = and **v** commands (disables passing of line number to editor).
-o*file*	When input is from a pipe, copy output to *file* as well as to screen. (Prompt for overwrite authority if *file* exists.)

-p*pattern*
> At startup, search for first occurrence of *pattern*.
>
> | | |
> |---|---|
> | m | Set medium prompt (specified by **-m**). |
> | M | Set long prompt (specified by **-M**). |
> | = | Set message printed by = command. |

-q	Disable ringing of bell on attempts to scroll past *EOF* or before beginning of file. Attempt to use visual bell instead.
-r	Display "raw" control characters, instead of using ^*x* notation. Sometimes leads to display problems.
-s	Print successive blank lines as one line.
-t*tag*	Edit file containing *tag*. Consult *./tags* (constructed by **ctags**).
-u	Treat backspaces and carriage returns as printable input.

-w	Print lines after *EOF* as blanks instead of tildes (~).
-x*n*	Set tab stops to every *n* characters. Default is 8.
-y*n*	Never scroll forward more than *n* lines at once.
-B	Do not automatically allocate buffers for data read from a pipe. If -b specifies a number of buffers, allocate that many. If necessary, allow information from previous screens to be lost.
-C	Redraw screen by clearing it and then redrawing from top.
-E	Automatically exit after reaching *EOF* once.
-G	Never highlight matching search strings.
-I	Make searches case-insensitive, even when the search string contains uppercase letters.
-M	Prompt more verbosely than with -m, including percentage, line number, and total lines.
-N	Print line number before each line.
-O*file*	Similar to -o, but does not prompt when overwriting file.
-P[m,M,=]*prompt*	Set *prompt* (as defined by -m, -M, or =). Default is short prompt (-m).
-Q	Never ring terminal bell.
-S	Cut, do not fold, long lines.
-T*file*	With the -t option or :t command, read *file* instead of ./**tags**.
-U	Treat backspaces and carriage returns as control characters.
-X	Do not send initialization and deinitialization strings from termcap to terminal.

Commands

Commands can be preceded by an argument.

SPACE, ˆV, f, ˆF
  Scroll forward the default number of lines (usually one windowful).

z
  Similar to SPACE, but allows the number of lines to be specified, in which case it resets the default to that number.

RETURN, ˆN, e, ˆE, j, ˆJ
  Scroll forward, a default of one line. Display all lines, even if the default is more lines than the screen size.

d, ˆD
  Scroll forward, a default of one half the screen size. The number of lines may be specified, in which case the default is reset.

→

b, ˆB, ESC-v
> Scroll backward, a default of one windowful.

w   Like **b**, but allows the number of lines to be specified, in which case it resets the default to that number.

y, ˆY, ˆP, k, ˆK
> Scroll backward, a default of 1 line. Display all lines, even if the default is more lines than the screen size.

u, ˆU   Scroll backward, a default of one half the screen size. The number of lines may be specified, in which case the default is reset.

r, ˆR, ˆL
> Redraw screen.

R   Like **r**, but discard buffered input.

F   Scroll forward. When an *EOF* is reached, continue trying to find more output, behaving similarly to **tail -f**.

g, <, ESC-<
> Skip to a line, default 1.

G, >, ESC->
> Skip to a line, default being the last one.

p, %   Prompt for a number between 0 and 100; then skip to a position *number* percent of the way into the file.

{   If the top line on the screen includes a {, find its matching }. If the top line contains multiple {, prompt for a number to determine which one to use in finding a match.

}   If the bottom line on the screen includes a }, find its matching {. If the bottom line contains multiple }, prompt for a number to determine which one to use in finding a match.

(If the top line on the screen includes a (, find its matching). If the top line contains multiple (, prompt for a number to determine which one to use in finding a match.

)   If the bottom line on the screen includes a), find its matching (. If the bottom line contains multiple), prompt for a number to determine which one to use in finding a match.

[If the top line on the screen includes a [, find its matching]. If the top line contains multiple [, prompt for a number to determine which one to use in finding a match.

]   If the bottom line on the screen includes a], find its matching [. If the bottom line contains multiple], prompt for a number to determine which one to use in finding a match.

ESC-^F	Behaves like {, but prompts for two characters, which it substitutes for { and } in its search.
ESC-^B	Behaves like }, but prompts for two characters, which it substitutes for { and } in its search.
m	Prompts for a lowercase letter, and then uses that letter to mark the current position.
'	Prompts for a lowercase letter, and then goes to the position marked by that letter. There are some special characters.

    '   Return to position before last "large movement."

    ^   Beginning of file.

    $ End of file.

^X^X   Same as '.

/pattern

    Find next occurrence of *pattern*, starting at second line displayed. Some special characters can be entered before *pattern*.

    !   Find lines that do not contain *pattern*.

    *   If current file does not contain *pattern*, continue through the rest of the files in the command line list.

    @   Search from the first line in the first file specified on the command line, no matter what the screen currently displays.

?pattern

    Search backwards, beginning at the line before the top line. Treats !, *, and @ as special characters when they begin *pattern*, as / does.

ESC-*/pattern*

    Same as /*.

ESC-*?pattern*

    Same as ?*.

n	Repeat last *pattern* search.
N	Repeat last *pattern* search, in the reverse direction.
ESC-n	Repeat previous search command, but as though it were prefaced by *.
ESC-N	Repeat previous search command, but as though it were prefaced by *, and in the opposite direction.
ESC-u	Toggle search highlighting.

:e [*filename*]

    Read in *filename* and insert it into the command-line list of filenames. Without *filename*, re-read the current file. *filename* may contain special characters.

    %   Name of current file

    #   Name of previous file

→

^X^V, E
: Same as :e.

:n Read in next file in command-line list.

:p Read in previous file in command-line list.

:x Read in first file in command-line list.

:f, =, ^G
: Print filename, position in command-line list, line number on top of window, total lines, byte number, and total bytes.

- Expects to be followed by a command-line option letter. Toggles the value of that option, or, if appropriate, prompts for its new value.

-+ Expects to be followed by a command-line option letter. Resets that option to its default.

-- Expects to be followed by a command-line option letter. Resets that option to the opposite of its default, where "opposite" can be determined.

_ Expects to be followed by a command-line option letter. Display that option's current setting.

+*cmd* Execute *cmd* each time a new file is read in.

q, :q, :Q, ZZ
: Exit.

v Not valid for all versions. Invoke editor specified by $VISUAL or $EDITOR, or **vi**.

! *command*
: Not valid for all versions. Invoke $SHELL or **sh**. If *command* is given, run it and exit. Special characters:

% Name of current file

Name of previous file

!! Last shell command

| *<mark-letter> command*
: Not valid for all versions. Pipe fragment of file (from first line on screen to *mark-letter*) to *command*. *mark-letter* may also be:

^ Beginning of file

$ End of file

., **newline** Current screen is piped

Prompts

The prompt interprets certain sequences specially. Those beginning with % are always evaluated. Those beginning with ? are evaluated if certain conditions are true.

Some prompts determine the position of particular lines on the screen. These sequences require that a method of determining that line be specified. There are five possibilities:

t   top of the screen

m   middle of the screen

b   bottom of the screen

B   line after the bottom of the screen

j   "target" line

%b{t,m,b,B,j}
> The byte offset into the file.

%B   Size of current file.

%E   Name of editor.

%f   Current file.

%i   Position of current file in command-line list.

%l{t,m,b,B,j}
> Line number in file of a specific line on screen.

%L   Line number of last line in current file.

%m   Total number of lines in all files.

%p{t,m,b,B,j}
> Percent into current input file.

%s   Same as %B.

%t   Remove trailing spaces.

%x   Next input file in command-line list.

?a   True if prompt so far is nonnull.

?b{t,m,b,B,j}
> True if specified line's byte offset can be determined.

?B   True if current file's size can be determined.

?e   True if *EOF* has been reached.

?f   True if reading from a file, not a pipe.

?l{t,m,b,B,j}
> True if line number can be determined.

?L   True if final line number can be determined.

?m   True if there are multiple input files.

?n   True if this is the first prompt in the current file.

?p{t,m,b,B,j}
> True if percent into current file can be determined.

?s   Same as ?B.

?x   True if current file is not the last one.

---

ln [*options*] *sourcename* [*destname*]   **ln**
ln [*options*] *sourcenames destdirectory*

Create pseudonyms (links) for files, allowing them to be accessed by different names. In the first form, link *sourcename*

→

ln

←

to *destname*, where *destname* is usually a new filename, or (by default) the current directory. If *destname* is an existing file, it is overwritten; if *destname* is an existing directory, a link named *sourcename* is created in that directory. In the second form, create links in *destdirectory*, each link having the same name as the file specified.

Options

-b, --backup
: Back up files before removing the originals.

-d, -F, --directory
: Allow hard links to directories. Available to privileged users.

-f
: Force the link to occur (don't prompt for overwrite permission).

-i, --interactive
: Prompt for permission before removing files.

-n, --no-dereference
: Replace symbolic links to directories instead of dereferencing them. --force is useful with this option.

-s
: Create a symbolic link. This lets you link across file systems and also see the name of the link when you run **ls** -l (otherwise there's no way to know the name that a file is linked to).

-S *suffix*, --suffix *suffix*
: Append *suffix* to files when making backups, instead of the default ˜.

-V, --version-control {numbered,existing,simple}
: Control the types of backups made.

t, numbered	Numbered
nil, existing	Simple (˜) unless a numbered backup exists; then make a numbered backup.
never, simple	Simple

---

locate

locate [*options*] *pattern*

Search database(s) of filenames and print matches. *, ?, [, and] are treated specially; / and . are not. Matches include all files that contain *pattern*, unless *pattern* includes metacharacters, in which case **locate** requires an exact match.

Option

-d *path*, --database=*path*
: Search databases in *path*. *path* must be a colon-separated list.

---

lockfile [options] filename

Create semaphore file(s), used to limit access to a file. When
lockfile fails to create some of the specified files, it pauses for 8
seconds and tries the last one on which it failed. The command
processes flags as they are encountered (i.e., a flag that is specified after a file will not affect that file).

Options

-!   Invert return value.

-r retries Stop trying to create *files* after *retries* retries. The
default is -1 (never stop trying). When giving up,
remove all created files.

login [name | option]

Log in to the system. login asks for a username (*name* can be
supplied on the command line), and password (if appropriate).

If successful, login updates accounting files, sets various environment variables, notifies users if they have mail, and executes
startup shell files.

No user except root is able to log in when */etc/nologin* exists.
That file will be displayed before the connection is terminated.
root may connect only on a tty that is included in */etc/securetty*.
If ~/.hushlogin exists, execute a quiet login. If */var/adm/lastlog*
exists, print the time of the last login.

Options

-f   Suppress second login authentication.

-h host Specify name of remote host. Normally used by
servers, not humans; may be used only by root.

-p   Preserve previous environment.

logname

Consult */etc/utmp* for user's login name. If found, print it; otherwise, exit with an error message.

look [options] string [file]

Search for lines in *file* (*/usr/dict/words* by default) that begin
with *string*.

Options

-d Compare only alphanumeric characters.

-f Search is not case-sensitive.

-t *character*
Examine only characters up to and including *character*.

lpq	## lpq [*options*] [*name*]

Check the print spool queue for status of print jobs. For each job, display username, rank in the queue, filenames, job number, and total file size (in bytes). If *name* is specified, display information only for that user.

Options

-P*printer*
    Specify which printer to query. Without this option, *lpq* uses the default system printer or the printer set in the PRINTER environment variable.

-1   Print information about each file comprising a job.

#*num*   Check status for a particular job number. |
| **lpr** | ## lpr [*options*] *files*

Send *files* to the printer spool queue.

Options

-c   Expect data produced by **cifplot**.

-d   Expect data produced by TEX in the DVI (device-independent) format.

-f   Use a filter that interprets the first character of each line as a standard carriage control character.

-g   Expect standard plot data as produced by the **plot** routines.

-1   Use a filter that allows control characters to be printed and suppresses page breaks.

-n   Expect data from **ditroff** (device-independent **troff**).

-p   Use **pr** to format the files (equivalent to **print**).

-t   Expect data from **troff** (cat phototypesetter commands).

-v   Expect a raster image for devices like the Benson Varian.

-P*printer*
    Output to *printer*.

-h   Do not print the burst page.

-m   Mail on completion.

-r   Remove the file upon completion of spooling or printing (with the -s option).

-s   Use symbolic links instead of copying files to the spool directory. This can save time and disk space for large files. Files should not be modified or removed until they have been printed.

-#*num*
    Print *num* copies of listed files. |

-C *string*
> Replace system name on the burst page with *string*.

-J *string*
> Replace the printed file's name on the burst page with *string*.

-T *title*
> Use *title* as the title name when using **pr**.

-i [*cols*]
> Indent the output. Default is 8 columns. Specify number of columns to indent with the *cols* argument.

-w *num*
> Set *num* characters as the page width for **pr**.

---

lprm [*options*] [*jobnum*] [*user*]

Remove a print job from the print spool queue. You must specify a job number or numbers, which can be obtained from **lpq**. A privileged user may use the *user* parameter to remove all files belonging to a particular user or users.

Options

-P*printer*
> Specify printer name. Normally, the default printer or printer specified in the PRINTER environment variable is used.

–
> Remove all jobs in the spool owned by *user*.

---

ls [*options*] [*names*]

List contents of directories. If no *names* are given, list the files in the current directory. With one or more *names*, list files contained in a directory *name* or that match a file *name*. *names* can include filename metacharacters. The options let you display a variety of information in different formats. The most useful options include –F, –R, –l, and –s. Some options don't make sense together; e.g., –u and –c.

Options

-1, --format=single-column
> Print one entry per line of output.

-a
> List all files, including the normally hidden files whose names begin with a period.

-b, --escape
> Display nonprinting characters in octal and alphabetic format.

-c, --time-ctime, --time=status
> List files by status change time (not creation/modification time).

$\rightarrow$

ls

←

-d, --directory
> Report only on the directory, not its contents.

-f
> Print directory contents in exactly the order in which they are stored, without attempting to sort them.

-i, --inode
> List the inode for each file.

-k, --kilobytes
> If file sizes are being listed, print them in kilobytes. This overrides the environment variable POSIXLY_CORRECT.

-l, --format=long, --format=verbose
> Long format listing (includes permissions, owner, size, modification time, etc.).

-m, --format=commas
> Merge the list into a comma-separated series of names.

-n, --numeric-uid-gid
> Like -l, but use group ID and user ID numbers instead of owner and group names.

-p
> Mark directories by appending / to them.

-q, --hide-control-chars
> Show nonprinting characters as **?**.

-r, --reverse
> List files in reverse order (by name or by time).

-s, --size
> Print size of the files in blocks.

-t, --sort=time
> Sort files according to modification time (newest first).

-u, --time=atime, --time=access, --time=use
> Sort files according to the file access time.

-x, --format=across, --format=horizontal
> List files in rows going across the screen.

-A, --almost-all
> List all files, including the normally hidden files whose names begin with a period. Does not include . and ..

-B, --ignore-backups
> Do not list files ending in '~', unless given as arguments.

-C, --format=vertical
> List files in columns (the default format).

-F, --classify
> Flag filenames by appending / to directories, * to executable files, @ to symbolic links, | to FIFOs, and = to sockets.

-G, --no-group
> In long format, do not display group name.

-L, --dereference
> List the file or directory referenced by a symbolic link rather than the link itself.

-N, --literal
> Do not list filenames.

-Q, --quote-name
> Quote filenames with "; quote nongraphic characters with alphabetic and octal backslash sequences.

-R, --recursive
> Recursively list subdirectories as well as the specified (or current) directory.

-S, --sort=size
> Sort by file size, largest to smallest.

-U, --sort=none
> Do not sort files. Similar to –f, but displays in long format.

-X, --sort=extension
> Sort by file extension.

Examples

List all files in the current directory and their sizes; use multiple columns and mark special files:

```
ls -asCF
```

List the status of directories /bin and /etc:

```
ls -ld /bin /etc
```

List C source files in the current directory, the oldest first:

```
ls -rt *.c
```

Count the files in the current directory:

```
ls | wc -l
```

---

lsattr [options] [files]

Print attributes of files on a Linux Second Extended File System. See also chattr.

Options

-a   List all files in specified directories.

-d   List directories' attributes, not the attributes of the contents.

-R   List directories and their contents recursively.

-v   List version of files.

mail   mail [*options*] [*users*]

Read mail or send mail to other *users*. The **mail** utility allows
you to compose, send, receive, forward, and reply to mail. **mail**
has two main modes: compose mode, where you create a message; and command mode, where you manage your mail.

While **mail** is a powerful utility, it can be tricky for a novice
user. Most Linux distributions include **pine** and **elm**, which are
much easier to use.

This section presents **mail** commands, options, and files. To get
you started, here are two of the most basic commands.

To enter interactive mail-reading mode, type:

    mail

To begin writing a message to *user*, type:

    mail *user*

Command-line options

-b *list*   Set blind carbon copy field to comma-separated *list*.

-c *list*   Set carbon copy field to comma-separated *list*.

-f [*file*]

            Process contents of *file*, or mbox, instead of
            /var/spool/mail/$user.

-i   Do not respond to tty interrupt signals.

-n   Do not consult */etc/mail.rc* when starting up.

-p   Read mail in POP mode.

-s *subject*

            Set subject to *subject*.

-u   Process contents of */var/spool/mail/$user*. Default.

-v   Verbose. Print information about mail delivery to
            standard out.

-I   Interactive—even when standard input has been
            redirected from the terminal.

-N   When printing a mail message or entering a mail
            folder, do not display message headers.

-P   Disable POP mode.

Compose mode commands

~!   Execute a shell escape from compose mode.

~?   List compose mode escapes.

~b   Add or change the *Bcc:* header.

~c   Add or change the *Cc:* header.

~d   Read in the *dead.letter* file.

~e   Invoke text editor.

~fmessages
        Insert *messages* into message being composed.

~Fmessages
        Similar to ~f, but include message headers.

~h   Add or change all the headers.

~mmessages
        Similar to ~f, but indent with a tab.

~Mmessages
        Similar to ~m, but include message headers.

~p   Print message header fields and message being sent.

~q   Abort current message composition.

~r   Append file to current message.

~s   Add or change *Subject:* header.

~t   Add names to *To:* list.

~v   Invoke editor specified with the VISUAL environment variable.

~|command
        Pipe message through *command*.

~:mail-command
        Execute *mail-command*.

~string Insert *string*. If string contains a ~, it must be escaped with a \.

Command-mode commands

?	List summary of commands (help screen).
!	Execute a shell command.
– num	Print *num*th previous message; defaults to immediately previous.
alias (a)	Print or create alias lists.
alternates (alt)	Specify remote accounts on remote machines that are yours. Tells mail not to reply to them.
chdir (c)	**cd** to home or specified directory.
copy (co)	Similar to save, but does not mark message for deletion.
delete (d)	Delete message.
dp	Delete current message and display next one.
edit (e)	Edit message.
exit (ex, x)	Exit mail without updating folder.
file (fi)	Switch folders.
folder (fold)	Read messages saved in a file. Files can be:

#	previous
%	system mailbox
%user	*user*'s system mailbox
&	mbox

→

mail	+*folder*	File in *folder* directory.
←	folders	List folders.
	headers (h)	List message headers at current prompt.
	headers+ (h+)	Move forward one window of headers.
	headers- (h-)	Move back one window of headers.
	help	Same as ?.
	hold (ho)	Hold messages in system mailbox.
	ignore	Append list of fields to ignored fields.
	mail *user* (m)	Compose message to *user*.
	mbox	Default. Move specified messages to mbox on exiting.
	next (n)	Type next message, or next message that matches argument.
	preserve (pr)	Synonym for **hold**.
	print [*list*] (p)	Display each message in *list*.
	Print [*list*] (P)	Similar to **print**, but include header fields.
	quit (q)	Exit mail and update folder.
	reply (r)	Send mail to all on distribution list.
	Reply (R)	Send mail to author only.
	respond	Same as **reply**.
	retain	Always include this list of header fields when printing messages. With no arguments, list retained fields.
	save (s)	Save message to folder.
	saveignore	Remove ignored fields when saving.
	saveretain	Override **saveignore** to retain specified fields.
	set (se)	Set or print **mail** options.
	shell (sh)	Enter a new shell.
	size	Print size of each specified message.
	source	Read commands from specified file.
	top	Print first few lines of each specified message.
	type (t)	Same as **print**.
	Type (T)	Same as **Print**.
	unalias	Discard previously defined aliases.
	undelete (u)	Restore deleted message.
	unread (U)	Mark specified messages as unread.
	unset (uns)	Unset **mail** options.
	visual (v)	Edit message with editor specified by the VISUAL environment vairable.
	write (w)	Write message, without header, to file.
	xit (x)	Same as **exit**.
	z	Move **mail**'s attention to next windowful of text. Use **z-** to move it back.

mail options

These options are used inside of the *.mailrc* file. The syntax is "set *option*" or "unset *option*".

append	Append (do not prepend) messages to mbox.	**mail**
ask	Prompt for subject.	
askcc	Prompt for carbon copy recipients.	
asksub	Prompt for **Subject:** line.	
chron	Display messages in chronological order, most recent last.	
debug	Same as **-d** on command line.	
dot	Interpret a solitary . as an *EOF*.	
folder	Define directory to hold mail folders.	
hold	Keep message in system mailbox upon quitting.	
ignore	Ignore interrupt signals from terminal. Print them as @.	
ignoreeof	Do not treat ^D as an *EOF*.	
metoo	Do not remove sender from groups when mailing to them.	
noheader	Same as **-N** on command line.	
nokerberos	Retrieve POP mail via POP3, not KPOP, protocol.	
nosave	Do not save aborted letters to *dead.letter*.	
pop-mail	Retrieve mail with POP3 protocol, and save it in *mbox.pop*.	
prompt	Set prompt to a different string.	
Replyall	Switch roles of **Reply** and **reply**.	
quiet	Do not print version at startup.	
searchheaders	When given the specifier /*x*:*y*, expand all messages that contain the string *y* in the *x* header field.	
verbose	Same as -v on command line.	
verbose-pop	Display status while retrieving POP mail.	

Special files

calendar	Contains reminders that the operating system mails to you.
.maildelivery	Mail delivery configuration file.
.mailrc	Mail configuration file.
triplog	Keeps track of your automatic response recipients.
tripnote	Contains automatic message.

man [*options*] [*section*] [*title*]

man

Display information from the online reference manuals. **man** locates and prints the named *title* from the designated reference *section*.

→

Options

-7, --ascii
> Expect a pure ASCII file, and format it for a 7-bit terminal or terminal emulator.

-a, --all
> Show all pages matching *title*.

-b   Leave blank lines in output.

-d, --debug
> Display debugging information. Suppress actual printing of manual pages.

-f, --whatis
> Same as **whatis** command.

-k, --apropos
> Same as **apropos** command.

-l, --local-file
> Search local files, not system files, for manual pages. If **i** is given as *filename*, search standard input.

-m *systems*, --systems=*systems*
> Search *systems'* manual pages. *systems* should be a comma-separated list.

-p *preprocessors*, --preprocessor=*preprocessors*
> Preprocess manual pages with *preprocessors* before turning them over to **nroff**, **troff**, or **groff**. Always runs **soelim** first.

-r *prompt*, --prompt=*prompt*
> Set prompt if **less** is used as pager.

-t, --troff
> Format the manual page with */usr/bin/groff -Tgv -mandoc*. Implied by *-T* and *-Z*.

-u, --update
> Perform a consistency check between manual page cache and filesytem.

-w, --where, --location
> Print pathnames of entries on standard output.

-D, --default
> Reset all options to their defaults.

-L *locale*, --locale=*locale*
> Assume current locale to be *locale*; do not consult setlocale().

-M *path*, --manpath=*path*
> Search for manual pages in *path*. Ignore -m option.

-P*pager*, —pager=*pager*
> Select paging program *pager* to display the entry.

-T *device*, --troff-device[=*device*]
> Format **groff** or **troff** output for *device*, such as **dvi**, **latin1**, **X75**, and **X100**.

-Z, --ditroff
> Do not allow postprocessing of manual page after **groff** has finished formatting it.

Section names

Manual pages are divided into sections, depending on their intended audience.

1   Executable programs or shell commands

2   System calls (functions provided by the kernel)

3   Library calls (functions within system libraries)

4   Special files (usually found in */dev*)

5   File formats and conventions, e.g. */etc/passwd*

6   Games

7   Macro packages and conventions

8   System administration commands (usually only for a privileged user)

9   Kernel routines (nonstandard)

---

manpath [*options*]

Attempt to determine path to manual pages. Check $MANPATH first; if that is not set, consult */etc/manpath.conf*, user environment variables, and the current working directory.

Options

-q, --quiet
> Do not print warning messages.

-d, --debug
> Print debugging information.

-c, --catpath
> Convert the determined **manpath** to its relative **cat-path**.

-g, --global
> Construct **manpath** from the list of paths that */etc/manpath.conf* designates as global.

-m *systems*, --systems=*systems*
> Search *systems* for the path.

---

mesg [*option*]

Change the ability of other users to send **write** messages to your terminal. With no options, display the permission status.

Options

n   Forbid **write** messages.

y   Allow **write** messages (the default).

mkdir	**mkdir** [*options*] *directories*

Create one or more *directories*. You must have write permission in the parent directory in order to create a directory. See also **rmdir**. The default mode of the new directory is 0777, modified by the system or user's **umask**.

Options

-m, --mode *mode*
> Set the access *mode* for new directories. See **chmod** for an explanation of acceptable formats for *mode*.

-p, --parents
> Create intervening parent directories if they don't exist.

Examples

Create a read-only directory named **personal**:

```
mkdir -m 444 personal
```

The following sequence:

```
mkdir work; cd work
mkdir junk; cd junk
mkdir questions; cd ../..
```

could be accomplished by typing this:

```
mkdir -p work/junk/questions
```

more	**more** [*options*] [*files*]

Display the named *files* on a terminal, one screenful at a time. See **less** for an alternative to **more**. Some commands can be preceded by a number.

Options

+*num*   Begin displaying at line number *num*.

+/*pattern*
> Begin displaying two lines before *pattern*.

-c   Repaint screen from top instead of scrolling.

-d   Display the prompt "Hit space to continue, Del to abort" in reponse to illegal commands; disable bell.

-f   Count logical rather than screen lines. Useful when long lines wrap past the width of the screen.

-l   Ignore formfeed (**CTRL-L**) characters. Cause carriage return to be of the form **CTRL-M**.

-num *number*
> Set screen size to *number* lines.

-p   Page through the file by clearing each window instead of scrolling. This is sometimes faster.

`-r`	Force display of control characters, in the form $\hat{}x$.
`-s`	Squeeze; display multiple blank lines as one.
`-u`	Suppress underline characters.

Commands

All commands in **more** are based on **vi** commands. An argument can be entered before many commands.

SPACE	Display next screen of text.
z	Display next *lines* of text, and redefine a screenful to *lines* lines. Default is one screenful.
RETURN	Display next *lines* of text, and redefine a screenful to *lines* lines. Default is one line.
d, ^D	Scroll *lines* of text, and redefine scroll size to *lines* lines. Default is one line.
q, Q, INTERRUPT	
	Quit.
s	Skip forward one line of text.
f	Skip forward one screen of text.
b, ^B	Skip backward one screen of text.
'	Return to point where previous search began.
=	Print number of current line.
/*pattern*	Search for *pattern*, skipping to *num*th occurrence if an argument is specified.
n	Repeat last search, skipping to *num*th occurrence if an argument is specified.
!*cmd*, :!*cmd*	
	Invoke shell and execute *cmd* in it.
v	Invoke **vi** editor on the file, at the current line.
^L	Redraw screen.
:n	Skip to next file.
:p	Skip to previous file.
:f	Print current filename and line number.
.	Re-execute previous command.

Examples

Page through *file* in "clear" mode, and display prompts:

```
more -cd file
```

Format *doc* to the screen, removing underlines:

```
nroff doc | more -u
```

View the man page for the **grep** command; begin near the word "BUGS" and compress extra white space:

```
man grep | more +/BUGS -s
```

	mv [option] sources target
mv	Move or rename files and directories. The source (first column) and target (second column) determine the result (third column):

Source	Target	Result
File	name (nonexistent)	Rename file as name.
File	Existing file	Overwrite existing file with source file.
Directory	name (nonexistent)	Rename directory as name.
Directory	Existing directory	Move directory to be a sub-directory of existing directory.
One or more files	Existing directory	Move files to directory.

Options

-b, --backup
: Back up files before removing.

-f
: Force the move, even if *target* file exists; suppress messages about restricted access modes.

-i, --interactive
: Query user before removing files.

-u, --update
: Do not remove a file or link if its modification is the same as or newer than its replacement.

---

newgrp

newgrp [*group*]

Similar to **login**. Changes user's group identification, by default to the login group identification.

---

nice

nice [*option*] *command* [*arguments*]

Execute a *command* and *arguments* with lower priority (i.e., be "nice" to other users). Without arguments, print the default scheduling priority (niceness). If **nice** is a child process, it prints the parent process's scheduling priority. Niceness has a range of −20 (highest priority) to 19 (lowest priority).

Option

-*adjustment*, --adjustment=*adjustment*
: Run *command* with niceness incremented by *adjustment* (1–19); default is 10. A privileged user can raise priority by specifying a negative *adjustment* (e.g., −5).

nohup *command* [*arguments*]

Continue to execute the named *command* and optional command *arguments* after you log out (make command immune to hangups; i.e., **no hangup**). TTY output is appended to the file *nohup.out* by default. Modern shells preserve background commands by default; this command is necessary only in the original Bourne shell.

nohup

passwd [*user*]

Create or change a password associated with a *user* name. Only the owner or a privileged user may change a password. Owners need not specify their *user* name.

passwd

paste [*options*] *files*

Merge corresponding lines of one or more *files* into vertical columns, separated by a tab. See also **cut**, **join**, **newform**, and **pr**.

paste

Options

-         Replace a filename with the standard input.

-d'*char*'   Separate columns with *char* instead of a tab. Note: You can separate columns with different characters by supplying more than one *char*.

-s, --serial
> Merge subsequent lines from one file.

Examples

Create a three-column *file* from files *x*, *y*, and *z*:

```
paste x y z > file
```

List users in two columns:

```
who | paste - -
```

Merge each pair of lines into one line:

```
paste -s -d"\t\n" list
```

pathchk [*options*] *filenames*

Determine validity and portability of *filenames*. Specifically, determine if all directories within the path are searchable, and if the length of the *filenames* is acceptable.

pathchk

Option

-p, --portability
> Check portability for all POSIX systems.

perl	**perl** A powerful text-processing language that combines many of the most useful features of shell programs, C, **awk**, and **sed**, as well as adding extended features of its own. For more information, see *Learning Perl* by Randal L. Schwartz and *Programming Perl*, Second Edition, by Larry Wall, Tom Christiansen, and Randal L. Schwartz.

pidof	**pidof** [*options*] *programs*
	
	Display the process IDs of the listed program or programs. **pidof** is actually a symbolic link to **killall5**.
	
	Options
	
	  -s Return a single process ID.
	  -o *pids*
	         Omit all processes with the specified process ID. You may list several process IDs.

popclient	**popclient** [*options*] *host*
	
	Retrieve mail via the Post Office Protocol. Supports POP2 and POP3.
	
	Options
	
	  -2 Use POP2.
	  -3 Use POP3.
	  -c Write retrieved messages to standard output.
	  -f *folder*
	         Retrieve *folder* from remote server.
	  -k Do not delete messages from folder on remote mail-server after retrieval.
	  -o *folder*
	         Append retrieved messages to *folder* on local machine instead of to system default.
	  -p *password*
	         Use *password* to log in to remote machine. By default, prompt for a password.
	  -s Silent mode. Do not provide any progress messages during connection.
	  -u *user*
	         Log in to remote server as *user*, by default your login name on local machine.
	  -v Verbose mode. Pass all control messages to the standard error stream. Override -s.

pr [*file*]

Convert a text file to a paginated, columned version, with headers. If – is provided as the filename, read from standard input.

Options

+*num*   Discard first *num*-1 pages, and begin printing on page *num*.

-*num*   Print in *num* columns.

-a   Print columns horizontally, not vertically.

-b   At the end of the file, balance columns.

-c   Convert control characters to hat notation (such as ^C) and other unprintable characters to octal backslash.

-d   Double space.

-e[*tab-char*[*width*]]

Convert tabs (or *tab-chars*) to spaces. If *width* is specified, convert tabs to *width* characters (default is 8).

-f, -F Separate pages with formfeeds, not newlines.

-h *header*

Use *header* for a header instead of the filename.

-l *lines*

Set page length to *lines* (default 66). If *lines* is less than 10, omit headers and footers.

-m   Print one file per column.

-n[*delimiter*[*digits*]]

Number columns, or, with the –m option, number lines. Append *delimiter* to each number (default is a tab) and limit the size of numbers to *digits*.

-o *width*

Set left margin to *width*.

-r   Continue silently when unable to open an input file.

-s[*delimiter*]

Separate columns with *delimiter* (default is a tab) instead of spaces.

-t   Suppress headers, footers, and fills at end of pages.

-v   Convert unprintable characters to octal backslash.

ps [*options*]

Report on active processes. Note that you do not need to include a – before options. In options, *list* arguments should either be separated by commas or be put in double quotes. In comparing the amount of output produced, note that -e prints more than -a and -l prints more than -f.

→

Options

pids   Include only specified processes, which are given in a comma-delimited list.

a   List all processes.

c   Consult **task_struct** for command name.

e   Include environment.

f   "Forest" family tree format.

h   Suppress header.

j   Jobs format.

l   Produce a long listing.

m   Memory format.

n   Print user IDs and WCHAN numerically.

r   Exclude processes that are not running.

s   Signal format.

--sort*delimiter*[+|-]*key*[,[+|-]*key*[, ...]]

     Similar to O, but designed to protect multiletter sort keys. See *Sort keys*.

t*tty*   Display only processes runing on *tty*.

u   Include username and start time.

v   *vm* format.

w   Wide format. Don't truncate long lines.

x   Include processes without an associated terminal.

O[+|-]*key*[,[+|-]*key*[, ...]]

     Sort processes. (See *Sort keys.*)

     +   Return key to default direction.

     –   Reverse default direction on key.

S   Include child processes' CPU time and page faults.

Sort keys

c, cmd	Name of executable.
C, cmdline	Whole command line.
f, flags	Flags.
g, pgrp	Group ID of process.
G, tpgid	Group ID of associated tty.
j, cutime	Cumulative user time.
J, cstime	Cumulative system time.
k, utime	User time.
K, stime	System time.
m, min_flt	Amount of minor page faults.
M, maj_flt	Amount of major page faults.
n, cmin_flt	Total minor page faults.
N, cmaj_flt	Total major page faults.
o, session	Session ID.

p, pid	Process ID.
P, ppid	Parent's process ID.
r, rss	Resident set size.
R, resident	Resident pages.
s, size	Kilobytes of memory used.
S, share	Number of shared pages.
t, tty	tty.
T, start_time	Process's start time.
U, uid	User ID.
u, user	User's name.
v, vsize	Bytes of VM used.
y, priority	Kernel's scheduling priority.

Fields

PRI	Process's scheduling priority. A higher number indicates lower priority.
NI	Process's nice value. A higher number indicates less CPU time.
SIZE	Size of virtual image.
RSS	Resident set size (amount of physical memory), in kilobytes.
WCHAN	Kernel function in which process resides.
STAT	Status.

	R	Runnable
	T	Stopped
	D	Asleep and not interruptible
	S	Asleep
	Z	Zombie
	W	No resident pages (second field)
	N	Positive nice value (third field)

TT	Associated tty.
PAGEIN	Amount of major page faults.
TRS	Size of resident text.
SWAP	Amount of swap used, in kilobytes.
SHARE	Shared memory.

---

pwd

Print the full pathname of the current working directory. Note: The built-in versions **pwd** (Bourne and Korn shells) and **dirs** (C shell) are faster, so you might want to define the following C-shell alias:

```
alias pwd dirs -l
```

rcp	**rcp** [*options*] *file1 file2* **rcp** [*options*] *file* ... *directory* Copy files between two machines. Each *file* or *directory* is either a remote filename of the form *rhost:path*, or a local filename. *Options* -k Attempt to get tickets for remote host; query **krb_real-mofhost** to determine realm. -p Preserve modification times and modes of the source files. -r If any of the source files are directories, **rcp** copies each subtree rooted at that name.
renice	**renice** [*priority*] [*options*] [*target*] Control the scheduling priority of various processes as they run. May be applied to a process, process group, or user (*target*). A privileged user may alter the priority of other users' processes. *priority* must, for ordinary users, lie between 0 and the environment variable PRIO_MAX (normally 20), with a higher number indicating increased niceness. A privileged user may set a negative priority, as low as PRIO_MIN, to speed up processes. *Options* +*num* Specify number by which to increase current priority of process, rather than an absolute priority number. -*num* Specify number by which to decrease current priority of process, rather than an absolute priority number. -g Interpret *target* parameters as process group IDs. -p Interpret *target* parameters as process IDs (default). -u Interpret *target* parameters as usernames.
reset	**reset** Clear screen (reset terminal).
rlogin	**rlogin** *rhost* [*options*] Remote login. **rlogin** connects the terminal on the current local host system to the remote host system *rhost*. The remote terminal type is the same as your local terminal type. The terminal or window size is also copied to the remote system if the server supports it. *Options* -8 Allow an eight-bit input data path at all times. -e*c* Specify escape character *c* (default is ~).

-d	Debugging mode.	rlogin
-k	Attempt to get tickets from remote host, requesting them in the realm as determined by **krb_real-mofhost**.	

-l *username*
> Specify a different *username* for the remote login. Default is the same as your local username.

-E
> Do not interpret any character as an escape character.

-K
> Suppress all Kerberos authentication.

-L
> Allow **rlogin** session to be run without any output postprocessing (in **litout** mode).

---

rm [*options*] *files*

Delete one or more *files*. To remove a file, you must have write permission in the directory that contains the file, but you need not have permission on the file itself. If you do not have write permission on the file, you will be prompted (**y** or **n**) to override.

Options

-d, --directory
> Remove directories, even if they are not empty; use **unlink**, not **rmdir**, to do so. Available only to a privileged user.

-f, --force
> Remove write-protected files without prompting.

-i, --interactive
> Prompt for **y** (remove the file) or **n** (do not remove the file).

-r, -R, --recursive
> If *file* is a directory, remove the entire directory and all its contents, including subdirectories. Be forewarned: use of this option can be dangerous.

--
> Mark the end of options. Use this when you need to supply a filename beginning with -.

---

rmdir [*options*] *directories*

Delete the named *directories* (not the contents). *directories* are deleted from the parent directory and must be empty (if not, **rm** -r can be used instead). See also **mkdir**.

Option

-p, --parents
> Remove *directories* and any intervening parent directories that become empty as a result; useful for removing subdirectory trees.

rpcinfo	**rpcinfo** [*options*] [*version*]

NFS/NIS command. Probe a remote RPC server and report information on it. Programs may be specified by name or number. If *version* is unknown, specify a *version* of 0, which tells **rpcinfo** to attempt to guess the version.

Options

-b *program version*
> Using the User Datagram Protocol, make an RPC broadcast for *program* and *version*. Report which hosts respond.

-d *program version*
> Privileged user only. Remove registration of *program*.

-n *portnum*
> Make RPC requests to *portnum*.

-p [*host*]
> Print all registered RPC programs that result from a query to *host* (or, if not specified, query **$hostname** for the name of the local host).

-u *host program*
> Attempt to make an RPC call to *program* on *host*, and report whether the attempt was successful.

-t
> Use TCP to attempt to make an RPC call to *program* on *host*, and report whether the attempt was successful.

rsh	**rsh** [*options*] *host* [*command*]

Execute *command* on remote host, or, if no command is specified, begin an interactive shell on the remote host using **rlogin**.

Options

-K
> Suppress Kerberos authentication.

-d
> Enable socket debugging.

-l *username*
> Attempt to log in as *username*. By default, the name of the user executing **rsh** is used.

-n
> Redirects the input to **rsh** from the special device */dev/null*. (This should be done when backgrounding **rsh** from a **csh** prompt, to direct the input away from the terminal.)

rstat	**rstat** *host*

Summarize *host*'s status: uptime, load averages, and current time.

run-parts [*options*] *directory*

Run scripts in specified directory. Consider every file with a filename consisting entirely of alphanumeric characters, underscores, and hyphens to be a script. Ignore others. Sort filenames lexically and run them in that order.

Options

   --   Do not consider anything after this option to be an option. Useful for protecting filenames beginning with −.

   --test   Test mode. Print information about scripts which it would run, but do not actually run them.

   --umask=*umask*
            Reset umask to *umask* (default is 022).

ruptime [*options*]

Show host status of local machines. These status lines are formed from packets broadcast by each host on the network once a minute. Machines for which no status report has been received for eleven minutes are shown as being down.

Options

   -l   Sort listing by load average.

   -r   Reverse sort order.

   -t   Sort listing by uptime.

   -u   Sort listing by number of users.

rusers [*options*] [*host* ...]

List who is logged in on local machines (RPC version). **rusers** produces output similar to the **who** command. When *host* arguments are given, **rusers** queries only the list of specified hosts. A remote host will respond only if it is running the **rusersd** daemon. Broadcasting does not work through gateways (this is a bug).

Options

   -a   Give a report for a machine even if no users are logged on.

   -l   Give a longer listing in the style of **who**.

rwall *hostname* [*file*]

Write to all users over a network. **rwall** reads a message from standard input until *EOF*. It then sends this message, preceded by the line Broadcast Message . . . , to all users logged in on *hostname*. If *file* is specified, it is sent instead of the standard input.

script	**script** [*options*] [*file*] Copy all output from terminal to the file *typescript* or specified name. Stop copying when shell exits. *Option* -a Append to file rather than overwriting.

sed	**sed** [*options*] [*command*] [*files*]
	
	Stream editor—edit one or more *files* without user interaction. See Chapter 10, *The sed Editor*, for more information.
	
	Options
	
	-e '*instruction*', --**expression**='*instruction*'
	        Apply the editing *instruction* to the files.
	-f *script*, --**file**=*script*
	        Apply the set of instructions from the editing *script*.
	-n, --**quiet**, --**silent**
	        Suppress default output.

setfdprm	**setfdprm** [*options*] *device* [*name*]
	
	Load disk parameters used when auto-configuring floppy devices.
	
	Options
	
	-c *device*
	        Clear parameters of *device*.
	-n *device*
	        Disable format-configuring messages for *device*.
	-p *device* [*name* | *parameter*]
	        Permanently reset parameters of *device*. You may specify **dev**, **size**, **sect**, **heads**, **tracks**, **stretch**, **gap**, **rate**, **spec1**, or **fmt_gap**. Consult */etc/fdprm* for original values. *name* specifies the configuration.
	-y *device*
	        Enable format-configuring messages for *device*.

sh	**sh** [*options*] [*file* [*arguments*]] The standard UNIX shell, a command interpreter into which all other commands are entered. On Linux, this is just another name for the **bash** shell. For more information, see Chapter 4, *bash: The Bourne Again Shell*.

showmount [*options*] [*host*]

NFS/NIS command. Show information about an NFS server. This information is maintained by the **mountd** server on *host*. The default value for *host* is the value returned by **hostname**. With no options, show the clients that have mounted directories from the host.

Options

-a, --all
> Print all remote mounts in the format
>
> > *hostname:directory*
>
> where *hostname* is the name of the client and *direc-tory* is the root of the filesystem that has been mounted.

-d, --directories
> List directories that have been remotely mounted by clients.

-e, --exports
> Print the list of exported filesystems.

--no-headers
> Do not print headers.

sleep *amount* [*units*]

Wait a specified *amount* of time before executing another command. The default for *units* is seconds.

Time	Units
s	seconds
m	minutes
h	hours
d	days

sort [*options*] [*files*]

Sort the lines of the named *files*. Compare specified fields for each pair of lines, or, if no fields are specified, compare them by byte, in machine collating sequence. See also **uniq**, **comm**, join.

Options

-b
> Ignore leading spaces and tabs.

-c
> Check whether *files* are already sorted, and if so, produce no output.

-d
> Sort in dictionary order.

→

sort	-f	"Fold"—ignore uppercase/lowercase differences.
←	-i	Ignore nonprinting characters (those outside ASCII range 040–176).
	-m	Merge (i.e., sort as a group) input files.
	-n	Sort in arithmetic order.
	-o*file*	Put output in *file*.
	-r	Reverse the order of the sort.
	-t*c*	Separate fields with *c* (default is a tab).
	-u	Identical lines in input file appear only one (unique) time in output.
	-z*recsz*	Provide *recsz* bytes for any one line in the file. This option prevents abnormal termination of **sort** in certain cases.
	+*n* [-*m*]	Skip *n* fields before sorting, and sort up to field position *m*. If *m* is missing, sort to end of line. Positions take the form *a.b*, which means character *b* of field *a*. If *.b* is missing, sort at the first character of the field.
	-k *n*[,*m*]	Similar to +. Skip *n*–1 fields and stop at *m*–1 fields (i.e., start sorting at the *n*th field, where the fields are numbered beginning with 1).
	-M	Attempt to treat the first three characters as a month designation (JAN, FEB, etc). In comparisons, treat JAN < FEB < *invalid month name*.
	-T *tempdir*	Directory pathname to be used for temporary files.

Examples

List files by decreasing number of lines:

```
wc -l * | sort -r
```

Alphabetize a list of words, remove duplicates, and print the frequency of each word:

```
sort -fd wordlist | uniq -c
```

Sort the password file numerically by the third field (user ID):

```
sort +2n -t: /etc/passwd
```

split	**split** [*option*] [*infile*] [*outfile*]
	Split *infile* into a specified number of line segments. *infile* remains unchanged, and the results are written to *outfile*aa, *outfile*ab, etc. (default is **xaa, xab**, etc.). If *infile* is - (or missing), standard input is read. See also **csplit**.

Options

-*n*, -l *n*, --lines=*n*
    Split *infile* into *n* line segments (default is 1000).

-b *n*[bkm], --bytes=*n*[bkm]
    Split *infile*. By default, split it to *n* byte segements.
    Alternate block sizes may be specified:

    b   512 bytes
    k   1 kilobyte
    m   1 megabyte

-C *bytes*[bkm], --line-bytes=*bytes*[bkm]
    Put a maximum of *bytes* into file; insist on adding
    complete lines.

-          Take input from the standard input.

Examples

Break *bigfile* into 1000-line segments:

    split *bigfile*

Join four files, then split them into ten-line files named
new.aa, *new.ab*, etc. Note that without the –, **new.** would be
treated as a nonexistent input file:

    cat list[1-4] | split -10 - new.

---

stty [*options*] [*modes*]   **stty**

Set terminal I/O options for the current standard input device.
Without options, **stty** reports the terminal settings that differ
from those set by running **stty sane**, where a ^ indicates the
CONTROL key and ^` indicates a null value. Most modes can
be negated using an optional – (shown in brackets). The corresponding description is also shown in brackets. Some arguments
use non-POSIX extensions; these are marked with a *.

    stty [*options*] [*modes*] [< *device*]

Options

    -a, --all   Report all option settings.
    -g   Report settings in hex.

Control modes

    n   Set terminal baud rate to *n* (e.g., 2400).
    [-]clocal   [Enable]disable modem control.
    [-]cread   [Disable]enable the receiver.
    cs*bits*   Set character size to *bits*, which must be 5, 6,
                   7, or 8.
    [-]cstopb   [One]two stop bits per character.

→

[-]hup	[Do not]hang up connection on last close.
[-]hupcl	Same as previous.
ispeed *n*	Set terminal input baud rate to *n*.
ospeed *n*	Set terminal output baud rate to *n*.
[-]parenb	[Disable]enable parity generation and detection.
[-]parodd	Use [even]odd parity.
[-]crtscts*	[Disable]enable RTS/CTS handshaking.

Flow control modes

The following flow control modes are available by combining the *ortsfl*, *ctsflow*, and *rtsflow* flags:

Flag settings	Flow control mode
ortsfl rtsflow ctsflow	Enable unidirectional flow control.
ortsfl rtsflow -ctsflow	Assert RTS when ready to send.
ortsfl -rtsflow ctsflow	No effect.
ortsfl -rtsflow -ctsflow	Enable bidirectional flow control.
-ortsfl rtsflow ctsflow	Enable bidirectional flow control.
-ortsfl rtsflow -ctsflow	No effect.
-ortsfl -rtsflow ctsflow	Stop transmission when CTS drops.
-ortsfl -rtsflow -ctsflow	Disable hardware flow control.

Input modes

[-]brkint	[Do not]signal INTR on break.
[-]icrnl	[Do not]map CR to NL on input.
[-]ignbrk	[Do not]ignore break on input.
[-]igncr	[Do not]ignore CR on input.
[-]ignpar	[Do not]ignore parity errors.
[-]inlcr	[Do not]map NL to CR on input.
[-]inpck	[Disable]enable input parity checking.
[-]istrip	[Do not]strip input characters to seven bits.
[-]iuclc*	[Do not]map uppercase to lowercase on input.
[-]ixany*	Allow [XON]any character to restart output.
[-]ixoff [-]tandem	[Do not]send START/STOP characters when queue is nearly empty/full.
[-]ixon	[Disable]enable START/STOP output control.
[-]parmrk	[Do not]mark parity errors.
[-]imaxbel*	When input buffer is too full to accept a new character, [flush the input buffer]beep; do not flush the input buffer.

Output modes

bs*n*	Select style of delay for backspaces (0 or 1).
cr*n*	Select style of delay for carriage returns (0–3).
ff*n*	Select style of delay for formfeeds (0 or 1).
nl*n*	Select style of delay for linefeeds (0 or 1).
tab*n*	Select style of delay for horizontal tabs (0–3).
vt*n*	Select style of delay for vertical tabs (0 or 1).
[-]ocrnl*	[Do not]map CR to NL on output.
[-]ofdel*	Set fill character to [NULL]DEL.
[-]ofill*	Delay output with [timing]fill characters.
[-]olcuc*	[Do not]map lowercase to uppercase on output.
[-]onlcr*	[Do not]map NL to CR-NL on output.
[-]onlret*	On the terminal, NL performs [does not perform] the CR function.
[-]onocr*	Do not [do] output CRs at column zero.
[-]opost	[Do not]postprocess output.

Local modes

[-]echo	[Do not]echo every character typed.
[-]echoe, [-]crterase	
	[Do not]echo ERASE character as BS-space-BS string.
[-]echok	[Do not]echo NL after KILL character.
[-]echonl	[Do not]echo NL.
[-]icanon	[Disable]enable canonical input (ERASE, KILL, WERASE, and RPRINT processing).
[-]iexten	[Disable]enable extended functions for input data.
[-]isig	[Disable]enable checking of characters against INTR, SUSPEND, and QUIT.
[-]noflsh	[Enable]disable flush after INTR or QUIT.
[-]tostop*	[Do not]send SIGTTOU when background processes write to the terminal.
[-]xcase*	[Do not]change case on local output.
[-]echoprt, [-]prterase*	
	When erasing characters, echo them backward, enclosed in \ and /.
[-]echoctl. [-]ctlecho*	
	Do not echo control characters literally. Use hat notation (e.g. ^Z).
[-]echoke [-]crtkill*	
	Erase characters as specified by the **echoprt** and **echoe** settings (default **echoctl** and **echok** settings).

$\rightarrow$

Control assignments

ctrl-char c   Set control character to *c*. *ctrl-char* is: **dsusp** (flush input and then send stop), **eof**, **eol**, **eol2** (alternate end-of-line), **erase**, **intr**, **lnext** (treat next character literally), **kill**, **rprnt** (redraw line), **quit**, **start**, **stop**, **susp**, **swtch**, or **werase** (erase previous word). *c* can be a literal control character, a character in hat notation (e.g. ^Z), in hex (must begin with 0x), in octal (must begin with 0), or in decimal. Disable the control character with values of ^- or **undef**.

min *n*   Set the minimum number of characters that will satisfy a read until the time value has expired when –**icanon** is set.

time *n*   Set the number of tenths of a second before reads time out if the **min** number of characters have not been read when –**icanon** is set.

line *i*   Set line discipline to *i* (1–126).

Combination modes

cooked   Same as –**raw**.

[–]evenp [–]parity
      Same as [-]**parenb** and **cs**[8]**7**.

[–]parity   Same as [-]**parenb** and **cs**[8]**7**.

ek   Reset ERASE and KILL characters to **CTRL-h** and **CTRL-u**, their defaults.

[–]lcase   [Un]set **xcase**, **iuclc**, and **olcuc**.

[–]LCASE   Same as [-]**lcase**.

[–]nl   [Un]set **icrnl** and **onlcr**. –**nl** also unsets **inlcr**, **igncr**, **ocrnl**, and **onlret**, **icrnl**, **onlcr**.

[–]oddp   Same as [-]**parenb**, [-]**parodd**, and **cs7**[8].

[–]raw   [Disable]enable raw input and output (no ERASE, KILL, INTR, QUIT, EOT, SWITCH, or output postprocessing).

sane   Reset all modes to reasonable values.

[–]tabs*   [Expand to spaces]preserve output tabs.

[–]cbreak   Same as –**icanon**.

[–]pass8   Same as –**parenb** –**istrip cs8**.

[–]litout   Same as –**parenb** –**istrip cs8**.

[–]decctlq*   Same as –**ixany**.

crt   Same as **echoe echoctl echoke**.

dec   Same as **echoe echoctl echoke** –**ixany**. Additionally, set INTERRUPT to ^C, ERASE to DEL, and KILL to ^U.

Special settings	stty

    ispeed *speed*   Specify input speed.

    ospeed *speed* Specify output speed.

    rows *rows**   Specify number of rows.

    cols *columns*, **columns** *columns**

                Specify number of columns.

    size*   Display current row and column settings.

    line *discipline**

                Specify line discipline.

    speed   Display terminal speed.

---

su [*option*] [*user*] [*shell_args*]	su

Create a shell with the effective user ID of another *user*. If no *user* is specified, create a shell for a privileged user (that is, become a superuser). Enter *EOF* to terminate. You can run the shell with particular options by passing them as *shell_args* (e.g., if the shell runs **sh**, you can specify −c *command* to execute *command* via **sh**, or −r to create a restricted shell).

Options

    −, −l, −−login

        Go through the entire login sequence (i.e., change to *user*'s environment).

    −c *command*, −−command=*command*

        Execute *command* in new shell and exit immediately. If *command* is more than one word, it should be enclosed in quotes—for example,

```
su -c 'find / -name \*.c -print' nobody
```

    −f, −−fast

        Start shell with -f option. In **csh** and **tcsh**, this suppresses the reading of the *.cshrc* file. In **bash**, this suppresses filename pattern expansion.

    −m, −p, −−preserve-environment

        Retain original values for HOME, USER, LOGNAME, and SHELL. Execute $SHELL, not the shell specified in */etc/passwd*, unless $SHELL is a restricted shell.

    −s *shell*, −−shell *shell*

        Execute *shell*, not the shell specified in */etc/passwd*, unless *shell* is restricted.

---

symlinks [*options*] *directories*	symlinks

Provide listing of and information about symbolic links. Examine *directories* for symbolic links, and specify whether each is **relative**, **absolute**, **dangling**, or **other_fs**.

→

symlinks ←	*Options* -c Convert absolute links to relative links, except absolute links from other filesystems. -r Recursively descend through subdirectories in search of symbolic links. -v Include relative links.

systat	**systat** [*options*] *host*
	
	Query *host* for system information. Attempt to query the host's **systat** service; if unable to do so, use its **netstat** or **daytime** services.
	
	Options
	
	-n, --netstat
	    Consult host's **netstat** service.
	
	-p *port*, --**port** *port*
	    Direct query to host's *port*.
	
	-s, --systat
	    Consult host's **systat** service (default).
	
	-t, --time
	    Consult host's **daytime** service.

tac	**tac** [*options*] [*file*]
	
	Named for the common command **cat**, **tac** prints files in reverse. Without a filename, or with -, it reads from standard input. By default, it reverses the order of the lines, printing the last line first.
	
	Options
	
	-b, --before
	    Print separator (by default a newline) before string that it delimits.
	
	-r, --regex
	    Expect separator to be a regular expression.
	
	-s *string*, --**separator**=*string*
	    Specify alternate separator (default is newline).

tail	**tail** [*options*] [*file*] Print the last ten lines of the named *file* (or standard input if - is specified) on standard output. *Options* -*n*[*k*] Begin printing at *n*th item from end of file. *k* specifies the item to count: 1 (lines, the default), **b** (blocks), or **c** (characters).

-*k*	Same as –*n*, but use the default count of 10.	**tail**
+*n*[*k*]	Like -*n*, but start at *n*th item from beginning of file.	
+*k*	Like -*k*, but count from beginning of file.	

-c *num*{bkm}, --bytes *num*{bkm}
:   Print last *num* bytes. An alternate block size may be specified:

b	512 bytes
k	1 kilobyte
m	1 megabyte

-f
:   Don't quit at the end of file; "follow" file as it grows. End with a **CTRL-C**.

-n *num*, --lines *num*
:   Print last *num* lines.

-q, --quiet, --silent
:   Suppress filename headers.

Examples

Show the last 20 lines containing instances of .**Ah**:

```
grep '\.Ah' file | tail -20
```

Show the last ten characters of variable **name**:

```
echo "$name" | tail -c
```

Print the last two blocks of **bigfile**:

```
tail -2b bigfile
```

---

talk *person* [*ttyname*]   **talk**

Talk to another user. *person* is either the login name of some-one on your own machine, or *user@host* on another host. To talk to a user who is logged in more than once, use *ttyname* to indicate the appropriate terminal name. Once communication has been established, the two parties may type simultaneously, with their output appearing in separate windows. To redraw the screen, type **CTRL-L**. To exit, type your interrupt character; **talk** then moves the cursor to the bottom of the screen and restores the terminal.

---

tcsh [*options*] [*file* [*arguments*]]   **tcsh**

An extended version of the C shell, a command interpreter into which all other commands are entered. For more information, see Chapter 5, *csh and tcsh*.

---

tee [*option*] *files*   **tee**

Accept output from another command and send it both to the standard output and to *files* (like a T or fork in a road).

$\rightarrow$

tee
←
	Option
	  -a append to *files*, do not overwrite
	
	Example
	
	  ls -l | tee savefile *View listing and save for later*

telnet	**telnet** [*options*] [*host* [*port*]]
	
	Access remote systems. **telnet** is the user interface that communicates with another host using the TELNET protocol. If telnet is invoked without *host*, it enters command mode, indicated by its prompt, telnet>, and accepts and executes the commands listed after the following options. If invoked with arguments, **telnet** performs an **open** command (see the entry following) with those arguments. *host* indicates the host's official name. *port* indicates a port number (default is the TELNET port).
	
	Options
	  -a Automatic login into the remote system.
	  -d Turn on socket level debugging.
	  -e [*escape_char*]
	      Set initial TELNET escape character to *escape_char*. If *escape_char* is omitted, there will be no predefined escape character.
	  -l *user*
	      When connecting to remote system, and if remote system understands ENVIRON, send *user* to the remote system as the value for variable USER.
	  -n *tracefile*
	      Open *tracefile* for recording the trace information.
	
	Commands
	  CTRL-Z
	      Suspend **telnet**.
	  ! [*command*]
	      Execute a single command in a subshell on the local system. If *command* is omitted, an interactive subshell will be invoked.
	  ? [*command*]
	      Get help. With no arguments, print a help summary. If a command is specified, print the help information for just that command.
	  close Close a TELNET session and return to command mode.
	  display *argument* ...
	      Display all, or some, of the **set** and **toggle** values.

mode [*type*]

Depending on state of TELNET session, *type* is one of several options:

?   Print out help information for the **mode** command.

character   Disable TELNET LINEMODE option, or, if remote side does not understand the option, enter "character at a time" mode.

[-]edit   Attempt to [disable]enable the EDIT mode of the TELNET LINEMODE option.

[-]isig   Attempt to [disable]enable the TRAPSIG mode of the LINEMODE option.

line   Enable LINEMODE option, or, if remote side does not understand the option, attempt to enter "old line by line" mode.

[-]softtabs Attempt to [disable]enable the SOFT_TAB mode of the LINEMODE option.

[-]litecho [Disable]enable LIT_ECHO mode.

open [-l *user*] *host* [*port*]

Open a connection to the named *host*. If no *port* number is specified, attempt to contact a TELNET server at the default port.

quit   Close any open TELNET session and exit telnet.

status   Show current status of **telnet**. This includes the peer one is connected to as well as the current mode.

send *arguments*

Send one or more special character sequences to the remote host. Following are the arguments that may be specified:

?   Print out help information for **send** command.

abort   Send TELNET ABORT sequence.

ao   Send TELNET AO sequence, which should cause the remote system to flush all output from the remote system to the user's terminal.

ayt   Send TELNET AYT (Are You There) sequence.

brk   Send TELNET BRK (Break) sequence.

ec   Send TELNET EC (Erase Character) sequence, which causes the remote system to erase the last character entered.

el   Send TELNET EL (Erase Line) sequence, which causes the remote system to erase the last line entered.

eof   Send TELNET EOF (End Of File) sequence.

eor   Send TELNET EOR (End Of Record) sequence.

→

telnet
←

escape	Send current TELNET escape character (initially ^).
ga	Send TELNET GA (Go Ahead) sequence.
getstatus	If the remote side supports the TELNET STATUS command, **getstatus** sends the subnegotiation request that the server send its current option status.
ip	Send TELNET IP (Interrupt Process) sequence, which causes the remote system to abort the currently running process.
nop	Send TELNET NOP (No OPeration) sequence.
susp	Send TELNET SUSP (SUSPend process) sequence.
synch	Send TELNET SYNCH sequence, which causes the remote system to discard all previously typed (but not read) input.

set *argument value*

unset *argument value*

Set any one of a number of telnet variables to a specific value or to "TRUE". The special value "off" disables the function associated with the variable. **unset** disables any of the specified functions. The values of variables may be interrogated with the aid of the **display** command. The variables which may be specified are:

?	Display legal **set** and **unset** commands.
ayt	If TELNET is in **localchars** mode, this character is taken to be the alternate AYT character.
echo	This is the value (initially ^E) which, when in line-by-line mode, toggles between doing local echoing of entered characters and suppressing echoing of entered characters.
eof	If **telnet** is operating in LINEMODE or in the old line-by-line mode, entering this character as the first character on a line will cause the character to be sent to the remote system.
erase	If **telnet** is in **localchars** mode and operating in the character-at-a-time mode, then when this character is entered, a TELNET EC sequence will be sent to the remote system.
escape	This is the TELNET escape character (initially ^[), which causes entry into the

TELNET command mode when connected to a remote system.

flushoutput
If **telnet** is in **localchars** mode and the
flushoutput character is entered, a TEL-
NET AO sequence is sent to the remote
host.

forw1   If TELNET is in **localchars** mode, this
character is taken to be an alternate
end-of-line character.

forw2   If TELNET is in **localchars** mode, this
character is taken to be an alternate
end-of-line character.

interrupt If TELNET AO is in **localchars** mode and
the **interrupt** character is entered, a TEL-
NET IP sequence is sent to the remote
host.

kill   If TELNET IP is in **localchars** mode and
operating in the "character-at-a-time"
mode, then when this character is
entered, a TELNET EL sequence is sent
to the remote system.

lnext   If TELNET EL is in LINEMODE or in the
old "line-by-line" mode, then this character is taken to be the terminal's **lnext**
character.

quit   If TELNET EL is in **localchars** mode and
the **quit** character is entered, a TELNET
BRK sequence is sent to the remote host.

reprint   If TELNET BRK is in LINEMODE or in
the old "line-by-line" mode, this character is taken to be the terminal's **reprint**
character.

start   If the TELNET TOGGLE-FLOW-CON-
TROL option has been enabled, this
character is taken to be the terminal's
start character.

stop   If the TELNET TOGGLE-FLOW-CON-
TROL option has been enabled, this
character is taken to be the terminal's
stop character.

susp   If TELNET is in **localchars** mode, or if the
LINEMODE is enabled and the **suspend**
character is entered, a TELNET SUSP
sequence is sent to the remote host.

tracefile File to which output generated by **net-
data** is written.

worderase If TELNET BRK is in LINEMODE or in
the old "line-by-line" mode, this character is taken to be the terminal's

telnet

→

worderase character. Defaults for these are the terminal's defaults.

slc [*state*]

Set state of special characters when TELNET LINEMODE option has been enabled.

?	List help on the **slc** command.
check	Verify current settings for current special characters. If discrepancies are discovered, convert local settings to match remote ones.
export	Switch to local defaults for the special characters.
import	Switch to remote defaults for the special characters.

environ [*arguments* [...]]

Manipulate variables that may be sent through the TELNET ENVIRON option. Valid arguments for **environ** are:

define *variable value*

Define *variable* to have a value of *value*.

undefine *variable*

Remove *variable* from the list of environment variables.

export *variable*

Mark *variable* to have its value exported to the remote side.

unexport *variable*

Mark *variable* to not be exported unless explicitly requested by the remote side.

list	Display current variable values.
	Send environment variable.

toggle *arguments* [...]

Toggle various flags that control how TELNET responds to events. The flags may be set explicitly to TRUE or FALSE using the **set** and **unset** commands listed previously. The valid arguments are:

?	Display legal **toggle** commands.
autoflush	If **autoflush** and **localchars** are both TRUE, then when the **ao** or **quit** characters are recognized, TELNET refuses to display any data on the user's terminal until the remote system acknowledges it has processed those TELNET sequences.
autosynch	If **autosynch** and **localchars** are both TRUE, then when the **intr** or **quit** character is entered, the resulting TELNET sequence sent is followed by the TELNET SYNCH sequence. Initial value for this **toggle** is FALSE.
binary	Enable or disable the TELNET BINARY option on both the input and the output.

inbinary	Enable or disable the TELNET BINARY option on the input.	**telnet**
outbinary	Enable or disable the TELNET BINARY option on the output.	
crlf	If this **toggle** value is TRUE, carriage returns are sent as CR-LF. If FALSE, carriage returns are sent as CR-NUL. Initial value is FALSE.	
crmod	Toggle carriage return mode. Initial value is FALSE.	
debug	Toggle socket level debugging mode. Initial value is FALSE.	
localchars	If the value is TRUE, **flush**, **interrupt**, **quit**, **erase**, and **kill** characters are recognized locally, then transformed into appropriate TELNET control sequences. Initial value is TRUE.	
netdata	Toggle display of all network data. Initial value is FALSE.	
options	Toggle display of some internal **telnet** protocol processing pertaining to TELNET options. Initial value is FALSE.	
prettydump	When **netdata** is enabled, and if **prettydump** is enabled, the output from the **netdata** command is reorganized into a more user-friendly format; spaces are put between each character in the output, and an asterisk precedes any TELNET escape sequence.	
skiprc	Toggle whether to process ~/.telnetrc file. Initial value is FALSE, meaning the file is processed.	
termdata	Toggle printing of hexadecimal terminal data. Initial value is FALSE.	

---

test *expression*
    or
[*expression*]

test

Shell built-in also exists for most shells.

Evaluate an *expression* and, if its value is true, return a zero exit status; otherwise, return a nonzero exit status. In shell scripts, you can use the alternate form [*expression*]. This command is generally used with conditional constructs in shell programs.

$\rightarrow$

File testers

The syntax for all of these options is **test** *option file.* If the specified file does not exist, they return FALSE. Otherwise, they will test the file as specified in the option description.

-b   Is the file block special?

-c   Is the file character special?

-d   Is the file a directory?

-e   Does the file exist?

-f   Is the file a regular file?

-g   Does the file have the set group ID bit set?

-k   Does the file have the sticky bit set?

-L   Is the file a symbolic link?

-p   Is the file a named pipe?

-r   Is the file readable by the current user?

-s   Is the file nonempty?

-S   Is the file a socket?

-t [*file-descriptor*]
    Is the file associated with *file-descriptor* (or 1, standard output, by default) connected to a terminal?

-u   Does the file have the set user ID bit set?

-w   Is the file writable by the current user?

-x   Is the file executable?

-O   Is the file owned by the process's effective user ID?

-G   Is the file owned by the process's effective group ID?

File comparisons

The syntax for file comparisons is **test** *file1 option file2.* A string by itself, without options, returns TRUE if it's at least one character long.

-nt   Is *file1* newer than *file2*? Check modification, not creation, date.

-ot   Is *file1* older than *file2*? Check modification, not creation, date.

-ef   Do the files have identical device and inode numbers?

String tests

The syntax for string tests is test *option string.*

-z   Is the string zero characters long?

-n   Is the string at least one character long?

= *string*
    Are the two strings equal? Strings with the same characters in different orders are considered equal.

!= *string*
    Are the strings unequal?

Expression tests

Note that an expression could consist of any of the previous tests.

! *expression*
> Is the expression false?

expression -a *expression*
> Are the expressions both true?

expression -o *expression*
> Is either expression true?

Integer tests

The syntax for integer tests is **test** *integer1 option integer2*. You may substitute -l *string* for an integer; this evaluates to *string*'s length.

-eq   Are the two integers equal?

-ne   Are the two integers unequal?

-lt   Is *integer1* less than *integer2*?

-le   Is *integer1* less than or equal to *integer2*?

-gt   Is *integer1* greater than *integer2*?

-ge   Is *integer1* greater than or equal to *integer2*?

---

tftp [*host* [*port*]]

User interface to the TFTP (Trivial File Transfer Protocol) protocol, which allows users to transfer files to and from a remote machine. The remote *host* may be specified, in which case **tftp** uses *host* as the default host for future transfers.

Commands

Once **tftp** is running, it issues the prompt:

```
tftp>
```

and recognizes the following commands:

? [*command-name*...]
> Print help information.

ascii   Shorthand for mode ASCII

binary   Shorthand for mode binary

connect *hostname* [*port*]
> Set the *hostname*, and optionally **port**, for transfers.

get *filename*

get *remotename localname*

get *filename1 filename2 filename3 ... filenameN*
> Get a file or set of files from the specified remote sources.

mode *transfer-mode*
> Set the mode for transfers. *transfer-mode* may be one of ASCII or binary. The default is ASCII.

→

tftp
←
	put *filename*
	put *localfile remotefile*
	put *filename1 filename2 ...filenameN remote-directory*
	    Transfer file or a set of files to the specified remote file or directory.
	quit Exit **tftp**.
	rexmt *retransmission -timeout*
	    Set the per-packet retransmission timeout, in seconds.
	status Print status information: whether **tftp** is connected to a remote host (i.e., whether a host has been specified for the next connection), the current mode, whether verbose and tracing modes are on, and the values for **retransmission timeout** and **total transmission timeout**.
	timeout *total-transmission-timeout*
	    Set the total transmission timeout, in seconds.
	trace Toggle packet tracing.
	verbose
	    Toggle verbose mode.

tload	**tload** [*options*] [*tty*]
	
	Display system load average in graph format. If *tty* is specified, print it to that tty.
	
	Options
	  -d Specify the delay, in seconds, between updates.
	  -s Specify scale (number of characters between each graph tick). A smaller number results in a larger scale.

top	**top**
	
	Provide information (frequently refreshed) about the most CPU-intensive processes currently running. See **ps** for explanations of the field descriptors.
	
	Options
	  -d Specify delay between refreshes.
	  -i Suppress display of idle and zombie processes.
	  -q Refresh without any delay. As a privileged user, run with highest priority.
	  -s Secure mode. Disable some (dangerous) interactive commands.
	  -S Cumulative mode. Print total CPU time of each process, including dead children.

ˆL   Redraw screen.

k   Prompt for process ID and signal; send signal to pro-
          cess ID.

i   Toggle suppression of idle and zombie processes.

n, #   Prompt for number of processes to show. If 0 is
          entered, show as many as will fit on the screen
          (default).

q   Exit.

r   Apply **renice** to a process. Prompt for PID and **renice**
          value. Suppressed in secure mode.

S   Toggle cumulative mode. (See the **-S** option.)

s   Change delay between refreshes. Prompt for new
          delay time, which should be in seconds. Suppressed
          in secure mode.

---

tr [*options*] [*string1* [*string2*]]   tr

Translate characters—copy standard input to standard output,
substituting characters from *string1* to *string2* or deleting characters in *string1*.

Options

  -c, --complement
          Complement characters in *string1* with respect to
          ASCII 001-377.

  -d, --delete
          Delete characters in *string1* from output.

  -s, --squeeze-repeats
          Squeeze out repeated output characters in *string2*.

Special characters

  \a   ˆG (bell)
  \b   ˆH (backspace)
  \f   ˆL (form feed)
  \n   ˆJ (newline)
  \r   ˆM (carriage return)
  \t   ˆI (tab)
  \v   ˆK (vertical tab)
  \nnn   Character with octal value *nnn*.
  \\   Literal backslash.

  char1-char2
          All of the characters in the range *char1* through
          char2. If *char1* does not sort before *char2*, produce
          an error.

→

tr
←
	[*char*number*]
	The brackets should be literally included. Expand char to number occurrences. [x*4] expands to **xxxx**, for instance.
	
	[:*class*]
	The brackets should be literally included. Expand to all characters in *class*.
	
	    alnum Letters and digits
	    alpha Letters
	    blank Whitespace
	    cntrl Control characters
	    digit Digits
	    graph All printable characters except space
	    lower Lowercase letters
	    print All printable characters
	    punct Punctuation
	    space Whitespace (horizontal or vertical)
	    upper Uppercase letters
	    xdigit Hexadecimal digits

[=*char*=]

The class of characters in which *char* belongs. Not fully implemented.

Examples

Change uppercase to lowercase in a file:

```
cat file | tr '[A-Z]' '[a-z]'
```

Turn spaces into newlines (ASCII code 012):

```
tr ' ' '\012' < file
```

Strip blank lines from **file** and save in **new.file** (or use **011** to change successive tabs into one tab):

```
cat file | tr -s "" "\012" > new.file
```

Delete colons from **file**; save result in **new.file**:

```
tr -d : < file > new.file
```

---

true

true

A null command that returns a successful (zero) exit status. See also **false**.

---

ul

ul [*options*] [*names*]

Translate underscores to underlining. The correct sequence with which to do this will vary by terminal type. Some terminals are unable to handle underlining.

Options

-i   Translate –, when on a separate line, to underline, instead of _.

-t *terminal -type*
          Specify terminal type. By default, TERM is consulted.

umount *argument*   umount

Unmount filesystems. For details, see the **mount** command.

unexpand [*options*] [*files*]   unexpand

Convert strings of initial whitespace, consisting of at least two spaces and/or tabs, to tabs. Read from standard input if given no file or a file named -.

Options

-, -t, --tabs *tab -stops*
          tab-stops is a comma-separated list of integers that specify the placement of tab stops. If exactly one integer is provided, the tab stops are set to every *integer* space. By default, tab stops are eight spaces apart. Implies -a. With -t and --tabs, the list may be separated by whitespace instead of commas.

-a, --all
          Convert all, not just initial, strings of spaces and tabs.

uniq [*options*] [*file1* [*file2*]]   uniq

Remove duplicate adjacent lines from sorted *file1*, sending one copy of each line to *file2* (or to standard output). Often used as a filter. Specify only one of -c, -d, or -u. See also **comm** and ᴄort.

Options

-*n*, -f *n*, --skip-fields=*n*
          Ignore first *n* fields of a line. Fields are separated by spaces or by tabs.

+*n*, -s *n*, --skip-chars=*n*
          Ignore first *n* characters of a field.

-c, --count
          Print each line once, counting instances of each.

-d, --repeated
          Print duplicate lines once, but no unique lines.

-u, --unique
          Print only unique lines (no copy of duplicate entries is kept).

→

uniq ←	-w *n*, --check-chars=*n* Compare only first *n* characters per line (beginning after skipped fields and characters). ***Examples*** Send one copy of each line from **list** to output file **list.new**: `uniq list list.new` Show which names appear more than once: `sort names	uniq -d`      Show which lines appear exactly three times:        `sort names	uniq -c	grep "3 "`
uptime	**uptime** Print the current time, amount of time logged in, number of users logged in, and system load averages. This output is also produced by the first line of the **w** command.
users	**users** [*file*] Print a space-separated list of each login session on the host. Note that this may include the same user multiple times. Consult *file* or, by default, */etc/utmp*.
vi	**vi** [*options*] [*files*] A screen-oriented text editor based on **ex**. For more information on **vi**, see Chapter 8, *The vi Editor*.

vrfy	**vrfy** [*options*] *address* [*host*]
	
	Query remote host to verify the accuracy of an email address. If *host* is provided, query that host directly; otherwise the query may go to a mail exchange. Print information about the address and, if provided by the remote host, about the user. With the **-f** and **-p** options, do not require the specification of an address on the command line.
	
	Options
	
	    -a Query each mail exchange host, not just primary.
	    -c *secs* Timeout connection attempts after *secs* seconds. The default is 6.
	    -d Enable debugging output.
	    -dd Enable more verbose debugging output.
	    -e Use EXPN, not VRFY, command when connected to the sendmail port on the remote host.

-f *file*	Consult file for list of email addresses to verify.
-l	Specify local error-handling mode.
-p *domain*	
	Determine whether domain's mail exchangers are presently accepting SMTP requests.
-s	Strip all comments from hosts' addresses.
-n	Use RCPT, not VRFY, command when connected to the sendmail port on the remote host. Disables recursion, as RCPT cannot support it.
-t *secs*	Time out read attempts after *secs* seconds. The default is 60.
-v	Verbose.
-vv	Very verbose.
-vvv	Amazingly verbose.
-L *levels*	Recursively verify *levels* levels of the address. -L recognizes mail loops and local users, and stops checking when it encounters them.
-R	Same as -L 17. 17 hops are the maximum in real mailings. Implies -s.

w [*options*] [*users*]

Print summaries of system usage, currently logged-in users, and what they are doing. **w** is essentially a combination of **uptime**, **who**, and **ps -a**. Display output for one user by specifying *user*.

Options

-h	Suppress headings and **uptime** information.
-i	Sort output by idle time.

wc [*options*] [*files*]

Print a character, word, and line count for *files*. If no *files* are given, read standard input. See other examples under **ls** and **sort**.

Options

-c, -bytes, --chars	
	Print character count only.
-l, --lines	Print line count only.
-w, --words	Print word count only.

Examples

Count the number of users logged in:

```
who | wc -l
```

$\rightarrow$

wc
←
	Count the words in three essay files:
	
	`wc -w essay.[123]`
	
	Count lines in variable **$file** (don't display filename):
	
	`wc -l < $file`

whatis	**whatis** [*options*] *keyword*
	
	Search each manual page's short description for *keyword*. Print a one-line description for each match.
	
	Options
	
	-d, --debug
	    Enable debugging mode.
	
	-m *systems*, --systems=*systems*
	    Search other operating systems' manual pages.
	
	-r, --regex
	    Treat *keyword* as a regular expression.
	
	-w, --wildcard
	    Allow *keyword* to contain wildcards.
	
	-M *path*, --manpath=*path*
	    Search *path* for manual pages.

who	**who** [*options*] [*file*]
	who am i
	
	Display information about the current status of the system. With no options, list the names of users currently logged in to the system, their terminal, the time they have been logged in, and the name of the host from which they have logged on. An optional system *file* (default is */etc/utmp*) can be supplied to give additional information.
	
	Options
	
	am i Print the username of the invoking user.
	
	-m Same as **who am i**.
	
	-i, -u, --idle
	    Include idle times. An idle time of . indicates activity within the last minute; one of **old** indicates no activity in more than a full day.
	
	-q, --count
	    "Quick." Display only the usernames and total number of users.
	
	-w, -T, --mesg, --message, --writable
	    Display user's message status.
	
	    + mesg y (**write** messages allowed)
	
	    - mesg n (**write** messages refused)

```
    ?    unknown
```

-H, --heading
>   Print headings.

Example

This sample output was produced at 8 a.m. on April 17:

```
who -uH
NAME    LINE   TIME         IDLE   PID   COMMENTS
Earvin  ttyp3  Apr 16 08:14 16:25  2240
Larry   ttyp0  Apr 17 07:33   .    15182
```

Since Earvin has been idle since yesterday afternoon (16 hours), it appears that Earvin isn't at work yet. He simply left himself logged in. Larry's terminal is currently in use.

---

whoami

Print current user ID. Equivalent to **who am i** and **id -un**.

---

write *user* [*tty*]
message

Initiate or respond to an interactive conversation with *user*. A **write** session is terminated with *EOF*. If the user is logged in to more than one terminal, specify a *tty* number. See also **talk**.

---

xargs [*options*] [*command*]

Execute *command* (with any initial arguments), but read remaining arguments from standard input instead of specifying them directly. **xargs** passes these arguments in several bundles to *command*, allowing *command* to process more arguments than it could normally handle at once. The arguments are typically a long list of filenames (generated by **ls** or **find**, for example) that get passed to **xargs** via a pipe.

Options

-0, --null
>   Expect filenames to be terminated by NULL. Do not treat quotes or backlashes specially.

-e[*string*], --eof[=*string*]
>   Set *EOF* to _ or, if specified, to *string*.

-i[*string*], --replace[=*string*]
>   Edit all occurences of {}, or *string*, to the names read in on standard input. Unquoted blanks are not considered argument terminators. Implies -x and -l 1.

-l[*lines*], --max-lines[=*lines*]
>   Allow no more than 1, or *lines*, nonblank input lines on the command line. Implies -x.

→

xargs ←	**-n** *args*, **--max-args**=*args* Allow no more than *args* arguments on the command line. May be overridden by **-s**. **-p**, **--interactive** Prompt for confirmation before running each command line. Implies **-t**. **-r**, **--no-run-if-empty** Do not run command if it is made up entirely of blanks. **-s** *max*, **--max-chars**=*max* Allow no more than *max* characters per command line. **-t**, **--verbose** Verbose mode. **-x**, **--exit** If the maximum size (as specified by **-s**) is exceeded, exit. **-P** *max*, **--max-procs**=*max* Allow no more than *max* processes to run at once. The default is 1. A maximum of 0 allows as many as possible to run at once. *Examples* **grep** for *pattern* in all files on the system: `find / -print	xargs grep pattern > out &`  Run **diff** on file pairs (e.g., **f1.a** and **f1.b**, **f2.a** and **f2.b** ...):  `echo $*	xargs -n2 diff`  The previous line would be invoked as a shell script, specifying filenames as arguments.  Display *file*, one word per line (same as **deroff -w**):  `cat file	xargs -n1`  Move files in *olddir* to *newdir*, showing each command:  `ls olddir	xargs -i -t mv olddir/{} newdir/{}`
ypchfn	**ypchfn** [*options*] [*user*] NFS/NIS command. Change the information that is stored in */etc/passwd* and is displayed when a user is fingered; distribute the change over NIS. Without options, **ypchfn** will enter interactive mode and prompt for changes. To make a field blank, enter the keyword **none**. See also **yppasswd** and **ypchsh**.

Options

-f	Behave like **ypchfn** (default).
-l	Behave like **ypchsh**.
-p	Behave like **yppasswd**.

ypchfn

ypchsh [*options*] [*user*]

ypchsh

NFS/NIS command. Change your login shell and distribute this information over NIS. Warn if *shell* does not exist in */etc/shells*. See also **yppasswd** and **ypchfn**.

Options

-f	Behave like **ypchfn**.
-l	Behave like **ypchsh** (default).
-p	Behave like **yppasswd**.

yppasswd [*options*] [*user*]

yppasswd

NFS/NIS command. Create or change a password associated with *user*, and distribute the new password over NIS. Only the owner or a privileged user may change a password. Owners need not specify their *user* name. See also **ypchfn** and **ypchsh**.

Options

-f	Behave like **ypchfn**.
-l	Behave like **ypchsh**.
-p	Behave like **yppasswd** (default).

zcat [*file*]

zcat

Read one or more *files* that have been compressed with **gzip** or **compress** and write them to standard output. Read standard input if no *files* are specified or if - is specified as one of the files; end input with *EOF*.

zcmp [*options*] *files*

zcmp

Read compressed files and pass them, uncompressed, to the **cmp** command, along with any command-line options. If a second file is not specified for comparison, look for a file called *file*.**gz**.

zdiff [*options*] *files*

zdiff

Read compressed files and pass them, uncompressed, to the **diff** command, along with any command-line options. If a second file is not specified for comparison, look for a file called *file*.**gz**.

zforce	**zforce** [*names*] Rename all **gzipped** files to *filename*.**gz**, unless file already has a .**gz** extension.
zgrep	**zgrep** [*options*] [*files*] Read compressed *files*; pass them, uncompressed, to **grep**, along with any command-line arguments. If no files are provided, read from (and attempt to uncompress) standard input. May be invoked as **zegrep** or **zfgrep**, and will in those cases invoke **egrep** or **fgrep**.
zmore	**zmore** [*files*] Similar to **more**. Print compressed files, uncompressed, one screenful at a time.

Commands

    space Print next screenful.

    i[*number*]

            Print next screenful, or *number* lines. Set *i* to *number* lines.

    ^D   Print next *i*, or 11, lines.

    d   Same as ^D.

    *i*z   Print next *i* lines, or a screenful.

    *i*s   Skip *i* lines. Print next screenful.

    *i*f   Skip *i* screens. Print next screenful.

    q, Q   Go to next file, or, if current file is the last, exit **zmore**.

    e   Exit.

    s   Skip next file and continue.

    =   Print line number.

    i/*expr* Search forward for *i*th occurrence (in all files) of *expr*, which should be a regular expression. Display occurrence, including the two previous lines of context.

    *i*n   Search forward for the *i*th occurrence of the last regular expression searched for.

    !*command*

            Execute *command* in shell. If *command* is not specified, execute last shell command. To invoke a shell without passing it a command, enter \!.

    :q, :Q Skip to the next file. Same as q.

    .   Previous command.

znew [*options*] [*files*]

Uncompress **.Z** files and recompress them in **.gz** format.

Options

-9   Optimal (and slowest) compression method.

-f   Recompress even if *filename*.**gz** already exists.

-t   Test **.gz** files before removing **.Z** files.

-v   Verbose mode.

-K   If the original file is smaller than the **.gz** file, keep it.

-P   Pipe data to conversion program. This saves disk space.

CHAPTER 3

The UNIX Shell:
An Overview

The shell is a program that acts as a buffer between you and the operating system. In its role as a command interpreter, it should (for the most part) act invisibly. It can also be used for simple programming.

This section introduces three shells commonly used on Linux systems—the Bourne Again shell (**bash**), the C shell (**csh**), and **csh**'s enhanced version, **tcsh**—and summarizes the major differences between them. Details on them are provided in Chapter 4, *bash: The Bourne Again Shell*, and Chapter 5, *csh and tcsh*.

The following topics are presented:

- Purpose of the shell

- Shell flavors

- Common features

- Differing features

Purpose of the Shell

There are three main uses for the shell:

- Interactive use

- Customization of your Linux session

- Programming

Interactive Use

When the shell is used interactively, it waits for you to issue commands, processes them (to interpret special characters, such as wildcards), and executes them. Shells also provide a set of commands, known as built-ins, to supplement Linux commands.

Customization of Your Linux Session

A Linux shell defines variables, such as the locations of your home directory and mail spool, to control the behavior of your session. Some variables are preset by the system; you can define others in startup files that your shell reads when you log in. Startup files can also contain Linux or shell commands or special shell commands, for execution immediately after login.

Programming

A series of individual commands (be they shell or other Linux commands available on the system) combined into one program is called a shell script. Batch files in MS-DOS are a similar concept. **bash** is considered a powerful programming shell, while scripting in **csh** is rumored to be hazardous to your health.

Shell Flavors

Many different Linux shells are available. This book describes the three most popular shells:

- The Bourne Again shell (**bash**), which is based on the Bourne shell and is standard for Linux

- The C shell (**csh**), which uses C syntax and has many conveniences

- **tcsh**, an extension of **csh**, which is less standard but has additional interesting features

Most systems have more than one shell, and people will often use one shell for writing shell scripts and another for interactive use.

When you log in, the system determines which shell to run by consulting your entry in */etc/passwd*. The last field of each entry calls a program to run as the default shell. For example:

If the program name is:	Your shell will be the:
/bin/sh	Bourne Again shell
/bin/bash	Bourne Again shell
/bin/csh	C shell
/bin/tcsh	**tcsh**

You can change to another shell by typing the program name at the command line. For example, to change from **bash** to **tcsh**, type:

```
$ exec tcsh
```

Common Features

The table below is a sampling of features that are common to **bash**, **csh**, and **tcsh**. Note that **tcsh** is an enhanced version of **csh**; therefore, **tcsh** includes all features of **csh**, plus some others.

Symbol/Command	Meaning/Action
>	Redirect output.
>>	Append output to file.
<	Redirect input.
<<	"Here" document (redirect input).
|	Pipe output.
&	Run process in background.
;	Separate commands on same line.
*	Match any character(s) in filename.
?	Match single character in filename.
!*n*	Repeat command number *n*.
[ ]	Match any characters enclosed.
( )	Execute in subshell.
` `	Substitute output of enclosed command.
" "	Partial quote (allows variable and command expansion).
' '	Full quote (no expansion).
\	Quote following character.
$*var*	Use value for variable.
$$	Process ID.
$0	Command name.
$*n*	*n*th argument ($0 < n \leq 9$).
$*	All arguments as a simple word.
#	Begin comment.
bg	Background execution.
break	Break from loop statements.
cd	Change directories.
continue	Resume a program loop.
echo	Display output.
eval	Evaluate arguments.
exec	Execute a new shell or other program.
fg	Foreground execution.
jobs	Show active jobs.
kill	Terminate running jobs.
newgrp	Change to a new group.
shift	Shift positional parameters.
stop	Suspend a background job.

Symbol/Command	Meaning/Action
suspend	Suspend a foreground job.
umask	Set or list permissions on files to be created.
unset	Erase variable or function definitions.
wait	Wait for a background job to finish.

Differing Features

The table below is a sampling of features that are different among the three shells.

Meaning/Action	bash	csh	tcsh
Default prompt.	$	%	%
Force redirection.	>|	>!	>!
Force append.		>>!	>>!
Variable assignment.	*var=value*	**set** *var=value*	**set** *var=value.*
Set environment variable.	**export** *var*	**setenv** *var val*	**setenv** *var val*
Number of arguments.	**$#**	**$#argv**	**$#**
Exit status.	**$?**	**$status**	**$?**
Execute commands in *file*.	**. *file***	**source** *file*	**source** *file*
End a loop statement.	**done**	**end**	**end**
End **case** or **switch**.	**esac**	**endsw**	**endsw**
Loop through variables.	**for/do**	**foreach**	**foreach**
Sample **if** statement.	**if [$i –eq 5]**	**if ($i==5)**	**if ($i==5)**
End **if** statement.	**fi**	**endif**	**endif**
Set resource limits.	**ulimit**	**limit**	**limit**
Read from terminal.	**read**	**$<**	**$<**
Make a variable read-only.	**readonly**		**set –r**
File inquiry operator: tests for nonzero size.		**–s**	
Complete current word.	**TAB**		**TAB**
Ignore interrupts.	**trap 2**	**onintr**	**onintr**
Begin **until** loop.	**until/do**	**until**	**until**
Begin **while** loop.	**while/do**	**while**	**while**

CHAPTER 4

bash: The Bourne Again Shell

This chapter presents the following topics:

- Overview of features
- Invoking the shell
- Syntax
- Variables
- Arithmetic expressions
- Command history
- Built-in commands
- Job control

Overview of Features

bash is the standard shell and provides the following features:

- Input/output redirection
- Wildcard characters (metacharacters) for filename abbreviation
- Shell variables for customizing your environment
- Powerful programming capabilities
- Command-Line editing (using **vi**- or Emacs-style editing commands)
- Access to previous commands (command history)
- Integer arithmetic
- Arithmetic expressions
- Command name abbreviation (aliasing)
- Job control

- Integrated programming features
- Control structures
- Directory stacking (using **pushd** and **popd**)
- Brace/tilde expansion
- Key bindings

Invoking the Shell

The command interpreter for **bash** can be invoked as follows:

> **bash** [*options*] [*arguments*]

bash can execute commands from a terminal (when -i is specified), from a file (when the first *argument* is an executable script), or from standard input (if no arguments remain or if -s is specified).

Options

-, --
  Treat all subsequent strings as arguments, not options.

-c *str*
  Read commands from string *str*.

-i Create an interactive shell (prompt for input).

-login
  Behave like a login shell.

-nobraceexpansion
  Disable brace expansion.

-nolineediting
  Disable line editing with arrow and control keys.

-noprofile
  Do not process */etc/profile*, ˜*/.bash_profile*, ˜*/.bash_login*, or ˜*/.profile* on startup.

-norc
  Do not process ˜*/.bashrc* on startup.

-p Start up as a privileged user; don't process *$HOME/.profile*.

-posix
  Conform to POSIX standard.

-quiet
  Default. Do not print startup information.

-rcfile *file*
  Substitute *file* for *.bashrc* on startup.

-s Read commands from standard input; output from built-in commands goes to file descriptor 1; all other shell output goes to file descriptor 2.

The remaining options to **bash** are listed under the **set** built-in command.

Arguments

Arguments are assigned, in order, to the positional parameters $1, $2, etc. If the first argument is an executable script, commands are read from it and remaining arguments are assigned to $1, $2, etc.

Syntax

This subsection describes the many symbols peculiar to **bash**. The topics are arranged as follows:

- Special files
- Filename metacharacters
- Command-Line editing
- Quoting
- Command forms
- Redirection forms
- Coprocesses

Special Files

/etc/profile	Executed automatically at login.
$HOME/.bash_profile	Executed automatically at login.
$HOME/.bashrc	Executed automatically at shell startup.
$HOME/.bash_logout	Executed automatically at logout.
$HOME/.bash_history	Record of last session's commands.
/etc/passwd	Source of home directories for ˜*name* abbreviations.

Filename Metacharacters

*	Match any string of zero or more characters.
?	Match any single character.
[abc...]	Match any one of the enclosed characters; a hyphen can be used to specify a range (e.g., a-z, A-Z, 0-9).
[!abc...]	Match any character *not* among the enclosed characters.
~name	HOME directory of user *name*
~+	Current working directory (PWD)
~-	Previous working directory (OLDPWD)

Patterns can be a sequence of patterns separated by |; if any of the subpatterns match, the entire sequence is considered matching. This extended syntax resembles that available to **egrep** and **awk**.

Examples

```
$ ls new*      List new and new.1
$ cat ch?      Match ch9 but not ch10
$ vi [D-R]*    Match files that begin with uppercase D through R
```

Command-line Editing

Command lines can be edited like lines in either Emacs or vi. Emacs is the default. See the section Line-Edit Mode for more information.

vi mode has two sub-modes, insert mode and command mode. The default mode is insert; you can toggle modes by pressing ESC, or, in command mode, typing **a** (append) or **i** (insert) will return you to insert mode.

Basic Emacs-Mode Commands

Command	Description
CTRL-B	Move backward one character (without deleting).
CTRL-F	Move forward one character.
DEL	Delete one character backward.
CTRL-D	Delete one character forward.

Emacs-Mode Word Commands

Command	Description
ESC b	Move one word backward.
ESC f	Move one word forward.
ESC DEL	Kill one word backward.
ESC d	Kill one word forward.
CTRL-Y	Retrieve ("yank") last item killed.

Emacs-Mode Line Commands

Command	Description
CTRL-A	Move to beginning of line.
CTRL-E	Move to end of line.
CTRL-K	Kill forward to end of line.

Emacs-Mode Commands for Moving Through the History File

Command	Description
CTRL-P	Move to previous line.
CTRL-N	Move to next line.
CTRL-R	Search backward.
ESC <	Move to first line of history file.
ESC >	Move to last line of history file.

Completion Commands

Command	Description
TAB	Attempt to perform general completion of the text.
ESC ?	List the possible completions.
ESC /	Attempt filename completion.
CTRL-X /	List the possible filename completions.
ESC ~	Attempt username completion.
CTRL-X ~	List the possible username completions.
ESC $	Attempt variable completion.
CTRL-X $	List the possible variable completions.
ESC @	Attempt hostname completion.
CTRL-X @	List the possible hostname completions.
ESC !	Attempt command completion.
CTRL-X !	List the possible command completions.
ESC TAB	Attempt completion from previous commands in the history list.

Emacs-Mode Miscellaneous Commands

Command	Description
CTRL-J	Same as RETURN.
CTRL-L	Clear the screen, placing the current line at the top of the screen.
CTRL-M	Same as RETURN.
CTRL-O	Same as RETURN, then display next line in command history.
CTRL-T	Transposes character left of and under the cursor.
CTRL-U	Kill the line from the beginning to point.
CTRL-V	Insert keypress instead of interpreting it as a command.
CTRL-[	Same as ESC (most keyboards).
ESC c	Capitalize word under or after cursor.
ESC u	Change word under or after cursor to all capital letters.
ESC l	Change word under or after cursor to all lowercase letters.
ESC .	Insert last word in previous command line after point.
ESC _	Same as ESC.

Editing Commands in vi Input Mode

Command	Description
DEL	Delete previous character.
CTRL-W	Erase previous word (i.e., erase until a blank).
CTRL-V	Insert keypress instead of interpreting it as a command.
ESC	Enter control mode (see next section).

Basic vi Control Mode Commands

Command	Description
h	Move left one character.
l	Move right one character.
b	Move left one word.
w	Move right one word.
B	Move to beginning of preceding nonblank word.
W	Move to beginning of next nonblank word.
e	Move to end of current word.
E	Move to end of current nonblank word.
0	Move to beginning of line.
^	Move to first nonblank character in line.
$	Move to end of line.

Commands for Entering vi Input Mode

Command	Description
i	Text inserted before current character (insert).
a	Text inserted after current character (append).
I	Text inserted at beginning of line.
A	Text inserted at end of line.
R	Text overwrites existing text.

Some vi-Mode Deletion Commands

Command	Description
dh	Delete one character backward.
dl	Delete one character forward.
db	Delete one word backward.
dw	Delete one word forward.
dB	Delete one nonblank word backward.
dW	Delete one nonblank word forward.
d$	Delete to end of line.
d0	Delete to beginning of line.

Abbreviations for vi-Mode Delete Commands

Command	Description
D	Equivalent to d$ (delete to end of line).
dd	Equivalent to 0d$ (delete entire line).
C	Equivalent to c$ (delete to end of line, enter input mode).
cc	Equivalent to 0c$ (delete entire line, enter input mode).
X	Equivalent to dl (delete character backward).
x	Equivalent to dh (delete character forward).

vi Control Mode Commands for Searching the Command History

Command	Description
k or –	Move backward one line.
j or +	Move forward one line.
G	Move to line given by repeat count.
/*string*	Search backward for *string*.
?*string*	Search forward for *string*.
n	Repeat search in same direction as previous.
N	Repeat search in opposite direction of previous.

vi-Mode Character-finding Commands

Command	Description
f*x*	Move right to next occurrence of *x*.
F*x*	Move left to previous occurrence of *x*.
t*x*	Move right to next occurrence of *x*, then back one space.
T*x*	Move left to previous occurrence of *x*, then forward one space.
;	Redo last character-finding command.
,	Redo last character-finding command in opposite direction.

Miscellaneous vi-Mode Commands

Command	Description
~	Invert (toggle) case of current character(s).
_	Append last word of previous command, enter input mode.
CTRL-L	Clear the screen and redraw the current line on it; good for when your screen becomes garbled.
#	Prepend # (comment character) to the line and send it to the history file; useful for saving a command to be executed later, without having to retype it.

Quoting

Quoting disables a character's special meaning and allows it to be used literally, as itself. The following characters have special meaning to **bash**:

;	Command separator
&	Background execution
( )	Command grouping (enter a subshell)
{ }	Command block
|	Pipe
> < &	Redirection symbols
* ? [ ] ~ !	Filename metacharacters
" ' \	Used in quoting other characters
`	Command substitution

`$`	Variable substitution (or command substitution)
newline space tab	Word separators
`#`	Comment.

The following characters can be used for quoting:

`" "`	Everything between `"` and `"` is taken literally, except for the following characters that keep their special meaning:

`$`	Variable substitution will occur.
`` ` ``	Command substitution will occur.
`"`	This marks the end of the double quote.

`' '`	Everything between `'` and `'` is taken literally, except for another `'`.
`\`	The character following a `\` is taken literally. Use within `" "` to escape `"`, `$`, and `` ` ``. Often used to escape itself, spaces, or newlines.

Examples

```
$ echo 'Single quotes "protect" double quotes'
Single quotes "protect" double quotes

$ echo "Well, isn't that \"special\"?"
Well, isn't that "special"?

$ echo "You have `ls|wc -1` files in `pwd`"
You have      43 files in /home/bob

$ echo "The value of \$x is $x"
The value of $x is 100
```

Command Forms

`cmd &`	Execute *cmd* in background.
`cmd1 ; cmd2`	Command sequence; execute multiple *cmd*s on the same line.
`(cmd1 ; cmd2)`	Subshell; treat *cmd1* and *cmd2* as a command group.
`cmd1	cmd2`	Pipe; use output from *cmd1* as input to *cmd2*.
`cmd1 `cmd2``	Command substitution; use *cmd2* output as arguments to *cmd1*.
`cmd1 $(cmd2)`	Command substitution; nesting is allowed.
`cmd1 && cmd2`	AND; execute *cmd2* only if *cmd1* succeeds.
`cmd1 || cmd2`	OR; execute *cmd2* only if *cmd1* fails.
`{ cmd1 ; cmd2 }`	Execute commands in the current shell.

Examples

`$ nroff file &`	*Format in the background*
`$ cd; ls`	*Execute sequentially*
`$ (date; who; pwd) > logfile`	*All output is redirected*
`$ sort file	pr -3	lp`	*Sort file, page output, then print*

```
$ vi `grep -1 ifdef *.c`          Edit files found by grep
$ egrep '(yes|no)' `cat list`     Specify a list of files to search
$ egrep '(yes|no)' $(cat list)    bash version of previous
$ egrep '(yes|no)' $(<list)       Same, but faster
$ grep XX file && lp file         Print file if it contains the pattern
$ grep XX file || echo "XX not found"   Echo an error message if
                                        the pattern is not found
```

Redirection Forms

File Descriptor	Name	Common Abbreviation	Typical Default
0	Standard input	stdin	Keyboard
1	Standard output	stdout	Terminal
2	Standard error	stderr	Terminal

The usual input source or output destination can be changed as follows:

I/O Redirectors

Redirector	Function
> *file*	Direct standard output to *file*.
< *file*	Take standard input from *file*.
cmd1 | cmd2	Pipe; take standard output of *cmd1* as standard input to *cmd2*.
>> *file*	Direct standard output to *file*; append to *file* if it already exists.
>| *file*	Force standard output to *file* even if **noclobber** is set.
n>| *file*	Force output from the file descriptor to *file* even if **noclobber** is set.
<> *file*	Use *file* as both standard input and standard output.
<< *text*	Read standard input up to a line identical to *text* (*text* can be stored in a shell variable). Input is usually typed on the screen or in the shell program. Commands that typically use this syntax include **cat**, **echo**, **ex**, and **sed**. If *text* is enclosed in quotes, standard input will not undergo variable substitution, command substitution, etc.
n> *file*	Direct file descriptor *n* to *file*.
n< *file*	Set *file* as file descriptor *n*.
>&*n*	Duplicate standard output to file descriptor *n*.
<&*n*	Duplicate standard input from file descriptor *n*.
&>*file*	Direct standard output and standard error to *file*.
<&-	Close the standard input.
>&-	Close the standard output.
n>&-	Close the output from file descriptor *n*.
n<&-	Close the input from file descriptor *n*.

Examples

```
$ cat part1 > book
$ cat part2 part3 >> book
$ mail tim < report

$ sed 's/^/XX /' << END_ARCHIVE
> This is often how a shell archive is "wrapped",
> bundling text for distribution. You would normally
> run sed from a shell program, not from the command line.
> END_ARCHIVE
XX This is often how a shell archive is "wrapped",
XX bundling text for distribution. You would normally
XX run sed from a shell program, not from the command line.
```

To redirect standard output to standard error:

```
$ echo "Usage error:  see administrator" 1>&2
```

The following command sends output (files found) to *filelist* and sends error messages (inaccessible files) to file *no_access*:

```
$ find / -print > filelist 2>no_access
```

Coprocesses

Coprocesses are a feature of **bash** only.

cmd1 | *cmd2* |&	Coprocess; execute the pipeline in the background. The shell sets up a two-way pipe, allowing redirection of both standard input and standard output.
read -p *var*	Read coprocess input into variable *var*.
print -p *string*	Write *string* to the coprocess.
cmd <&p	Take input for *cmd* from the coprocess.
cmd >&p	Send output of *cmd* to the coprocess.

Examples

```
cat memo                            Print contents of file
Sufficient unto the day is
A word to the wise.
ed - memo |&                        Start coprocess
print -p /word/                     Send ed command to coprocess
read -p search                      Read output of ed command into variable search
print "$search"                     Show the line on standard output
A word to the wise.
```

Variables

This subsection describes:

* Variable substitution
* Built-in shell variables

Variable Substitution

Substitution Operators

Operator	Substitution
${varname:-word}	If *varname* exists and isn't null, return its value; otherwise return *word*.
Purpose:	Returning a default value if the variable is undefined.
Example:	${count:-0} evaluates to 0 if **count** is undefined.
${varname:=word}	If *varname* exists and isn't null, return its value; otherwise set it to *word* and then return its value. Positional and special parameters cannot be assigned this way.
Purpose:	Setting a variable to a default value if it is undefined.
Example:	${count:=0} sets **count** to 0 if it is undefined.
${varname:?message}	If *varname* exists and isn't null, return its value; otherwise print *varname*: followed by *message*, and abort the current command or script (non-interactive shells only). Omitting *message* produces the default message **parameter null or not set**.
Purpose:	Catching errors that result from variables being undefined.
Example:	{count:?"undefined!"} prints "count: undefined!" and exits if **count** is undefined.
${varname:+word}	If *varname* exists and isn't null, return *word*; otherwise return null.
Purpose:	Testing for the existence of a variable.
Example:	${count:+1} returns 1 (which could mean "true") if **count** is defined.

bash

Pattern-Matching Operators

Operator	Meaning
${variable#pattern}	If the pattern matches the beginning of the variable's value, delete the shortest part that matches and return the rest.
${variable##pattern}	If the pattern matches the beginning of the variable's value, delete the longest part that matches and return the rest.
${variable%pattern}	If the pattern matches the end of the variable's value, delete the shortest part that matches and return the rest.
${variable%%pattern}	If the pattern matches the end of the variable's value, delete the longest part that matches and return the rest.

Built-in Shell Variables

Built-in variables are automatically set by the shell and are typically used inside shell scripts. Built-in variables can make use of the variable substitution patterns already shown above. Variables are shown here without them, but they are always needed when referencing them.

Basic Shell Options

Option	Description
emacs	Enter Emacs editing mode (on by default).
ignoreeof	Don't allow use of a single **CTRL-D** to log off; use the **exit** command to log off. This has the same effect as setting the shell variable IGNOREEOF=1.
noclobber	Don't allow output redirection (>) to overwrite an existing file.
noglob	Don't expand filename wildcards like * and ? (wildcard expansion is sometimes called *globbing*).
nounset	Indicate an error when trying to use a variable that is undefined.
vi	Enter **vi** editing mode.

Standard Variables

Variable	Meaning
COLUMNS	The number of columns your display has.
EDITOR	Pathname of your text editor.
LINES	The number of lines your display has.
SHELL	Pathname of the shell you are running.
TERM	The type of terminal that you are using.

History Variables

Variable	Meaning
HISTCMD	The history number of the current command.
HISTCONTROL	If HISTCONTROL is set to the value of **ignorespace**, lines beginning with a space are not entered into the history list. If set to **ignoredups**, lines matching the last history line are not entered. Setting it to **ignoreboth** enables both options.
HISTFILE	Name of history file, on which the editing modes operate.
HISTFILESIZE	The maximum number of lines to store in the history file. The default is 500.
HISTSIZE	The maximum number of commands to remember in the command history. The default is 500.
FCEDIT	Pathname of editor to use with the **fc** command.

Mail Variables

Variable	Meaning
MAIL	Name of file to check for incoming mail.
MAILCHECK	How often, in seconds, to check for new mail (default is 60 seconds).
MAILPATH	List of filenames, separated by colons (:), to check for incoming mail.

Status Variables

Variable	Meaning
HOME	Name of your home (login) directory.
SECONDS	Number of seconds since the shell was invoked.
BASH	Pathname of this instance of the shell you are running.
BASH_VERSION	The version number of the shell you are running.
PWD	Current directory.
OLDPWD	Previous directory before the last **cd** command.

Arithmetic Expressions

The **let** command performs integer arithmetic. **bash** provides a way to substitute integer values (for use as command arguments or in variables); base conversion is also possible:

$((expr))   Use the value of the enclosed arithmetic expression.

Operators

bash uses arithmetic operators from the C programming language; the following list is in decreasing order of precedence. Use parentheses to override precedence.

-	Unary minus
! ~	Logical negation; binary inversion (one's complement)
* / %	Multiplication; division; modulus (remainder)
+ -	Addition; subtraction
<< >>	Bitwise left shift; bitwise right shift
<= >=	Less than or equal to; greater than or equal to
< >	Less than; greater than
== !=	Equality; inequality (both evaluated left to right)
&	Bitwise AND
^	Bitwise exclusive OR
|	Bitwise OR
&&	Logical AND
||	Logical OR

=	Assign value.
+= -=	Reassign after addition/subtraction.
*= /= %=	Reassign after multiplication/division/remainder.
&= ^= |=	Reassign after bitwise AND/XOR/OR.
<<= >>=	Reassign after bitwise shift left/right.

Examples

See the **let** command for more information and examples.

```
let "count=0" "i = i + 1"     Assign i and count
let "num % 2"                 Test for an even number
```

Command History

bash lets you display or modify previous commands. This is similar to the C shell's history mechanism. Commands in the history list can be modified using:

- Line-Edit mode

- The **fc** command

In addition, the command substitutions described in Chapter 5, *csh and tcsh*, also work in **bash**.

Line-Edit Mode

Line-edit mode lets you emulate many features of the **vi** or Emacs editors. The history list is treated like a file. When the editor is invoked, you type editing keystrokes to move to the command line you want to execute. You can also change the line before executing it. When you're ready to issue the command, press RETURN.

Line-edit mode can be started in several ways. For example, these are equivalent:

```
$ VISUAL=vi
$ EDITOR=vi
$ set -o vi        Overrides value of VISUAL or EDITOR
```

Note that **vi** starts in input mode; to type a **vi** command, press ESCAPE first.

Common Editing Keystrokes

vi	Emacs	Result
k	CTRL-P	Get previous command.
j	CTRL-N	Get next command.
/*string*	CTRL-R *string*	Get previous command containing *string*.
h	CTRL-B	Move back one character.
l	CTRL-F	Move forward one character.
b	ESC-B	Move back one word.
w	ESC-F	Move forward one word.

vi	Emacs	Result
X	DEL	Delete previous character.
x	CTRL-D	Delete one character.
dw	ESC-D	Delete word forward.
db	ESC-H	Delete word back.
xp	CTRL-T	Transpose two characters.

The fc Command

Use fc -l to list history commands and fc -e to edit them. See the entry under built-in commands for more information.

Examples

`$ history`	*List the last 16 commands*
`$ fc -l 20 30`	*List commands 20 through 30*
`$ fc -l -5`	*List the last five commands*
`$ fc -l cat`	*List the last command beginning with* cat
`$ fc -ln 5 > doit`	*Save command 5 to file* doit
`$ fc -e vi 5 20`	*Edit commands 5 through 20 using* vi
`$ fc -e emacs`	*Edit previous command using Emacs.*
`$ !!`	*Reexecute previous command*
`$ !cat`	*Reexecute last* cat *command.*
`$ !cat foo-file`	*Reexecute last command, adding* foo-file *to the end of the argument list*

Command Substitution

!	Begin a history substitution.
!!	Previous command.
!*N*	Command number *N* in history list.
!-*N*	*N*th command back from current command.
!*string*	Most recent command that starts with *string*.
!?*string*?	Most recent command that contains *string*.
!?*string*?%	Most recent command argument that contains *string*.
!$	Last argument of previous command.
!!*string*	Previous command, then append *string*.
!*N string*	Command *N*, then append *string*.
!{*s1*}*s2*	Most recent command starting with string *s1*, then append string *s2*.
^*old*^*new*^	Quick substitution; change string *old* to *new* in previous command; execute modified command.

Built-in Commands

Examples to be entered as a command line are shown with the **$** prompt. Otherwise, examples should be treated as code fragments that might be included in a shell script. For convenience, some of the reserved words used by multiline commands are also included.

#	#
	Ignore all text that follows on the same line. # is used in shell scripts as the comment character, and is not really a command.

#!	*#!shell*
	Used as the first line of a script to invoke the named *shell* (with optional arguments). Some older, non-Linux systems do not support scripts starting with this line. For example:

```
#!/bin/bash
```

:	:
	Null command. Returns an exit status of 0. Sometimes used as the first character in a file to denote a **bash** script. Shell variables can be placed after the : to expand them to their values.

Example

Check whether someone is logged in:

```
if who | grep $1 > /dev/null
then :                      # do nothing
                            # if pattern is found
else echo "User $1 is not logged in"
fi
```

.	. *file* [*arguments*]
	Same as **source**.

---

alias	**alias** [*name*[='*cmd*']]
	Assign a shorthand *name* as a synonym for *cmd*. If ='*cmd*' is omitted, print the alias for *name*; if *name* is also omitted, print all aliases. If *cmd* is followed by a space, check subsequent command-line argument for another alias. See also **unalias**.

---

bg	**bg** [*jobIDs*]
	Put current job or *jobIDs* in the background. See "Job Control" later in this chapter.

---

bind [*options*]
bind [*options*] *keys:function*

Print or set key and function bindings.

Options

-m *keymap*
   Specify a keymap for future bindings. Possible keymaps are **emacs**, **emacs-standard**, **emacs-meta**, **emacs-ctlx**, **vi**, **vi-move**, **vi-command**, and **vi-insert**.

-l Print all read-line functions.

-v Print all function names.

-d Display function names and bindings, suitable for rereading.

-f *filename*
   Consult *filename* for bindings.

-q *function*
   Display the bindings that invoke *function*.

---

break [*n*]

Exit from the innermost (most deeply nested) **for**, **while**, or **until** loop, or from the *n* innermost levels of the loop. Also exits from a **select** list.

---

built-in *command* [*arguments*]

Execute *command*, which must be a shell built-in. Useful for invoking built-ins within scripts of the same name.

---

case *string*
in
  regex)
  commands
    ;;
    ...
  esac

If *string* matches regular expression *regex*, perform the following *commands*. Procede down the list of regular expressions until one is found (to catch all remaining strings, use * as *regex* at the end).

---

cd [*dir*]

With no arguments, change to home directory of user. Otherwise, change working directory to *dir*. If *dir* is a relative pathname but is not in the current directory, then the CDPATH variable is searched.

command	command [*options*] *command* [*arguments*]
	
	Execute *command*; do not perform function look up (i.e., refuse to run any command that is neither in PATH or a built-in). Set exit status to that returned by *command*, unless *command* cannot be found, in which case exit with a status of 127.
	
	  -p Search default path, ignoring the PATH variable's value.
	
	  -- Treat everything that follows as an argument, not an option.

continue	continue [*n*] Skip remaining commands in a **for, while,** or **until** loop, resuming with the next iteration of the loop (or skipping *n* loops).

declare	declare [*options*] [*name*[=*value*]]
	typeset [*options*] [*name*[=*value*]]
	
	Print or set variables. Options prefaced by + instead of − are inverted in meaning.
	
	  -f Use only function names.
	
	  -r Do not allow variables to be reset later.
	
	  -x Mark variables for subsequent export.
	
	  -i Expect variable to be an integer, and evaluate its assigned value.

dirs	dirs [*options*]
	
	Print directories currently remembered for **pushd/popd** operations.
	
	Options
	
	  +*entry*
	      Print *entry*th entry (starting with zero).
	
	  -*entry*
	      Print *entry*th entry from end of list.
	
	  -l Long listing.

echo	echo [*options*] [*string*]
	
	Write *string* to standard output, terminated by a newline. If no *string* is supplied, echo a newline. In **bash**, echo is just an alias for **print −**. (See also **echo** in Chapter 2, *Linux User Commands.*)
	
	  -n Do not append a newline to the output.
	
	  -e Enable interpretation of escape characters.
	
	     \a Audible alert
	     \b Backspace
	     \c Suppress the terminating newline (same as −**n**)
	     \f Form feed

enable [−*n*] [−*a*|−*all*] [*built−in* ...]

Enable (or when -*n* is specified, disable) built-in shell commands. Without *built-in*, print enabled built-ins; with -*a* or -*all* print the status of all built-ins. You can disable shell commands so as to define your own functions with the same names.

eval [*command args...*]

Perform *command*, passing *args*.

exec [[−] *command*]

Execute *command* in place of the current process (instead of creating a new process). **exec** is also useful for opening, closing, or copying file descriptors. If − is provided, pass − as zeroth argument to the new process.

Examples

```
trap 'exec 2>&-' 0        Close standard error when
                          shell script exits (signal 0)
$ exec /bin/csh           Replace current shell with C shell
$ exec < infile           Reassign standard input to infile
```

exit [*n*]

Exit a shell script with status *n* (e.g., **exit 1**). *n* can be 0 (success) or nonzero (failure). If *n* is not given, exit status will be that of the most recent command. **exit** can be issued at the command line to close a window (log out).

Example

```
if [ $# -eq 0 ]; then
    echo "Usage:  $0 [-c] [-d] file(s)"
    exit 1                # Error status
fi
```

export [*options*] [*variables*]
export [*options*] [*name=[value]*] . . .

Pass (export) the value of one or more shell *variables*, giving global meaning to the variables (which are local by default). For example, a variable defined in one shell script must be exported if its value will be used in other programs called by the script. If no *variables* are given, **export** lists the variables exported by the current shell. If *name* and *value* are specified, assign *value* to a variable *name*.

$\rightarrow$

export ←	*Options* -- Treat all subsequent strings as arguments, not options. -f Expect *variables* to be functions. -n Unexport variable. -p List variables exported by current shell.

fc	**fc** [*options*] [*first*] [*last*]
	fc -e - [*old=new*] [*command*]
	
	Display or edit commands in the history list. (Use only one of -l or -e.) **fc** provides capabilities similar to the C shell's **history** and ! syntax. *first* and *last* are numbers or strings specifying the range of commands to display or edit. If *last* is omitted, **fc** applies to a single command (specified by *first*). If both *first* and *last* are omitted, **fc** edits the previous command or lists the last 16.
	
	The second form of **fc** takes a history *command*, replaces *old* string with *new* string, and executes the modified command. If no strings are specified, *command* is just reexecuted. If no *command* is given either, the previous command is reexecuted. *command* is a number or string like *first*. See examples under "Command History."
	
	Options
	
	-e [*editor*]
	    Invoke *editor* to edit the specified history commands. The default *editor* is set by shell variable FCEDIT.
	-l [*first last*]
	    List the specified command or range of commands, or list the last 16.
	-n Suppress command numbering from the -l listing.
	-r Reverse the order of the -l listing.
	-s *pattern=newpattern*
	    Edit command(s), replacing all occurrences of *pattern* with *newpattern*. Then reexecute.

fg	**fg** [*jobIDs*] Bring current job or *jobIDs* to the foreground. See "Job Control."
for	**for** *x* [**in** *list*] **do** *commands* **done** Assign each word in list to *x* in turn and execute commands. If *list* is omitted, $@ (positional parameters) is assumed.

Examples

Paginate all files in the current directory; save each result:

```
for $file in * do
        pr $file > $file.tmp
done
```

Search chapters for a list of words (like **fgrep -f**):

```
for item in `cat program_list`
do
        echo "Checking chapters for"
        echo "references to program $item..."
        grep -c "$item.[co]" chap*
done
```

---

function *command*
{

Define a function. Refer to arguments the same way as positional parameters in a shell script (**$1**, etc.) and terminate with **}**.

---

getopts *string name* [*args*]

Process command-line arguments (or *args*, if specified) and check for legal options. **getopts** is used in shell script loops and is intended to ensure standard syntax for command-line options. *string* contains the option letters to be recognized by **getopts** when running the shell script. Valid options are processed in turn and stored in the shell variable *name*. If an option letter is followed by a colon, the option must be followed by one or more arguments. **getopts** uses the shell variables OPTARG and OPTIND.

---

hash [**-r**] [*commands*]

Search for *commands* and remember the directory in which each command resides. Hashing causes the shell to remember the association between a "name" and the absolute pathname of an executable, so that future executions don't require a search of PATH. With no arguments, **hash** lists the current hashed commands. The display shows *hits* (the number of times the command is called by the shell) and *command* (the full pathname).

---

help [*string*]

Print help text on all built-in commands, or those matching *string*.

history	**history** [*options*] **history** [*lines*] Print a numbered command history, denoting modified commands with a *. Include commands from previous sessions. You may specify how many lines of history to print. ***Options*** -a **bash** maintains a file called *.bash_history* in the user's home directory, a record of previous sessions' commands. Ask **bash** to append the current session's commands to *.bash_history*. -n Append to the history list those lines in the *bash_history* file that have not yet been included. -r Use *.bash_history* as the history list, instead of the working history list. -w Overwrite *.bash_history* with working history list.

if	**if** *test–cmds*
	
	Begin a conditional statement. Possible formats are:
	
	<pre>if test-cmds if test-cmds if test-cmds
	then then then
	   cmds1 cmds1 cmds1
	fi else elif test-cmds
	                       cmds2 then
	                    fi cmds2
	                                         ...
	                                         else
	                                            cmdsn
	                                         fi</pre>
	Usually, the initial **if** and any **elif** lines execute one **test** or [] command (although any series of commands is permitted). When **if** succeeds (that is, the last of its *test-cmds* returns zero), *cmds1* are performed; otherwise each succeeding **elif** or **else** line is tried.

jobs	**jobs** [*options*] [*jobIDs*] List all running or stopped jobs, or those specified by *jobIDs*. For example, you can check whether a long compilation or text format is still running. Also useful before logging out. See also "Job Control" later in this chapter. ***Options*** -l List job IDs and process group IDs. -n List only jobs whose status changed since last notification.

-p List process group IDs only.

-x *command* [*arguments*]
    Execute *command*. If *jobIDs* are specified, replace them with
    command.

---

kill [*options*] *IDs*

Terminate each specified process *ID* or job *ID*. You must own the
process or be a privileged user. See also "Job Control."

Options

-*signal*
    The signal number (from **ps -f**) or name (from **kill -l**). With a
    signal number of 9, the kill cannot be caught. The default is
    TERM.

-- Consider all subsequent strings to be arguments, not options.

-l List the signal names. (Used by itself.)

-s *signal*
    Specify *signal*. May be a name.

---

let *expressions*

Perform arithmetic as specified by one or more integer *expressions*.
expressions consist of numbers, operators, and shell variables (which
don't need a preceding $). Expressions must be quoted if they con-
tain spaces or other special characters. For more information and
examples, see "Arithmetic Expressions" earlier in this section. See
also **expr** in Chapter 2.

Examples

Both of the following examples add 1 to variable **i**.

```
let i=i+1
let "i = i + 1"
```

---

local [*variable*[=*value*]] [*variable2*[=*value*]] ...

Without arguments, print all local variables. Otherwise, create (and
set, if specified) a local variable.

---

logout

Exit shell. Can be used only if it is a login shell. Otherwise, use **exit**.

---

popd [*options*]

Manipulate the directory stack. By default, remove the top directory
and **cd** to it.

→

popd ←	*Options* +*n* Remove the *n*th directory in the stack, counting from 0. -*n* Remove *n*th entry from the bottom of the stack, counting from 0.
pushd	**pushd** *directory* **pushd** [*options*] By default, switch top two directories on stack. If specified, add a new directory to the top of the stack instead, and **cd** to it. *Options* +*n* Rotate the stack to place the *n*th (counting from 0) directory at the top. -*n* Rotate the stack to place the *n*th directory from the bottom of the stack at the top.
pwd	**pwd** Display the current working directory's absolute pathname. If the built-in **-P** option is set, this pathname will not contain symbolic links.

read	**read** [*options*] *variable1* [*variable2* ...]
	
	Read one line of standard input, and assign each word (as defined by IFS) to the corresponding *variable*, with all leftover words assigned to the last variable. If only one variable is specified, the entire line will be assigned to that variable. See the following example; also see **case**. The return status is 0 unless *EOF* is reached. If no variable names are provided, read the entire string into the environment variable REPLY.
	
	Options
	
	-**r** Raw mode; ignore \ as a line continuation character.
	
	Example
	
	```$ read first last address```
	```Sarah Caldwell 123 Main Street```
	
	```$ echo "$last, $first\n$address"```
	```Caldwell, Sarah```
	```123 Main Street```

readonly	**readonly** [*options*] [*variable1 variable2* ...] Prevent the specified shell variables from being assigned new values. Variables can be accessed (read) but not overwritten. In **bash**, the syntax *variable=value* can be used to assign a new value that cannot be changed.

Options

    -- Treat all subsequent strings as arguments, not options.
    -f [*variable(s)*]
        Set *variable(s)* to read-only, so that they cannot be changed.
    -p Display all read-only variables (default).

---

return [*n*]

Used inside a function definition. Exit the function with status *n* or with the exit status of the previously executed command.

---

select *name* [*in wordlist ;*]
do
  commands
done

Choose a value for *name* by displaying the words in *wordlist* to the user and prompting for a choice. Store user input in the variable **REPLY** and the chosen word in *name*. Then execute *commands* repeatedly until they execute a **break** or **return**.

---

set [*options*] [*arg1 arg2* ...]

With no arguments, **set** prints the values of all variables known to the current shell. Options can be enabled (*–option*) or disabled (*+option*). Options can also be set when the shell is invoked, via **bash**. Arguments are assigned in order to **$1**, **$2**, etc.

Options

    -    Turn off -v and -x, and turn off option processing.
    --   Used as the last option; -- turns off option processing so
         that arguments beginning with – are not misinterpreted as
         options. (For example, you can set $1 to –1.) If no argu-
         ments are given after --, unset the positional parameters.
    -a   From now on, automatically mark variables for export after
         defining or changing them.
    -b   Report background job status at termination, instead of wait-
         ing for next shell prompt.
    -d   Do not hash commands after looking them up.
    -e   Exit if a command yields a nonzero exit status.
    -f   Do not expand filename metacharacters (e.g., * ? [ ]).
    -h   Locate commands as they are defined, and remember them.
    -k   Assignment of environment variables (*var=value*) will take
         effect regardless of where they appear on the command line.
         Normally, assignments must precede the command name.
    -l   When a **for** command uses a variable that is already bound,
         restore that variable's original value after the **for** command
         exits.

$\rightarrow$

-m
    Monitor mode. Enable job control; background jobs executes in a separate process group. -m is usually set automatically.

-n Read commands but don't execute; useful for checking errors. Useful for noninteractive shells.

-o [*m*]
    List shell modes, or turn on mode *m*. Many modes can be set by other options. Modes are:

allexport	Same as -a.
braceexpand	Default. Enable brace expansion.
emacs	Default. Enable Emacs-style command-line editing.
errexit	Same as -e.
histexpand	Same as -H.
ignoreeof	Do not exit on *EOF*. To exit the shell, type **exit**.
interactive-comments	
	Treat all words beginning with #, and all subsequent words, as comments.
monitor	Same as -m.
noclobber	Same as -C.
noexec	Same as -n.
noglob	Same as -f.
notify	Same as -b.
nounset	Same as -u.
physical	Same as -P.
posix	Match POSIX standard.
privileged	Same as -p.
verbose	Same as -v.
vi	Enable vi-style command-line editing.
xtrace	Same as -x.

-p Start up as a privileged user; don't process *$HOME/.profile*.

-t Exit after one command is executed.

-u In substitutions, treat unset variables as errors.

-v Show each shell command line when read.

-x Show commands and arguments when executed, preceded by a +. This provides step-by-step debugging of shell scripts. (Same as -o **xtrace**.)

-C Same as **noclobber**

-H Default. Enable ! and !! commands.

-P Print absolute pathnames in response to **pwd**. By default, **bash** includes symbolic links in its response to **pwd**.

Examples

`set -- "$num" -20 -30`	*Set $1 to $num, $2 to –20, $3 to –30.*
`set -vx`	*Read each command line; show it;*
	execute it; show it again (with arguments)
`set +x`	*Stop command tracing*

`set -o noclobber`	*Prevent file overwriting*	set
`set +o noclobber`	*Allow file overwriting again*	

shift [*n*]

Shift positional arguments (e.g., **$2** becomes **$1**). If *n* is given, shift to the left *n* places.

source *file* [*arguments*]

Read and execute lines in *file*. *file* does not have to be executable but must reside in a directory searched by PATH.

suspend [-f]

Same as **CTRL-Z**. Often used to stop an **su** command.

Option

    -f   Force suspend, even if shell is a login shell.

bash

test *condition*
    or
[*condition*]

Evaluate a *condition* and, if its value is true, return a zero exit status; otherwise, return a nonzero exit status. An alternate form of the command uses [ ] rather than the word *test*. *condition* is constructed using the expressions below. Conditions are true if the description holds true.

File conditions

-b *file*	*file* exists and is a block special file.
-c *file*	*file* exists and is a character special file.
-d *file*	*file* exists and is a directory.
-e *file*	*file* exists.
-f *file*	*file* exists and is a regular file.
-g *file*	*file* exists and its set-group-id bit is set.
-k *file*	*file* exists and its sticky bit is set.
-p *file*	*file* exists and is a named pipe (fifo).
-r *file*	*file* exists and is readable.
-s *file*	*file* exists and has a size greater than zero.
-t [*n*]	The open file descriptor *n* is associated with a terminal device; default *n* is 1.
-u *file*	*file* exists and its set-user-id bit is set.
-w *file*	*file* exists and is writable.
-x *file*	*file* exists and is executable.
-G *file*	*file* exists and its group is the process's effective group ID.

→

test		
←	-L *file*	*file* exists and is a symbolic link.
	-O *file*	*file* exists and its owner is the process's effective user ID.
	-S *file*	*file* exists and is a socket.
	f1 -ef *f2*	Files *f1* and *f2* are linked (refer to same file).
	f1 -nt *f2*	File *f1* is newer than *f2*.
	f1 -ot *f2*	File *f1* is older than *f2*.

String conditions

-n *s1*	String *s1* has nonzero length.
-z *s1*	String *s1* has zero length.
s1 = *s2*	Strings *s1* and *s2* are identical.
s1 != *s2*	Strings *s1* and *s2* are *not* identical.
string	*string* is not null.

Integer comparisons

n1 -eq *n2*	*n1* equals *n2*.
n1 -ge *n2*	*n1* is greater than or equal to *n2*.
n1 -gt *n2*	*n1* is greater than *n2*.
n1 -le *n2*	*n1* is less than or equal to *n2*.
n1 -lt *n2*	*n1* is less than *n2*.
n1 -ne *n2*	*n1* does not equal *n2*.

Combined forms

! *condition*	True if *condition* is false.
condition1 -a *condition2*	True if both conditions are true.
condition1 -o *condition2*	True if either condition is true.

Examples

Each of the following examples shows the first line of various statements that might use a test condition:

```
while test $# -gt 0        While there are arguments . . .
while [ -n "$1" ]          While the first argument is nonempty . . .
if [ $count -lt 10 ]       If $count is less than 10 . . .
if [ -d RCS ]              If the RCS directory exists . . .
if [ "$answer" != "y" ]    If the answer is not  y . . .
if [ ! -r "$1" -o ! -f "$1" ]  If the first argument is not a
                               readable file or a regular file . . .
```

---

times	**times**
	Print accumulated process times for user and system.

---

trap	**trap** [–l] [[*commands*] *signals*]
	Execute *commands* if any of *signals* is received. Common signals include 0, 1, 2, and 15. Multiple commands should be quoted as a

group and separated by semicolons internally. If *commands* is the null string (i.e., **trap ""** *signals*), then *signals* will be ignored by the shell. If *commands* is omitted entirely, reset processing of specified signals to the default action. If both *commands* and *signals* are omitted, list current trap assignments. See examples at the end of this entry and under **exec**.

Option

-l   List signals.

Signals

Signals are listed along with what triggers them.

0	Exit from shell (usually when shell script finishes)
1	Hangup (usually logout)
2	Interrupt (usually **CTRL-C**)
3	Quit
4	Illegal instruction
5	Trace trap
6	Abort
7	Unused
8	Floating-point exception
9	Termination
10	User-defined
11	Reference to invalid memory
12	User-defined
13	Write to a pipe without a process to read it
14	Alarm timeout
15	Software termination (usually via **kill**)
16	Coprocessor stack fault
17	Termination of child process
18	Continue (if stopped)
19	Stop process
20	Stop typed at tty
21	Background process has tty input
22	Background process has tty output
23	I/O error
24	CPU time limit exceeded
25	File size limit exceeded
27	Profile
28	Window resize

Examples

```
trap "" 2          Ignore signal 2 (interrupts)
trap 2             Obey interrupts again
```

→

trap ←	Remove a $tmp file when the shell program exits, or if the user logs out, presses **CTRL-C**, or does a **kill**: `trap "rm -f $tmp; exit" 0 1 2 15`

type	**type** [*options*] *commands*
	
	Report absolute pathname of programs invoked for *commands*, and whether or not they are hashed.
	
	`--` Consider all subsequent strings to be arguments, not options.
	
	`-a, -all` Print all occurrences of *command*, not just that which would be invoked.
	
	`-p, -path` Print the hashed value of *command*, which may differ from the first appearance of *command* in the PATH.
	
	`-t, -type` Determine and state if *command* is an alias, keyword, function, built-in, or file.
	
	Example
	
	`$ type mv read`
	`mv is /bin/mv`
	`read is a shell built-in`

typeset	**typeset** See **declare**.
ulimit	**ulimit** [*options*] [*n*] Print the value of one or more resource limits, or, if *n* is specified, set a resource limit to *n*. Resource limits can be either hard (`-H`) or soft (`-S`). By default, **ulimit** sets both limits or prints the soft limit. The options determine which resource is acted on. *Options* `--` Consider all subsequent strings to be arguments, not options. `-a` Print all current limits. `-H` Hard resource limit. `-S` Soft resource limit. *Specific limits* These options limit specific resource sizes. `-c` Core files. `-d` Size of processes' data segments. `-f` Size of shell-created files. `-m` Resident set size.

-n	Number of file descriptors. On many systems, this cannot be set.	**ulimit**
-p	Pipe size, measured in blocks of 512 bytes.	
-s	Stack size.	
-t	Amount of CPU time, counted in seconds.	
-u	Number of processes per user.	
-v	Virtual memory used by shell.	

umask [*nnn*]
umask [-*S*]

Display file creation mask or set file creation mask to octal value *nnn*. The file creation mask determines which permission bits are turned off (e.g., **umask 002** produces **rw-rw-r--**).

Option

-S   Display **umask** symbolically, rather than in octal.

unalias [-*a*] *names*

Remove *names* from the alias list. See also **alias**.

Option

-a   Remove all aliases.

unset [*options*] *names*

Erase definitions of functions or variables listed in *names*.

Options

-f   Expect *name* to refer to a function.

-v   Expect *name* to refer to a variable (default).

until
    test-commands
do
    commands
done

Execute *test-commands* (usually a **test** or [] command) and if the exit status is non-zero (that is, the test fails), perform *commands*; repeat.

wait [*ID*]

Pause in execution until all background jobs complete (exit status 0 will be returned), or pause until the specified background process *ID* or job *ID* completes (exit status of *ID* is returned). Note that the shell variable $! contains the process ID of the most recent background process. If job control is not in effect, *ID* can be only a process ID number. See "Job Control."

→

wait ←	*Example*
	wait $! *Wait for last background process to finish*

while	while
	    test-commands
	do
	    commands
	done
	
	Execute *test-commands* (usually a **test** or [] command) and if the exit status is zero, perform *commands*; repeat.

Job Control

Job control lets you place foreground jobs in the background, bring background jobs to the foreground, or suspend (temporarily stop) running jobs. Job control is enabled by default. Once disabled, it can be reenabled by any of the following commands:

```
bash -m -i
set -m
set -o monitor
```

Many job control commands take *jobID* as an argument. This argument can be specified as follows:

%*n*	Job number *n*
%*s*	Job whose command line starts with string *s*
%?*s*	Job whose command line contains string *s*
%%	Current job
%+	Current job (same as above)
%-	Previous job

bash provides the following job control commands. For more information on these commands, see "Built-in Commands" earlier in this chapter.

bg	Put a job in the background.
fg	Put a job in the foreground.
jobs	List active jobs.
kill	Terminate a job.
stop	Suspend a background job.
stty tostop	Stop background jobs if they try to send output to the terminal.
wait	Wait for background jobs to finish.
CTRL-Z	Suspend a foreground job. Then use **bg** or **fg**. (Your terminal may use something other than **CTRL-Z** as the suspend character.)

CHAPTER 5

csh and tcsh

This chapter describes the C shell and its enhancement, **tcsh**. On some versions of Linux, **tcsh** is used as the C shell, so all the features in this chapter work even if you run **csh**. The C shell was so named because many of its programming constructs and symbols resemble those of the C programming language. The following topics are presented:

- Overview of features
- Invoking the shell
- Syntax
- Variables
- Expressions
- Command history
- Command-line manipulation
- Built-in commands
- Job control

Overview of Features

Features of the C shell include:

- Input/output redirection
- Wildcard characters (metacharacters) for filename abbreviation
- Shell variables for customizing your environment
- Integer arithmetic
- Access to previous commands (command history)
- Command-name abbreviation (aliasing)

- A built-in command set for writing shell programs
- Job control

The **tcsh** shell includes all of these features. In addition, it has some extensions:

- Command-line editing and editor commands
- Word completion (tab completion)
- Spell checking
- Extended history commands
- Extended handling of directory manipulation (**cd**, **pushd**, **popd**, **dirs**)
- Scheduled events, such as logout or terminal locking after a set idle period, and delayed commands
- New shell built-ins: **hup**, **ls-F**, **newgrp**, **printenv**, **which**, and **where**
- New shell variables (**gid**, **loginsh**, **oid**, **shlvl**, **tcsh**, **tty**, **uid**, and **version**) and environment variables (**HOST**, **REMOTEHOST**, **VENDOR**, **OSTYPE**, and **MACH-TYPE**)
- New formatting sequences for the PROMPT variable, as well as two new prompts (in loops and spelling correction)
- Read-only variables

Invoking the Shell

A shell command interpreter can be invoked as follows:

> csh [*options*] [*arguments*]
> tcsh [*options*] [*arguments*]

csh and tcsh use syntax resembling C and execute commands from a terminal or a file. Options -n, -v, and -x are useful when debugging scripts.

Options

-b	Allow the remaining command-line options to be interpreted as options to a specified command, rather than as options to **csh** itself.
-c	Execute command specified following the argument.
-e	Exit if a command produces errors.
-f	Fast startup; start **csh** without executing *.cshrc* or *.login*.
-i	Invoke interactive shell (prompt for input).
-n	Parse commands but do not execute.
-s	Read commands from the standard input.
-t	Exit after executing one command.
-v	Display commands before executing them; expand history substitutions, but don't expand other substitutions (e.g., filename, variable, and command). Same as setting **verbose**.
-V	Same as -v, but also display *.cshrc*.
-x	Display commands before executing them, but expand all substitutions. Same as setting **echo**.

-X   Same as -**x**, but also display *.cshrc*.

Arguments

Arguments are assigned, in order, to the positional parameters **$1**, **$2**, etc. If the first argument is an executable script, commands are read from it and remaining arguments are assigned to **$1**, **$2**, etc.

Syntax

This section describes the many symbols peculiar to **csh** and **tcsh**. The topics are arranged as follows:

- Special files
- Filename metacharacters
- Quoting
- Command forms
- Redirection forms

Special Files

˜/.cshrc	Executed at each instance of shell startup
˜/.login	Executed by login shell after *.cshrc* at login
˜/.logout	Executed by login shell at logout
/etc/passwd	Source of home directories for ˜*name* abbreviations

Filename Metacharacters

*	Match any string of zero or more characters.
?	Match any single character.
[*abc*...]	Match any one of the enclosed characters; a hyphen can be used to specify a range (e.g., a-z, A-Z, 0-9).
{*abc,xxx,* ...}	Expand each comma-separated string inside braces.
˜	Home directory for the current user.
˜*name*	Home directory of user *name*.

Examples

% **ls new***	*Match* new *and* new.1
% **cat ch?**	*Match* ch9 *but not* ch10
% **vi [D-R]***	*Match files that begin with uppercase D through R*
% **ls {ch,app}?**	*Expand, then match* ch1, ch2, app1, app2
% **cd ˜tom**	*Change to* tom's *home directory*

Quoting

Quoting disables a character's special meaning and allows it to be used literally, as itself. The following characters have special meaning to the C shell:

;	Command separator

&	Background execution
( )	Command grouping
|	Pipe
* ? [ ] ~	Filename metacharacters
{ }	String expansion characters (usually don't require quoting)
> < & !	Redirection symbols
! ^	History substitution, quick substitution
**" ' **	Used in quoting other characters
`	Command substitution
$	Variable substitution
newline space tab	Word separators

The characters that follow can be used for quoting:

" " Everything between **"** and **"** is taken literally, except for the following characters that keep their special meaning:

$	Variable substitution will occur.
`	Command substitution will occur.
"	This marks the end of the double quote.
****	Escape next character.
!	The history character
newline	The newline character

' ' Everything between **'** and **'** is taken literally except for **!** (history) and another **'**, and newline.

** The character following a **** is taken literally. Use within **" " to escape **"**, **$**, and **`**. Often used to escape itself, spaces, or newlines. Always needed to escape a history character (usually **!**).

Examples

```
% echo 'Single quotes "protect" double quotes'
Single quotes "protect" double quotes

% echo "Well, isn't that \"special\"?"
Well, isn't that "special"?

% echo "You have `ls|wc -1` files in `pwd`"
You have 43 files in /home/bob

% echo "The value of \$x is $x"
The value of $x is 100
```

Command Forms

cmd **&**	Execute *cmd* in background.
cmd1 **;** *cmd2*	Command sequence; execute multiple *cmd*s on the same line.
(*cmd1* **;** *cmd2* **)**	Subshell; treat *cmd1* and *cmd2* as a command group.
cmd1 **|** *cmd2*	Pipe; use output from *cmd1* as input to *cmd2*.
cmd1 **`** *cmd2* **`**	Command substitution; use *cmd2* output as arguments to *cmd1*.

cmd1 || *cmd2*	OR; execute *cmd1* and then (if *cmd1* succeeds) *cmd2*.
cmd1 && *cmd2*	AND; execute either *cmd1* or (if *cmd1* fails) *cmd2*.

Examples

% `nroff file &`	*Format in the background*
% `cd; ls`	*Execute sequentially*
% `(date; who; pwd) > logfile`	*All output is redirected*
% `sort file | pr -3 | lp`	*Sort file, page output, then print*
% `vi `grep -l ifdef *.c``	*Edit files found by* grep
% `egrep '(yes|no)' `cat list``	*Specify a list of files to search*
% `grep XX file || lp file`	*Print file if it contains the pattern*
% `grep XX file && echo XX not found`	*Echo an error message if* XX *not found*

Redirection Forms

File Descriptor	Name	Common Abbreviation	Typical Default
0	Standard input	stdin	Keyboard
1	Standard output	stdout	Terminal
2	Standard error	stderr	Terminal

The usual input source or output destination can be changed as follows:

Simple redirection

cmd `>` *file*	Send output of *cmd* to *file* (overwrite).
cmd `>!` *file*	Same as above, even if **noclobber** is set.
cmd `>>` *file*	Send output of *cmd* to *file* (append).
cmd `>>!` *file*	Same as above, even if **noclobber** is set.
cmd `<` *file*	Take input for *cmd* from *file*.
cmd `<<` *text*	Read standard input up to a line identical to *text* (*text* can be stored in a shell variable). Input is usually typed on the screen or in the shell program. Commands that typically use this syntax include **cat**, **echo**, **ex**, and **sed**. If *text* is enclosed in quotes, standard input will not undergo variable substitution, command substitution, etc.

Multiple redirection

cmd `>&` *file*	Send both standard output and standard error to *file*.
cmd `>&!` *file*	Same as above, even if **noclobber** is set.
cmd `>>&` *file*	Append standard output and standard error to end of *file*.
cmd `>>&!` *file*	Same as above, even if **noclobber** is set.
cmd1 `|&` *cmd2*	Pipe standard error together with standard output.
(*cmd* `>` *f1*) `>&` *f2*	Send standard output to file *f1*, and standard error to file *f2*.
cmd `| tee` *files*	Send output of *cmd* to standard output (usually the terminal). and to *files*. (See the example in Chapter 2 under **tee**.)

Examples

`% cat part1 > book`	*Copy* `part1` *to book*
`% cat part2 part3 >> book`	*Append parts 2 and 3 to same file at* `part1`
`% mail tim < report`	*Take input to message from* `report`
`% cc calc.c >& error_out`	*Store all messages, including errors*
`% cc newcalc.c >&! error_out`	*Overwrite old file*
`% grep UNIX ch* |& pr`	*Pipe all messages, including errors*
`% (find / -print > filelist) >& no_access`	*Separate error messages from list of files*
`% sed 's/^/XX /' << "END_ARCHIVE"`	*Supply text right after command*

```
This is often how a shell archive is "wrapped",
bundling text for distribution. You would normally
run sed from a shell program, not from the command line
"END_ARCHIVE"
```

Variables

This subsection describes the following:

- Variable substitution
- Variable modifiers
- Predefined shell variables
- Sample *.cshrc* file
- Environment variables

Variable Substitution

In the following substitutions, braces ({ }) are optional, except when needed to separate a variable name from following characters that would otherwise be a part of it.

`${var}`	The value of variable *var*.
`${var[i]}`	Select word or words in position *i* of *var*. *i* can be a single number, a range *m–n*, a range *-n* (missing *m* implies 1), a range *m-* (missing *n* implies all remaining words), or * (select all words). *i* can also be a variable that expands to one of these values.
`${#var}`	The number of words in *var*.
`${#argv}`	The number of arguments.
`$0`	Name of the program.
`${#argv[n]}`	Individual arguments on command line (positional parameters); $1 \leq n \leq 9$.
`${n}`	Same as ${argv[*n*]}.
`${#argv[*]}`	All arguments on command line.
`$*`	Same as $argv[*].
`$argv[$#argv]`	The last argument.
`${?var}`	Return 1 if *var* is set, 0 if *var* is not set.

$$	Process number of current shell; useful as part of a filename for creating temporary files with unique names.
$?0	Return 1 if input filename is known, 0 if not.

Examples

Sort the third through last arguments and save the output in a file whose name is unique to this process:

```
sort $argv[3-] > tmp.$$
```

Process *.cshrc* commands only if the shell is interactive (i.e., the **prompt** variable must be set).

```
if ($?prompt) then
    set commands,
    alias commands,
    etc.
endif
```

Variable Modifiers

Except for $?*var*, $$, and $?0, the variable substitutions in the preceding section may be followed by one of these modifiers. When braces are used, the modifier goes inside them.

:r	Return the variable's root (the portion before the last dot).
:e	Return the variable's extension.
:h	Return the variable's header (the directory portion).
:t	Return the variable's tail (the portion after the last slash).
:gr	Return all roots.
:ge	Return all extensions.
:gh	Return all headers.
:gt	Return all tails.
:q	Quote a wordlist variable, keeping the items separate. Useful when the variable contains filename metacharacters that should not be expanded.
:x	Quote a pattern, expanding it into a wordlist.

Examples using pathname modifiers

The following table shows the use of pathname modifiers on the following variable:

```
set aa=(/progs/num.c /book/chap.ps)
```

Variable Portion	Specification	Output Result
Normal variable	echo $aa	/progs/num.c /book/chap.ps
Second root	echo $aa[2]:r	/book/chap
Second header	echo $aa[2]:h	/book
Second tail	echo $aa[2]:t	chap.ps
Second extension	echo $aa[2]:e	ps

Variable Portion	Specification	Output Result
Root	`echo $aa:r`	`/progs/num /book/chap.ps`
Global root	`echo $aa:gr`	`/progs/num /book/chap`
Header	`echo $aa:h`	`/progs /book/chap.ps`
Global header	`echo $aa:gh`	`/progs /book`
Tail	`echo $aa:t`	`num.c /book/chap.ps`
Global tail	`echo $aa:gt`	`num.c chap.ps`
Extension	`echo $aa:e`	`c /book/chap.ps`
Global extension	`echo $aa:ge`	`c ps`

Examples using quoting modifiers

Unless quoted, the shell expands variables to represent files in current directory.

```
% set a="[a-z]*" A="[A-Z]*"
% echo "$a" "$A"
[a-z]* [A-Z]*

% echo $a $A
at cc m4 Book Doc

% echo $a:x $A
[a-z]* Book Doc

% set d=($a:q $A:q)
% echo $d
at cc m4 Book Doc

% echo $d:q
[a-z]* [A-Z]*

% echo $d[1] +++ $d[2]
at cc m4 +++ Book Doc

% echo $d[1]:q
[a-z]*
```

Predefined Shell Variables

Variables can be set in one of two ways, by assigning a value:

```
set var=value
```

or by simply turning the variable on:

```
set var
```

In the following list, variables that accept values are shown with the equal sign followed by the type of value they accept; the value is then described. (Note, however, that variables such as **argv**, **cwd**, or **status** are never explicitly assigned.) For variables that are turned on or off, the table describes what they do when set. **tcsh** automatically sets (and, in some cases, updates) the variables **addsuffix**, **argv**, autologout, cwd, dirstack, echo-style, edit, gid, home, loginsh, logout, oid, owd, path, prompt, prompt2, prompt3, shell, shlvl, status, tcsh, term tty, uid, user and version. Variables in italics are specific to tcsh.

addsuffix	Append / to directories and a space to files during tab completion to indicate a precise match.
ampm	Display all times in 12-hour format.
argv=(*args*)	List of arguments passed to current command; default is ( ).
autocorrect	Check spelling before attempting to complete commands.
autoexpand	Expand history (such as ! references) during command completion.
autolist[=ambiguous]	Print possible completions when correct one is ambiguous. If **ambiguous** is specified, print possible completions only when completion adds no new characters.
autologout=logout-minutes [*locking-minutes*]	Log out after *logout-minutes* of idle time. Lock the terminal after *locking-minutes* of idle time, requiring a password before continuing.
backslash_quote	Always allow backslashes to quote \, ', and ".
cdpath=*dirs*	List of alternate directories to search when locating arguments for **cd**, **popd**, or **pushd**.
complete=enhance	When **enhance**, ignore case in completion, treat ., –, and _ as word separators, and consider _ and – to be the same.
correct={cmd| complete|all}	When *cmd*, spell-check commands. When *complete*, complete commands. When *all*, spell-check whole command line.
cwd=*dir*	Full pathname of current directory.
dirsfile=file	History file consulted by **dirs –S** and **dirs –L**. Default is `~/.cshdirs`.
dirstack	Directory stack, in array format. *dirstack[0]* is always equivalent to **cwd**. The other elements can be artificially changed.
dunique	Make sure that each directory exists only once in the stack.
echo	Redisplay each command line before execution; same as **csh –x** command.
echo_style={bsd| sysv|both|none}	Don't echo a newline with **-n** option (bsd) | parse escaped characters (sysv) | do both | do neither.
edit	Enable command-line editor.
ellipsis	For use with **prompt** variable. Represent skipped directories with `. . . .`
fignore=chars	List of filename suffixes to ignore during filename completion (see **filec**).

`filec`	If set, a filename that is partially-typed on the command line can be expanded to its full name when ESC is pressed. If more than one filename would match, type *EOF* to list possible completions. Ignored in **tcsh**.
gid	User's group ID.
`histchars=ab`	A two-character string that sets the characters to use in history-substitution and quick-substitution (default is !ˆ).
histdup={all|prev}	Maintain a record only of unique history events (**all**), or do not enter new event when it is the same as the previous one (**prev**).
histfile=file	History file consulted by **history –S** and **history –L**. Default is ˜/.*history*.
histlit	Do not expand history lines when recalling them.
`history=n format`	The first word indicates the number of commands to save in the history list. The second indicates the format with which to display that list (**tcsh** only; see **Prompt** section for possible formats).
`home=dir`	Home directory of user, initialized from HOME. The ~ character is shorthand for this value.
`ignoreeof`	Ignore an end-of-file (*EOF*) from terminals; prevents accidental logout.
inputmode= {insert|overwrite}	Control editor's mode.
listjobs=long	When a job is suspended, list all jobs (in long format, if specified).
listlinks	In **ls -F** command, include type of file to which links point.
listmax=num	Do not allow **list-choices** to print more than *num* choices before prompting.
listmaxrows=num	Do not allow **list-choices** to print more than *num* rows of choices before prompting.
loginsh	Set if shell is a login shell.
logout	Indicates status of an imminent logout (**normal, automatic,** or **hangup**).
`mail=(n files)`	One or more files checked for new mail every five minutes or (if *n* is supplied) every *n* seconds.
matchbeep= {never|nomatch| ambiguous|notunique}	Specifies cirumstances under which completion should beep: never, if no match exists, if multiple matches exist, or if multiple matches exist and one is exact.
nobeep	Disable beeping.
`noclobber`	Don't redirect output to an existing file; prevents accidental destruction of files.
`noglob`	Turn off filename expansion; useful in shell scripts.
nokanji	Disable Kanji (if supported).

nonomatch	Treat filename metacharacters as literal characters, if no match exists; e.g., **vi ch*** creates new file **ch*** instead of printing "No match."
nostat=*directory-list*	Do not stat *directory-list* during completion.
notify	Declare job completions when they occur.
owd	Old working directory.
path=(*dirs*)	List of pathnames in which to search for commands to execute. Initialized from PATH; the default is: . /usr/ucb /usr/bin
printexitvalue	Print all nonzero exit values.
prompt='*str*'	String that prompts for interactive input; default is %. See the section "Formatting for the Prompt Variable" later in this chapter for formatting information.
prompt2='*str*'	String that prompts for interactive input in **foreach** and **while** loops and continued lines (those with escaped newlines). See "Formatting for the Prompt Variable" for formatting information.
prompt3='*str*'	String that prompts for interactive input in automatic spelling correction. See "Formatting for the Prompt Variable" for formatting information.
pushdtohome	Change to home directory when **pushd** is invoked without arguments.
pushdsilent	Do not print directory stack when **pushd** and **popd** are invoked.
recexact	Consider completion to be concluded on first exact match.
recognize_only_executables	When command completion is invoked, print only executable files.
rmstar	Prompt before executing the command **rm ***.
savedirs	Execute **dirs -S** before exiting.
savehist=*max* [merge]	Execute **history -S** before exiting. Save no more than *max* lines of history. If specified, merge those lines with previous history saves, and sort by time.
sched=*string*	Format for **sched**'s printing of events. See "Formatting for the Prompt Variable" for formatting information.
shell=*file*	Pathname of the shell program currently in use; default is */bin/csh*.
shlvl	Number of nested shells.
showdots[=-A]	Show hidden files with **ls -F**. If **-A** is specified, do not show . or .. entries.
status=*n*	Exit status of last command. Built-in commands return 0 (success) or 1 (failure).

symlinks= {chase|ignore|expand}	Specify manner in which to deal with symbolic links. Expand them to real directory name in *cwd* (chase); treat them as real directories (ignore); or expand arguments that resemble pathnames (expand).
tcsh	Version of **tcsh**.
term	Terminal type.
time=*'n %c'*	If command execution takes more than *n* CPU seconds, report user time, system time, elapsed time, and CPU percentage. Supply optional *%c* flags to show other data.
tperiod	Number of minutes between executions of **periodic** alias.
tty	Name of tty, if applicable.
uid	User ID.
user	Username.
verbose	Display a command after history substitution; same as the command **csh -v**.
version	Shell's version and additional information, including options set at compile time.
visiblebell	Flash screen instead of beeping.
watch=([n] user terminal...)	Watch for *user* logging in at *terminal*, where *terminal* can be a tty name or **any**. Check every *n* minutes, or 10 by default.
who=string	Specify information to be printed by **watch**.
wordchars=chars	List of all nonalphanumeric characters that may be part of a word. Default is *?_-.[]~=.

Formatting for the Prompt Variable

tcsh provides a list of substitutions that can be used in formatting the prompt. (**csh** allows only plain-string prompts and the ! history substitution below.) The list of available substitutions includes:

%%	Literal %
%/	The present working directory
%~	The present working directory, in ~ notation
%#	# for the superuser, > for others
%?	Previous command's exit status
%b	End boldfacing
%c[[0]n], %.[[0]n]	The last *n* (default 1) components of the present working directory. If 0 is specified, replace removed components with /<skipped>.
%d	Day of the week (e.g., Mon, Tue)
%h, %!, !	Number of current history event
%l	Current tty
%m	First component of hostname

%n	Username
%p	Current time, with seconds (12-hour mode)
%s	End standout mode (reverse video)
%t, %@	Current time (12-hour format)
%u	End underlining
%w	Month (e.g., Jan, Feb)
%y	Year (e.g., 94, 95)
%B	Begin boldfacing
%C	Similar to %c, but uses full pathnames instead of ~ notation
%D	Day of month (e.g., 09, 10)
%M	Fully-qualified hostname
%P	Current time, with seconds (24-hour format)
%S	Begin standout mode (reverse video)
%T	Current time (24-hour format)
%U	Begin underlining
%W	Month (e.g., 09, 10)
%Y	Year (e.g., 1994, 1995)

Sample .cshrc File

```
# PREDEFINED VARIABLES

set path=(~ ~/bin /usr/ucb /bin /usr/bin . )
set mail=(/usr/mail/tom)

if ($?prompt) then              # settings for interactive use
  set echo
  set noclobber ignoreeof

  set cdpath=(/usr/lib /usr/spool/uucp)
# Now I can type cd macros
# instead of cd /usr/lib/macros

  set history=100
  set prompt='tom \!% '         # includes history number
  set time=3

# MY VARIABLES

  set man1="/usr/man/man1"     # lets me do    cd $man1, ls $man1
  set a="[a-z]*"               # lets me do    vi $a
  set A="[A-Z]*"               # or            grep string $A

# ALIASES

  alias c "clear; dirs"        # use quotes to protect ; or |
  alias h "history|more"
  alias j jobs -l
  alias ls ls -sFC             # redefine ls command
  alias del 'mv \!* ~/tmp_dir' # a safe alternative to rm
endif
```

Environment Variables

The C shell maintains a set of *environment variables*, which are distinct from shell variables and aren't really part of the C shell. Shell variables are meaningful only within the current shell, but environment variables are automatically exported, making them available globally. For example, C-shell variables are accessible only to a particular script in which they're defined, whereas environment variables can be used by any shell scripts, mail utilities, or editors you might invoke.

Environment variables are assigned as follows:

```
setenv VAR value
```

By convention, environment variable names are all uppercase. You can create your own environment variables, or you can use the predefined environment variables that follow.

These environment variables have corresponding C-shell variables. When either one changes, the value is copied to the other:

HOME   Home directory; same as **home**.

PATH   Search path for commands; same as **path**.

TERM   Terminal type; same as **term**.

Other environment variables include the following (italics means specific to **tcsh**):

EXINIT   A string of **ex** commands similar to those found in the startup *.exrc* file (e.g., **set ai**). Used by **vi** and **ex**.

IHOST   Name of machine.

LOGNAME   Another name for the USER variable.

MAIL   The file that holds mail. Used by mail programs. This is not the same as the C shell **mail** variable, which only checks for new mail.

IOSTYPE   Operating system.

PWD   The current directory; the value is copied from **cwd**.

REMOTEHOST

Machine name of remote host.

SHELL   Undefined by default; once initialized to **shell**, the two are identical.

TERMCAP   The file that holds the cursor-positioning codes for your terminal type. Default is */etc/termcap*.

Expressions

Expressions are used in @, **if**, and **while** statements to perform arithmetic, string comparisons, file testing, etc. **exit** and **set** can also specify expressions. Expressions are formed by combining variables and constants with operators that resemble those in the C programming language. Operator precedence is the same as in C but can be remembered as follows:

1. `* / %`

2. `+ -`

Group all other expressions inside ( )s. Parentheses are required if the expression contains <, >, &, or |.

Operators

Operators can be one of the following types:

Assignment operators

`=`	Assign value
`+=` `-=`	Reassign after addition/subtraction
`*=` `/=` `%=`	Reassign after multiplication/division/remainder
`&=` `^=` `|=`	Reassign after bitwise AND/XOR/OR
`++`	Increment
`--`	Decrement

Arithmetic operators

`*` `/` `%`	Multiplication; integer division; modulus (remainder)
`+` `-`	Addition; subtraction

Bitwise and logical operators

`~`	Binary inversion (one's complement)
`!`	Logical negation
`<<` `>>`	Bitwise left shift; bitwise right shift
`&`	Bitwise AND
`^`	Bitwise exclusive OR
`|`	Bitwise OR
`&&`	Logical AND
`||`	Logical OR
`{ command }`	Return 1 if command is successful; 0 otherwise. Note that this is the opposite of *command*'s normal return code. The **$status** variable may be more practical.

Comparison operators

`==` `!=`	Equality; inequality
`<=` `>=`	Less than or equal to; greater than or equal to
`<` `>`	Less than; greater than

File inquiry operators

Command substitution and filename expansion are performed on *file* before the test is performed.

`-d` *file*	The file is a directory.
`-e` *file*	The file exists.
`-f` *file*	The file is a plain file.
`-o` *file*	The user owns the file.
`-r` *file*	The user has read permission.
`-w` *file*	The user has write permission.
`-x` *file*	The user has execute permission.
`-z` *file*	The file has zero size.
`!`	Reverse the sense of any inquiry above.

Examples

The following examples show @ commands and assume **n** = 4:

Expression	Value of $x
@ x = ($n > 10 || $n < 5)	1
@ x = ($n >= 0 && $n < 3)	0
@ x = ($n << 2)	16
@ x = ($n >> 2)	1
@ x = $n % 2	0
@ x = $n % 3	1

The following examples show the first line of **if** or **while** statements:

Expression	Meaning
while ($#argv != 0)	While there are arguments . . .
if ($today[1] == "Fri")	If the first word is "Fri". . .
if (-f $argv[1])	If the first argument is a plain file. . .
if (! -d $tmpdir)	If **tmpdir** is not a directory. . .

Command History

Previously executed commands are stored in a history list. The C shell lets you access this list so you can verify commands, repeat them, or execute modified versions of them. The **history** built-in command displays the history list; the predefined variables **histchars** and **history** also affect the history mechanism. There are three ways to use the history list:

- Making command substitutions (using ! and ^).
- Making argument substitutions (specific words within a command).
- Using modifiers to extract or replace parts of a command or word.

Command Substitution

!	Begin a history substitution
!!	Previous command
!*N*	Command number *N* in history list
!-*N*	*N*th command back from current command
!*string*	Most recent command that starts with *string*
!?*string*?	Most recent command that contains *string*
!?*string*?%	Most recent command argument that contains *string*
!$	Last argument of previous command
!!*string*	Previous command, then append *string*
!*N string*	Command *N*, then append *string*
!{*s1*}*s2*	Most recent command starting with string *s1*, then append string *s2*
^*old*^*new*^	Quick substitution; change string *old* to *new* in previous command; execute modified command

Command Substitution Examples

The following command is assumed:

```
%3 vi cprogs/01.c ch002 ch03
```

Event Number	Command Typed	Command Executed
4	^00^0	vi cprogs/01.c ch02 ch03
5	nroff !*	nroff cprogs/01.c ch02 ch03
6	nroff !$	nroff ch03
7	!vi	vi cprogs/01.c ch02 ch03
8	!6	nroff ch03
9	!?01	vi cprogs/01.c ch02 ch03
10	!{nr}.new	nroff ch03.new
11	!!|lp	nroff ch03.new | lp
12	more !?pr?%	more cprogs/01.c

Word Substitution

Colons may precede any word specifier.

:0	Command name
:n	Argument number n
^	First argument
$	Last argument
:n-m	Arguments n through m
-m	Words 0 through m; same as :0-m
:n-	Arguments n through next-to-last
:n*	Arguments n through last; same as n-$
*	All arguments; same as ^-$ or 1-$
#	Current command line up to this point; fairly useless

Word Substitution Examples

The following command is assumed:

```
%13 cat ch01 ch02 ch03 biblio back
```

Event Number	Command Typed	Command Executed
14	ls !13^	ls ch01
15	sort !13:*	sort ch01 ch02 ch03 biblio back
16	lp !cat:3*	more ch03 biblio back
17	!cat:0-3	cat ch01 ch02 ch03
18	vi !-5:4	vi biblio

History Modifiers

Command and word substitutions can be modified by one or more of the following:

Printing, substitution, and quoting

:p	Display command but don't execute.
:s/*old*/*new*	Substitute string *new* for *old*, first instance only.
:gs/*old*/*new*	Substitute string *new* for *old*, all instances.
:&	Repeat previous substitution (:s or ^ command), first instance only.
:g&	Repeat previous substitution, all instances.
:q	Quote a wordlist.
:x	Quote separate words.

Truncation

:r	Extract the first available pathname root (the portion before the last period).
:gr	Extract all pathname roots.
:e	Extract the first available pathname extension (the portion after the last period).
:ge	Extract all pathname extensions.
:h	Extract the first available pathname header (the portion before the last slash).
:gh	Extract all pathname headers.
:t	Extract the first available pathname tail (the portion after the last slash).
:gt	Extract all pathname tails.
:u	Make first lowercase letter uppercase (**tcsh** only).
:l	Make first uppercase letter lowercase (**tcsh** only).
:a	Apply modifier(s) following a as many times as possible to a word. If used with g, a is applied to all words (**tcsh** only).

History Modifier Examples

From above, command number 17 is:

```
%17 cat ch01 ch02 ch03
```

Event Number	Command Typed	Command Executed
19	!17:s/ch/CH/	cat CH01 ch02 ch03
20	!17g&	cat CH01 CH02 CH03
21	!more:p	more cprogs/01.c *(displayed only)*
22	cd !$:h	cd cprogs
23	vi !mo:$:t	vi 01.c
24	grep stdio !$	grep stdio 01.c
25	^stdio^include stdio^:q	grep "include stdio" 01.c
26	nroff !21:t:p	nroff 01.c *(is that what I wanted?)*
27	!!	nroff 01.c *(execute it)*

Command-Line Manipulation

Completion

Both **tcsh** and **csh** provide word completion. **tcsh** automatically completes words and commands when the **TAB** key is hit; **csh** does so only when the *filec* variable is set, after the **ESC** key is hit. If the completion is ambiguous (i.e., more than one file matches the provided string), the shell completes as much as possible and beeps to notify you that the completion is not finished. You may request a list of possible completions with **CTRL-D**. **tcsh** will also notify you when a completion is finished by appending a space to complete filenames or commands and a / to complete directories.

Both **csh** and **tcsh** recognize ~ notation for home directories. The shells assume that words at the beginning of a line and subsequent to |, &, ;, | |, or && are commands, and modify their search paths appropriately. Completion can be done midword; only the letters to the left of the prompt are checked for completion. **CTRL-D** will list possible completions mid-word only in **vi** bindings, not Emacs bindings.

Related shell variables

- autolist
- fignore
- listmax
- listmaxrows

Related command-line editor commands

- complete-word-back
- complete-word-forward
- expand-glob
- list-glob

Related shell built-ins

- complete
- uncomplete

Command-Line Editing

tcsh lets you move your cursor around in the command line, editing it as you type it. There are two main modes for editing the command line, based on the two most common text editors: Emacs and **vi**. You can switch between them with:

```
bindkey -e     Select Emacs bindings
bindkey -v     Select vi bindings
```

The main difference between Emacs and **vi** bindings is that Emacs bindings are modeless; i.e., they always work. With **vi** bindings, you must switch between insert and command modes; different commands are useful in each mode. Additionally:

- Emacs mode is simpler; **vi** mode allows finer control.

- Emacs mode allows you to yank cut text and set a mark; **vi** mode does not.

- The command history searching capabilities differ.

Emacs mode

The following tables describe the various editing keystrokes available in Emacs mode.

Cursor Positioning Commands (Emacs Mode)

Command	Description
CTRL-B	Move cursor back (left) one character.
CTRL-F	Move cursor forward (right) one character.
ESC b	Move cursor back one word.
ESC f	Move cursor forward one word.
CTRL-A	Move cursor to beginning of line.
CTRL-E	Move cursor to end of line.

Text Deletion Commands (Emacs Mode)

Command	Description
DEL or CTRL-H	Delete character to left of cursor.
CTRL-D	Delete character under cursor.
ESC d	Delete word.
ESC DEL or ESC CTRL-H	Delete word backward.
CTRL-K	Delete from cursor to end of line.
CTRL-U	Delete entire line.

Command Control (Emacs Mode)

Command	Description
CTRL-P	Previous command.
CTRL-N	Next command.
Up Arrow	Previous command.
Down Arrow	Next command.
cmd-fragment ESC p	Search history for cmd-fragment, which must be the beginning of a command.
cmd-fragment ESC n	Like ESC p, but search forward.
esc num	Repeat next command num times.
CTRL-Y	Yank previously deleted string.

vi mode

vi mode has two submodes, insert mode and command mode. The default mode is insert. You can toggle modes by hitting ESC; alternatively, in command mode, typing a (append) or i (insert) will return you to insert mode.

Commands Availible in Insert and Command Mode (vi Mode)

Command	Description
CTRL-P	Previous command.
CTRL-N	Next command.
Up Arrow	Previous command.
Down Arrow	Next command.
ESC	Toggle mode.

Editing Commands (vi Insert Mode)

Command	Description
CTRL-B	Move cursor back (left) one character.
CTRL-F	Move cursor forward (right) one character.
CTRL-A	Move cursor to beginning of line.
CTRL-E	Move cursor to end of line.
DEL or CTRL-H	Delete character to left of cursor.
CTRL-W	Delete word backward.
CTRL-U	Delete from beginning of line to cursor.
CTRL-K	Delete from cursor to end of line.

Cursor Positioning Commands (vi Command Mode)

Command	Description
h or CTRL-H	Move cursor back (left) one character.
l or SPACE	Move cursor forward (right) one character.
w	Move cursor forward (right) one word.
b	Move cursor back (left) one word.
e	Move cursor to next word ending.
W, B, E	Like w, b, and e, but treats whitespace as word separator instead of all non-alphanumeric characters.
ˆ or CTRL-A	Move cursor to beginning of line (first nonwhitespace character).
0	Move cursor to beginning of line.
$ or CTRL-E	Move cursor to end of line.

Text Insertion Commands (vi Command Mode)

Command	Description
a	Append new text after cursor until **ESC**.
i	Insert new text before cursor until **ESC**.
A	Append new text after end of line until **ESC**.
I	Insert new text before beginning of line until **ESC**.

Text Deletion Commands (vi Command Mode)

Command	Description
x	Delete character under cursor.
X or **DEL**	Delete character to left of cursor.
dm	Delete from cursor to end of motion command m.
D	Same as **d$**.
CTRL-W	Delete word backward.
CTRL-U	Delete from beginning of line to cursor.
CTRL-K	Delete from cursor to end of line.

Text Replacement Commands (vi Command Mode)

Command	Description
cm	Change characters from cursor to end of motion command m until **ESC**.
C	Same as **c$**.
rc	Replace character under cursor with character c.
R	Replace multiple characters until **ESC**.
s	Substitute character under cursor with characters typed until **ESC**.

Character-Seeking Motion Commands (vi Command Mode)

Command	Description
fc	Move cursor to next instance of c in line.
Fc	Move cursor to previous instance of c in line.
tc	Move cursor just before next instance of c in line.
Tc	Move cursor just after previous instance of c in line.
;	Repeat previous **f** or **F** command.
,	Repeat previous **f** or **F** command in opposite direction.

Built-in csh and tcsh Commands

@ [*variable* [*n*]=*expression*]	@

Assign the value of the arithmetic *expression* to *variable*, or to the *n*th element of *variable* if the index *n* is specified. With no *variable* or *expression* specified, print the values of all shell variables (same as **set**). Expression operators as well as examples are listed under "Expressions," earlier in this chapter. Two special forms are also valid:

@ *variable*++   Increment *variable* by one.
@ *variable*––   Decrement *variable* by one.

#   #

Ignore all text that follows on the same line. # is used in shell scripts as the comment character, and is not really a command.

#!shell   #!

Used as the first line of a script to invoke the named *shell* (with optional arguments). Not supported in all shells. For example:

```
#!/bin/csh -f
```

:   :

Null command. Returns an exit status of 0. The colon command is often put as the first character of a Bourne- or Korn-shell script to act as a place-holder to keep a # (hash) from accidentally becoming the first character.

---

alias [*name* [*command*]]   **alias**

Assign *name* as the shorthand name, or alias, for *command*. If *command* is omitted, print the alias for *name*; if *name* is also omitted, print all aliases. Aliases can be defined on the command line, but they are more often stored in *.cshrc* so that they take effect upon logging in. (See the sample *.cshrc* file previously in this chapter.) Alias definitions can reference command-line arguments, much like the history list. Use \!* to refer to all command-line arguments, \!ˆ for the first argument, \!\!:2 for the second, \!$ for the last, etc. An alias *name* can be any valid UNIX command; however, you lose the original command's meaning unless you type *name*. See also **unalias** and the "Special Aliases in tcsh" section.

→

alias ←	*Examples* Set the size for **xterm** windows under the X Window System: `alias R 'set noglob; eval `resize`; unset noglob'` Show aliases that contain the string **ls**: `alias	grep ls`  Run **nroff** on all command-line arguments:      `alias ms 'nroff -ms \!*'`  Copy the file that is named as the first argument:      `alias back 'cp \!^ \!^.old'`  Use the regular **ls**, not its alias:      `% \ls`
alloc	**alloc** Print totals of used and free memory.

bg	**bg** [*jobIDs*]
	
	Put the current job or the *jobIDs* in the background.
	
	Example
	To place a time-consuming process in the background, you might begin with:
	
	    `4% nroff -ms report CTRL-Z`
	
	and then issue any one of the following:
	
	    `5% bg`
	    `5% bg %` *Current job*
	    `5% bg %1` *Job number 1*
	    `5% bg %nr` *Match initial string nroff*
	    `5% % &`

bindkey	**bindkey** [*options*] [*key*] [*command*]
	
	tcsh only. Display all key bindings, or bind a key to a command.
	
	    `-a` List standard and alternate key bindings.
	    `-b` *key* Expect *key* to be one of the following: a control character (in hat notation, e.g., ^B, or C notation, e.g., C-B); a metacharacter (e.g., M-B); a function key (e.g., F-*string*); or an extended prefix key (e.g., X-B).
	    `-c` *command*
	        Interpret *command* as a shell, not editor, command.

-d *key* Bind key to its original binding.	**bindkey**
-e Bind to standard Emacs bindings.	
-k Expect *key* to refer to an arrow (**left**, **right**, **up**, or **down**).	
-l List and describe all editor commands.	
-r *key* Completely unbind *key*.	
-v Bind to standard **vi** bindings.	

break	**break**
Resume execution following the **end** command of the nearest enclosing **while** or **foreach**.	

breaksw	**breaksw**
Break from a **switch**; continue execution after the **endsw**.	

built-ins	**built-ins**
tcsh only. Print all built-in shell commands.	

bye	**bye**
tcsh only. Same as **logout**.	

case *pattern* :	**case**
Identify a *pattern* in a **switch**.	

cd [*dir*]	**cd**
Change working directory to *dir*; default is home directory of user. If *dir* is a relative pathname but is not in the current directory, the **cdpath** variable is searched. See the sample *cshrc* file earlier in this chapter. tcsh includes some options for **cd**:	
– Change to previous directory.	
-l Explicitly expand ~ notation.	
-p Print directory stack.	

chdir [*dir*]	**chdir**
Same as **cd**. Useful if you are redefining **cd**.	

complete [*string* [*word*/*pattern*/*list*[:*select*]/[*suffix*]]]	**complete**
tcsh only. List all completions, or, if specified, all completions for *string* (which may be a pattern). Further options can be specified. Options for *word* are:	
	→

complete ←	c	Complete current word only, and without referring to *pattern*.
	C	Complete current word only, referring to *pattern*.
	n	Complete previous word.
	N	Complete word before previous word.
	P	Expect *pattern* to be a range of numbers. Perform completion within that range.

Various *lists* of strings can be searched for possible completions. Some *list* options include:

(*string*)
> Members of the list *string*

`command`
> Output from *command*

a	Aliases
b	Bindings
c	Commands
C	External (not built-in) commands
d	Directories
D	Directories whose names begin with *string*
e	Environment variables
f	Filenames
F	Filenames that begin with *string*
g	Groups
t	Text files
T	Text files whose names begin with *string*
u	Users

select should be a glob-pattern. Completions are limited to words that match this pattern. *suffix* is appended to all completions.

---

continue

continue

Resume execution of nearest enclosing **while** or **foreach**.

---

default

default :

Label the default case (typically last) in a **switch**.

---

dirs

dirs [*options*]

Print the directory stack, showing the current directory first. See also **popd** and **pushd**. All options except -1 are **tcsh** extensions.

-1	Expand the home directory symbol (~) to the actual directory name.
-n	Wrap output.

-v Print one directory per line.	**dirs**

-L *file*   Recreate stack from *file*, which should have been created by **dirs -S** *file*.

-S *file*   Print a series of **pushd** and **popd** commands, which will replicate the stack, to *file*.

---

echo [-n] *string*	**echo**

Write *string* to standard output; if **-n** is specified, the output is not terminated by a newline. Unlike the UNIX version (*/bin/echo*) and the Bourne-shell version, the C shell's **echo** doesn't support escape characters. See also **echo** in Chapter 2, *Linux User Commands*, and Chapter 4, *bash: The Bourne Again Shell*.

---

echotc [*options*] *arguments*	**echotc**

Display terminal capabilities, or move cursor on screen, depending on the argument. Some possible arguments are:

    baud   Display current baud.

    cols   Display current column.

    cm *column row*

            Move cursor to specified coordinates.

    home   Move cursor to home position.

    lines   Print number of lines per screen.

    meta   Does this terminal have meta capacity (usually the ALT key)?

    tabs   Does this terminal have tab capacity?

csh and tcsh

---

else	**else**

Reserved word for interior of **if ... endif** statement.

---

end	**end**

Reserved word that ends a **foreach** or **switch** statement.

---

endif	**endif**

Reserved word that ends an **if** statement.

---

endsw	**endsw**

Reserved word that ends a **switch** statement.

---

eval *args*	**eval**

Typically, **eval** is used in shell scripts, and *args* is a line of code that may contain shell variables. **eval** forces variable expansion to happen first and then runs the resulting command. This

$\rightarrow$

eval
←
	"double-scanning" is useful any time shell variables contain input/output redirection symbols, aliases, or other shell variables. (For example, redirection normally happens before variable expansion, so a variable containing redirection symbols must be expanded first using **eval**; otherwise, the redirection symbols remain uninterpreted.)
	
	Examples
	
	The following line can be placed in the .login file to set up terminal characteristics:
	
	```set noglob eval `tset -s xterm` unset noglob```
	
	The following commands show the effect of **eval**:
	
	```% set b='$a'```
	```% set a=hello```
	```% echo $b``` *Read the command line once*
	```$a```
	```% eval echo $b``` *Read the command line twice*
	```hello```
	
	Another example of **eval** can be found under **alias**.

exec	**exec** *command* Execute *command* in place of current shell. This terminates the current shell, rather than creating a new process under it.
exit	**exit** [(*expr*)] Exit a shell script with the status given by *expr*. A status of zero means success; nonzero means failure. If *expr* is not specified, the exit value is that of the **status** variable. **exit** can be issued at the command line to close a window (log out).

fg	**fg** [*jobIDs*]
	
	Bring the current job or the *jobIDs* to the foreground. *jobID* can be %*job-number*.
	
	Example
	
	If you suspend a **vi** editing session (by pressing **CTRL-Z**), you might resume **vi** using any of these commands:
	
	```% %```
	```% fg```
	```% fg %```
	```% fg %vi``` *Match initial string*

filetest *– op files*	**filetest**

tcsh only. Apply *op* file tester to *files*. Print results in a list. See "File inquiry operators" for a list of file testers.

foreach *name (wordlist)* *commands* **end**	**foreach**

Assign variable *name* to each value in *wordlist* and execute *commands* between **foreach** and **end**. You can use **foreach** as a multiline command issued at the C-shell prompt (first example below), or you can use it in a shell script (second example).

Examples

Rename all files that begin with a capital letter:

```
% foreach i ([A-Z]*)
? mv $i $i.new
? end
```

Check whether each command-line argument is an option or not:

```
foreach arg ($argv)
    # does it begin with - ?
    if ("$arg" =~ -*) then
        echo "Argument is an option"
    else
        echo "Argument is a filename"
    endif
end
```

glob *wordlist*	**glob**

Do filename, variable, and history substitutions on *wordlist*. No \ escapes are recognized in its expansion, and words are delimited by null characters. **glob** is typically used in shell scripts to "hardcode" a value so that it remains the same for the rest of the script.

goto *string*	**goto**

Skip to a line whose first nonblank character is *string* followed by a **:** and continue execution below that line. On the **goto** line, *string* can be a variable or filename pattern, but the label branched to must be a literal, expanded value and must not occur within a **foreach** or **while**.

hashstat	**hashstat** Display statistics that show the hash table's level of success at locating commands via the **path** variable.
history	**history** [*options*] Display the list of history events. (History syntax is discussed earlier, in "Command History.") ***Options*** -c tcsh only. Clear history list. -h Print history list without event numbers. -r Print in reverse order; show oldest commands last. *n* Display only the last *n* history commands, instead of the number set by the **history** shell variable. -L *file* tcsh only. Load series of **pushd** and **popd** commands from *file* in order to recreate a saved stack. -M *file* tcsh only. Merge the current directory stack and the stack saved in *file*. Save both, sorted by time, in *file*, as a series of **pushd** and **popd** commands. -S *file* tcsh only. Print a series of pushd and popd commands, which will replicate the stack, to *file*. ***Example*** To save and execute the last five commands: ``` history -h 5 > do_it source do_it ```
hup	**hup** [*command*] tcsh only. Start *command* but make it exit when sent a hangup signal, which is sent when shell exits. By default, configure shell script to exit on hangup signal.

if	**if**
	
	Begin a conditional statement. The simple format is:
	
	``
	if (expr) cmd
	``
	
	There are three other possible formats, shown side-by-side:
	
	``
	if (expr) then if (expr) then if (expr) then
	    cmds cmds1 cmds1
	endif else else if (expr) then
	                      cmds2 cmds2
	                  endif else
	                                        cmds3
	                                    endif
	``

In the simplest form, execute *cmd* if *expr* is true; otherwise do nothing (redirection still occurs; this is a bug). In the other forms, execute one or more commands. If *expr* is true, continue with the commands after **then**; if *expr* is false, branch to the commands after **else** (or branch to after the **else if** and continue checking). For more examples, see "Expressions" earlier in this chapter, or **shift** or **while**.

if

Example

Take a default action if no command-line arguments are given:

```
if ($#argv == 0) then
    echo "No filename given. Sending to Report."
    set outfile = Report
else
    set outfile = $argv[1]
endif
```

---

jobs [-1]

jobs

List all running or stopped jobs; -1 includes process IDs. For example, you can check whether a long compilation or text format is still running. Also useful before logging out.

---

kill [*options*] *ID*

kill

Terminate each specified process *ID* or job *ID*. You must own the process or be a privileged user. This built-in is similar to */bin/kill* described in Chapter 2 but also allows symbolic job names. Stubborn processes can be killed using signal 9.

Options

-1   List the signal names. (Used by itself.)

-*signal*   The signal number or name (obtained from **kill -1**). Default is TERM.

Signals

Signals are defined in */usr/include/sys/signal.h* and are listed here without the SIG prefix.

HUP	1	Hangup
INT	2	Interrupt
QUIT	3	Quit
ILL	4	Illegal instruction
TRAP	5	Trace trap
IOT	6	IOT instruction
EMT	7	EMT instruction
FPE	8	Floating point exception
KILL	9	Kill
BUS	10	Bus error
SEGV	11	Segmentation violation

csh and tcsh

→

kill	SYS	12	Bad argument to system call
←	PIPE	13	Write to pipe, but no process to read it
	ALRM	14	Alarm clock
	TERM	15	Software termination (the default signal)
	USR1	16	User-defined signal 1
	USR2	17	User-defined signal 2
	CLD	18	Child process died
	PWR	19	Restart after power failure

Examples

If you've issued the following command:

```
44% nroff -ms report &
```

you can terminate it in any of the following ways:

45% **kill 19536**	*Process ID*
45% **kill %**	*Current job*
45% **kill %1**	*Job number 1*
45% **kill %nr**	*Initial string*
45% **kill %?report**	*Matching string*

---

limit

limit [-h] [*resource* [*limit*]]

Display limits or set a *limit* on resources used by the current process and by each process it creates. If no *limit* is given, the current limit is printed for *resource*. If *resource* is also omitted, all limits are printed. By default, the current limits are shown or set; with **-h**, hard limits are used. A hard limit imposes an absolute limit that can't be exceeded. Only a privileged user may raise it. See also **unlimit**.

Option

-h   Use hard, not current, limits.

Resource

cputime	Maximum number of seconds the CPU can spend; can be abbreviated as **cpu**.
filesize	Maximum size of any one file.
datasize	Maximum size of data (including stack).
stacksize	Maximum size of stack.
coredumpsize	Maximum size of a core dump file.

Limit

A number followed by an optional character (a unit specifier).

For **cputime**:	nh (for n hours)
	nm (for n minutes)
	mm:ss (minutes and seconds)
For others:	nk (for n kilobytes, the default)
	nm (for n megabytes)

log

tcsh only. Consult **watch** variable for list of users being watched. Print list of those who are presently logged in. If – is entered as an option, reset environment as if user had logged in with new group.

login [*user* | -p]

Replace *user*'s login shell with */bin/login*. -p is used to preserve environment variables.

logout

Terminate the login shell.

ls-F [*options*] [*files*]

tcsh only. Faster alternative to **ls -F**. If given any options, invokes **ls**.

newgrp [–] [*group*]

tcsh only. Change user's group ID to specified group ID, or, if none is specified, to original group ID. If – is entered as an option, reset environment as if user had logged in with new group.

nice [±*n*] *command*

Change the execution priority for *command*, or, if none is given, change priority for the current shell. (See also **nice** in Chapter 2.) The priority range is –20 to 20, with a default of 4. The range seems backwards: –20 gives the highest priority (fastest execution); 20 gives the lowest. Only a privileged user may specify a negative number.

+*n*   Add *n* to the priority value (lower job priority).
-*n*   Subtract *n* from the priority value (raise job priority). Privileged users only.

nohup [*command*]

"No hangup signals." Do not terminate *command* after terminal line is closed (i.e., when you hang up from a phone or log out). Use without *command* in shell scripts to keep script from being terminated. (See also **nohup** in Chapter 2.)

notify	**notify** [*jobID*] Report immediately when a background job finishes (instead of waiting for you to exit a long editing session, for example). If no *jobID* is given, the current background job is assumed.

onintr	**onintr** *label*
	onintr -
	onintr
	
	"On interrupt." Used in shell scripts to handle interrupt signals (similar to **bash**'s **trap 2** and **trap "" 2** commands). The first form is like a **goto** *label*. The script will branch to *label*: if it catches an interrupt signal (e.g., **CTRL-C**). The second form lets the script ignore interrupts. This is useful at the beginning of a script or before any code segment that needs to run unhindered (e.g., when moving files). The third form restores interrupt handling that was previously disabled with **onintr** -.
	
	Example
	
	``
	onintr cleanup # go to "cleanup" on interrupt
	   .
	   . # shell script commands
	   .
	cleanup: # label for interrupts
	  onintr - # ignore additional interrupts
	  rm -f $tmpfiles # remove any files created
	  exit 2 # exit with an error status
	``

popd	**popd** [*options*] Remove the current entry from the directory stack, or remove the *n*th entry from the stack. The current entry has number 0 and appears on the left. See also **dirs** and **pushd**. *Options* +*n* Specify *n*th entry. -l Expand ~ notation. -n Wrap long lines. -v Print precisely one directory per line.
printenv	**printenv** [*variable*] Print all (or one specified) environment variables and their values.

pushd *name*
pushd [*options*]
pushd

The first form changes the working directory to *name* and adds it to the directory stack. The second form rotates the *n*th entry to the beginning, making it the working directory. (Entry numbers begin at 0.) With no arguments, **pushd** switches the first two entries and changes to the new current directory. The +*n*, -l, -n, and −*v* options behave the same as in popd. See also **dirs** and popd.

Examples

```
% dirs
/home/bob /usr
% pushd /etc              Add /etc to directory stack
/etc /home/bob /usr
% pushd +2                Switch to third directory
/usr /etc /home/bob
% pushd                   Switch top two directories
/etc /usr /home/bob
% popd                    Discard current entry; go to next
/usr /home/bob
```

rehash

Recompute the hash table for the PATH variable. Use **rehash** whenever a new command is created during the current session. This allows the PATH variable to locate and execute the command. (If the new command resides in a directory not listed in PATH, add this directory to PATH before rehashing.) See also **unhash**.

repeat *n command*

Execute *n* instances of *command*.

Examples

Print three copies of **memo**:

```
% repeat 3 pr memo | lp
```

Read 10 lines from the terminal and store in **item_list**:

```
% repeat 10 line > item_list
```

Append 50 boilerplate files to **report**:

```
% repeat 50 cat template >> report
```

sched	**sched** [*options*] **sched** *time command* tcsh only. Without options, print all scheduled events. The second form schedules an event. *time* should be specified in *hh:mm* form (e.g., 13:00). *Options* +*hh:mm* Schedule event to take place *hh:mm* from now. -*n* Remove *n*th item from schedule.
set	**set** *variable* = *value* **set** [*options*] *variable* [*n*] = *value* **set** Set *variable* to *value*, or if multiple values are specified, set the variable to the list of words in the value list. If an index *n* is specified, set the *n*th word in the variable to *value*. (The variable must already contain at least that number of words.) With no arguments, display the names and values of all set variables. See also "Predefined Shell Variables" earlier in this chapter. *Options* -r tcsh only. List only read-only variables, or set specified variable to read-only. *Examples* `% set list=(yes no mabye)` *Assign a wordlist* `% set list[3]=maybe` *Assign an item in existing wordlist* `% set quote="Make my day"` *Assign a variable* `% set x=5 y=10 history=100` *Assign several variables* `% set blank` *Assign a null value to* `blank`
setenv	**setenv** [*name* [*value*]] Assign a *value* to an environment variable *name*. By convention, *name* is uppercase. *value* can be a single word or a quoted string. If no *value* is given, the null value is assigned. With no arguments, display the names and values of all environment variables. **setenv** is not necessary for the PATH variable because it is automatically exported from **path**.
settc	**settc** *capability value* Set terminal *capability* to *value*.
setty	**setty** [*options*] [+|−*mode*] tcsh only. Do not allow shell to change specified tty modes. By default, act on execute set.

Options

+*mode*	Without arguments, list all modes in specified set that are on. Otherwise, set specified mode to on.
-*mode*	Without arguments, list all modes in specified set that are off. Otherwise, set specified mode to on.
-a	List all modes in specified set.
-d	Act on edit set of modes (used when editing commands).
-q	Act on quote set of modes (used when entering characters verbatim).
-x	Act on execute set of modes (default) (used when executing examples).

shift [*variable*]

If *variable* is given, shift the words in a wordlist variable; i.e., *name*[2] becomes *name*[1]. With no argument, shift the positional parameters (command-line arguments); i.e., **$2** becomes **$1**. **shift** is typically used in a **while** loop. See additional example under **while**.

Example

```
while ($#argv)        # while there are arguments
    if (-f $argv[1])
        wc -l $argv[1]
    else
        echo "$argv[1] is not a regular file"
    endif
    shift             # get the next argument
end
```

source [-h] *script*

Read and execute commands from a C-shell script. With -h, the commands are added to the history list but aren't executed.

Example

```
source ~/.cshrc
```

stop [*jobIDs*]

Suspend the current background jobs or the background jobs specified by *jobIDs*; this is the complement of **CTRL-Z** or **suspend**.

suspend	**suspend** Suspend the current foreground job; same as **CTRL-Z**. Often used to stop an **su** command.
switch	**switch** Process commands depending on the value of a variable. When you need to handle more than three choices, **switch** is a useful alternative to an **if-then-else** statement. If the *string* variable matches *pattern1*, the first set of *commands* is executed; if *string* matches *pattern2*, the second set of *commands* is executed, and so on. If no patterns match, execute commands under the **default** case. *string* can be specified using command substitution, variable substitution, or filename expansion. Patterns can be specified using pattern-matching symbols *, ?, and [ ]. **breaksw** is used to exit the **switch** after *commands* are executed. If **breaksw** is omitted (which is rarely done), the **switch** continues to execute another set of commands until it reaches a **breaksw** or **endsw**. Below is the general syntax of **switch**, side-by-side with an example that processes the first command-line argument.

```
switch (string)              switch ($argv[1])
   case pattern1:               case -[nN]:
      commands                     nroff $file | lp
      breaksw                      breaksw
   case pattern2:               case -[Pp]:
      commands                     pr $file | lp
      breaksw                      breaksw
   case pattern3:               case -[Mm]:
      commands                     more $file
      breaksw                      breaksw
         .                      case -[Ss]:
         .                         sort $file
         .                         breaksw
   default:                     xdefault:
      commands                     echo "Error--no such option"
                                   exit 1
      breaksw                      breaksw
endsw                        endsw
```

telltc	**telltc** Print all terminal capabilities and their values.
time	**time** [*command*] Execute a *command* and show how much time it uses. With no argument, **time** can be used in a shell script to time the script.

umask [*nnn*] Display file creation mask or set file creation mask to octal *nnn*. The file creation mask determines which permission bits are turned off. **umask** is also a standard command. See the **umask** entry in Chapter 2 for examples.	umask
unalias *name* Remove *name* from the alias list. See **alias** for more information.	unalias
uncomplete *pattern* tcsh only. Remove completions (specified by **complete**).	uncomplete
unhash Remove internal hash table. The C shell will stop using hashed values and will spend time searching the **path** directories to locate a command. See also **rehash**.	unhash
unlimit [*resource*] Remove the allocation limits on *resource*. If *resource* is not specified, remove limits for all resources. See **limit** for more information. With **–h**, specify removal of hard limits. This command only be run only by a privileged user.	unlimit
unset *variables* Remove one or more *variables*. Variable names may be specified as a pattern, using filename metacharacters. See **set**.	unset
unsetenv *variable* Remove an environment variable. Filename matching is *not* valid. See **setenv**.	unsetenv
wait Pause in execution until all child processes complete, or until an interrupt signal is received.	wait
watchlog Same as **log**.	watchlog

where	**where** *command*
	tcsh only. Display all aliases, built-ins, and executables named *command*.
which	**which** *command*
	tcsh only. Report which version of command will be executed. Same as the executable **which**, but faster, and checks **tcsh** built-ins.
while	**while** (*expression*) *commands* **end**
	As long as *expression* is true (evaluates to nonzero), evaluate *commands* between **while** and **end**. **break** and **continue** can be used to terminate or continue the loop. See also example under **shift**.
	Example

```
set user = (alice bob carol ted)
while ($argv[1] != $user[1])
   #Cycle through each user, checking for a match
   shift user
   #If we cycled through with no match...
   if ($#user == 0) then
     echo "$argv[1] is not on the list of users"
     exit 1
   endif
end
```

Special Aliases in tcsh

Certain special aliases can be set in **tcsh**. These are executed when specific events occur.

beepcmd	At beep.
cwdcmd	When **cwd** changes.
periodic	Every few minutes. The exact amount of time is set by the *tperiod* shell variable.
precmd	Before printing a new prompt.
shell *shell*	If a script does not specify a shell, interpret it with *shell*.

Job Control

Job control lets you place foreground jobs in the background, bring background jobs to the foreground, or suspend (temporarily stop) running jobs. The C shell provides the following commands for job control. For more information on these commands, see "Built-in csh and tcsh Commands" earlier in this chapter.

bg	Put a job in the background.
fg	Put a job in the foreground.
jobs	List active jobs.
kill	Terminate a job.
notify	Notify when a background job finishes.
stop	Suspend a background job.
CTRL-Z	Suspend a foreground job.

Many job control commands take *jobID* as an argument. This argument can be specified as follows:

%*n*	Job number *n*.
%*s*	Job whose command line starts with string *s*.
%?*s*	Job whose command line contains string *s*.
%%	Current job.
%	Current job (same as above).
%+	Current job (same as above).
%-	Previous job.

CHAPTER 6

Pattern Matching

A number of Linux text-editing utilities let you search for, and in some cases change, text patterns rather than fixed strings. These utilities include the editing programs **ed**, **ex**, **vi**, and **sed**; the **awk** scripting language; and the commands **grep** and **egrep**. Text patterns (also called regular expressions) contain normal characters mixed with special characters (also called metacharacters).

This chapter presents the following information:

- Filenames versus patterns

- List of metacharacters available to each program

- Description of metacharacters

- Examples

A thorough guide to pattern matching can be found in the Nutshell Handbook *Mastering Regular Expressions*, by Jeffrey E. F. Friedl.

Filenames Versus Patterns

Metacharacters used in pattern matching are different from those used for filename expansion. When you issue a command on the command line, special characters are seen first by the shell, then by the program; therefore, unquoted metacharacters are interpreted by the shell for filename expansion. The command:

```
$ grep [A-Z]* chap[12]
```

could, for example, be interpreted by the shell as:

```
$ grep Array.c Bug.c Comp.c chap1 chap2
```

and **grep** would then try to find the pattern "Array.c" in files *Bug.c*, *Comp.c*, *chap1*, and *chap2*. To bypass the shell and pass the special characters to **grep**, use quotes:

```
$ grep "[A-Z]*" chap[12]
```

Double quotes suffice in most cases, but single quotes are the safest bet.

Note also that * and ? have subtly different meanings in pattern matching and filename expansion.

Metacharacters, Listed by Linux Program

Some metacharacters are valid for one program but not for another. Those that are available to a given program are marked by a square (■) in the following table. Full descriptions are provided after the table.

Symbol	ed	ex	vi	sed	awk	grep	egrep	Action
.	■	■	■	■	■	■	■	Match any character.
*	■	■	■	■	■	■	■	Match zero or more preceding.
^	■	■	■	■	■	■	■	Match beginning of line.
$	■	■	■	■	■	■	■	Match end of line.
\	■	■	■	■	■	■	■	Escape character following.
[ ]	■	■	■	■	■	■	■	Match one from a set.
\(\)	■	■		■				Store matched text for later replay.
\{ \}	■			■		■		Match a range of instances.
\< \>		■	■					Match word's beginning or end.
+					■		■	Match one or more preceding.
?					■		■	Match zero or one preceding.
|					■		■	Separate choices to match.
( )					■		■	Group expressions to match.

In **ed**, **ex**, and **sed**, note that you specify both a search pattern (on the left) and a replacement pattern (on the right). The metacharacters in this table are meaningful only in a search pattern.

In **ed**, **ex**, and **sed**, the following additional metacharacters are valid only in a replacement pattern:

Symbol	ex	sed	ed	Action
\	■	■	■	Escape character following.
\n	■	■	■	Reuse matched text stored in \(\).
&	■	■		Reuse previous search pattern.
~	■			Reuse previous replacement pattern.
\u \U	■			Change characters to uppercase.
\l \L	■			Change characters to lowercase.
\E	■			Turn off previous \U or \L.
\e	■			Turn off previous \u or \l.

Metacharacters

The following characters have special meaning only in search patterns:

.	Match any *single* character except newline.
*	Match any number (or none) of the single character that immediately precedes it. The preceding character can also be a regular expression, e.g., since . (dot) means any character, .* means "match any number of any character."
^	Match the following regular expression at the beginning of the line.
$	Match the preceding regular expression at the end of the line.
[ ]	Match any *one* of the enclosed characters.
	A hyphen (-) indicates a range of consecutive characters. A circumflex (^) as the first character in the brackets reverses the sense: it matches any one character *not* in the list. A hyphen or close bracket ( ]) as the first character is treated as a member of the list. All other metacharacters are treated as members of the list.
[^]	Do not match enclosed character(s).
\{n,m\}	Match a range of occurrences of the single character that immediately precedes it. The preceding character can also be a regular expression. \{n\} matches exactly n occurrences, \{n,\} matches at least n occurrences, and \{n,m\} matches any number of occurrences between n and m.
\	Turn off the special meaning of the character that follows.
\(\)	Save the matched text enclosed between \(and \) in a special holding space. Up to nine patterns can be saved on a single line. They can be "replayed" in substitutions by the escape sequences \1 to \9.
\< \>	Match characters at beginning (\<) or end (\>) of a word.
+	Match one or more instances of preceding regular expression.
?	Match zero or one instances of preceding regular expression.
|	Match the regular expression specified before or after.
( )	Group regular expressions.

The following characters have special meaning only in replacement patterns:

\	Turn off the special meaning of the character that follows.
\n	Restore the nth pattern previously saved by \(and \). n is a number from 1 to 9, with 1 starting on the left.
&	Reuse the search pattern as part of the replacement pattern.
~	Reuse the previous replacement pattern in the current replacement pattern.
\u	Convert first character of replacement pattern to uppercase.
\U	Convert replacement pattern to uppercase.
\l	Convert first character of replacement pattern to lowercase.
\L	Convert replacement pattern to lowercase.

Examples of Searching

When used with **grep** or **egrep**, regular expressions are surrounded by quotes. (If the pattern contains a $, you must use single quotes; e.g., *'pattern'*.) When used with **ed**, **ex**, **sed**, and **awk**, regular expressions are usually surrounded by / (although any delimiter works). Here are some sample patterns:

Pattern	What does it match?
bag	The string *bag*.
^bag	*bag* at beginning of line.
bag$	*bag* at end of line.
^bag$	*bag* as the only word on line.
[Bb]ag	*Bag* or *bag*.
b[aeiou]g	Second letter is a vowel.
b[^aeiou]g	Second letter is a consonant (or uppercase or symbol).
b.g	Second letter is any character.
^...$	Any line containing exactly three characters.
^\.	Any line that begins with a dot.
^\.[a-z][a-z]	Same, followed by two lowercase letters (e.g., troff requests).
^\.[a-z]\{2\}	Same as previous, **grep** or **sed** only.
^[^.]	Any line that doesn't begin with a dot.
bugs*	*bug*, *bugs*, *bugss*, etc.
"word"	A word in quotes.
"*word"*	A word, with or without quotes.
[A-Z][A-Z]*	One or more uppercase letters.
[A-Z]+	Same, **egrep** or **awk** only.
[A-Z].*	An uppercase letter, followed by zero or more characters.
[A-Z]*	Zero or more uppercase letters.
[a-zA-Z]	Any letter.
[0-9A-Za-z]*	Any alphanumeric sequence.

egrep or awk pattern	What does it match?
[567]	One of the numbers *5*, *6*, or *7*.
five|six|seven	One of the words five, six, or seven.
80[23]?86	*8086*, *80286*, or *80386*
compan(y|ies)	*company* or *companies*

ex or vi pattern	What does it match?
\<the	Words like *theater* or *the*
the\>	Words like *breathe* or *the*
\<the\>	The word *the*

sed or grep pattern	What does it match?
0\{5,\}	Five or more zeros in a row
[0-9]\{3\}-[0-9]\{2\}-[0-9]\{4\}	Social security number (*nnn-nn-nnnn*)

Examples of Searching and Replacing

The following examples show the metacharacters available to **sed** or **ex**. Note that **ex** commands begin with a colon. A space is marked by a □; a tab is marked by *tab*.

Command	Result
`s/.*/(&)/`	Reproduce the entire line, but add parentheses.
`s/.*/mv & &.old/`	Change a wordlist (one word per line) into **mv** commands.
`/^$/d`	Delete blank lines.
`:g/^$/d`	Same as previous, in **ex** editor.
`/^[□tab]*$/d`	Delete blank lines, plus lines containing spaces or tabs.
`:g/^[□tab]*$/d`	Same as previous, in **ex** editor.
`s/□□*/□/g`	Turn one or more spaces into one space.
`:%s/□□*/□/g`	Same as previous, in **ex** editor.
`:s/[0-9]/Item &/`	Turn a number into an item label (on the current line).
`:s`	Repeat the substitution on the first occurrence.
`:&`	Same as previous.
`:sg`	Same, but for all occurrences on the line.
`:&g`	Same as previous.
`:%&g`	Repeat the substitution globally.
`:.,$s/Fortran/\U&/g`	Change word to uppercase, on current line to last line.
`:%s/.*/\L&/`	Lowercase entire file.
`:s/\<./\u&/g`	Uppercase first letter of each word on current line. (Useful for titles.)
`:%s/yes/No/g`	Globally change a word (yes) to another word (No).
`:%s/Yes/~/g`	Globally change a different word to No (previous replacement).

Finally, here are some **sed** examples for transposing words. A simple transposition of two words might look like this:

    `s/die or do/do or die/`   *Transpose words*

The real trick is to use hold buffers to transpose variable patterns. For example:

    `s/\([Dd]ie\) or \([Dd]o\)/\2 or \1/`   *Transpose, using hold buffers*

CHAPTER 7

The Emacs Editor

This section presents the following topics:

- Introduction

- Typical problems

- Summary of Emacs commands by group

- Summary of Emacs commands by key

- Summary of Emacs commands by name

Introduction

Although Emacs is not part of Linux, this text editor is found on many UNIX systems because it is a popular alternative to **vi**. Many versions are available. This book documents GNU Emacs, which is available from the Free Software Foundation in Cambridge, Massachusetts. For more information, see the Nutshell Handbook *Learning GNU Emacs*, Second Edition, by Debra Cameron, Bill Rosenblatt, and Eric Raymond.

To start an Emacs editing session, type:

> emacs [*file*]

Typical Problems

A very common problem is that the DEL or Backspace key on the terminal does not delete the character before the cursor, as it should. Instead, it invokes a help prompt. This problem is caused by an incompatible terminal. A fairly robust fix is to create a file named *.emacs* in your home directory (or edit one that's already there) and add the following lines:

```
(keyboard-translate ?\C-h ?\C-?)
(keyboard-translate ?\C-\\ ?\C-h)
```

Now the DEL or Backspace kill should work, and you can invoke help by pressing C-\ (an arbitrarily chosen key sequence).

Another problem that could happen when you are logged in from a remote terminal is that C-s may cause the terminal to hang. This is caused by an old-fashioned handshake protocol between the terminal and the system. You can restart the terminal by pressing C-q, but that doesn't help you enter commands that contain the sequence C-s. The only solution (aside from using a more modern dial-in protocol) is to create new key-bindings that replace C-s.

Notes on the Tables

Emacs commands use the Control key and the Meta key. Most modern terminals provide a key named Alt that functions as a Meta key. In this section, the notation C- indicates that the Control key is pressed at the same time as the character that follows, while M- indicates that the Meta or Alt key is pressed along with the character that follows. (Instead of Meta, you can press the ESCAPE key, release it, and press the character.)

In the command tables that follow, the first column lists the keystroke and the last column describes it. When there is a middle column, it lists the command name. The command can be executed by typing M-x followed by the command name. If you're unsure of the name, you can type a space or a carriage return, and Emacs will list possible completions of what you've typed so far.

Because Emacs is such a comprehensive editor, containing hundreds of commands, some commands must be omitted for the sake of preserving a "quick" reference. You can browse the command set by typing C-h (for help) or M-x (for command names).

Absolutely Essential Commands

If you're just getting started with Emacs, here's a short list of the most important commands to know:

Binding	Action
C-h	Enter the online help system.
C-x C-s	Save the file.
C-x C-c	Exit Emacs.
C-x u	Undo last edit (can be repeated).
C-g	Get out of current command operation.
C-p	Up by line or character.
C-n	Down by line or character.
C-f	Forward by line or character.
C-b	Back by line or character.
C-v	Forward by one screen.

Binding	Action
M-v	Backward by one screen.
C-s	Search for characters.
C-d	Delete current character.
DEL	Delete previous character.
Backspace	Delete previous character.

Summary of Commands by Group

Reminder: Tables list keystrokes, command name, and description. C- indicates the Control key; M- indicates the Meta key.

File-handling Commands

Binding	Command	Action
C-x C-f	find-file	Find file and read it.
C-x C-v	find-alternate-file	Read another file; replace the one read with C-x C-f.
C-x i	insert-file	Insert file at cursor position.
C-x C-s	save-buffer	Save file.
C-x C-w	write-file	Write buffer contents to file.
C-x C-c	save-buffers-kill-emacs	Exit Emacs.
C-z	suspend-emacs	Suspend Emacs (use **exit** or **fg** to restart).

Cursor Movement Commands

Some words are emphasized in the **Action** column to help you remember the binding for the command.

Binding	Command	Action
C-f	forward-char	Move *forward* one character (right).
C-b	backward-char	Move *backward* one character (left).
C-p	previous-line	Move to *previous* line (up).
C-n	next-line	Move to *next* line (down).
M-f	forward-word	Move one word *forward*.
M-b	backward-word	Move one word *backward*.
C-a	beginning-of-line	Move to beginning of line.
C-e	end-of-line	Move to *end* of line.
M-a	backward-sentence	Move backward one sentence.
M-e	forward-sentence	Move forward one sentence.
M-{	backward-paragraph	Move backward one paragraph.
M-}	forward-paragraph	Move forward one paragraph.
C-v	scroll-up	Move forward one screen.
M-v	scroll-down	Move backward one screen.
C-x [	backward-page	Move backward one page.
C-x]	forward-page	Move forward one page.
M->	end-of-buffer	Move to end of file.
M-<	beginning-of-buffer	Move to beginning of file.

Binding	Command	Action
(none)	goto-line	Go to line *n* of file.
(none)	goto-char	Go to character *n* of file.
C-l	recenter	Redraw screen with current line in the center.
M-*n*	digit-argument	Repeat the next command *n* times.
C-u *n*	universal-argument	Repeat the next command *n* times.

Deletion Commands

Binding	Command	Action
DEL	backward-delete-char	Delete previous character.
C-d	delete-char	Delete character under cursor.
M-DEL	backward-kill-word	Delete previous word.
M-d	kill-word	Delete the word the cursor is on.
C-k	kill-line	Delete from cursor to end of line.
M-k	kill-sentence	Delete sentence the cursor is on.
C-x DEL	backward-kill-sentence	Delete previous sentence.
C-y	yank	Restore what you've deleted.
C-w	kill-region	Delete a marked region (see next section).
(none)	backward-kill-paragraph	Delete previous paragraph.
(none)	kill-paragraph	Delete from the cursor to the end of the paragraph.

Paragraphs and Regions

Binding	Command	Action
C-@	set-mark-command	Mark the beginning (or end) of a region.
C-SPACE	(same as above)	(same as above)
C-x C-p	mark-page	Mark page.
C-x C-x	exchange-point-and-mark	Exchange location of cursor and mark.
C-x h	mark-whole-buffer	Mark buffer.
M-q	fill-paragraph	Reformat paragraph.
M-g	fill-region	Reformat individual paragraphs within a region.
M-h	mark-paragraph	Mark paragraph.
M-{	backward-paragraph	Move backward one paragraph.
M-}	forward-paragraph	Move forward one paragraph.
(none)	backward-kill-paragraph	Delete previous paragraph.
(none)	kill-paragraph	Delete from the cursor to the end of the paragraph.

Stopping and Undoing Commands

Binding	Command	Action
C-g	keyboard-quit	Abort current command.
C-x u	advertised-undo	Undo last edit (can be done repeatedly).
(none)	revert-buffer	Restore buffer to the state it was in when the file was last saved (or auto-saved).

Transposition Commands

Binding	Command	Action
C-t	transpose-chars	Transpose two letters.
M-t	transpose-words	Transpose two words.
C-x C-t	transpose-lines	Transpose two lines.
(none)	transpose-sentences	Transpose two sentences.
(none)	transpose-paragraphs	Transpose two paragraphs.

Capitalization Commands

Binding	Command	Action
M-c	capitalize-word	Capitalize first letter of word.
M-u	upcase-word	Uppercase word.
M-l	downcase-word	Lowercase word.
M- – M-c	negative-argument; capitalize-word	Capitalize previous word.
M- – M-u	negative-argument; upcase-word	Uppercase previous word.
M- – M-l	negative-argument; downcase-word	Lowercase previous word.
(none)	capitalize-region	Capitalize initial letters in region.
C-x C-u	upcase-region	Uppercase region
C-x C-l	downcase-region	Lowercase region.

Incremental Search Commands

Binding	Command	Action
C-s	isearch-forward	Start or repeat incremental search forward.
C-r	isearch-backward	Start or repeat incremental search backward.
Return	(none)	Exit a successful search.
C-g	keyboard-quit	Cancel incremental search; return to starting point.
DEL	(none)	Delete incorrect character of search string.
M-C-r	isearch-backward-regexp	Incremental search backward for regular expression.
M-C-s	isearch-forward-regexp	Incremental search forward for regular expression.

Word Abbreviation Commands

Binding	Command	Action
(none)	abbrev-mode	Enter (or exit) word abbreviation mode.
C-x -	inverse-add-global-abbrev	Type global abbreviation, then definition.
C-x C-h	inverse-add-local- abbrev	Type local abbreviation, then definition.
(none)	unexpand-abbrev	Undo the last word abbreviation.
(none)	write-abbrev-file	Write the word abbreviation file.

Binding	Command	Action
(none)	edit-abbrevs	Edit the word abbreviations.
(none)	list-abbrevs	View the word abbreviations.
(none)	kill-all-abbrevs	Kill abbreviations for this session.

Buffer Manipulation Commands

Binding	Command	Action
C-x b	switch-to-buffer	Move to specified buffer.
C-x C-b	list-buffers	Display buffer list.
C-x k	kill-buffer	Delete specified buffer.
(none)	kill-some-buffers	Ask about deleting each buffer.
(none)	rename-buffer	Change buffer name to specified name.
C-x s	save-some-buffers	Ask whether to save each modified buffer.

Window Commands

Binding	Command	Action
C-x 2	split-window-horizontally	Divide the current window horizontally into two.
C-x 5	split-window-vertically	Divide the current window vertically into two.
C-x >	scroll-right	Scroll the window right.
C-x <	scroll-left	Scroll the window left.
C-x o	other-window	Move to the other window.
C-x 0	delete-window	Delete current window.
C-x 1	delete-other-windows	Delete all windows but this one.
(none)	delete-windows-on	Delete all windows on a given buffer.
C-x ^	enlarge-window	Make window taller.
(none)	shrink-window	Make window shorter.
C-x }	enlarge-window-horizontally	Make window wider.
C-x {	shrink-window-horizontally	Make window narrower.
M-C-v	scroll-other-window	Scroll other window.
C-x 4 f	find-file-other-window	Find a file in the other window.
C-x 4 b	switch-to-buffer-other-window	Select a buffer in the other window.
(none)	compare-windows	Compare two buffers; show first difference.

Special Shell Mode Characters

Binding	Command	Action
C-c C-c	interrupt-shell-subjob	Terminate the current job.
C-c C-d	shell-send-eof	End of file character.
C-c C-u	kill-shell-input	Erase current line.
C-c C-w	backward-kill-word	Erase the previous word.
C-c C-z	stop-shell-subjob	Suspend the current job.

Indentation Commands

Binding	Command	Action
C-x .	set-fill-prefix	Prepend each line in paragraph with characters from beginning of line up to cursor column; cancel prefix by typing this command in column 1.
(none)	indented-text-mode	Major mode: each tab defines a new indent for subsequent lines.
(none)	text-mode	Exit indented text mode; return to text mode.
M-C-\	indent-region	Indent a region to match first line in region.
M-m	back-to-indentation	Move cursor to first character on line.
M-C-o	split-line	Split line at cursor; indent to column of cursor.
(none)	fill-individual-paragraphs	Reformat indented paragraphs, keeping indentation.

Centering Commands

Binding	Command	Action
M-s	center-line	Center line that cursor is on.
(none)	center-paragraph	Center paragraph that cursor is on.
(none)	center-region	Center currently defined region.

Macro Commands

Binding	Command	Action
C-x (	start-kbd-macro	Start macro definition.
C-x)	end-kbd-macro	End macro definition.
C-x e	call-last-kbd-macro	Execute last macro defined.
M-n C-x e	digit-argument and call-last-kbd-macro	Execute last macro defined, n times.
C-u C-x (	start-kbd-macro	Execute last macro defined, then add keystrokes.
(none)	name-last-kbd-macro	Name last macro you created (before saving it).
(none)	insert-last-keyboard-macro	Insert the macro you named into a file.
(none)	load-file	Load macro files you've saved.
(none)	macroname	Execute a keyboard macro you've saved.
C-x q	kbd-macro-query	Insert a query in a macro definition.
C-u C-x q	(none)	Insert a recursive edit in a macro definition.
M-C-c	exit-recursive-edit	Exit a recursive edit.

Detail Information Help Commands

Binding	Command	Action
C-h a	command-apropos	What commands involve this concept?
(none)	apropos	What commands, functions, and variables involve this concept?
C-h c	describe-key-briefly	What command does this keystroke sequence run?

Emacs

Binding	Command	Action
C-h b	describe-bindings	What are all the key bindings for this buffer?
C-h k	describe-key	What command does this keystroke sequence run, and what does it do?
C-h l	view-lossage	What are the last 100 characters I typed?
C-h w	where-is	What is the key binding for this command?
C-h f	describe-function	What does this function do?
C-h v	describe-variable	What does this variable mean, and what is its value?
C-h m	describe-mode	Tell me about the mode the current buffer is in.
C-h s	describe-syntax	What is the syntax table for this buffer?

Help Commands

Binding	Command	Action
C-h t	help-with-tutorial	Run the Emacs tutorial.
C-h i	info	Start the info documentation reader.
C-h n	view-emacs-news	View news about updates to Emacs.
C-h C-c	describe-copying	View the Emacs General Public License.
C-h C-d	describe-distribution	View information on ordering Emacs from FSF.
C-h C-w	describe-no-warranty	View the (non)warranty for Emacs.

Summary of Commands by Key

Emacs commands are presented next in two alphabetical lists. Tables list keys-trokes, command name, and description. C- indicates the Control key; M- indicates the Meta key.

Control-Key Sequences

Binding	Command	Action
C-@	set-mark-command	Mark the beginning (or end) of a region.
C-SPACE	(same as above)	(same as above)
C-]	(none)	Exit recursive edit and exit query-replace.
C-a	beginning-of-line	Move to beginning of line.
C-b	backward-char	Move *backward* one character (left).
C-c C-c	interrupt-shell-subjob	Terminate the current job.
C-c C-d	shell-send-eof	End of file character.
C-c C-u	kill-shell-input	Erase current line.
C-c C-w	backward-kill-word	Erase the previous word.
C-c C-z	stop-shell-subjob	Suspend the current job.
C-d	delete-char	Delete character under cursor.
C-e	end-of-line	Move to *end* of line.
C-f	forward-char	Move *forward* one character (right).
C-g	keyboard-quit	Abort current command.
C-h	help-command	Enter the online help system.
C-h a	command-apropos	What commands involve this concept?
C-h b	describe-bindings	What are all the key bindings for this buffer?

Binding	Command	Action
C-h C-c	describe-copying	View the Emacs General Public License.
C-h C-d	describe-distribution	View information on ordering Emacs from FSF.
C-h C-w	describe-no-warranty	View the (non)warranty for Emacs.
C-h c	describe-key-briefly	What command does this keystroke sequence run?
C-h f	describe-function	What does this function do?
C-h i	info	Start the info documentation reader.
C-h k	describe-key	What command does this keystroke sequence run, and what does it do?
C-h l	view-lossage	What are the last 100 characters I typed?
C-h m	describe-mode	Tell me about the mode the current buffer is in.
C-h n	view-emacs-news	View news about updates to Emacs.
C-h s	describe-syntax	What is the syntax table for this buffer?
C-h t	help-with-tutorial	Run the Emacs tutorial.
C-h v	describe-variable	What does this variable mean, and what is its value?
C-h w	where-is	What is the key binding for this command?
C-k	kill-line	Delete from cursor to end of line.
C-l	recenter	Redraw screen with current line in the center.
C-n	next-line	Move to *next* line (down).
C-p	previous-line	Move to *previous* line (up).
C-r	isearch-backward	Start or repeat nonincremental search backward.
C-r	(none)	Enter recursive edit (during query replace).
C-r	isearch-backward	Start incremental search backward.
C-s	isearch-forward	Start or repeat nonincremental search forward.
C-s	isearch-forward	Start incremental search forward.
C-t	transpose-chars	Transpose two letters.
C-u *n*	universal-argument	Repeat the next command *n* times.
C-u C-x (	start-kbd-macro	Execute last macro defined, then add keystrokes.
C-u C-x q	(none)	Insert recursive edit in a macro definition.
C-v	scroll-up	Move forward one screen.
C-w	kill-region	Delete a marked region.
C-x (	start-kbd-macro	Start macro definition.
C-x)	end-kbd-macro	End macro definition.
C-x [	backward-page	Move backward one page.
C-x]	forward-page	Move forward one page.
C-x ^	enlarge-window	Make window taller.
C-x {	shrink-window-horizontally	Make window narrower.
C-x }	enlarge-window-horizontally	Make window wider.
C-x <	scroll-left	Scroll the window left.
C-x >	scroll-right	Scroll the window right.
C-x -	inverse-add-global-abbrev	Type global abbreviation, then definition.
C-x .	set-fill-prefix	Prepend each line in paragraph with characters from beginning of line up to cursor column; cancel prefix by typing this command in column 1.
C-x 0	delete-window	Delete current window.
C-x 1	delete-other-windows	Delete all windows but this one.

Emacs

Binding	Command	Action
C-x 2	split-window-horizon-tally	Divide current window horizontally into two.
C-x 4 b	switch-to-buffer-other-window	Select a buffer in the other window.
C-x 4 f	find-file-other-window	Find a file in the other window.
C-x 5	split-window-vertically	Divide current window vertically into two.
C-x b	switch-to-buffer	Move to the buffer specified.
C-x C-b	list-buffers	Display the buffer list.
C-x C-c	save-buffers-kill-emacs	Exit Emacs.
C-x C-f	find-file	Find file and read it.
C-x C-h	inverse-add-local-abbrev	Type local abbreviation, then definition.
C-x C-l	downcase-region	Lowercase region.
C-x C-p	mark-page	Place cursor and mark around whole page.
C-x C-q	(none)	Toggle read-only status of buffer.
C-x C-s	save-buffer	Save file.
C-x C-t	transpose-lines	Transpose two lines.
C-x C-u	upcase-region	Uppercase region.
C-x C-v	find-alternate-file	Read an alternate file, replacing the one read with C-x C-f.
C-x C-w	write-file	Write buffer contents to file.
C-x C-x	exchange-point-and-mark	Exchange location of cursor and mark.
C-x DEL	backward-kill-sentence	Delete previous sentence.
C-x e	call-last-kbd-macro	Execute last macro defined.
C-x h	mark-whole-buffer	Place cursor and mark around whole buffer.
C-x i	insert-file	Insert file at cursor position.
C-x k	kill-buffer	Delete the buffer specified.
C-x o	other-window	Move to the other window.
C-x q	kbd-macro-query	Insert a query in a macro definition.
C-x s	save-some-buffers	Ask whether to save each modified buffer.
C-x u	advertised-undo	Undo last edit (can be done repeatedly).
C-y	yank	Restore what you've deleted.
C-z	suspend-emacs	Suspend Emacs (use **exit** or **fg** to restart).

Meta-Key Sequences

Binding	Command	Action
M- – M-c	negative-argument; capitalize-word	Capitalize previous word.
M- – M-l	negative-argument; downcase-word	Lowercase previous word.
M- – M-u	negative-argument; upcase-word	Uppercase previous word.
M-$	spell-word	Check spelling of word after cursor.
M-<	beginning-of-buffer	Move to beginning of file.
M->	end-of-buffer	Move to end of file.
M-{	backward-paragraph	Move backward one paragraph.

Binding	Command	Action
M-}	forward-paragraph	Move forward one paragraph.
M-^	delete-indentation	Join this line to the previous one.
M-*n*	digit-argument	Repeat the next command *n* times.
M-*n* C-x e	digit-argument and call-last-kbd-macro	Execute the last defined macro *n* times.
M-a	backward-sentence	Move backward one sentence.
M-b	backward-word	Move one word *backward*.
M-C-\	indent-region	Indent a region to match first line in region.
M-C-c	exit-recursive-edit	Exit a recursive edit.
M-C-o	split-line	Split line at cursor; indent to column of cursor.
M-C-r	isearch-backward-regexp	Incremental search backward for regular expression.
M-C-s	isearch-forward-regexp	Incremental search forward for regular expression.
M-C-v	scroll-other-window	Scroll other window.
M-c	capitalize-word	Capitalize first letter of word.
M-d	kill-word	Delete word that cursor is on.
M-DEL	backward-kill-word	Delete previous word.
M-e	forward-sentence	Move forward one sentence.
M-f	forward-word	Move one word *forward*.
M-g	fill-region	Reformat individual paragraphs within a region.
M-h	mark-paragraph	Place cursor and mark around whole paragraph.
M-k	kill-sentence	Delete sentence the cursor is on.
M-l	downcase-word	Lowercase word.
M-m	back-to-indentation	Move cursor to first nonblank character on line.
M-q	fill-paragraph	Reformat paragraph.
M-s	center-line	Center line that cursor is on.
M-t	transpose-words	Transpose two words.
M-u	upcase-word	Uppercase word.
M-v	scroll-down	Move backward one screen.
M-x	(none)	Execute a command by typing its name.

Summary of Commands by Name

The Emacs commands below are presented alphabetically by command name. Use M-x to access the command name. Tables list command name, keystroke, and description. C- indicates the Control key; M- indicates the Meta key.

Command	Binding	Action
macroname	(none)	Execute a keyboard macro you've saved.
abbrev-mode	(none)	Enter (or exit) word abbreviation mode.
advertised-undo	C-x u	Undo last edit (can be done repeatedly).
apropos	(none)	What functions and variables involve this concept?
back-to-indentation	M-m	Move cursor to first nonblank character on line.
backward-char	C-b	Move backward one character (left).
backward-delete-char	DEL	Delete previous character.
backward-kill-paragraph	(none)	Delete previous paragraph.

Command	Binding	Action
backward-kill-sentence	C-x DEL	Delete previous sentence.
backward-kill-word	C-c C-w	Erase previous word.
backward-kill-word	M-DEL	Delete previous word.
backward-page	C-x [	Move backward one page.
backward-paragraph	M-{	Move backward one paragraph.
backward-sentence	M-a	Move backward one sentence.
backward-word	M-b	Move backward one word.
beginning-of-buffer	M-<	Move to beginning of file.
beginning-of-line	C-a	Move to beginning of line.
call-last-kbd-macro	C-x e	Execute last macro defined.
capitalize-region	(none)	Capitalize region.
capitalize-word	M-c	Capitalize first letter of word.
center-line	M-s	Center line that cursor is on.
center-paragraph	(none)	Center paragraph that cursor is on.
center-region	(none)	Center currently defined region.
command-apropos	C-h a	What commands involve this concept?
compare-windows	(none)	Compare two buffers; show first difference.
delete-char	C-d	Delete character under cursor.
delete-indentation	M-^	Join this line to previous one.
delete-other-windows	C-x 1	Delete all windows but this one.
delete-window	C-x 0	Delete current window.
delete-windows-on	(none)	Delete all windows on a given buffer.
describe-bindings	C-h b	What are all the key bindings for in this buffer?
describe-copying	C-h C-c	View the Emacs General Public License.
describe-distribution	C-h C-d	View information on ordering Emacs from FSF.
describe-function	C-h f	What does this function do?
describe-key	C-h k	What command does this keystroke sequence run, and what does it do?
describe-key-briefly	C-h c	What command does this keystroke sequence run?
describe-mode	C-h m	Tell me about the mode the current buffer is in.
describe-no-warranty	C-h C-w	View the (non)warranty for Emacs.
describe-syntax	C-h s	What is the syntax table for this buffer?
describe-variable	C-h v	What does this variable mean, and what is its value?
digit-argument	M-n	Repeat next command n times.
downcase-region	C-x C-l	Lowercase region.
downcase-word	M-l	Lowercase word.
edit-abbrevs	(none)	Edit word abbreviations.
end-kbd-macro	C-x)	End macro definition.
end-of-buffer	M->	Move to end of file.
end-of-line	C-e	Move to end of line.
enlarge-window	C-x ^	Make window taller.
enlarge-window-horizontally	C-x }	Make window wider.
exchange-point-and-mark	C-x C-x	Exchange location of cursor and mark.
exit-recursive-edit	M-C-c	Exit a recursive edit.

Command	Binding	Action
fill-individual-paragraphs	(none)	Reformat indented paragraphs, keeping indentation.
fill-paragraph	M-q	Reformat paragraph.
fill-region	M-g	Reformat individual paragraphs within a region.
find-alternate-file	C-x C-v	Read an alternate file, replacing the one read with C-x C-f.
find-file	C-x C-f	Find file and read it.
find-file-other-window	C-x 4 f	Find a file in the other window.
forward-char	C-f	Move forward one character (right).
forward-page	C-x]	Move forward one page.
forward-paragraph	M-}	Move forward one paragraph.
forward-sentence	M-e	Move forward one sentence.
forward-word	M-f	Move forward one word.
goto-char	(none)	Go to character n of file.
goto-line	(none)	Go to line n of file.
help-command	C-h	Enter the online help system.
help-with-tutorial	C-h t	Run the Emacs tutorial.
indent-region	M-C-\	Indent a region to match first line in region.
indented-text-mode	(none)	Major mode: each tab defines a new indent for subsequent lines.
info	C-h i	Start the info documentation reader.
insert-file	C-x i	Insert file at cursor position.
insert-last-keyboard-macro	(none)	Insert the macro you named into a file.
interrupt-shell-subjob	C-c C-c	Terminate the current job.
inverse-add-global-abbrev	C-x -	Type global abbreviation, then definition.
inverse-add-local-abbrev	C-x C-h	Type local abbreviation, then definition.
isearch-backward	C-r	Start incremental search backward.
isearch-backward-regexp	M-C-r	Same, but search for regular expression.
isearch-forward	C-s	Start incremental search forward.
isearch-forward-regexp	M-C-s	Same, but search for regular expression.
kbd-macro-query	C-x q	Insert a query in a macro definition.
keyboard-quit	C-g	Abort current command.
kill-all-abbrevs	(none)	Kill abbreviations for this session.
kill-buffer	C-x k	Delete the buffer specified.
kill-line	C-k	Delete from cursor to end of line.
kill-paragraph	(none)	Delete from cursor to end of paragraph.
kill-region	C-w	Delete a marked region.
kill-sentence	M-k	Delete sentence the cursor is on.
kill-shell-input	C-c C-u	Erase current line.
kill-some-buffers	(none)	Ask about deleting each buffer.
kill-word	M-d	Delete word the cursor is on.
list-abbrevs	(none)	View word abbreviations.
list-buffers	C-x C-b	Display buffer list.
load-file	(none)	Load macro files you've saved.
mark-page	C-x C-p	Place cursor and mark around whole page.
mark-paragraph	M-h	Place cursor and mark around whole paragraph.
mark-whole-buffer	C-x h	Place cursor and mark around whole buffer.

Command	Binding	Action
name-last-kbd-macro	(none)	Name last macro you created (before saving it).
negative-argument; capitalize-word	M- – M-c	Capitalize previous word.
negative-argument; downcase-word	M- – M-l	Lowercase previous word.
negative-argument; upcase-word	M- – M-u	Uppercase previous word.
next-line	C-n	Move to next line (down).
other-window	C-x o	Move to the other window.
previous-line	C-p	Move to previous line (up).
query-replace-regexp	(none)	Query-replace a regular expression.
recenter	C-l	Redraw screen, with current line in center.
rename-buffer	(none)	Change buffer name to specified name.
replace-regexp	(none)	Replace a regular expression unconditionally.
re-search-backward	(none)	Simple regular expression search backward.
re-search-forward	(none)	Simple regular expression search forward.
revert-buffer	(none)	Restore buffer to the state it was in when the file was last saved (or auto-saved).
save-buffer	C-x C-s	Save file.
save-buffers-kill-emacs	C-x C-c	Exit Emacs.
save-some-buffers	C-x s	Ask whether to save each modified buffer.
scroll-down	M-v	Move backward one screen.
scroll-left	C-x <	Scroll the window left.
scroll-other-window	M-C-v	Scroll other window.
scroll-right	C-x >	Scroll the window right.
scroll-up	C-v	Move forward one screen.
set-fill-prefix	C-x .	Prepend each line in paragraph with characters from beginning of line up to cursor column; cancel prefix by typing this command in column 1.
set-mark-command	C-@ or C-SPACE	Mark the beginning (or end) of a region.
shell-send-eof	C-c C-d	End of file character.
shrink-window	(none)	Make window shorter.
shrink-window-horizontally	C-x {	Make window narrower.
spell-buffer	(none)	Check spelling of current buffer.
spell-region	(none)	Check spelling of current region.
spell-string	(none)	Check spelling of string typed in minibuffer.
spell-word	M-$	Check spelling of word after cursor.
split-line	M-C-o	Split line at cursor; indent to column of cursor.
split-window-horizontally	C-x 2	Divide current window horizontally into two.
split-window-vertically	C-x 5	Divide current window vertically into two.
start-kbd-macro	C-x (	Start macro definition.
stop-shell-subjob	C-c C-z	Suspend current job.
suspend-emacs	C-z	Suspend Emacs (use exit or fg to restart).
switch-to-buffer	C-x b	Move to the buffer specified.
switch-to-buffer-other-window	C-x 4 b	Select a buffer in the other window.

Command	Binding	Action
text-mode	(none)	Enter text mode.
transpose-chars	C-t	Transpose two letters.
transpose-lines	C-x C-t	Transpose two lines.
transpose-paragraphs	(none)	Transpose two paragraphs.
transpose-sentences	(none)	Transpose two sentences.
transpose-words	M-t	Transpose two words.
unexpand-abbrev	(none)	Undo the last word abbreviation.
universal-argument	C-u n	Repeat the next command n times.
upcase-region	C-x C-u	Uppercase region.
upcase-word	M-u	Uppercase word.
view-emacs-news	C-h n	View news about updates to Emacs.
view-lossage	C-h l	What are the last 100 characters I typed?
where-is	C-h w	What is the key binding for this command?
write-abbrev-file	(none)	Write the word abbreviation file.
write-file	C-x C-w	Write buffer contents to file.
yank	C-y	Restore what you've deleted.

Emacs

CHAPTER 8

The vi Editor

Linux systems usually provide an enhanced **vi** called **vim** or **nvi**. This section presents the following topics:

- Review of **vi** operations
- Movement commands
- Edit commands
- Saving and exiting
- Accessing multiple files
- Interacting with the shell
- Macros
- Miscellaneous commands
- Alphabetical list of keys
- Setting up **vi**

Review of vi Operations

This subsection provides a review of the following:

- Command-Line syntax
- **vi** modes
- Syntax of **vi** commands
- Status-Line commands

For more information on **vi**, refer to the Nutshell Handbook *Learning the vi Editor*, by Linda Lamb.

Command-line Syntax

The three most common ways of starting a **vi** session are:

> **vi** *file*
> **vi** *+n file*
> **vi** *+/pattern file*

You can open *file* for editing, optionally at line *n* or at the first line matching *pattern*. If no *file* is specified, **vi** opens with an empty buffer.

Command Mode

Once the file is opened, you are in command mode. From command mode, you can:

- Invoke insert mode
- Issue editing commands
- Move the cursor to a different position in the file
- Invoke **ex** commands
- Invoke a Linux shell
- Save or exit the current version of the file

Insert Mode

In insert mode, you can enter new text in the file. Press the ESCAPE key to exit insert mode and return to command mode. The following commands invoke insert mode:

a   Append after cursor.
A   Append at end of line.
c   Begin change operation.
C   Change to end of line.
i   Insert before cursor.
I   Insert at beginning of line.
o   Open a line below current line.
O   Open a line above current line.
R   Begin overwriting text.
s   Substitute a character.
S   Substitute entire line.

Syntax of vi Commands

In **vi**, commands have the following general form:

> *[n] operator [m] object*

The basic editing *operators* are:

c	Begin a change.
d	Begin a deletion.
y	Begin a yank (or copy).

If the current line is the object of the operation, then the operator is the same as the object: **cc**, **dd**, **yy**. Otherwise, the editing operators act on objects specified by cursor-movement commands or pattern-matching commands. *n* and *m* are the number of times the operation is performed, or the number of objects the operation is performed on. If both *n* and *m* are specified, the effect is *n* × *m*.

An object can represent any of the following text blocks:

word	Includes characters up to a space or punctuation mark. A capitalized object is a variant form that recognizes only blank spaces.
sentence	Extends to ., !, ? followed by two spaces.
paragraph	Extends to next blank line or paragraph macro defined by **para=** option.
section	Extends to next section heading defined by **sect=** option.

Examples

2cw	Change the next two words.
d}	Delete up to next paragraph.
d^	Delete back to beginning of line.
5yy	Copy the next five lines.
y]]	Copy up to the next section.

Status-Line Commands

Most commands are not echoed on the screen as you input them. However, the status line at the bottom of the screen is used to echo input for the following commands:

/	Search forward for a pattern.
?	Search backward for a pattern.
:	Invoke an **ex** command.
!	Invoke a shell command that takes as its input an object in the buffer and replaces it with output from the command.

Commands that are input on the status line must be entered by pressing the RETURN key. In addition, error messages and output from the **CTRL-G** command are displayed on the status line.

Movement Commands

A number preceding a command repeats the movement. Movement commands are also objects for change, delete, and yank operations.

Character

h, j, k, l	Left, down, up, right ($\leftarrow$, $\downarrow$, $\uparrow$, $\rightarrow$)
SPACEBAR	Right

Text

w, W, b, B	Forward, backward by word
e, E	End of word
), (	Beginning of next, current sentence
}, {	Beginning of next, current paragraph
]], [[	Beginning of next, current section

Lines

0, $	First, last position of current line
^	First nonblank character of current line
+, -	First character of next, previous line
RETURN	First character of next line
n		Column n of current line
H	Top line of screen
M	Middle line of screen
L	Last line of screen
nH	n lines after top line
nL	n lines before last line

Screens

CTRL-F, CTRL-B	Scroll forward, backward one screen.
CTRL-D, CTRL-U	Scroll down, up one-half screen.
CTRL-E, CTRL-Y	Show one more line at bottom, top of window.
z RETURN	Reposition line with cursor to top of screen.
z .	Reposition line with cursor to middle of screen.
z -	Reposition line with cursor to bottom of screen.
CTRL-L, CTRL-R	Redraw screen (without scrolling).

Searches

/pattern	Search forward for *pattern*.
/	Repeat forward search.
/pattern/+n	Go to line n after *pattern*.
?pattern	Search backward for *pattern*.
?	Repeat previous search backward.
?pattern?-n	Go to line n before *pattern*.
n	Repeat previous search.

N	Repeat search in opposite direction.
%	Find match of current parenthesis, brace, or bracket.
f*x*	Move forward to *x* on current line.
F*x*	Move backward to *x* on current line.
t*x*	Move forward to just before *x* in current line.
T*x*	Move back to just after *x* in current line.
,	Reverse search direction of last f, F, t, or T.
;	Repeat last character search (f, F, t, or T).

Line numbering

CTRL-G	Display current line number.
*n*G	Move to line number *n*.
G	Move to last line in file.
:*n*	Move to line number *n*.

Marking position

m*x*	Mark current position with character *x*.
`*x*	(backquote) Move cursor to mark *x*.
'*x*	(apostrophe) Move to start of line containing *x*.
``	(backquotes) Return to previous mark (or to location prior to a search).
''	(apostrophes) Like above, but return to start of line.

Edit Commands

Recall that c, d, and y are the basic editing operators.

Inserting New Text

a	Append after cursor.
A	Append to end of line.
i	Insert before cursor.
I	Insert at beginning of line.
o	Open a line below cursor.
O	Open a line above cursor.
ESC	Terminate insert mode.
TAB	Insert a tab.
BACKSPACE	Move back one character.
RETURN	Move down one line.
CTRL-J	Move down one line.
CTRL-I	Insert a tab.
CTRL-T	Move to next tab setting.
CTRL-D	Move to previous tab setting.
CTRL-H	Move back one character.
CTRL-U	Delete current line.
CTRL-V	Insert next character verbatim.
CTRL-W	Move back one word.

The last four control characters are set by **stty**. Your terminal settings may differ.

Changing and Deleting Text

cw	Change word.
cc	Change line.
c	Change text from current position to end of line.
dd	Delete current line.
ndd	Delete n lines.
D	Delete remainder of line.
dw	Delete a word.
d}	Delete up to next paragraph.
d^	Delete back to beginning of line.
d/pat	Delete up to first occurrence of pattern.
dn	Delete up to next occurrence of pattern.
dfa	Delete up to and including a on current line.
dta	Delete up to (not including) a on current line.
dL	Delete up to last line on screen.
dG	Delete to end of file.
p	Insert last deleted text after cursor.
P	Insert last deleted text before cursor.
rx	Replace character with x.
Rtext	Replace *text* beginning at cursor.
s	Substitute character.
ns	Substitute n characters.
S	Substitute entire line.
u	Undo last change.
U	Restore current line.
x	Delete current cursor position.
X	Delete back one character.
nX	Delete previous n characters.
.	Repeat last change.
~	Reverse case.

Copying and moving

Y	Copy current line to new buffer.
yy	Copy current line.
"xyy	Yank current line to buffer x.
"xd	Delete into buffer x.
"Xd	Delete and append into buffer x.
"xp	Put contents of buffer x.
y]]	Copy up to next section heading.
ye	Copy to end of word.

Saving and Exiting

Writing a file means saving the edits and updating the file's modification time.

ZZ	Quit **vi**, writing the file only if changes were made.
:x	Same as **ZZ**.
:wq	Write and quit file.
:w	Write file.

:w *file*	Save copy to *file*.
:n1,n2w *file*	Write lines *n1* to *n2* to new *file*.
:n1,n2w >> *file*	Append lines *n1* to *n2* to existing *file*.
:w!	Write file (overriding protection).
:w! *file*	Overwrite *file* with current buffer.
:w %.new	Write current buffer named *file* as *file.new*.
:q	Quit file.
:q!	Quit file (discarding edits).
Q	Quit **vi** and invoke **ex**.
:vi	Return to **vi** after **Q** command.
:e *file2*	Edit *file2* without leaving **vi**.
:n	Edit next file.
:e!	Return to version of current file at time of last write.
:e#	Edit alternate file.
%	Current filename.
#	Alternate filename.

Accessing Multiple Files

:e *file*	Edit another *file*; current file becomes alternate.
:e!	Restore last saved version of current file.
:e + *file*	Begin editing at end of *file*.
:e +*n* *file*	Open *file* at line *n*.
:e #	Open to previous position in alternate file.
:ta *tag*	Edit file at location *tag*.
:n	Edit next file.
:n!	Force next file.
:n *files*	Specify new list of *files*.
CTRL-G	Show current file and line number.
:args	Display multiple files to be edited.
:rew	Rewind list of multiple files to top.

Interacting with the Shell

:r *file*	Read in contents of *file* after cursor.
:r !*command*	Read in output from *command* after current line.
:nr !*command*	Like above, but place after line *n* (0 for top of file).
:!*command*	Run *command*, then return.
!*object command*	Send buffer *object* to *command*; replace with output.
:n1,n2! *command*	Send lines *n1* – *n2* to *command*; replace with output.
n!!*command*	Send *n* lines to *command*; replace with output.
!!	Repeat last system command.
:sh	Create subshell; return to file with *EOF*.
CTRL-Z	Suspend editor, resume with **fg**.
:so *file*	Read and execute commands from *file*.

Macros

:ab *in out*	Use *in* as abbreviation for *out*.
:unab *in*	Remove abbreviation for *in*.
:ab	List abbreviations.
:map *c sequence*	Map character *c* as *sequence* of commands.
:unmap *c*	Disable map for character *c*.
:map	List characters that are mapped.
:map! *c sequence*	Map character *c* to input mode *sequence*.
:unmap! *c*	Disable input mode map (you may need to quote the character with **CTRL-V**).
:map!	List characters that are mapped to input mode.

The following characters are unused in command mode and can be mapped as user-defined commands.

Letters:	g K q V v
Control keys:	^A ^K ^O ^T ^W ^X
Symbols:	_ * \ =

(Note: The = is used by **vi** if Lisp mode is set.)

Miscellaneous Commands

J	Join two lines.
:j!	Join two lines, preserving blank spaces.
<<	Shift this line left one shift width (default is 8 spaces).
>>	Shift this line right one shift width (default is 8 spaces).
>}	Shift right to end of paragraph.
<%	Shift left until matching parenthesis, brace, bracket, etc. (Cursor must be on the matching symbol.)

Alphabetical List of Keys

For brevity, control characters are marked by ^.

a	Append text after cursor.
A	Append text at end of line.
^A	Unused.
b	Back up to beginning of word in current line.
B	Back up to word, ignoring punctuation.
^B	Scroll backward one window.
c	Change operator.
C	Change to end of current line.
^C	Unused in command mode; ends insert mode.
d	Delete operator.
D	Delete to end of current line.
^D	Scroll down half-window; in insert mode, unindent to **shiftwidth** if **autoindent** is set.
e	Move to end of word.

E	Move to end of word, ignoring punctuation.
^E	Show one more line at bottom of window.
f	Find next character typed forward on current line.
F	Find next character typed backward on current line.
^F	Scroll forward one window.
g	Unused.
G	Go to specified line or end of file.
^G	Print information about file on status line.
h	Left arrow cursor key.
H	Move cursor to Home position.
^H	Left arrow cursor key; Backspace key in insert mode.
i	Insert text before cursor.
I	Insert text before first nonblank character on line.
^I	Unused in command mode; in insert mode, same as TAB key.
j	Down arrow cursor key.
J	Join two lines.
^J	Down arrow cursor key; in insert mode, move down a line.
k	Up arrow cursor key.
K	Unused.
^K	Unused.
l	Right arrow cursor key.
L	Move cursor to Last position in window.
^L	Redraw screen.
m	Mark the current cursor position in register (a-z).
M	Move cursor to Middle position in window.
^M	Carriage return.
n	Repeat the last search command.
N	Repeat the last search command in reverse direction.
^N	Down arrow cursor key.
o	Open line below current line.
O	Open line above current line.
^O	Unused.
p	Put yanked or deleted text after or below cursor.
P	Put yanked or deleted text before or above cursor.
^P	Up arrow cursor key.
q	Unused.
Q	Quit **vi** and invoke **ex**.
^Q	Unused. (On some terminals, resume data flow.)
r	Replace character at cursor with the next character you type.
R	Replace characters.
^R	Redraw the screen.
s	Change the character under the cursor to typed characters.
S	Change entire line.
^S	Unused. (On some terminals, stop data flow.)

t	Move cursor forward to character before next character typed.
T	Move cursor backward to character after next character typed.
^T	Unused in command mode; in insert mode, move to next tab setting.
u	Undo the last change made.
U	Restore current line, discarding changes.
^U	Scroll the screen upward a half-window.
v	Unused.
V	Unused.
^V	Unused in command mode; in insert mode, insert next character verbatim.
w	Move to beginning of next word.
W	Move to beginning of next word, ignoring punctuation.
^W	Unused in command mode; in insert mode, back up to beginning of word.
x	Delete character under cursor.
X	Delete character before cursor.
^X	Unused.
y	Yank or copy operator.
Y	Make copy of current line.
^Y	Show one more line at top of window.
z	Reposition line containing cursor. z must be followed either by: RETURN (reposition line to top of screen), . (reposition line to middle of screen), or – (reposition line to bottom of screen).
ZZ	Exit the editor, saving changes.
^Z	Suspend **vi**.

Setting Up vi

This subsection describes the following:

- The :**set** command

- Options available with :**set**

- Sample *.exrc* file

The :set Command

The :**set** command lets you specify options that change characteristics of your editing environment. Options may be put in the *.exrc* file or set during a vi session.

The colon should not be typed if the command is put in *.exrc*.

:set *x*	Enable option *x*.
:set no*x*	Disable option *x*.
:set *x=val*	Give *value* to option *x*.
:set	Show changed options.
:set all	Show all options.
:set *x?*	Show value of option *x*.

Options Used by :set

The following table describes the options to :set. The first column includes the optional abbreviation, if there is one, and uses an equal sign to show that the option takes a value. The second column gives the default, and the third column describes the behavior of the enabled option.

Option	Default	Description
autoindent (ai)	noai	In insert mode, indent each line to the same level as the line above or below. Use with **shiftwidth** option.
autoprint (ap)	ap	Display changes after each editor command. (For global replacement, display last replacement.)
autowrite (aw)	noaw	Automatically write (save) file if changed, before opening another file with :n or before giving Linux command with :!.
beautify (bf)	nobf	Ignore all control characters during input (except tab, newline, or formfeed).
directory= (dir)	/tmp	Name the directory in which **ex** stores buffer files. (Directory must be writable.)
edcompatible	noedcompatible	Use **ed**-like features on substitute commands.
errorbells (eb)	errorbells	Sound bell when an error occurs.
exrc (ex)	noexrc	Allow the execution of .*exrc* files that reside outside the user's home directory.
hardtabs= (ht)	8	Define boundaries for terminal hardware tabs.
ignorecase (ic)	noic	Disregard case during a search.
lisp	nolisp	Insert indents in appropriate Lisp format. ( ), { }, [[, and]] are modified to have meaning for Lisp.
list	nolist	Print tabs as ^I; mark ends of lines with $. (Use **list** to tell if end character is a tab or a space.)
magic	magic	Wildcard characters . (dot), * (asterisk), and [ ] (brackets) have special meaning in patterns.
mesg	mesg	Permit system messages to display on terminal while editing in **vi**.

Option	Default	Description
number (nu)	nonu	Display line numbers on left of screen during editing session.
open	open	Allow entry to open mode from **ex**.
optimize (opt)	noopt	Abolish carriage returns at the end of lines when printing multiple lines; speeds output on dumb terminals when printing lines with leading white space (blanks or tabs).
paragraphs= (para)	IPLPPPQPLI pplpipbp	Define paragraph delimiters for movement by { or }. The pairs of characters in the value are the names of nroff/troff macros that begin paragraphs.
prompt	prompt	Display the **ex** prompt (:) when vi's **Q** command is given.
readonly (ro)	noro	Any writes (saves) of a file will fail unless you use ! after the write (works with **w**, **ZZ**, or **autowrite**).
redraw (re)	noredraw	Terminal redraws screen whenever edits are made (in other words, insert mode pushes over existing characters, and deleted lines immediately close up). Default depends on line speed and terminal type. **noredraw** is useful at slow speeds on a dumb terminal: deleted lines show up as @, and inserted text appears to overwrite existing text until you press ESC.
remap	remap	Allow nested map sequences.
report=	5	Display a message on the prompt line whenever you make an edit that affects at least a certain number of lines. For example, 6dd reports the message "6 lines deleted."
scroll=	<1/2 window>	Amount of screen to scroll.
sections= (sect)	SHNHH HU	Define section delimiters for [[ ]] movement. The pairs of characters in the value are the names of nroff/troff macros that begin sections.
shell= (sh)	/bin/sh	Pathname of shell used for shell escape (:!) and shell command (:sh). Default value is derived from SHELL variable.
shiftwidth= (sw)	8	Define number of spaces used by the indent commands (^T, ^D, >>, and <<).

Option	Default	Description
showmatch (sm)	nosm	In **vi**, when) or } is entered, cursor moves briefly to matching (or {. (If the match is not on the screen, rings the error message bell.) Very useful for programming.
showmode	noshowmode	In insert mode, displays a message on the prompt line indicating the type of insert you are making. For example, "Open Mode" or "Append Mode."
slowopen (slow)		Hold off display during insert. Default depends on line speed and terminal type.
tabstop= (ts)	8	Define number of spaces that a tab indents during editing session. (Printer still uses system tab of 8.)
taglength= (tl)	0	Define number of characters that are significant for tags. Default (zero) means that all characters are significant.
tags=	tags /usr/lib/tags	Define pathname of files containing tags (see the **ctags** command in Chapter 12). By default, the system looks for files **tags** (in the current directory) and */usr/lib/tags*.
term=		Set terminal type.
terse	noterse	Display shorter error messages.
timeout (to)	timeout	Keyboard maps "time out" after 1 second.
ttytype=		Set terminal type. Default is inherited from TERM environment variable.
warn	warn	Display the message, "No write since last change."
window= (w)		Show a certain number of lines of the file on the screen. Default depends on line speed and terminal type.
wrapmargin= (wm)	0	Define right margin. If greater than zero, automatically insert carriage returns to break lines.
wrapscan (ws)	ws	Searches wrap around either end of file.
writeany (wa)	nowa	Allow saving to any file.

Sample .exrc File

```
set nowrapscan wrapmargin=7
set sections=SeAhBhChDh nomesg
map q :w^M:n^M
map v dwElp
ab ORA O'Reilly & Associates, Inc.
```

CHAPTER 9

The ex Editor

ex is a line editor that serves as the foundation for the screen editor **vi**. **ex** commands work on the current line or on a range of lines in a file. On Linux, **ex** is often called **hex**.

Most often, you use **ex** from within **vi**. In **vi**, **ex** commands are preceded by a colon and entered by pressing RETURN.

But you can invoke **ex** on its own—from the command line—just as you would invoke **vi**. (You could execute an **ex** script this way.) You can also use the **vi** command **Q** to quit the **vi** editor and enter **ex**.

This section presents the following topics:

- Syntax of **ex** commands

- Alphabetical summary of commands

For more information, see the Nutshell Handbook *Learning the vi Editor* by Linda Lamb.

Syntax of ex Commands

To enter an **ex** command from **vi**, type:

>   :[*address*] *command* [*options*]

An initial : indicates an **ex** command. As you type the command, it is echoed on the status line. Enter the command by pressing RETURN. *address* is the line number or range of lines that are the object of *command. options* and *addresses* are described in the following sections. **ex** commands are described in the alphabetical summary.

You can exit **ex** in several ways:

    :x Exit (save changes and quit).

    :q! Quit without saving changes.

    :vi Enter the **vi** editor.

Options

!	Indicates a variant command form, overriding the normal behavior.
count	The number of times the command is to be repeated. Unlike **vi** commands, **ex** commands cannot be preceded by *count*, because a number preceding an **ex** command is treated as a line address. For example, **d3** deletes three lines beginning with the current line; **3d** deletes line 3.
file	The name of a file that is affected by the command. % stands for current file; # stands for previous file.

Addresses

If no address is given, the current line is the object of the command. If the address specifies a range of lines, the format is:

    x,y

where *x* and *y* are the first and last addressed lines (*x* must precede *y* in the buffer). *x* and *y* may be line numbers or symbols. Using ; instead of , sets the current line to *x* before interpreting *y*. The notation **1,$** addresses all lines in the file, as does %.

Address Symbols

1,$	All lines in the file
%	All lines; same as **1,$**
x,y	Lines *x* through *y*
x;y	Lines *x* through *y*, with current line reset to *x*
0	Top of file
.	Current line
n	Absolute line number *n*
$	Last line
x-n	*n* lines before *x*
x+n	*n* lines after *x*
-[n]	One or *n* lines previous
+[n]	One or *n* lines ahead
'x	Line marked with *x*
' '	Previous mark
/pattern/	Forward to line matching *pattern*
?pattern?	Backward to line matching *pattern*

See Chapter 6, *Pattern Matching*, for more information on using patterns.

Alphabetical Summary of ex Commands

ex commands can be entered by specifying any unique abbreviation. In this listing, the full name appears in the margin, and the shortest possible abbreviation is used in the syntax line. Examples are assumed to be typed from **vi**, so they include the : prompt.

---

ab [*string text*]

Define *string* when typed to be translated into *text*. If *string* and *text* are not specified, list all current abbreviations.

Examples

> Note: ^M appears when you type **CTRL-V** followed by RETURN.

```
:ab ora O'Reilly & Associates, Inc.
:ab id Name:^MRank:^MPhone:
```

abbrev

[*address*] **a**[!]
text
.

Append *text* at specified *address*, or at present address if none is specified. Add a ! to switch the **autoindent** setting that will be used during input (e.g., if **autoindent** was enabled, ! disables it).

append

---

ar

Print filename arguments (the list of files to edit). The current argument is shown in brackets ([ ]).

args

[*address*] **c**[!]
text
.

Replace the specified lines with *text*. Add a ! to switch the **autoindent** setting during input of *text*.

change

[*address*] **co** *destination*

Copy the lines included in *address* to the specified *destination* address. The command **t** is the same as **copy**.

Example

```
:1,10 co 50        Copy first 10 lines to just after line 50
```

copy

[*address*] **d** [*buffer*]

Delete the lines included in *address*. If *buffer* is specified, save or append the text to the named buffer.

delete

→

ex Editor

delete	*Examples*	
←	`:/Part I/,/Part II/-1d`	*Delete to line above "Part II"*
	`:/main/+d`	*Delete line below "main"*
	`:.,$d`	*Delete from this line to last line*

edit

e[!] [+*n*] [*file*]

Begin editing *file*. Add a ! to discard any changes to the current file. If no *file* is given, edit another copy of the current file. With the +*n* argument, begin editing on line *n*.

Examples

`:e file`	
`:e#`	*Return to editing the previous file*
`:e!`	*Discard edits since last save*

file

f [*filename*]

Change the name of the current file to *filename*, which is considered "not edited." If no *filename* is specified, print the current status of the file.

Example

`:f %.new`

global

[*address*] g[!]/*pattern*/[*commands*]

Execute *commands* on all lines that contain *pattern* or, if *address* is specified, on all lines within that range. If *commands* are not specified, print all such lines. If ! is used, execute *commands* on all lines that don't contain *pattern*. See **v**.

Examples

`:g/Unix/p`	*Print all lines containing "Unix"*
`:g/Name:/s/tom/Tom/`	*Change "tom" to "Tom" on all lines containing "Name:"*

insert

address i[!]
text
.

Insert *text* at line before the specified *address*, or at present address if none is specified. Add a ! to switch the **autoindent** setting during input of *text*.

join

[*address*] j[!] [*count*]

Place the text in the specified *address* on one line, with whitespace adjusted to provide two blank characters after a period (.), no blank characters after a), and one blank character otherwise. Add a ! to prevent whitespace adjustment.

Example	<div align="right">join</div>

```
:1,5j!          Join first five lines, preserving whitespace
```

[*address*] k *char* k

Mark the given *address* with *char*. Return later to the line with *char*.

[*address*] l [*count*] list

Print the specified lines so that tabs display as ^I, and the ends of lines display as $. l is a temporary version of :set **list**.

---

map[!] [*char commands*] map

Define a keyboard macro named *char* as the specified sequence of *commands*. *char* is usually a single character, or the sequence #*n*, representing a function key on the keyboard. Use a ! to create a macro for input mode. With no arguments, list the currently defined macros.

Examples

```
:map  K  dwwP           Transpose two words
:map  q  :w^M:n^M       Write current file; go to next
:map! + ^[bi(^[ea)      Enclose previous word in parentheses
```

[*address*] ma *char* mark

Mark the specified line with *char*, a single lowercase letter. Return later to the line with *char*. Same as **k**.

[*address*] m *destination* move

Move the lines specified by *address* to the *destination* address.

Example

```
:.,/Note/m /END/     Move text block after line containing "END"
```

---

n[!] [[+*command*] *filelist*] next

Edit the next file from the command-line argument list. Use **args** to list these files. If *filelist* is provided, replace the current argument list with *filelist* and begin editing on the first file; if *command* is given (containing no spaces), execute *command* after editing the first such file.

Example

```
:n chap*      Start editing all "chapter" files
```

number	[*address*] **nu** [*count*]
	Print each line specified by *address*, preceded by its buffer line number. Use **#** as an alternate abbreviation for **number**. *count* specifies the number of lines to show, starting with *address*.

open	[*address*] **o** [/*pattern*/]
	Enter **vi**'s open mode at the lines specified by *address*, or at the lines matching *pattern*. Enter and exit open mode with **Q**. Open mode lets you use the regular **vi** commands, but only one line at a time. May be useful on slow dialup lines.

preserve	**pre**
	Save the current editor buffer as though the system had crashed.

print	[*address*] **p** [*count*]
	Print the lines specified by *address*. *count* specifies the number of lines to print, starting with *address*. **P** is another abbreviation.
	Example
	`:100;+5p` *Show line 100 and the next five lines*

put	[*address*] **pu** [*char*]
	Restore the lines that were previously deleted or yanked from named buffer *char*, and put them after the line specified by *address*. If *char* is not specified, restore the last deleted or yanked text.

quit	**q**[!]
	Terminate current editing session. Use **!** to discard changes made since the last save. If the editing session includes additional files in the argument list that were never accessed, quit by typing **q!** or by typing **q** twice.

read	[*address*] **r** *file*
	Copy in the text from *file* on the line below the specified *address*. If *file* is not specified, the current filename is used.
	Example
	`:0r $HOME/data` *Read file in at top of current file*

[*address*] **r** !*command*	**read**

Read the output of Linux *command* into the text after the line specified by *address*.

Example

```
:$r !cal                   Place a calendar at end of file
```

rec [*file*]	**recover**

Recover *file* from system save area.

rew[!]	**rewind**

Rewind argument list and begin editing the first file in the list. The ! flag rewinds, discarding any changes to the current file that haven't been saved.

se *parameter1 parameter2* ...	**set**

Set a value to an option with each *parameter*, or if no *parameter* is supplied, print all options that have been changed from their defaults. For Boolean-valued options, each *parameter* can be phrased as *option* or **no***option*; other options can be assigned with the syntax *option=value*. Specify **all** to list current settings.

Examples

```
:set nows wm=10
:set all
```

sh	**shell**

Create a new shell. Resume editing when the shell is terminated.

so *file*	**source**

Read and execute **ex** commands from *file*.

Example

```
:so $HOME/.exrc
```

[*address*] **s** [/*pattern*/*replacement*/] [*options*] [*count*]	**substitute**

Replace each instance of *pattern* on the specified lines with *replacement*. If *pattern* and *replacement* are omitted, repeat last substitution. *count* specifies the number of lines on which to substitute, starting with *address*. For more examples, see "Examples of Searching and Replacing" in Chapter 6.

→

substitute ←	**Options** c Prompt for confirmation before each change. g Substitute all instances of *pattern* on each line. p Print the last line on which a substitution was made. **Examples** <code>:1,10s/yes/no/g</code> *Substitute on first 10 lines* <code>:%s/[Hh]ello/Hi/gc</code> *Confirm global substitutions* <code>:s/Fortran/\U&/ 3</code> *Uppercase first instance of "Fortran"* *on next three lines*
t	[*address*] **t** *destination* Copy the lines included in *address* to the specified *destination* address. **t** is an alias for **copy**. **Example** <code>:%t$</code> *Copy the file and add it to the end*
tag	[*address*] **ta** *tag* Switch the editing session to the file containing *tag*. **Example** Run **ctags**, then switch to the file containing *myfunction*: <code>:!ctags *.c</code> <code>:tag</code> *myfunction*
unabbreviate	**una** *word* Remove *word* from the list of abbreviations.
undo	**u** Reverse the changes made by the last editing command.
unmap	**unm**[!] *char* Remove *char* from the list of keyboard macros. Use ! to remove a macro for input mode.
v	[*address*] **v**/*pattern*/[*commands*] Execute *commands* on all lines *not* containing *pattern*. If *commands* are not specified, print all such lines. **v** is equivalent to **g!**. **Example** <code>:v/#include/d</code> *Delete all lines except "#include" lines*

ve	version

Print the editor's current version number.

[*address*] **vi** [*type*] [*count*]	visual

Enter visual mode (**vi**) at the line specified by *address*. Exit with Q. *type* can be one of -, ^, or . (See the **z** command.) *count* specifies an initial window size.

vi [*+n*] file	vi

Begin editing *file* in visual mode (**vi**), optionally at line *n*.

[*address*] **w**[!] [[>>] *file*]	write

Write lines specified by *address* to *file*, or write full contents of buffer if *address* is not specified. If *file* is also omitted, save the contents of the buffer to the current filename. If >> *file* is used, write contents to the end of an existing *file*. The ! flag forces the editor to write over any current contents of *file*.

[*address*] **w** !*command*	write

Write lines specified by *address* to *command*.

Examples

```
:1,10w name_list        Copy first 10 lines to name_list
:50w >> name_list       Now append line 50
```

wq[!]	wq

Write and quit the file in one command. The ! flag forces the editor to write over any current contents of *file*.

x	xit

Write the file if it was changed since the last write; then quit.

[*address*] **ya** [*char*] [*count*]	yank

Place lines specified by *address* in named buffer *char*. If no *char* is given, place lines in general buffer. *count* specifies the number of lines to yank, starting with *address*.

Example

```
:101,200 ya a
```

z	[*address*] z [*type*] [*count*]
	
	Print a window of text, with the line specified by *address* at the top. *count* specifies the number of lines to be displayed.
	
	Type
	
	   + Place specified line at top of window (the default).
	   - Place specified line at bottom of window.
	   . Place specified line in center of window.
	   ^ Move up one window.
	   = Place specified line in center of window, and leave this line as the current line.

!	[*address*] !*command* Execute Linux *command* in a shell. If *address* is specified, apply the lines contained in *address* as standard input to *command*, and replace the lines with the output. **Examples** `:!ls` *List files in the current directory* `:11,20!sort -f` *Sort lines 11–20 of current file*
=	[*address*] = Print the line number of the next line matching *address*. If no address is given, print the number of the last line.
<>	[*address*] < [*count*] [*address*] > [*count*] Shift lines specified by *address* either left (<) or right (>). Only blanks and tabs are removed in a left shift. *count* specifies the number of lines to shift, starting with *address*.
address	*address* Print the line specified in *address*.
RETURN	RETURN Print the next line in the file.
&	& [*options*] [*count*] Repeat the previous substitution (s) command. *count* specifies the number of lines on which to substitute, starting with *address*.

Examples

```
:s/Overdue/Paid/      Substitute once on current line
:g/Status/&           Redo substitution on all "Status" lines
```

[*address*] ~ [*count*]   ~

Replace the previous regular expression with the previous
replacement pattern from a substitute (**s**) command.

ex
Editor

CHAPTER 10

The sed Editor

This chapter presents the following topics:

- Conceptual overview of **sed**

- Command-line syntax

- Syntax of **sed** commands

- Group summary of **sed** commands

- Alphabetical summary of **sed** commands

For more information, see the Nutshell Handbook *sed & awk*, Second Edition, by Dale Dougherty and Arnold Robbins.

Conceptual Overview

sed is a noninteractive, or **stream-oriented**, editor. It interprets a script and performs the actions in the script. **sed** is stream-oriented because, as with many UNIX programs, input flows through the program and is directed to standard output. For example, **sort** is stream-oriented; **vi** is not. **sed**'s input typically comes from a file, but can be directed from the keyboard. Output goes to the screen by default, but can be captured in a file instead.

Typical uses of **sed** include:

- Editing one or more files automatically

- Simplifying repetitive edits to multiple files

- Writing conversion programs

sed operates as follows:

- Each line of input is copied into a pattern space.

- All editing commands in a **sed** script are applied in order to each line of input.

- Editing commands are applied to all lines (globally) unless line addressing restricts the lines affected.

- If a command changes the input, subsequent commands are applied to the changed line, not to the original input line.

- The original input file is unchanged because the editing commands modify a copy of the original input line. The copy is sent to standard output (but can be redirected to a file).

Command-Line Syntax

The syntax for invoking **sed** has two forms:

> **sed** [*options*] '*command*' *file(s)*
> **sed** [*options*] -f *scriptfile file(s)*

The first form allows you to specify an editing command on the command line, surrounded by single quotes. The second form allows you to specify a *scriptfile*, a file containing **sed** commands. If no files are specified, **sed** reads from standard input.

The following *options* are recognized:

-e *cmd*
> Next argument is an editing command; not needed unless specifying two or more editing commands.

-f *file*
> Next argument is a file containing editing commands.

-g Treat all substitutions as global.

-n Suppress the default output; **sed** displays only those lines specified with the **p** command, or with the **p** flag of the **s** command.

Syntax of sed Commands

sed commands have the general form:

> [*address*][,*address*][!]*command* [*arguments*]

sed commands consist of *addresses* and editing *commands*. *commands* consist of a single letter or symbol; they are described later, alphabetically and by group. *arguments* include the label supplied to **b** or **t**, the filename supplied to **r** or **w**, and the substitution flags for **s**. *addresses* are described in the next section.

Pattern Addressing

A **sed** command can specify zero, one, or two addresses. An address can be a line number, the symbol $ (for last line), or a regular expression enclosed in slashes (*/pattern/*). Regular expressions are described in Chapter 6, *Pattern Matching*.

Additionally, \n can be used to match any newline in the pattern space (resulting from the N command), but not the newline at the end of the pattern space.

If the command specifies:	Then the command is applied to:
No address	Each input line.
One address	Any line matching the address. Some commands accept only one address: **a**, **i**, **r**, **q**, and **=**.
Two comma-separated addresses	First matching line and all succeeding lines up to and including a line matching the second address.
An address followed by !	All lines that do *not* match the address.

Examples

`s/xx/yy/g`	*Substitute on all lines (all occurrences)*
`/BSD/d`	*Delete lines containing* BSD
`/^BEGIN/,/^END/p`	*Print between* BEGIN *and* END, *inclusive*
`/SAVE/!d`	*Delete any line that doesn't contain* SAVE
`/BEGIN/,/END/!s/xx/yy/g`	*Substitute on all lines, except between* BEGIN *and* END

Braces ({}) are used in **sed** to nest one address inside another or to apply multiple commands at the same address:

```
[/address/][,/address/]{
command1
command2
}
```

The opening curly brace must end a line, and the closing curly brace must be on a line by itself. Be sure there are no blank spaces after the braces.

Group Summary of sed Commands

In the lists below, the **sed** commands are grouped by function and are described tersely. Full descriptions, including syntax and examples, can be found afterward in the alphabetical summary.

Basic Editing

a	Append text after a line.
c	Replace text (usually a text block).
i	Insert text before a line.
d	Delete lines.
s	Make substitutions.
y	Translate characters (like **tr** in Chapter 2, *Linux User Commands*).

Line Information

=	Display line number of a line.
l	Display control characters in ASCII.
p	Display the line.

Input/Output Processing

n	Skip current line and go to line below.
r	Read another file's contents into the input.
w	Write input lines to another file.
q	Quit the **sed** script (no further output).

Yanking and Putting

h	Copy pattern space into hold space; wipe out what's there.
H	Copy pattern space into hold space; append to what's there.
g	Get the hold space back; wipe out the pattern space.
G	Get the hold space back; append to pattern space.
x	Exchange contents of hold space and pattern space.

Branching Commands

b	Branch to *label* or to end of script.
t	Same as **b**, but branch only after substitution.
:*label*	Label branched to by **t** or **b**.

Multiline Input Processing

N	Read another line of input (creates embedded newline).
D	Delete up to the embedded newline.
P	Print up to the embedded newline.

Alphabetical Summary of sed Commands

:	*:label* Label a line in the script for the transfer of control by **b** or **t**. *label* may contain up to seven characters.
=	*[/pattern/]*= Write to standard output the line number of each line containing *pattern*.
a	*[address]*a\ *text* Append *text* following each line matched by *address*. If *text* goes over more than one line, newlines must be "hidden" by preceding them with a backslash. The *text* will be terminated by the first newline that is not hidden in this way. The *text* is not available in the pattern space, and subsequent commands cannot be applied to it. The results of this command are sent to standard output when the list of editing commands is finished, regardless of what happens to the current line in the pattern space.

Example

```
$a\
This goes after the last line in the file\
(marked by $). This text is escaped at the\
end of each line, except for the last one.
```

a

*[address1][,address2]*b*[label]*

b

Transfer control unconditionally to *:label* elsewhere in script. That is, the command following the *label* is the next command applied to the current line. If no *label* is specified, control falls through to the end of the script, so no more commands are applied to the current line.

Example

Ignore lines between .TS and .TE; resume script after .TE:

```
/^\.TS/,/^\.TE/b
```

*[address1][,address2]*c\
text

c

Replace the lines selected by the address with *text*. When a range of lines is specified, all lines as a group are replaced by a single copy of *text*. The newline following each line of *text* must be escaped by a backslash, except the last line. The contents of the pattern space are, in effect, deleted and no subsequent editing commands can be applied.

Example

Replace first 100 lines in a file:

```
1,100c\
\
<First 100 names to be supplied>
```

*[address1][,address2]*d

d

Delete the addressed line (or lines) from the pattern space. Thus, the line is not passed to standard output. A new line of input is read, and editing resumes with the first command in the script.

Example

Delete all blank lines:

```
/^$/d
```

*[address1][,address2]*D

D

Delete first part (up to embedded newline) of multiline pattern space created by **N** command, and resume editing with first command in script. If this command empties the pattern space, then a new line of input is read, as if the **d** had been executed.

→

D
←
	Example
	
	Strip multiple blank lines, leaving only one:
	
	``
	/^$/{
	N
	/^\n$/D
	}
	``

g	*[address1][,address2]*g Paste the contents of the hold space (see **h** or **H** command) back into the pattern space, wiping out the previous contents of the pattern space. The example shows a simple way to copy lines. *Example* This script collects all lines containing the word *Item:* and copies them to a place marker later in the file. The place marker is overwritten. ``` /Item:/H /<Replace this line with the item list>/g ```

G	*[address1][,address2]*G
	
	Same as **g**, except that the hold space is pasted below the address instead of overwriting it. The example shows a simple way to "cut and paste" lines.
	
	Example
	
	This script collects all lines containing the word *Item*: and moves them after a place marker later in the file. The original *Item*: lines are deleted.
	
	``
	/Item:/{
	H
	d
	}
	/Summary of items:/G
	``

h	*[address1][,address2]*h
	
	Copy the pattern space into the hold space, a special temporary buffer. The previous contents of the hold space are obliterated. You can use **h** to save a line before editing it.
	
	Example
	
	``
	# Edit a line; print the change; replay the original
	/Linux/{
	h
	s/.* Linux \(.*\) .*/\1:/
	p
	x
	}
	``

Sample input:

```
This describes the Linux ls command.
This describes the Linux cp command.
```

Sample output:

```
ls:
This describes the Linux ls command.
cp:
This describes the Linux cp command.
```

[*address1*][,*address2*]H

Append the contents of the pattern space (preceded by a newline) to the contents of the hold space. Even if the hold space is empty, **H** still appends a newline. **H** is like an incremental copy. See examples under **g** and **G**.

[*address1*]i\
text

Insert *text* before each line matched by *address*. (See **a** for details on *text*.)

Example

```
/Item 1/i\
The five items are listed below:
```

[*address1*][,*address2*]l

List the contents of the pattern space, showing nonprinting characters as ASCII codes. Long lines are wrapped.

[*address1*][,*address2*]n

Read next line of input into pattern space. The current line is sent to standard output, and the next line becomes the current line. Control passes to the command following **n** instead of resuming at the top of the script.

Example

In the **ms** macros, a section header occurs on the line below an .NH macro. To print all lines of header text, invoke this script with **sed -n**:

```
/^\.NH/{
n
p
}
```

[*address1*][,*address2*]N

Append next input line to contents of pattern space; the two lines are separated by an embedded newline. (This command is designed to allow pattern matches across two lines.) Using \n to match the embedded newline, you can match patterns across multiple lines. See example at **D**.

→

N
←
	Examples
	
	Like previous example, but print .NH line as well as header title:
	
	``
	/^\.NH/{
	N
	p
	}
	``
	
	Join two lines (replace newline with space):
	
	``
	/^\.NH/{
	N
	s/\n/ /
	p
	}
	``

p	[*address1*][,*address2*]p Print the addressed lines. Unless the -n command-line option is used, this command will cause duplicate lines to be output. Also, it is typically used before commands that change flow control (d, N, b) and that might prevent the current line from being output. See examples at h, n, and N.
P	[*address1*][,*address2*]P Print first part (up to embedded newline) of multiline pattern created by N command. Same as p if N has not been applied to a line.
q	[*address*]q Quit when *address* is encountered. The addressed line is first written to output (if default output is not suppressed), along with any text appended to it by previous a or r commands. *Examples* Delete everything after the addressed line: ``` /Garbled text follows:/q ``` Print only the first 50 lines of a file: ``` 50q ```
r	[*address*]r *file* Read contents of *file* and append after the contents of the pattern space. Exactly one space must be put between the r and the filename. *Example* ``` /The list of items follows:/r item_file ```

[*address1*][,*address2*]s/*pattern*/*replacement*/[*flags*]

Substitute *replacement* for *pattern* on each addressed line. If pattern addresses are used, the pattern // represents the last pattern address specified. The following flags can be specified:

n   Replace *n*th instance of /*pattern*/ on each addressed line. *n* is any number in the range 1 to 512; the default is 1.

g   Replace all instances of /*pattern*/ on each addressed line, not just the first instance.

p   Print the line if a successful substitution is done. If several successful substitutions are done, multiple copies of the line will be printed.

w *file*
   Write the line to a *file* if a replacement was done.

Examples

Here are some short, commented scripts:

```
# Change third and fourth quote to ( and ):
/function/{
s/"/(/3
s/"/)/4
}

# Remove all quotes on a given line:
/Title/s/"//g

# Remove first colon or all quotes; print resulting lines:
s/://p
s/"//gp

# Change first "if" but leave "ifdef" alone:
/ifdef/!s/if/    if/
```

[*address1*][,*address2*]t [*label*]

Test if any substitutions have been made on addressed lines, and if so, branch to line marked by :*label*. (See **b** and **:**.) If *label* is not specified, control falls through to bottom of script. The **t** command is like a case statement in the C programming language or the shell programming languages. You test each case: when it's true, you exit the construct.

Example

Suppose you want to fill empty fields of a database. You have this:

```
ID: 1    Name: greg    Rate: 45
ID: 2    Name: dale
ID: 3
```

You want this:

```
ID: 1    Name: greg    Rate: 45    Phone: ??
ID: 2    Name: dale    Rate: ??    Phone: ??
ID: 3    Name: ????    Rate: ??    Phone: ??
```

You need to test the number of fields already there. Here's the script (fields are tab-separated):

```
/ID/{
s/ID: .* Name: .* Rate: .*/&    Phone: ??/p
t
s/ID: .* Name: .*/&    Rate: ??    Phone: ??/p
t
s/ID: .*/&    Name: ??    Rate: ??    Phone: ??/p
}
```

---

w

[*address1*][,*address2*]**w** *file*

Append contents of pattern space to *file*. This action occurs when the command is encountered, rather than when the pattern space is output. Exactly one space must separate the **w** and the filename. This command will create the file if it does not exist; if the file exists, its contents will be overwritten each time the script is executed. Multiple write commands that direct output to the same file append to the end of the file.

Example

```
# Store tbl and eqn blocks in a file:
/^\.TS/,/^\.TE/w troff_stuff
/^\.EQ/,/^\.EN/w troff_stuff
```

---

x

[*address1*][,*address2*]**x**

Exchange contents of the pattern space with the contents of the hold space. See **h** for an example.

---

y

[*address1*][,*address2*]**y**/*abc*/*xyz*/

Translate characters. Change every instance of *a* to *x*, *b* to *y*, *c* to *z*, etc.

Example

```
# Change item 1, 2, 3 to Item A, B, C ...
/^item [1-9]/y/123456789/ABCDEFGHI/
```

CHAPTER 11

The gawk Scripting Language

This section presents the following topics:

- Conceptual overview

- Command-line syntax

- Patterns and procedures

- System variables

- Operators

- Variable and array assignment

- Group listing of commands

- Alphabetical summary of commands

For more information, see the Nutshell Handbook *sed & awk*, Second Edition, by Dale Dougherty and Arnold Robbins.

Conceptual Overview

gawk is the GNU version of **awk**, a powerful pattern-matching program for processing text files that may be composed of fixed or variable length records separated by some delineator (by default, a newline character). **gawk** may be used from the command line or in **gawk** scripts.

With **gawk**, you can:

- Conveniently process a text file as though it were made up of records and fields in a textual database.

- Use variables to change the database.

- Execute shell commands from a script.

- Perform arithmetic and string operations.

- Use programming constructs such as loops and conditionals.

- Define your own functions.

- Process the result of shell commands.

- Process command-line arguments more gracefully.

- Produce formatted reports.

Command-Line Syntax

The **awk** command will invoke **gawk** on almost all systems on which the latter is installed. **gawk**'s syntax has two forms:

> **gawk** [*options*] '*script*' *var=value file(s)*
> **gawk** [*options*] -f *scriptfile var=value file(s)*

You can specify a *script* directly on the command line, or you can store a script in a *scriptfile* and specify it with -f. Variables can be assigned a value on the command line. Using a *scriptfile* is preferred for very long **gawk** programs, as it avoids the possible `arg list too long` error message that might otherwise be returned by the shell. The value can be a literal, a shell variable (**$**_name_), or a command substitution (`` `cmd` ``), but the value is available only after a line of input is read (i.e., after the **BEGIN** statement). **gawk** operates on one or more *files*. If none are specified (or if - is specified), **gawk** reads from the standard input.

For example, to print the first three (colon-separated) fields on a separate line:

```
gawk -F: '{print $1; print $2; print $3}' /etc/passwd
```

Numerous examples are shown later in this section under "Patterns and Procedures."

Options

All options exist in both traditional POSIX (one-letter) format and GNU-style (long) format. Some recognized *options* are:

--
> Treat all subsequent text as commands or filenames, not options.

-f *file*, --**file-program**=*file*
> Read **gawk** commands from *file* instead of command line.

-v *var=value*, --**assign**=*var=value*
> Assign a *value* to variable *var*. This allows assignment before the script begins execution.

-F*c*, --**field-separator**=*c*
> Set the field separator to character *c*. This is the same as setting the variable **FS**. *c* may be a regular expression. Each input line, or record, is divided into fields by whitespace (blanks or tabs) or by some other user-definable record separator. Fields are referred to by the variables **$1**, **$2**,..., **$***n*. **$0** refers to the entire record.

-W *option*	All -W options are specific to **gawk**, as opposed to **awk**. An alternate syntax is *--option* (i.e., **--compat**). *option* may be one of:	
	compat	Behave exactly like **awk**.
	lint	Warn about commands that might not port to other versions of **awk**, or that **gawk** considers problematic.
	posix	Expect exact compatibility with POSIX; additionally, ignore \x escape sequences, the synonym function, ******, and ****=**.
source=*program*		Treat the rest of the command line as **gawk** commands, as though reading them out of a file.

Patterns and Procedures

gawk scripts consist of patterns and procedures:

> *pattern* {*procedure*}

Both are optional. If *pattern* is missing, {*procedure*} is applied to all lines. If {*procedure*} is missing, the matched line is printed.

Patterns

A pattern can be any of the following:

> /*regular expression*/
> *relational expression*
> *pattern-matching expression*
> *pattern,pattern*
> **BEGIN**
> **END**

- Expressions can be composed of quoted strings, numbers, operators, functions, defined variables, or any of the predefined variables described later under "gawk System Variables."

- Regular expressions use the extended set of metacharacters, and are described in Chapter 6, *Regular Expressions*.

- In addition, ^ and $ can be used to refer to the beginning and end of a field, respectively, rather than the beginning and end of a line.

- Relational expressions use the relational operators listed under "Operators" later in this chapter. Comparisons can be either string or numeric. For example, **$2 > $1** selects lines for which the second field is greater than the first.

- Pattern-matching expressions use the operators ~ (match) and !~ (don't match). See "Operators" later in this chapter.

- The **BEGIN** pattern lets you specify procedures that take place *before* the first input line is processed. (Generally, you set global variables here.)

- The **END** pattern lets you specify procedures that take place *after* the last input record is read.

- If there are multiple **BEGIN** or **END** patterns, their associated actions are taken in the order in which they appear in the script.

- *pattern,pattern* specifies a range of lines.

Except for **BEGIN** and **END**, patterns can be combined with the Boolean operators || (or), **&&** (and), and ! (not).

Procedures

Procedures consist of one or more commands, functions, or variable assignments, separated by newlines or semicolons, and contained within curly braces. Commands fall into four groups:

- Variable or array assignments

- Printing commands

- Built-in functions

- Control-flow commands

Simple Pattern-Procedure Examples

1. Print first field of each line (no pattern specified):

   ```
   { print $1 }
   ```

2. Print all lines that contain *pattern*:

   ```
   /pattern/
   ```

3. Print first field of lines that contain *pattern*:

   ```
   /pattern/{ print $1 }
   ```

4. Print records containing more than two fields:

   ```
   NF > 2
   ```

5. Interpret input records as a group of lines up to a blank line:

   ```
   BEGIN { FS = "\n"; RS = "" }
   ```

6. Print fields 2 and 3 in switched order, but only on lines whose first field matches the string "URGENT":

   ```
   $1 ~ /URGENT/ { print $3, $2 }
   ```

7. Count and print the number of *pattern* found:

   ```
   /pattern/ { ++x } END { print x }
   ```

8. Add numbers in second column and print total:

   ```
   {total += $2 }; END { print "column total is", total}
   ```

9. Print lines that contain fewer than 20 characters:

```
length($0) < 20
```

10. Print each line that begins with *Name:* and that contains exactly seven fields:

```
NF == 7 && /^Name:/
```

11. Reverse the order of fields:

```
{ for (i = NF; i >= 1; i--) print $i }
```

gawk System Variables

Variable	Description
$n	nth field in current record; fields are separated by FS
$0	Entire input record
ARGC	Number of arguments on command line
ARGIND	Current file's place in command line (starting with 0)
ARGV	An array containing the command-line arguments
CONVFMT	Conversion format for numbers (default is %.6g)
ENVIRON	An associative array of environment variables
ERRNO	Description of last system error
FIELDWIDTHS	List of field widths (whitespace separated)
FILENAME	Current filename
FNR	Like NR, but relative to the current file
FS	Field separator (default is any whitespace)
IGNORECASE	If true, make case-insensitive matches
NF	Number of fields in current record
NR	Number of the current record
OFMT	Output format for numbers (default is %.6g)
OFS	Output field separator (default is a blank)
ORS	Output record separator (default is a newline)
RLENGTH	Length of the string matched by **match** function
RS	Record separator (default is a newline)
RSTART	First position in the string matched by **match** function
SUBSEP	Separator character for array subscripts (default is \034)

Operators

The table below lists the operators, in order of increasing precedence, that are available in **gawk**.

Symbol	Meaning
= =+ -= *= /= %= ^=	Assignment
? :	C conditional expression
||	Logical OR
&&	Logical AND
~ !~	Match regular expression and negation
< <= > >= != ==	Relational operators
(blank)	Concatenation
+ -	Addition, subtraction
* / %	Multiplication, division, and modulus

Symbol	Meaning
+ - !	Unary plus and minus, and logical negation
^	Exponentiation
++ --	Increment and decrement, either prefix or postfix
$	Field reference

Variables and Array Assignments

Variables can be assigned a value with an = sign. For example:

```
FS = ","
```

Expressions using the operators +, -, /, and % (modulo) can be assigned to variables.

Arrays can be created with the **split** function (see the listing in the "Alphabetical Summary of Commands"), or they can simply be named in an assignment statement. Array elements can be subscripted with numbers (*array*[1], ..., *array*[*n*]) or with names. For example, to count the number of occurrences of a pattern, you could use the following script:

```
/pattern/ { array["/pattern/"]++ }
END { print array["/pattern/"] }
```

In **gawk**, variables need not be declared previous to their use, nor do arrays need to be dimensioned; they are activated upon first reference. All variables are stored as strings, but may be used either as strings or numbers. **gawk** will use the program script context to determine whether to treat a variable as a string or a number, but the distinction can also be forced by the user. To force a variable to be treated as a string, catenate a null to the variable:

```
var ""
```

To force a variable to be treated as a number, add zero to it:

```
var + 0
```

Group Listing of gawk Commands

gawk commands may be classified as follows:

Arithmetic Functions	String Functions	Control Flow Statements	Input/Output Processing	Time Functions	Miscellaneous
atan2	gsub	break	close	systime	delete
cos	index	continue	getline	strftime	function
exp	length	do/while	next		system
int	match	exit	print		
log	split	for	printf		
rand	sub	if	sprintf		
sin	substr	return			
sqrt	tolower	while			
srand	toupper				

Alphabetical Summary of Commands

The following alphabetical list of statements and functions includes all that are available in **gawk** in Linux.

atan2 (*y*,*x*) Return the arctangent of *y*/*x* in radians.	atan2
break Exit from a **while** or **for** loop.	break
close (*filename=expr*) **close**(*command-expr*) In most implementations of **gawk**, you can have only ten files open simultaneously and one pipe. Therefore, **gawk** provides a **close** statement that allows you to close a file or a pipe. It takes as an argument the same expression that opened the pipe or file.	close
continue Begin next iteration of **while** or **for** loop without reaching the bottom.	continue
cos (*x*) Return the cosine of *x*, an angle in radians.	cos
delete (*array*[*element*]) Delete *element* of *array*.	delete
do *body* **while** (*expr*) Looping statement. Execute statements in *body*, then evaluate *expr*. If *expr* is true, execute *body* again.	do
exit Do not execute remaining instruction, and read no new input. END procedures will be executed.	exit
exp (*arg*) Return the natural exponent of *arg* (the inverse of **log**).	exp

for	for (*i=lower*; *i<=upper*; *i++*) *command* While the value of variable *i* is in the range between *lower* and *upper*, do *command*. A series of commands must be put within braces. <= or any relational operator can be used; ++ or −− can be used to increment or decrement the variable.
for	for (*item* in *array*) *command* For each *item* in an associative *array*, do *command*. Multiple commands must be put inside braces. Refer to each element of the array as *array*[*item*]. Elements of **gawk** arrays are stored in an order that enables access of any element in essentially equivalent time. This order may appear to be indiscriminate; if the output is desired in sorted order, you must pipe it through the **sort** command.

function	function *name*(*parameter–list*) {
	    statements
	}
	
	Create *name* as a user-defined function consisting of **gawk** *statements* that apply to the specified list of parameters.

getline	**getline** [*var*] [<*file*] *command*	**getline** [*var*] The first form reads input from *file* or the next file on the command line, and the second form reads the output of *command*. Both forms read one line at a time, and each time the statement is executed it gets the next line of input. The line of input is assigned to $0 and is parsed into fields, setting **NF**, **NR**, and **FNR**. If *var* is specified, the result is assigned to *var*, and the $0 is not changed. Thus, if the result is assigned to a variable, the current line does not change. **getline** is actually a function, and it returns 1 if it reads a record successfully, 0 at *EOF*, and −1 if for some reason it is otherwise unsuccessful.
gsub	**gsub** (*r*, *s*, *t*) Globally substitute *s* for each match of the regular expression *r* in the string *t*. Return the number of substitutions. If *t* is not supplied, it defaults to $0.

if (*condition*)
    command1
[**else**]
    [*command2*]
	if

If *condition* is true, do *command1*; otherwise do *command2*. Condition can be an expression using any of the relational operators <, <=, ==, !=, >=, or >, as well as the pattern-matching operator ~. A series of commands must be put within braces.

Example

The following lines determine whether the first word in each line starts with A, uppercase or lowercase:

```
if ($1 ~ /[Aa]*/)
        ...begins with A or a
```

index (*substr,str*)	**index**

Return the position of a substring in a string. Returns 0 if *substr* is not contained in *str*.

int (*arg*)	**int**

Return the integer part of *arg*.

length (*arg*)	**length**

Return the length of *arg*. If *arg* is not supplied, $0 is assumed. Therefore, **length** can be used as a predefined variable that contains the length of the current record.

log (*arg*)	**log**

Return the natural logarithm of *arg* (the inverse of **exp**).

match (*s,r*)	**match**

Return position in *s* where regular expression *r* first matches or 0 if no occurrences are found. Sets the value of **RSTART** and **RLENGTH**.

next	**next**

Read next input line and start new cycle through pattern/procedures statements.

print [*args*] [*destination*]	**print**

Print *args* on output. Literal strings must be quoted. Fields are printed in the order they are listed. If separated by commas in the

$\rightarrow$

gawk

print ←	argument list, they are separated in the output by the character specified by OFS. If separated by spaces, they are concatenated in the output. *destination* is a shell redirection or pipe expression (e.g., > *file*) that redirects the default output.
printf	**printf** [*format* [, *expressions*]]

Formatted **print** statement. Expressions or variables can be formatted according to instructions in the *format* argument. The number of *expressions* must correspond to the number specified in the format sections.

format follows the conventions of the C-language **printf** statement. Here are a few of the most common formats:

%s	A string.
%d	A decimal number.
%*n.m*f	A floating point number; *n* = total number of digits. *m* = number of digits after decimal point.
%[-]*nc*	*n* specifies minimum field length for format type *c*, while – justifies value in field; otherwise value is right-justified.

The field width may be specified. For example, %3.2f limits a floating point number to three digits before the decimal point and two after.

format can also contain embedded escape sequences, \n (newline) and \t (tab) being the most common.

Spaces and literal text can be placed in the *format* argument by quoting the entire argument. If there are multiple expressions to be printed, multiple formats should be specified.

Example

Using the script:

```
{printf ("The sum on line %s is %d.\n", NR, $1+$2)}
```

the following input line:

```
5    5
```

produces this output, followed by a newline:

```
The sum on line 1 is 10.
```

rand	**rand** ()

Generate a random number between 0 and 1. This function returns the same series of numbers each time the script is executed, unless the random number generator is seeded using the **srand**() function.

return [*expr*] Used at end of user-defined functions to exit function, returning the value of *expr*.	**return**
sin (*x*) Return the sine of *x*, an angle in radians.	**sin**
split (*string,array*[*,sep*]) Split *string* into elements of array *array* [1], . . . ,*array* [*n*]. The string is split at each occurrence of separator *sep*. If *sep* is not specified, **FS** is used. The number of array elements created is returned.	**split**
sprintf [*format* [, *expression(s)*]] Return the value of one or more *expressions*, using the specified *format* (see **printf**). Data is formatted but not printed.	**sprintf**
sqrt (*arg*) Return square root of *arg*.	**sqrt**
srand (*expr*) Use *expr* to set a new seed for random number generator. Default is time of day.	**srand**
strftime (*format, time*) Return time (which should be input in same format as that returned by **systime()**) in specified format, which uses the same % tokens as the C function **strftime** or the **date** command discussed in Chapter 2.	**strftime**
sub (*r,s,t*) Substitute *s* for first match of the regular expression *r* in the string *t*. Return 1 if successful; 0 otherwise. If *t* is not supplied, defaults to $0.	**sub**
substr (*string,m*[*,n*]) Return substring of *string* beginning at character position *m* and consisting of the next *n* characters. If *n* is omitted, include all characters to the end of string.	**substr**

gawk

system	**system** (*command*)
	Execute the specified shell *command* and return its status. The status of the command that is executed typically indicates its success (1), completion (0), or unexpected error (–1). The output of the command is not available for processing within the **gawk** script. Use "*command* | **getline**" to read the output of a command into the script.
systime	**systime** ( )
	Return number of seconds since midnight UTC, January 1, 1970.
tolower	**tolower** (*str*)
	Translate all uppercase characters in *str* to lowercase and return the new string.
toupper	**toupper** (*str*)
	Translate all lowercase characters in *str* to uppercase and return the new string.
while	**while** (*condition*) *command*
	Do *command* while *condition* is true (see **if** for a description of allowable conditions). A series of commands must be put within braces.

CHAPTER 12

Programming Overview
and Commands

This section lists tables of commonly used programming commands.

Common Commands

Following are tables of commonly used software development commands. These commands, and more, are covered in detail in the next section, "Alphabetical Summary of Commands."

Creating Programs

ar	Create and update library files.
as	Generate object file.
bison	Generate parsing tables.
cpp	Preprocess C code.
g++	GNU C++ compiler.
gcc	GNU C compiler.
ld	Link editor.
flex	Lexical analyzer.
m4	Macro processor.
make	Create programs.
rpcgen	Translate RPC to C code.
yacc	Generate parsing tables.

Maintaining Programs

ctags	Generate symbol list for use with the **vi** editor.
etags	Generate symbol list for use with the Emacs editor.
gdb	GNU debugger.
gprof	Display object file's profile data.
imake	Generate makefiles for use with **make**.

273

make	Maintain, update, and regenerate related programs and files.
nm	Display object file's symbol table.
patch	Apply patches to source code.
size	Print the size of an object file in bytes.
strip	Strip symbols from an object file.

Alphabetical Summary of Commands

ar

ar [-V] *key* [*args*] [*posname*] *archive* [*files*]

Maintain a group of *files* that are combined into a file *archive*. Used most commonly to create and update library files as used by the link editor (**ld**). Only one key letter may be used, but each can be combined with additional *args* (with no separations between). *posname* is the name of a file in *archive*. When moving or replacing *files*, you can specify that they be placed before or after *posname*. -**V** prints the version number of **ar** on standard error.

Key

d   Delete *files* from *archive*.

m   Move *files* to end of *archive*.

p   Print *files* in *archive*.

q   Append *files* to *archive*.

r   Replace *files* in *archive*.

t   List the contents of *archive* or list the named *files*.

x   Extract contents from *archive* or only the named *files*.

Args

a   Use with **r** or **m** key to place *files* in the archive after *posname*.

b   Same as **a** but before *posname*.

c   Create *archive* silently.

i   Same as **b**.

l   For backwards compatibility; meaningless in Linux.

o   Preserve original time stamps.

s   Force regeneration of *archive* symbol table (useful after running **strip**).

u   Use with **r** to replace only *files* that have changed since being put in *archive*.

v   Verbose; print a description of actions taken.

Example

Replace **mylib.a** with object files from the current directory:

```
ar r mylib.a `ls *.o`
```

as [*options*] *files*

Generate an object file from each specified assembly language source *file*. Object files have the same root name as source files but replace the .s suffix with .o. There may be some additional system-specific options.

Options

    -- [| *files*]
        Read input files from standard input, or from *files* if the pipe is used.

    -a[dhlns][=*file*]
        With only the -a option, list source code, assembler listing, and symbol table. The other options specify additional things to list or omit:

-ad	Omit debugging directives.
-ah	Include the high level source code, if available.
-al	Include an assembly listing.
-an	Suppress forms processing.
-as	Include a symbol listing.
=*file*	Set the listing filename to *file*.

    -defsym *symbol=value*
        Define the *symbol* to have the value *value*, which must be an integer.

    -f Skip preprocessing.

    -o *objfile*
        Place output in object file *objfile* (default is *file*.o).

    -v Display the version number of the assembler.

    -I *path*
        Include *path* when searching for .include directives.

    -K Warn before altering difference tables.

    -L Do not remove local symbols, which begin with L.

    -R Combine both data and text in text section.

    -W Quiet mode.

Programming

---

bison [*options*] *file*

Given a *file* containing context-free grammar, convert into tables for subsequent parsing while sending output to *file.c*. This utility is both to a large extent compatible with **yacc** and named for it. All input files should use the suffix *.y*; output files will use the original prefix. All long options (those preceded by ––) may instead be preceded by +.

→

bison ←	**Options** **-b** *prefix*, **--file-prefix=***prefix* Use *prefix* for all output files. **-d**, **--defines** Generate *file.h*, producing **#define** statements that relate **bison**'s token codes to the token names declared by the user. **-r**, **--raw** Use **bison** token numbers, not **yacc**-compatible translations, in *file.h*. **-k**, **--token-table** Include token names and values of YYNTOKENS, YYNNTS, YYNRULES, and YYNSTATES in *file.c*. **-l**, **--no-lines** Exclude **#line** constructs from code produced in *file.c*. (Use after debugging is complete.) **-n**, **--no-parser** Suppress parser code in output, allowing only declarations. Assemble all translations into a switch statement body and print it to *file.act*. **-o** *file*, **--output-file=***file* Output to *file*. **-p** *prefix*, **--name-prefix=***prefix* Substitute *prefix* for **yy** in all external symbols. **-t**, **--debug** Compile runtime debugging code. **-v**, **--verbose** Verbose mode. Print diagnostics and notes about parsing tables to *file.output*. **-V**, **--version** Display version number. **-y**, **--yacc**, **--fixed-output-files** Duplicate **yacc**'s conventions for naming output files.
c++	**c++** [*options*] *files* See **g++**.
cc	**cc** [*options*] *files* See **gcc**.
cpp	**cpp** [*options*] [*ifile* [*ofile*]] GNU C language preprocessor. **cpp** is invoked as the first pass of any C compilation by the **gcc** command. The output of **cpp** is a form acceptable as input to the next pass of the C compiler, and **cpp** normally invokes **gcc** after it finishes processing. *ifile* and

ofile are, respectively, the input and output for the preprocessor; they default to standard input and standard output.

Options

- **-$**   Do not allow $ in identifiers.

- **-dM**   Suppress normal output. Print series of **#defines** that create the macros used in the source file.

- **-dD**   Similar to **-dM**, but excludes predefined macros and includes results of preprocessing.

- **-idirafter** *dir*

    Search *dir* for header files when a header file is not found in any of the included directories.

- **-imacros** *file*

    Process macros in *file* before processing main files.

- **-include** *file*

    Process *file* before main file.

- **-iprefix** *prefix*

    When adding directories with **–iwithprefix**, prepend *prefix* to the directory's name.

- **-iwithprefix** *dir*

    Append *dir* to the list of directories to be searched when a header file cannot be found in the main include path. If **–iprefix** has been set, prepend that prefix to the directory's name.

- **–lang-c, –lang-c++, –lang-objc, –lang-objc++**

    Expect the source to be in C, C++, Objective C, or Objective C++, respectively.

- **-lint**   Display all lint commands in comments as **#pragma lint** *command.*

- **-nostdinc**

    Search only specified, not standard, directories for header files.

- **-nostdinc++**

    Suppress searching of directories believed to contain C++–specific header files.

- **-pedantic**

    Warn verbosely.

- **-pedantic-errors**

    Produce a fatal error in every case in which **–pedantic** would have produced a warning.

- **-traditional**

    Behave like traditional C, not ANSI.

- **-undef**

    Suppress definition of all nonstandard macros.

- **-C**   Pass along all comments (except those found on **cpp** directive lines). By default, **cpp** strips C-style comments.

$\rightarrow$

cpp
←

-D*name*[*=def*]
     Define *name* with value *def* as if by a **#define**. If no *=def* is given, *name* is defined with value 1. -D has lower precedence than -U.

-H   Print pathnames of included files, one per line, on standard error.

-I*dir*   Search in directory *dir* for **#include** files whose names do not begin with / before looking in directories on standard list. **#include** files whose names are enclosed in double quotes and do not begin with / will be searched for first in the current directory, then in directories named on -I options, and last in directories on the standard list.

-M [-**MG**]
     Suppress normal output. Print a rule for **make** that describes the main source file's dependencies. If -**MG** is specified, assume that missing header files are actually generated files, and look for them in the source file's directory.

-**MD** *file*
     Similar to -**M**, but output to *file*; also compile the source.

-**MM**   Similar to -**M**. Describe only those files included as a result of **#include** "*file*".

-**MMD** *file*
     Similar to -**MD**, but descibe only the user's header files.

-P   Preprocess input without producing line control information used by next pass of C compiler.

-U*name*
     Remove any initial definition of *name*, where *name* is a reserved symbol predefined by the preprocessor or a name defined on a -**D** option. Names predefined by **cpp** are **unix** and **i386** (for Intel systems).

-Wcomment, -Wcomments
     Warn when encountering the beginning of a nested comment.

-Wtraditional
     Warn when encountering constructs that are interpreted differently in ANSI from traditional C.

Special names

cpp understands various special names, some of which are:

  __DATE__ Current date (e.g., Oct 10 1997)
  __FILE__ Current filename (as a C string)
  __LINE__ Current source line number (as a decimal integer)
  __TIME__ Current time (e.g., 12:00:00)

These special names can be used anywhere, including macros, just like any other defined names. **cpp**'s understanding of the line number and filename may be changed using a **#line** directive.

Directives

All **cpp** directive lines start with **#** in column 1. Any number of blanks and tabs is allowed between the **#** and the directive. The directives are:

#define *name token-string*

> Defines a macro called *name*, with a value of *token-string*. Subsequent instances of *name* are replaced with *token-string*.

#define *name(arg, . . . , arg) token-string*

> This allows substitution of a macro with arguments. *token-string* will be substituted for *name* in the input file. Each call to *name* in the source file includes arguments that are plugged into the corresponding *args* in *token-string*.

#undef *name*

> Remove definition of the macro *name*. No additional tokens are permitted on the directive line after *name*.

#ident *string*

> Put *string* into the comment section of an object file.

#include *"filename"*, **#include**<*filename*>

> Include contents of *filename* at this point in the program. No additional tokens are permitted on the directive line after the final " or >.

#line *integer-constant "filename"*

> Causes **cpp** to generate line-control information for the next pass of the C compiler. The compiler behaves as if *integer-constant* is the line number of the next line of source code and *filename* (if present) is the name of the input file. No additional tokens are permitted on the directive line after the optional *filename*.

#endif End a section of lines begun by a test directive (**#if**, **#ifdef**, or **#ifndef**). No additional tokens are permitted on the directive line.

#ifdef *name*

> Lines following this directive and up to matching **#endif** or next **#else** or **#elif** will appear in the output if *name* is currently defined. No additional tokens are permitted on the directive line after *name*.

#ifndef *name*

> Lines following this directive and up to matching **#endif** or next **#else** or **#elif** will appear in the output if *name* is not currently defined. No additional tokens are permitted on the directive line after *name*.

$\rightarrow$

cpp
←
	#if *constant-expression*
	      Lines following this directive and up to matching **#endif** or next **#else** or **#elif** will appear in the output if *constant-expression* evaluates to nonzero.
	
	#elif *constant-expression*
	      An arbitrary number of **#elif** directives are allowed between a **#if**, **#ifdef**, or **#ifndef** directive and a **#else** or **#endif** directive. The lines following the **#elif** and up to the next **#else**, **#elif**, or **#endif** directive will appear in the output if the preceding test directive and all intervening **#elif** directives evaluate to zero, and the *constant-expression* evaluates to nonzero. If *constant-expression* evaluates to nonzero, all succeeding **#elif** and **#else** directives will be ignored.
	
	#else Lines following this directive and up to the matching **#endif** will appear in the output if the preceding test directive evaluates to zero, and all intervening **#elif** directives evaluate to zero. No additional tokens are permitted on the directive line.
	
	#error Report fatal errors.
	
	#warning
	      Report warnings, but then continue processing.

ctags	**ctags** [*options*] *files*
	
	Create a list of function and macro names that are defined in the specified C, Pascal, FORTRAN, **yacc**, or **lex** source *files*. The output list (named **tags** by default) contains lines of the form:
	
	    name *file* *context*
	
	where *name* is the function or macro name, *file* is the source file in which *name* is defined, and *context* is a search pattern that shows the line of code containing *name*. After the list of tags is created, you can invoke **vi** on any file and type:
	
	    `:set tags=`*tagsfile*
	    `:tag` *name*
	
	This switches the **vi** editor to the source file associated with the *name* listed in *tagsfile* (which you specify with -t).
	
	etags produces an equivalent file for tags to be used with Emacs.
	
	Options
	
	  -a, --append
	      Append tag output to existing list of tags.
	  -d, --defines
	      Include tag entries for C preprocessor definitions.
	  -o *file*, --output=*file*
	      Write to *file*.

-t, --typedefs
> Include tag entries for **typedefs**.

-u, --update
> Update tags file to reflect new locations of functions (e.g., when functions are moved to a different source file). Old tags are deleted; new tags are appended.

-v, --vgrind
> Print to standard output a listing (index) of each function, source file, and page number (1 page = 64 lines).

-w, --no-warn
> Suppress warning messages.

-x, --cxref
> Produce a listing of each function, and its line number, source file, and context.

-B, --backward-search
> Search for tags backward through files.

-C, --c++
> Expect *.c* and *.h* files to contain C++, not C, code.

-S, --ignore-indentation
> Normally **ctags** uses indentation to parse the tag file; this option tells it to rely on it less.

-T, --typedefs-and-c++
> Include tag entries for typedefs, structs, enums, unions, and C++ member functions.

---

etags [*options*] *files*

Create a list of function and macro names that are defined in the specified C, Pascal, FORTRAN, **yacc**, or **flex** source *files*. The output list (named **tags** by default) contains lines of the form:

> *name*   *file*   *context*

where *name* is the function or macro name, *file* is the source file in which *name* is defined, and *context* is a search pattern that shows the line of code containing *name*. After the list of tags is created, you can invoke Emacs on any file and type:

```
ESC-x visit-tags-table
```

You will be prompted for the name of the tag table; the default is TAGS. To switch to the source file associated with the *name* listed in *tagsfile*, type:

```
ESC-x find-tag
```

You will be prompted for the tag you would like Emacs to search for. **ctags** produces an equivalent tags file for use with **vi**.

→

Programming

etags	**Options**
←	-a, --append
	Append tag output to existing list of tags.
	-i *file*, --include=*file*
	Consult *file* in addition to the normal input file.
	-o *file*, --output=*file*
	Write to *file*.
	-C, --c++
	Expect *.c* and *.h* files to contain C++, not C, code.
	-D, --no-defines
	Do not include tag entries for C preprocessor defini-tions.
	-S, --ignore-indentation
	Normally **etags** uses indentation to parse the tag file; this option tells it to rely on it less.

flex

flex [*options*] [*file*]

flex (Fast Lexical Analyzer Generator) is a faster variant of **lex**. It generates a lexical analysis program (named *lex.yy.c*) based on the regular expressions and C statements contained in one or more input *files*. See also **bison**, **yacc**, and the Nutshell Handbook *lex & yacc*, by John Levine, Tony Mason, and Doug Brown.

Options

-b   Generate backup information to *lex.backup*.

-d   Debug mode.

-f   Use faster compilation (limited to small programs).

-h   Help summary.

-i   Scan case-insensitively.

-l   Maximum **lex** compatibility.

-o *file*
    Write output to *file* instead of *lex.yy.c*.

-p   Print performance report.

-s   Exit if the scanner encounters input that does not match any of its rules.

-t   Print to standard out. (By default, **flex** prints to *lex.yy.c*.)

-v   Print a summary of statistics.

-w   Suppress warning messages.

-B   Generate batch (non-interactive) scanner.

-F   Use the fast scanner table representation.

-I   Generate an interactive scanner (default).

-L   Suppress #**line** directives in *lex.yy.c*.

-P *prefix*
    Change default **yy** prefix to *prefix* for all globally visible variable and function names.

-V Print version number.

-7 Generate a 7-bit scanner.

-8 Generate an 8-bit scanner (default).

-+ Generate a C++ scanner class.

-C Compress scanner tables but do not use equivalence classes.

-Ca
Align tables for memory access and computation. This creates larger tables, but gives faster performance.

-Ce
Construct equivalence classes. This creates smaller tables and sacrifices little performance (default).

-Cf Generate full scanner tables, not compressed.

-CF
Generate faster scanner tables, like **-F**.

-Cm
Construct meta-equivalence classes (default).

-Cr
Bypass use of the standard I/O library. Instead use **read**() system calls.

---

g++ [*options*] *files*

Invoke **gcc** with the options necessary to make it recognize C++. **g++** recognizes all the file extensions **gcc** does, in addition to C++ source files (*.C*, **.cc**, or **.cxx** files) and C++ preprocessed files (*.ii* files). See also **gcc**.

---

gcc [*options*] *files*

Compile one or more C source files (*file.c*), assembler source files (*file.s*), or preprocessed C source files (*file.i*). If the file suffix is not recognizable, assume that the file is an object file or library. **gcc** automatically invokes the link editor **ld** (unless **-c**, **-S**, or **-E** is supplied). In some cases, **gcc** generates an object file having a *.o* suffix and a corresponding root name. By default, output is placed in *a.out*. **gcc** accepts many system specific options, not covered here.

Note: **gcc** is the GNU form of **cc**; on most Linux systems, the command **cc** will invoke **gcc**. The command **g++** will invoke **gcc** with the appropriate options for interpreting C++.

Options

-a   Provide profile information for basic blocks.

-ansi   Enforce full ANSI conformance.

-b *machine*
Compile for use on *machine* type.

$\rightarrow$

-c Create linkable object file for each source file, but do not call linker.

-dD Print #**defines**.

-dM Suppress normal output. Print series of #**defines** that are in effect at the end of preprocessing.

-dN Print #**defines** with macro names only, not arguments or values.

-fno-ident
Do not respond to #**ident** commands.

-fsigned-char
Cause the type **char** to be signed.

-fsyntax-only
Check for syntax errors. Do not attempt to actually compile.

-funsigned-char
Cause the type **char** to be unsigned.

-g Include debugging information for use with **gdb**.

-glevel *level*
Provide *level* amount of debugging information. *level* must be 1, 2, or 3, with 1 providing the least amount of information. The default is 2.

-gxcoff
Include debugging information in XCOFF format, for use with the **dbx** debugger.

-idirafter *dir*
Include *dir* in the list of directories to search when an include file is not found in the normal include path.

-include *file*
Process *file* before proceeding to the normal input file.

-imacros *file*
Process the macros in *file* before proceeding to the normal input file.

-iprefix *prefix*
When adding directories with **-iwithprefix**, prepend *prefix* to the directory's name.

-iwithprefix *dir*
Append *dir* to the list of directories to be searched when a header file cannot be found in the main include path. If **-iprefix** has been set, prepend that prefix to the directory's name.

-l*lib* Link to *lib*.

-lobjc Provide support for linking Objective C programs.

-m486 Optimize code for an Intel 80x86 system where $x \geq 4$.

-mno-486
> Optimize code for a 386 system rather than a 486.

-mno-fp-ret-in-387
> Do not use the FPU registers for return values of functions.

-nostartfiles
> Force linker to ignore standard system startup files.

-nostdinc
> Search only specified, not standard, directories for header files.

-nostdinc++
> Suppress searching of directories believed to contain C++-specific header files.

-nostdlib
> Suppress linking to standard library files.

-o *file*   Specify output file as *file*. Default is *a.out*.

-pedantic
> Warn verbosely.

-pedantic-errors
> Err in every case in which -**pedantic** would have produced a warning.

-pg   Provide profile information for use with **gprof**.

-pipe   Transfer information between stages of compiler by pipes instead of temporary files.

-print-file-name=*library*
> Suppress normal output. Simply print the absolute pathname of the library file to which the executable would be linked.

-static   Suppress linking to shared libraries.

-traditional
> Attempt to behave like a traditional C compiler.

-traditional-cpp
> Cause the preprocessor to attempt to behave like a traditional C preprocessor.

-trigraphs
> Include trigraph support.

-u *symbol*
> Force the linker to search libraries for a definition of *symbol* and to link to them, if found.

-v   Verbose mode. Display commands as they are executed, **gcc** version number, and preprocessor version number.

-w   Suppress warnings.

-x *language*
> Expect input file to be written in *language*, which may be **c**, **objective-c**, **c-header**, **c++**, **cpp-output**,

→

assembler, or **assembler-with-cpp**. If **none** is specified as *language*, guess the language by filename extension.

-A*question*(*answer*)
: If the preprocessor encounters a conditional such as #**if** *question*, assert *answer* in response. To turn off standard assertions, use –**A**-.

-C
: Retain comments during preprocessing. Meaningful only with –**E**.

-D*name*[*=def*]
: Define *name* with value *def* as if by a #**define**. If no *=def* is given, *name* is defined with value 1. -**D** has lower precedence than –**U**.

-E
: Preprocess the source files, but do not compile. Print result to standard output.

-I*dir*
: Include *dir* in list of directories to search for include files. If *dir* is -, search those directories that were specified by -**I** *before* the -**I**- only when #**include** "**file**" is specified, not #include <file>.

-L*dir*
: Search *dir* in addition to standard directories.

-M, -MG
: Suppress normal output. Print a rule for **make** that describes the main source file's dependencies. Implies –**E**.

-MM [-MG]
: Similar to -**M**. Describe only those files included as a result of #**include** "*file*". Implies –**E**.

-H
: Print pathnames of included files, one per line, on standard error.

-O[*level*]
: Optimize. *level* should be 1, 2, 3, or 0. The default is 1. 0 turns off optimization; 3 optimizes the most.

-P
: Preprocess input without producing line control information used by next pass of C compiler. Meaningful only with –**E**.

-S
: Compile source files into assembler code, but do not assemble.

-U*name*
: Remove any initial definition of *name*, where *name* is a reserved symbol predefined by the preprocessor or a name defined on a -**D** option. Names predefined by **cpp** are **unix** and **i386**.

-V *version*
: Attempt to run **gcc** version *version*.

-W
: Warn more verbosely than normal.

-Wl,_option_
>   Invoke linker with _option_, which may be a comma-
>   separated list.

-Wa,_option_
>   Call assembler with _option_, which may be a comma-
>   separated list.

-Waggregate-return
>   Warn if any functions return structures or unions are
>   defined or called.

-Wall Enable **-W**, **-Wchar-subscripts**, **-Wcomment**, **-Wfor-**
>   **mat**, **-Wimplicit**, **-Wparentheses**, **-Wreturn-type**,
>   **-Wswitch**, **-Wtemplate-debugging**, **-Wtrigraphs**,
>   **-Wuninitialized**, and **-Wunused**.

-Wcast-align
>   Warn when encountering instances in which pointers
>   are cast to types that increase the required alignment
>   of the target from its original definition.

-Wcast-qual
>   Warn when encountering instances in which pointers
>   are cast to types that lack the type qualifier with
>   which the pointer was originally defined.

-Wchar-subscripts
>   Warn when encountering arrays with subscripts of
>   type **char**.

-Wcomment
>   Warn when encountering the beginning of a nested
>   comment.

-Wconversion
>   Warn in particular cases of type conversions.

-Werror
>   Exit at the first error.

-Wformat
>   Warn about inappropriately formatted **printfs** and
>   **scanfs**.

-Wimplicit
>   Warn when encountering implicit function or param-
>   eter declarations.

-Winline
>   Warn about illegal inline functions.

-Wmissing-declarations
>   Warn if a global function is defined without a previ-
>   ous declaration.

-Wmissing-prototypes
>   Warn when encountering global function definitions
>   without previous prototype declarations.

-Wnested-externs
>   Warn if an **extern** declaration is encountered within a
>   function.

$\rightarrow$

Programming

-Wno-import
> Don't warn about use of **#import**.

-Wparentheses
> Enable more verbose warnings about omitted parentheses.

-Wpointer-arith
> Warn when encountering code that attempts to determine the size of a function or void.

-Wredundant-decls
> Warn if anything is declared more than once in the same scope.

-Wreturn-type
> Warn about functions defined without return types, or with improper return types.

-Wshadow
> Warn when a local variable shadows another local varaible.

-Wstrict-prototypes
> Insist that argument types be specified in function declarations and definitions.

-Wswitch
> Warn about switches that skip the index for one of their enumerated types.

-Wtemplate-debugging
> Warn if debugging is not available for C++ templates.

-Wtraditional
> Warn when encountering code that produces different results in ANSI C and traditional C.

-Wtrigraphs
> Warn when encountering trigraphs.

-Wuninitialized
> Warn when encountering uninitialized automatic variables.

-Wunused
> Warn about unused variables and functions.

Pragma directives

#pragma interface [*header-file*]
> Used in header files to force object files to provide definition information via references, instead of including it locally in each file. C++–specific.

#pragma implementation [*header-file*]
> Used in main input files to force generation of full output from *header-file* (or, if it is not specified, from the header file with the same base name as the file containing the pragma directive). This information will be globally visible. Normally the specified header file contains a **#pragma interface** directive.

gdb [*options*] [*program* [*core*|*pid*]]   **gdb**

GDB (GNU DeBugger) allows you to step through C, C++, and
Modula-2 programs in order to find the point at which they
break. The program to be debugged is normally specified on the
command line; you can also specify a core, or, if you want to
investigate a running program, a process ID.

Options

-s *file*, -symbols=*file*
> Consult *file* for symbol table. With -e, also uses *file*
> as the executable.

-e *file*, -exec=*file*
> Use *file* as executable, to be read in conjunction with
> source code. May be used in conjunction with -s to
> read symbol table from the executable.

-c *file*, -core=*file*
> Consult *file* for information provided by a core
> dump.

-x *file*, -command=*file*
> Read **gdb** commands from *file*.

-d *directory*, -directory=*directory*
> Include *directory* in path that is searched for source
> files.

-n, -nx
> Ignore *.gdbinit* file.

-q, -quiet
> Suppress introductory and copyright messages.

-batch Exit after executing all the commands specified in
> *.gdbinit* and -x files. Print no startup messages.

-cd=*directory*
> Use *directory* as **gdb**'s working directory.

-f, -fullname
> Show full filename and line number for each stack
> frame.

-b *bps* Set line speed of serial device used by GDB to *bps*.

-tty=*device*
> Set standard in and standard out to *device*.

Common commands

These are just some of the more common **gdb** commands;
there are too many commands to list all of them here.

backtrace
> Print the current location within the program and a
> stack trace showing how the current location was
> reached. (**where** does the same thing.)

breakpoint
> Set a breakpoint in the program.

→

cd   Change the current working directory.

clear   Delete the breakpoint where you just stopped.

commands
        List commands to be executed when breakpoint is hit.

continue
        Continue execution from a breakpoint.

delete Delete a breakpoint or a watchpoint; also used in conjunction with other commands.

display
        Cause variables or expressions to be displayed when program stops.

down   Move down one stack frame to make another function the current one.

frame   Select a frame for the next **continue** command.

info   Show a variety of information about the program. For instance, **info breakpoints** shows all outstanding breakpoints and watchpoints.

jump   Start execution at another point in the source file.

kill   Abort the process running under **gdb**'s control.

list   List the contents of the source file corresponding to the program being executed.

next   Execute the next source line, executing a function in its entirety.

print   Print the value of a variable or expression.

pwd   Show the current working directory.

ptype   Show the contents of a data type, such as a structure or C++ class.

quit   Exit **gdb**.

reverse-search
        Search backward for a regular expression in the source file.

run   Execute the program.

search Search for a regular expression in the source file.

set variable
        Assign a value to a variable.

signal Send a signal to the running process.

step   Execute the next source line, stepping into a function if necessary.

undisplay
        Reverse the effect of the **display** command; keep expressions from being displayed.

until   Finish the current loop.

up   Move up one stack frame to make another function the current one.

watch Set a watchpoint (i.e., a data breakpoint) in the program.	**gdb**
whatis Print the type of a variable or function.	

gprof [*options*] [*object_file*]   **gprof**

Display the profile data for an object file. The file's symbol table is compared with the call graph profile file *gmon.out* (previously created by compiling with **gcc –pg**).

Options

- **-a** Do not display statically declared functions. Since their information might still be relevant, append it to the information about the functions loaded immediately before.
- **-b** Do not display information about each field in the profile.
- **-c** Consult the object file's text area to attempt to determine the program's static call graph. Display static-only parents and children with call counts of 0.
- **-e** *routine*
  Do not display entries for *routine* and its descendants.
- **-f** *routine*
  Print only *routine*, but include time spent in all routines.
- **-k** *from to*
  Remove arcs between the routines *from* and *to*.
- **-s** Summarize profile information in the file *gmon.sum*.
- **-v** Print version and exit.
- **-z** Include zero-usage calls.
- **-E** *routine*
  Do not display entries for *routine* and its descendants, or include time spent on them in calculations for total time.
- **-F** *routine*
  Print only information about *routine*. Do not include time spent in other routines.

imake *options*   **imake**

C preprocessor (**cpp**) interface to the **make** utility. **imake** (for *include make*) solves the portability problem of **make** by allowing machine dependencies to be kept in a central set of configuration files, separate from the descriptions of the various items to be built. The targets are contained in the *Imakefile*, a machine-independent description of the targets to be built, written as **cpp** macros. **imake** uses **cpp** to process the configuration files and the *Imakefile*, and to generate machine-specific *Makefile*s, which can then be used by **make**.

$\rightarrow$

Programming

One of the configuration files is a template file, a master file for **imake**. This template file (default is *Imake.tmpl*) **#include**s the other configuration files that contain machine dependencies such as variable assignments, site definitions, and **cpp** macros, and directs the order in which the files are processed. Each file affects the interpretation of later files and sections of *Imake.tmpl*.

Comments may be included in **imake** configuration files, but the initial # needs to be preceded with an empty C comment:

    /**/#

For more information, see **cpp** and **make**. Also check out the Nutshell Handbook *Sofware Portability with imake*, by Paul DuBois.

Options

  -D*define*

Set directory-specific variables. This option is passed directly to **cpp**.

  -e   Execute the generated *Makefile*. Default is to leave this to the user.

  -f *filename*

Name of per-directory input file. Default is *Imakefile*.

  -I*directory*

Directory in which **imake** template and configuration files may be found. This option is passed directly to **cpp**.

  -s *filename*

Name of **make** description file to be generated. If filename is a dash, the output is written to **stdout**. The default is to generate, but not execute, a *Makefile*.

  -T*template*

Name of master template file used by **cpp**. This file is usually located in the directory specified with the -I option. The default file is *Imake.tmpl*.

  -v   Print the **cpp** command line used to generate the *Makefile*.

Tools

Following is a list of tools used with **imake**:

makedepend [*options*] *files*

Create header file dependencies in *Makefile*s. **makedepend** reads the named input source *files* in sequence and parses them to process **#include**, **#define**, **#undef**, **#ifdef**, **#ifndef**, **#endif**, **#if**, and **#else** directives so it can tell which **#include** directives would be used in a compilation. **makedepend** determines the dependencies and writes them to the *Makefile*. **make** then knows which object files must be recompiled when a dependency has changed. **makedepend** has the following options:

-- options --
> Ignore any unrecognized options following double hyphen. A second double hyphen terminates this action. Recognized options between the hyphens are processed normally.

-a
> Append dependencies to any existing ones instead of replacing existing ones.

-f*filename* Write dependencies to *filename* instead of to *Makefile*.

-m
> Print a warning when encountering a multiple inclusion.

-s*string* Use *string* as delimiter in file, instead of **# DO NOT DELETE THIS LINE — make depend depends on it.**

-v
> Verbose. List all files included by main source file.

-D*name=value*

-D*name* Define *name* with the given value (first form) or with value 1 (second form).

-I*dir* Add directory *dir* to the list of directories searched.

-Y*dir* Search only *dir* for include files. Ignore standard include directories.

mkdirhier *dir...*
> Create directory *dir* and all missing parent directories during file installation operations.

xmkmf [*option*] [*topdir*] [*curdir*]
> Bootstrap a *Makefile* from an *Imakefile*. *topdir* specifies the location of the project root directory. *curdir* (usually omitted) is specified as a relative pathname from the top of the build tree to the current directory. The **-a** option is equivalent to the following command sequence:

```
% xmkmf
% make Makefiles
% make includes
% make depend
```

Configuration files

Following is a list of the **imake** configuration files:

Imake.tmpl
> Master template for **imake**. *Imake.tmpl* includes all the other configuration files, plus the *Imakefile* in the current directory.

→

Imake.params
> Contains definitions that apply across sites and vendors.

Imake.rules
> Contains **cpp** macro definitions that are configured for the current platform. The macro definitions are fed into **imake**, which runs **cpp** to process the macros. Newlines (line continuations) are indicated by the string @@\ (double at-sign, backslash).

site.def Contains site-specific (as opposed to vendor-specific) information, such as installation directories, what set of programs to build, and any special versions of programs to use during the build. The *site.def* file changes from machine to machine.

Project.tmpl
> File containing X-specific variables.

Library.tmpl
> File containing library rules.

Server.tmpl
> File containing server-specific rules.

cf The *.cf* files are the vendor-specific *VendorFiles* that live in *Imake.vb*. A *.cf* file contains platform-specific definitions, such as version numbers of the operating system and compiler, and workarounds for missing commands. The definitions in *.cf* files override the defaults, defined in *Imake.params*.

The Imakefile

The *Imakefile* is a per-directory file that indicates targets to be built and installed, and rules to be applied. **imake** reads the *Imakefile* and expands the rules into *Makefile* target entries. An *Imakefile* may also include definitions of **make** variables, and list the dependencies of the targets. The dependencies are expressed as **cpp** macros, defined in *Imake.rules*. Whenever you change an *Imakefile*, you need to rebuild the *Makefile* and regenerate header file dependencies. For more information on **imake**, see the Nutshell Handbook *Software Portability with imake*, by Paul DuBois.

---

ld

ld [*options*] *objfiles*

Combine several *objfiles*, in the specified order, into a single executable object module (*a.out* by default). **ld** is the link editor and is often invoked automatically by compiler commands.

Options

-c *file* Consult *file* for commands.

-d, -dc, -dp
: Force the assignment of space to common symbols.

-defsym *symbol* = *expression*
: Create the global *symbol* with the value *expression*.

-e *symbol*
: Set *symbol* as the address of the output file's entry point.

-i
: Produce a linkable output file; attempt to set its magic number to OMAGIC.

-l*arch* Include the archive file *arch* in the list of files to link.

-m *linker*
: Emulate *linker*.

-n
: Make text read only; attempt to set NMAGIC.

-noinhibit-exec
: Produce output file even if errors are encountered.

-o *output*
: Place output in *output*, instead of *a.out*.

-oformat *format*
: Specify output format.

-r
: Produce a linkable output file; attempt to set its magic number to OMAGIC.

-s
: Do not include any symbol information in output.

-sort-common
: Do not sort global common symbols by size.

-t
: Announce each input file's name as it is processed.

-u *symbol*
: Force *symbol* to be undefined.

-v, --version
: Show version number.

--verbose
: Print information about ld; print the names of input files while attempting to open them.

-warn-common
: Warn when encountering common symbols combined with other constructs.

-warn-once
: Provide only one warning per undefined symbol.

-x
: With -s or -S, delete all local symbols beginning with L.

-L *dir* Search directory *dir* before standard search directories (this option must precede the -l option that searches that directory).

-M
: Display a link map on standard out.

-Map *file*
: Print a link map to *file*.

→

ld ←	-N	Allow reading of and writing to both data and text; mark ouput if it supports UNIX magic numbers; do not page-align data.
	-R *file*	Obtain symbol names and addresses from *file*, but suppress relocation of *file* and its inclusion in output.
	-S	Do not include debugger symbol information in output.
	-Tbss *address*	Begin bss segment of output at *address*.
	-Tdata *address*	Begin data segment of output at *address*.
	-Ttext *address*	Begin text segment of output at *address*.
	-Ur	Synonymous with -r except when linking C++ programs, where it resolves constructor references.
	-X	With -s or -S, delete local symbols beginning with L.
	-V	Show version number and emulation linkers for -m option.

ldd

ldd [*options*] *programs*

Display a list of the shared libraries each *program* requires.

Options

-v	Display ldd's version.
-V	Display the linker's version.

m4

m4 [*options*] [*macros*] [*files*]

Macro processor for C and other files.

Options

-e
    Operate interactively, ignoring interrupts.

-d*flags*, --**debug**=*flags*
    Specify *flag*-level debugging.

-l*n*, --**arglength**=*n*
    Specify the length of debugging output.

-o *file*, --**error-output**=*file*
    Place output in *file*. Despite the name, print error messages on standard error.

-p, --**prefix-built-ins**
    Prepend m4_ to all built-in macro names.

-s, --**synclines**
    Insert #line directives for the C preprocessor.

-B*n*
    Set the size of the push-back and argument collection buffers to *n* (default is 4,096).

-D*name*[=*value*], --**define**=*name*[=*value*]   **m4**
> Define *name* as *value* or, if *value* is not specified,
> define *name* as null.

-E, --**fatal-warnings**
> Consider all warnings to be fatal, and exit after the
> first of them.

-F*file*, --**freeze-state** *file*
> Record **m4**'s frozen state in *file*, for subsequent
> reloading.

-G, --**traditional**
> Behave like traditional **m4**, ignoring GNU exten-
> sions.

-H*n*, --**hashsize**=*n*
> Set symbol-table hash array to *n* (default is 509).

-I*directory*, --**include**=*directory*
> Search *directory* for include files.

-Q, --**quiet**, --**silent**
> Suppress warning messages.

-R*file*, --**reload-state** *file*
> Load state from *file* before starting execution.

-U*name*, --**undefine**=*name*
> Undefine *name*.

---

make [*options*] [*targets*] [*macro definitions*]   **make**

Update one or more *targets* according to dependency instructions in a description file in the current directory. By default, this
file is called *makefile* or *Makefile*. Options, targets, and macro
definitions can be in any order. Macros definitions are typed as:

    name=string

For more information on **make**, see the Nutshell Handbook
Managing Projects with make, by Andrew Oram and Steve Tal-
bott.

Options

-b   Ignored, out of date.

-d, -dd, --**debug**
> Print detailed debugging information.

-e, --**environment-overrides**
> Override **makefile** macro definitions with environ-
> ment variables.

-f *makefile*, --**file** *makefile*, --**makefile** *makefile*
> Use *makefile* as the description file; a filename of
> – denotes standard input.

-h, --**help**
> Print options to **make** command.

$\rightarrow$

make
←

-i, --ignore-errors
> Ignore command error codes (same as .IGNORE).

-j [*jobs*], --jobs [*jobs*]
> Attempt to execute *jobs* jobs simultaneously, or, if no number is specified, as many jobs as possible.

-k, --keep-going
> Abandon the current target when it fails, but keep working with unrelated targets.

-l [*load*], --load-average [*load*], --max-load [*load*]
> Attempt to keep load below *load*, which should be a floating-point number. Used with –j.

-m
> Ignored, out of date.

-n, --just-print, --dry-run, --recon
> Print commands but don't execute (used for testing).

-o *file*, --old-file *file*, --assume-old *file*
> Never remake *file*, or cause other files to be remade on account of it.

-p, --print-data-base
> Print rules and variables in addition to normal execution.

-q, --question
> Query; return 0 if file is up to date; nonzero otherwise.

-r, --no-built-in-rules
> Do not use default rules.

-s, --silent, --quiet
> Do not display command lines (same as .SILENT).

-t, --touch
> Touch the target files, without remaking them.

-v, --version
> Show version of make.

-w, --print-directory
> Display the current working directory before and after execution.

--warn -undefined -variables
> Print warning if a macro is used without being defined.

-C *directory*, --directory *directory*
> cd to *directory* before beginning make operations. A subsequent -C directive will cause make to attempt to cd into a directory relative to the current working directory.

-I *directory*, --include-dir *directory*
> Include *directory* in list of directories that contain included files.

-S, --no-keep-going, --stop
> Cancel previous -k options. Useful in recursive makes.

-W *file*, --what-if *file*, --new-file *file assume-new file*
> Behave as though *file* has been recently updated.

Description file lines

Instructions in the description file are interpreted as single lines. If an instruction must span more than one input line, use a backslash (\) at the end of the line so that the next line is considered as a continuation. The description file may contain any of the following types of lines:

blank lines
> Blank lines are ignored.

comment lines
> . A pound sign (#) can be used at the beginning of a line or anywhere in the middle. **make** ignores everything after the #.

dependency lines
> Depending on one or more targets, certain commands that follow will be executed. Possible formats include:

```
targets : dependencies
targets : dependencies ; command
```

> Subsequent commands are executed if *dependency* files (the names of which may contain wildcards) do not exist or are newer than a target. If no prerequisites are supplied, then subsequent commands are *always* executed (whenever any of the targets are specified). No tab should precede any *targets*.

suffix rules
> These specify that files ending with the first suffix can be prerequisites for files ending with the second suffix (assuming the root filenames are the same). Either of these formats can be used:

```
.suffix.suffix:
.suffix:
```

> The second form means that the root filename depends on the filename with the corresponding suffix.

commands
> Commands are grouped below the dependency line and are typed on lines that begin with a tab. If a command is preceded by a hyphen (−), **make** ignores any error returned. If a command is preceded by an at-sign (@), the command line won't echo on the display (unless **make** is called with -n).

$\rightarrow$

macro definitions

These have the following form:

```
name = string
      or
define name
string
endef
```

Blank space is optional around the =.

include statements

Similar to the C include directive, these have the form:

```
include files
```

Internal macros

$?   The list of prerequisites that have been changed more recently than the current target. Can be used only in normal description file entries—not suffix rules.

$@   The name of the current target, except in description file entries for making libraries, where it becomes the library name. Can be used both in normal description file entries and in suffix rules.

$<   The name of the current prerequisite that has been modified more recently than the current target.

$*   The name—without the suffix—of the current prerequisite that has been modified more recently than the current target. Can be used only in suffix rules.

$%   The name of the corresponding .o file when the current target is a library module. Can be used both in normal description file entries and in suffix rules.

$^   A space-separated list of all dependencies, with no duplications.

$+   A space-separated list of all dependencies, including duplications.

Pattern rules

These are a more general application of the idea behind suffix rules. If a target and a dependency both contain %, GNU **make** will substitute any part of an existing filename. For instance, the standard suffix rule

```
$(cc) -o $@ $<
```

can be written as the following pattern rule:

```
%.o : %.c
    $(cc) -o $@ $<
```

D   The directory portion of any internal macro name
        except $?. Valid uses are:

        $(*D) $$(@D) $(?D) $(<D)
        ${%D) $(@D) $(ˆD)

F   The file portion of any internal macro name except
        $?. Valid uses are:

        $(*F) $$(@F) $(?F) $(<F)
        ${%F} $(@F) $(ˆF)

Functions

$(subst *from, to, string*)
        Replace all occurrences of *from* with *to* in *string*.
$(patsubst *pattern, to, string*)
        Similar to **subst**, but treats % as a wildcard within *pat-*
        tern. Substitutes *to* for any word in *string* that
        matches *pattern*.
$(strip *string*)
        Remove all extraneous whitespace.
$(findstring *substring, mainstring*)
        Return *substring* if it exists within *mainstring*; other-
        wise, return null.
$(filter *pattern, string*)
        Return those words in *string* that match at least one
        word in *pattern. pattern*s may include the wildcard
        %.
$(filter-out *pattern, string*)
        Remove those words in *string* that match at least one
        word in *pattern. pattern*s may include the wildcard
        %.
$(sort *list*)
        Return *list*, sorted in lexical order.
$(dir *list*)
        Return the directory part (everything up to the last
        slash) of each filename in *list*.
$(notdir *list*)
        Return the nondirectory part (everything after the
        last slash) of each filename in *list*.
$(suffix *list*)
        Return the suffix part (everything after the last
        period) of each filename in *list*.
$(basename *list*)
        Return everything but the suffix part (everything up
        to the last period) of each filename in *list*.
$(addsuffix *suffix,list*)
        Return each filename given in *list* with *suffix*
        appended.

→

$(addprefix *prefix,list*)

Return each filename given in *list* with *prefix* prepended.

$(join *list1,list2*)

Return a list formed by concatenating the two arguments, word by word; e.g., **$(join a b,.c .o)** becomes **a.c b.o**

$(word *n,string*)

Return the *n*th word of *string*.

$(words *string*)

Return the number of words in *string*.

$(firstword *list*)

Return the first word in the list *list*.

$(wildcard *pattern*)

Return a list of existing files in the current directory that match *pattern*.

$(origin *variable*)

Return one of the following strings that describes how *variable* was defined: **undefined**, **default**, **environment**, **environment override**, **file**, **command line**, **override**, or **automatic**.

$(shell *command*)

Return the results of *command*. Any newlines in the result are to be converted to spaces. This function works similarly to backquotes in most shells.

Macro string substitution

${ *macro:s1=s2***}**

Evaluates to the current definition of **${***macro***}**, after substituting the string *s2* for every occurrence of *s1* that occurs either immediately before a blank or tab, or at the end of the macro definition.

Special target names

.DEFAULT: Commands associated with this target are executed if **make** can't find any description file entries or suffix rules with which to build a requested target.

.EXPORT_ALL_VARIABLES:

If this target exists, export all macros to all child processes.

.IGNORE: Ignore error codes. Same as the −i option.

.PHONY: Always execute commands under a target, even if it is an existing, up-to-date file.

.PRECIOUS: Files you specify for this target are not removed when you send a signal (such as an interrupt) that aborts **make**, or when a command line in your description file returns an error.

.SILENT:	Execute commands but do not echo them. Same as the -s option.
.SUFFIXES:	Suffixes associated with this target are meaningful in suffix rules. If no suffixes are listed, the existing list of suffix rules is effectively "turned off."

make

nm [*options*] [*objfiles*]

nm

Print the symbol table (name list) in alphabetical order for one or more object files. If no object files are specified, perform operations on *a.out*. Output includes each symbol's value, type, size, name, etc. A key letter categorizing the symbol can also be displayed. If no object file is given, use *a.out*.

Options

-a, --debug-syms
> Print debugger symbols.

-f *format* Specify output format (**bsd**, **sysv**, or **posix**). Default is **bsd**.

-g, --extern-only
> Print external symbols only.

-n, -v, --numeric-sort
> Sort the external symbols by address.

-p, --no-sort
> Don't sort the symbols at all.

-r, --reverse-sort
> Sort in reverse, alphabetically or numerically.

--size-sort Sort by size.

-u, --undefined-only
> Report only the undefined symbols.

-A, -o, -print-file-name
> Print input filenames before each symbol.

-C, --demangle
> Translate low-level symbol names into readable versions.

-D, --dynamic
> Print dynamic, not normal, symbols. Useful only when working with dynamic objects (some kinds of shared libraries, for example).

-P, --portability
> Same as -f **posix**.

-V, --version
> Print **nm**'s version number on standard error.

Programming

| patch | **patch** [*options*] [*original* [*patchfile*]] |

Apply the patches specified in *patchfile* to *original*. Replace the original with the new, patched version; move the original to *original.orig* or *original˜*.

Options

+ [*options*] [*original2*]
> Apply patches again, with different options or a different original file.

-b *suffix*, --suffix=*suffix*
> Back up the original file in *original.suffix*.

-B *prefix*, --prefix=*prefix*
> Prepend *prefix* to the backup filename.

-c, --context
> Interpret *patchfile* as a context diff.

-d *dir*, --directory=*dir*
> **cd** to *directory* before beginning **patch** operations.

-D *string*, --ifdef=*string*
> Mark all changes with

```
#ifdef
string
#endif
```

-e, --ed   Treat the contents of *patchfile* as **ed** commands.

-E, --remove-empty-files
> If **patch** creates any empty files, delete them.

-f, --force   Force all changes, even those that look incorrect. Skip patches if the original file does not exist; force patches for files with the wrong version specified; assume patches are never reversed.

-t, --batch   Skip patches if the original file does not exist.

-F *num*, --fuzz=*num*
> Specify the maximum number of lines that may be ignored (fuzzed over) when deciding where to install a hunk of code. The default is 2. Meaningful only with context diffs.

-l, --ignore-whitespace
> Ignore whitespace while pattern matching.

-n, --normal
> Interpret patch file as a normal diff.

-N, --forward
> Ignore patches that appear to be reversed or to have already been applied.

-o *file*, --output=*file*
> Print output to *file*.

-p[*num*], --strip[=*num*]
> Specify how much of preceding pathname to strip. A *num* of 0 strips everything, leaving just the filename. 1 strips the leading /; each higher number after that strips another directory from the left.

-r *file*, --reject-file=*file*
> Place rejects (hunks of the patch file that **patch** fails to place within the original file) in *file*. Default is *original.rej*.

-R, --reverse
> Do a reverse patch: attempt to undo the damage done by patching with the old and new files reversed.

-s, --silent, --quiet
> Suppress commentary.

-S, --skip   Skip to next patch in the patch file.

-u, --unified
> Interpret patch file as a unified context diff.

-V *method*, --version-control=*method*
> Specify method for creating backup files (overridden by -B):
>
> t, numbered
> > Make numbered backups.
>
> nil, existing
> > Back up files according to preexisting backup schemes, with simple backups as the default. This is **patch**'s default behavior.
>
> never, simple
> > Make simple backups.

TMPDIR   Specify the directory for temporary files, */tmp* by default.

SIMPLE_BACKUP_SUFFIX
> Suffix to append to backup files instead of *.orig* or ˜.

VERSION_CONTROL
> Specify what method to use in naming backups (see -V).

---

rpcgen [*options*] *file*

Parse *file*, which should be written in the RPC language, and produce a program written in C that implements the RPC code. Place header code generated from *file.x* in *file.h*, XDR routines in *file_xdr.c*, server code in *file_svc.c*, and client code in *file_clnt.c*.

→

rpcgen	Lines preceded by % are not parsed. By default, **rpcgen** produces SunOS 4.1-compatible code.
←	

-a	Produce all files (client and server).
-5	Produce SVR4-compatible code.
-c	Create XDR routines. Cannot be used with other options.
-C	Produce ANSI C code (default).
-k	Produce K&R C code.
-D*name*[=*value*]	
	Define the symbol *name*, and set it equal to *value* or 1.
-h	Produce a header file. With -T, make the file support RPC dispatch tables. Cannot be used with other options.
-I	Produce an **inetd**-compatible server.
-K *secs*	Specify amount of time that the server should wait after replying to a request and before exiting. Default is 120. A *secs* of -1 prevents the program from ever exiting.
-l	Produce client code. Cannot be used with other options.
-m	Produce server code only, suppressing creation of a "main" routine. Cannot be used with other options.
-N	New style. Allow multiple arguments for procedures. Not necessarily backwards compatible.
-o [*file*]	Print output to *file* or standard output.
-Ss	Create skeleton server code only.
-t	Create RPC dispatch table. Cannot be used with other options.
-T	Include support for RPC dispatch tables.

size	size [*options*] [*objfile* ...]

Print the number of bytes of each section of *objfile*, and its total size. If *objfile* is not specified, *a.out* is used.

Options

-d	Display the size in decimal and hexadecimal.
--**format** *format*	
	Imitate the **size** command from either System V (--**format sysv**) or BSD (--**format berkeley**).
-o	Display the size in octal and hexadecimal.
--**radix** *num*	
	Specify how to display the size: in hexadecimal and decimal (if *num* is **10** or **16**) or hexadecimal and octal (if *num* is **8**.)

-x	Display the size in hexadecimal and decimal.	**size**
-A	Imitate System V's **size** command.	
-B	Imitate BSD's **size** command.	

strip [*options*] *files*   strip

Remove symbols from object *files*, thereby reducing file sizes and freeing disk space.

Options

    -F *format*, --**target**=*format*
           Expect the input file to be in the format *format*.

    -O *format*, --**output-target**=*format*
           Write output file in *format*.

    -R *section*, --**remove-section**=*section*
           Delete *section*.

    -s, --**strip-all**
           Strip all symbols.

    -S, -g, --**strip-debug**
           Strip debugging symbols.

    -x, --**discard-all**
           Strip nonglobal symbols.

    -X, --**discard-locals**
           Strip local symbols that were generated by the compiler.

    -v, --**verbose**
           Verbose mode.

Programming

yacc [*options*] *file*   yacc

Given a *file* containing context-free grammar, convert *file* into tables for subsequent parsing and send output to *y.tab.c*. This command name stands for yet another compiler-compiler. See also **flex**, **bison**, and the Nutshell Handbook *lex & yacc*, by John Levine, Tony Mason, and Doug Brown.

Options

-b *prefix*	Prepend *prefix*, instead of *y*, to the output file.
-d	Generate *y.tab.h*, producing **#define** statements that relate **yacc**'s token codes to the token names declared by the user.
-l	Exclude **#line** constructs from code produced in *y.tab.c*. (Use after debugging is complete.)
-t	Compile runtime debugging code.
-v	Generate *y.output*, a file containing diagnostics and notes about the parsing tables.

CHAPTER 13

System and
Network Administration Overview

Common Commands

Following are tables of commonly used system administration commands.

Archiving

cpio   Create and unpack file archives.
tar   Copy files to or restore files from an archive medium.

Clocks

clock   Manage CMOS clock.
netdate   Set clock according to *host*'s clock.
rdate   Manage time server.
zdump   Print list of time zones.
zic   Create time conversion information files.

Daemons

bootpd   Internet Boot Protocol daemon.
fingerd   Finger daemon.
ftpd   File Transfer Protocol daemon.
identd   Identify user running TCP/IP process.
imapd   IMAP protocol mailbox server daemon.
inetd   Internet services daemon.
kerneld   Provides automatic kernel module loading.
klogd   Manage syslogd.
lpd   Printer daemon.
mountd   NFS mount request server.
named   Internet domain name server.

nfsd	NFS daemon.
pop2d	POP server.
pop3d	POP server.
powerd	Monitor UPS connection.
pppd	Maintains point-to-point protocol (PPP) network connections.
rdistd	Remote file distribution server.
rexecd	Remote execution server.
rlogind	rlogin server.
routed	Routing daemon.
rwhod	Remote who server.
syslogd	System logging daemon.
tcpd	TCP network daemon.
tftpd	Trivial file transfer protocol daemon.
ypbind	NIS binder process.
yppasswdd	NIS password modification server.
ypserv	NIS server process.

Hardware

arp	Manage the ARP cache.
cfdisk	Maintain disk partitions.
fdisk	Maintain disk partitions.
kbdrate	Manage the keyboard's repeat rate.
ramsize	Print information about RAM disk.
setserial	Set serial port information.
slattach	Attach serial lines as network interfaces.

Host Information

dnsdomainname	Print DNS domain name.
domainname	Print NIS domain name.
host	Print host and zone information.

Installation

install	Copy files into locations that provide user access to them.
rdist	Distribute files to remote systems.
cpio	Copy file archives.
tar	Copy files to or restore files from an archive medium.

Mail

makemap	Update sendmail's database maps.
rmail	Handle uucp mail.
sendmail	Send and receive mail.

Managing the Kernel

insmod	Install new kernel module.
lsmod	List kernel modules.
modprobe	Load new module and its dependent modules.
rmmod	Remove module.

Managing Filesystems

To UNIX systems, a *filesystem* is some device (such as a hard drive, floppy, or CD-ROM) that is formatted to store files. Filesystems can be found on hard drives, floppies, CD-ROMs, or other storage media that permit random access.

The exact format and means by which the files are stored are not important; the system provides a common interface for all *filesystem types* that it recognizes. Under Linux, filesystem types include the Second Extended Filesystem, or *ext2fs*, which you probably use to store Linux files. The second extended filesystem was developed primarily for Linux and supports 256-character filenames, 4-terabyte maximum filesystem size, and other useful features. (It is "second" because it is the successor to the extended filesystem type.) Other common filesystem types include the MS-DOS filesystem, which allows files on MS-DOS partitions and floppies to be accessed under Linux, and the ISO 9660 filesystem used by CD-ROMs.

debugfs	Debug **extfs** filesystem.
dumpe2fs	Print super block/blocks group information.
e2fsck	Check and repair a second extended filesystem.
fsck	Check and repair filesystem.
fsck.minix	Check and repair a MINIX filesystem.
fuser	List processes using a filesystem.
mkfs	Make new filesystem.
mkfs.ext2	Make new second extended filesystem.
mkfs.minix	Make new MINIX filesystem.
mklost+found	Make *lost+found* directory.
mkswap	Designate swap space.
mount	Mount a filesystem.
rdev	Describe or change values for root filesystem.
rootflags	List or set flags to use in mounting root filesystem.
showmount	List exported directories.
swapdev	Display or set swap device information.
swapon	Begin using device for swapping.
swapoff	Cease using device for swapping.
sync	Write filesystem buffers to disk.
tune2fs	Manage second extended filesystem.
umount	Unmount a filesystem.

Miscellaneous

cron	Schedule commands for specific times.
dmesg	Print bootup messages after the system is up.
install	Copy files and set their permissions.
ldconfig	Update library links and do caching.

logger	Send messages to the system logger.
login	Sign onto system.
rdist	Transfer files between machines.
rstat	Display *host*'s system status.
run-parts	Run all scripts in *directory*.
script	Create typescript of terminal session.

Networking

gated	Manage routing tables between networks.
ifconfig	Manage network interfaces.
ipfwadm	Administrate accounting/firewall facilities.
named	Translate between domain names and IP addresses.
netstat	Print network status.
portmap	Map daemons to ports.
rarp	Manage RARP table.
route	Manage routing tables.
routed	Dynamically keep routing tables up to date.
rpcinfo	Report RPC information.
traceroute	Trace packets' route to remote host.

NIS Administration

domainname	Set or display name of current NIS domain.
makedbm	Rebuild NIS databases.
ypbind	Connect to NIS server.
ypcat	Print values in NIS database.
ypinit	Build new NIS databases.
ypmatch	Print value of one or more NIS *keys*.
yppasswd	Change user passwd in NIS database.
yppasswdd	Update NIS database in response to **yppasswd**.
yppoll	Determine version of NIS map at NIS server.
yppush	Propagate NIS map.
ypserv	NIS server daemon.
ypset	Point **ypbind** at a specific server.
ypwhich	Display name of NIS server or map master.
ypxfr	Transfer NIS database from server to local host.

Printing

| tunelp | Tune the printer parameters. |

Security and System Integrity

| badblocks | Search for bad blocks. |
| chroot | Change root directory. |

Starting and Stopping the System

bootpd	Internet Boot Protocol daemon.
bootpgw	Internet Boot Protocol gateway.
bootptest	Test **bootpd**.
halt	Stop or shutdown system.
reboot	Shut down, then reboot system.
runlevel	Print system runlevel.
shutdown	Shut down system.
telinit	Change the current runlevel.
uptime	Display uptimes of local machines.

System Activity and Process Management

A number of commands in Chapter 2, *Linux User Commands*, are particularly useful in controlling processes, including **kill**, **killall**, **killall5**, **pidof**, **ps**, and **who**.

fuser	Identify processes using file or filesystem.
netstat	Show network status.
psupdate	Update */boot/psupdate*.

Users

adduser	Add a new user.
rusers	Print **who**-style information on remote machines.
rwall	Print a message to remote users.
w	List logged-in users.
wall	Write to all users.

Networking Overview

Networks connect computers so that the different systems can share information. For users and system administrators, UNIX systems have traditionally provided a set of simple but valuable network services, which let you check whether systems are running, refer to files residing on remote systems, communicate via electronic mail, and so on.

For most commands to work over a network, each system must be continuously running a server process in the background, silently waiting to handle the user's request. This kind of process is called a *daemon*; common examples, on which you rely for the most basic functions of your Linux system, are **named** (which translates numeric IP addresses into the alphanumeric names that humans are so fond of), **lpd** (which sends documents to a printer, possibly over a network), and **ftpd** (which allows you to connect to another machine via **ftp**).

Most UNIX networking commands are based on Internet Protocols. These are standardized ways of communicating across a network on hierarchical layers. The protocols range from addressing and packet routing at a relatively low layer to finding users and executing user commands at a higher layer.

The basic user commands that most systems support over Internet Protocols are generally called TCP/IP commands, named after the two most common protocols. You can use all of these commands to communicate with other UNIX systems besides Linux systems. Many can also be used to communicate with non-UNIX systems, because a wide variety of systems support TCP/IP.

This section also covers NFS and NIS, which allow for transparent file and information sharing across networks, and **sendmail**.

TCP/IP Administration Commands

ftpd	Server for file transfers.
gated	Manage routing tables between networks.
named	Translate between domain names and IP addresses.
netstat	Print network status.
ifconfig	Configure network interface parameters.
nslookup	Query domain name servers.
ping	Check that a remote host is online and responding.
pppd	Create PPP serial connection.
rdate	Notify time server that date has changed.
route	Manage routing tables.
routed	Dynamically keep routing tables up to date.
slattach	Attach serial lines as network interfaces.
telnetd	Use TELNET to interface with remote system.
tftpd	Server for restricted set of file transfers.

NFS and NIS Administration Commands

portmap	DARPA port to RPC program number mapper.
rpcinfo	Report RPC information.
domainname	Set or display name of current NIS domain.
makedbm	Rebuild NIS databases.
ypbind	Connect to NIS server.
ypcat	Print values in NIS database.
ypinit	Build new NIS databases.
ypmatch	Print value of one or more NIS *keys*.
yppasswd	Change user password in NIS database.
yppasswdd	Update NIS database in response to **yppasswd**.
yppoll	Determine version of NIS map at NIS server.
yppush	Propagate NIS map.
ypserv	NIS server daemon.
ypset	Point **ypbind** at a specific server.
ypwhich	Display name of NIS server or map master.
ypxfr	Transfer NIS database from server to local host.

Overview of TCP/IP

TCP/IP is a set of communications protocols that define how different types of computers talk to each other. It's named for its two most common protocols, the Transmission Control Protocol and the Internet Protocol. The Internet Protocol moves data between hosts: it splits data into packets, which are then forwarded to machines via the network. The Transmission Control Protocol ensures that the packets in a message are reassembled in the correct order at their final destination, and that any missing datagrams are resent until they are correctly received. Other protocols provided as part of TCP/IP include:

Address Resolution Protocol (ARP)
   Translates between Internet and local hardware addresses (Ethernet et al.).

Internet Control Message Protocol (ICMP)
   Error-message and control protocol.

Point-to-Point Protocol (PPP)
   Provides both synchronous and asynchronous network connections.

Reverse Address Resolution Protocol (RARP)
   Translates between local hardware and Internet addresses (opposite of ARP).

Serial Line Internet Protocol (SLIP)
   Enables IP over serial lines.

Simple Mail Transport Protocol (SMTP)
   Used by **sendmail** to send mail via TCP/IP.

Simple Network Management Protocol (SNMP)
   Performs distributed network management functions via TCP/IP.

User Datagram Protocol (UDP)
   Provides data transfer, without the reliable delivery capabilities of TCP.

Background about TCP/IP is described in the three-volume set *Internetworking with TCP/IP*, by Douglas R. Comer, published by Prentice-Hall. The commands in this chapter and the next are described in more detail in *TCP/IP Network Administration*, by Craig Hunt, published by O'Reilly & Associates.

In the architecture of TCP/IP protocols, data is passed down the stack (toward the Network Access Layer) when it is being sent to the network, and up the stack when it is being received from the network (see Figure 13-1).

IP Addresses

The IP (Internet) address is a 32-bit binary number that differentiates your machine from all others on the network. Each machine must have a unique IP address. An IP address contains two parts: a network part and a host part. The number of address bits used to identify the network and host differ according to the class of the address. There are three main address classes: A, B, and C (see Figure 13-2). The left-most bits indicate what class each address is.

If you wish to connect to the Internet, contact the Network Information Center and have them assign you a network address. If you are not connecting to an outside network, you can choose your own network address, as long as it conforms to the IP address syntax. You should use special reserved addresses provided for in RFC

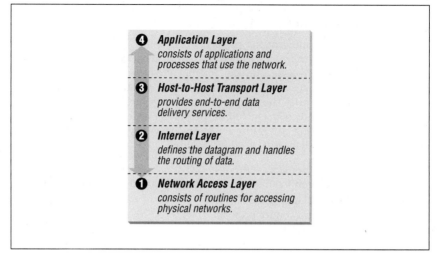

Figure 13-1: Layers in the TCP/IP protocol architecture

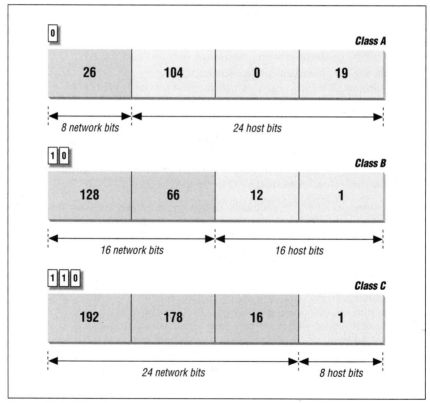

Figure 13-2: IP address structure

1597, which lists IP network numbers for private networks that don't have to be registered with the IANA (Internet Assigned Numbers Authority). An IP address is different from an Ethernet address, which is assigned by the manufacturer of the physical Ethernet card.

Gateways and Routing

Gateways are hosts responsible for exchanging routing information and forwarding data from one network to another. Each portion of a network that is under a separate local administration is called an autonomous system (AS). Autonomous systems connect to each other via exterior gateways. An AS may also contain its own system of networks, linked via interior gateways.

Gateway protocols

Gateway protocols include:

EGP (Exterior Gateway Protocol)

BGP (Border Gateway Protocol)
> Protocols for exterior gateways to exchange information.

RIP (Routing Information Protocol)
> Interior gateway protocol; most popular for LANs.

Hello protocol
> Interior gateway protocol.

Routing daemons

gated and **routed**, the routing daemons, can be run on a host to make it function as a gateway. Only one of them can run on a host at any given time. **gated** is the gateway routing daemon, and allows a host to function as both an exterior and interior gateway. It simplifies the routing configuration by combining the protocols RIP, Hello, BGP, and EGP into a single package.

routed, the network routing daemon, allows a host to function as an interior gateway only. **routed** manages the Internet Routing tables. For more details on **gated** and **routed**, see the TCP/IP commands in Chapter 14, *System and Network Administration Commands*.

Routing tables

Routing tables provide information needed to route packets to their destinations. This information includes destination network, gateway to use, route status, and number of packets transmitted. Routing tables can be displayed with the **netstat** command.

Name Service

Each host on a network has a name that points to information about the host. Hostnames can be assigned to any device that has an IP address. Name service translates the hostnames (easy for people to remember) to IP addresses (the numbers the computer deals with).

DNS and BIND

The Domain Name Service (DNS) is a distributed database of information about hosts on a network. Its structure is similar to that of the UNIX filesystem—an inverted tree, with the root at the top. The branches of the tree are called domains (or subdomains), and correspond to IP addresses. The most popular implementation of DNS is the BIND (Berkeley Internet Name Domain) software.

DNS works as a client-server model. The *resolver* is the client, the software that asks questions about host information. The *name server* is the process that answers the questions. The server side of BIND is the **named** daemon. You can interactively query name servers for host information with the **nslookup** command. For more details on **named** and **nslookup**, see the TCP/IP commands in Chapter 14.

As the name server of its domain, your machine would be responsible for keeping (and providing on request) the names of the machines in its domain. Other name servers on the network would forward requests for these machines to it.

Domain names

The full domain name is the sequence of names, starting from the current domain and going back to the root, with a period separating the names. For instance, *ora.com* indicates the domain *ora* (for O'Reilly & Associates) which is under the domain *com* (for commercial). One machine under this domain is *www.ora.com*. Top-level domains include:

com	Commercial organizations
edu	Educational organizations
gov	Government organizations
mil	Military departments
net	Commercial Internet organizations, usually Internet Service Providers
org	Miscellaneous organizations

Countries also have top-level domains.

Configuring TCP/IP

ifconfig

The network interface represents the way that the networking software uses the hardware—the driver, the IP address, and so forth. To configure a network interface, use the **ifconfig** command. With **ifconfig**, you can assign an address to a network interface, setting the netmask, broadcast address, and IP address at boot time. You can also set network interface parameters, including the use of ARP, the use of driver-dependent debugging code, the use of one-packet mode, and the address of the correspondent on the other end of a point-to-point link. For more information on **ifconfig**, see the TCP/IP commands in Chapter 14.

Serial-line communication

There are two protocols for serial line communication: Serial Line IP (SLIP) and Point-to-Point Protocol (PPP). These protocols let computers transfer information using the serial port instead of a network card and a serial cable in place of an Ethernet cable.

Under Linux, the SLIP driver is installed in the kernel. To convert a serial line to SLIP mode, use the **slattach** program (details on **slattach** are available in Chapter 14). Don't forget that, after putting the line in SLIP mode, you still have to run **ifconfig** to configure the network interface. For example, if your machine is named *tanuki* and you have dialed in to *ruby*:

```
# ifconfig sl0 tanuki pointopoint ruby
# route add ruby
# route add default gw ruby
```

This configures the interface as a point-to-point link to **ruby**, adds the route to **ruby**, and makes it a default route, specifying **ruby** as the gateway.

PPP was intended to remedy some of SLIP's failings; it can hold packets from non-Internet protocols, and it implements client authorization; it supports Van Jacobson header compression; and it dynamically configures each network protocol that passes through it. Under Linux, PPP exists as a driver in the kernel and as the daemon **pppd**. For more information on **pppd**, see Chapter 14.

Troubleshooting TCP/IP

The following commands can be used to troubleshoot TCP/IP. For more details on these commands, see the TCP/IP commands in Chapter 14.

ifconfig Provide information about the basic configuration of the network interface.

netstat Display network status.

ping Indicate whether a remote host can be reached.

nslookup Query the DNS name service.

traceroute Trace route taken by packets to reach network host.

Overview of NFS

NFS is a distributed filesystem that allows users to mount remote filesystems as if they were local. NFS uses a client-server model, where a server exports directories to be shared, and clients mount the directories to access the files in them. NFS eliminates the need to keep copies of files on several machines by letting the clients all share a single copy of a file on the server. NFS is an RPC-based application-level protocol. For more information on the architecture of network protocols, see the section "Overview of TCP/IP."

Administering NFS

Setting up NFS clients and servers involves starting the NFS daemons, exporting filesystems from the NFS servers, and mounting them on the clients. The */etc/exports* file is the NFS server configuration file; it controls which files and directories are exported and what kinds of access are allowed. Names and addresses for clients receiving services are kept in the */etc/hosts* file.

Daemons

NFS server daemons, called **nfsd** daemons, run on the server and accept RPC calls from clients. NFS servers also run the **mountd** daemon to handle mount requests. On the client, caching and buffering are handled by **biod**, the block I/O daemon. The **portmap** daemon maps RPC program numbers to the appropriate TCP/IP port numbers.

Exporting filesystems

To set up an NFS server, first check that all the hosts that will mount your filesystem can reach your host. Next, edit the */etc/exports* file to include the mount-point pathname of the filesystem to be exported. If you are running **mountd**, the files will be exported as the permissions in */etc/exports* allow.

Mounting filesystems

To enable an NFS client, mount a remote filesystem after NFS is started, either by using the **mount** command or by specifying default remote filesystems in */etc/fstab*. A **mount** request calls the server's **mountd** daemon, which checks the access permissions of the client and returns a pointer to a filesystem. Once a directory is mounted, it remains attached to the local filesystem until it is dismounted with the **umount** command, or until the local system is rebooted.

Usually, only a privileged user can mount filesystems with NFS. However, you can enable users to mount and unmount selected filesystems using the **mount** and **umount** commands if the "user" option is set in */etc/fstab*. This can reduce traffic by having filesystems mounted only when needed. To enable user mounting, create an entry in */etc/fstab* for each filesystem to be mounted.

Overview of NIS

NIS refers to the service formerly know as Sun Yellow Pages (YP). It is used to make configuration information consistent on all machines in a network. It does this by designating a single host as the master of all the system administration files and databases, and distributing this information to all other hosts on the network. The information is compiled into databases called maps. NIS is built on the RPC protocol. There are currently two NIS servers freely available for Linux, **yps** and **ypserv**.

Servers

In NIS, there are two types of servers—master and slave servers. Master servers are responsible for maintaining the maps and distributing them to the slave servers. The files are then available locally to requesting processes.

Domains

An NIS domain is a group of hosts that use the same set of maps. The maps are contained in a subdirectory of */var/yp* having the same name as the domain. The machines in a domain share password, hosts, and group file information. NIS domain names are set with the **domainname** command.

NIS maps

NIS stores information in database files called maps. Each map consists of a pair of **dbm** database files, one containing a directory of keys (a bitmap of indices), and the other containing data values. The non-ASCII structure of **dbm** files neccessitates using NIS tools such as **yppush** to move maps between machines.

The file */var/yp/YP_MAP_X_LATE* contains a complete listing of active NIS maps as well as NIS aliases for NIS maps. All maps must be listed here in order for NIS to serve them.

Map manipulation utilities

The following utilities are used to administer NIS maps:

makedbm
> Make **dbm** files. Modify only *ypservers* map and any nondefault maps.

ypinit   Build and install NIS databases. Manipulate maps when NIS is being initialized. Should not be used when NIS is already running.

yppush
> Transfer updated maps from the master server.

Administering NIS

NIS is enabled by setting up NIS servers and NIS clients. The descriptions given here describe NIS setup using **ypserv**, which does not support a master/slave server configuration. All NIS command depend on the RPC portmap program, so make sure it is installed and running before setting up NIS.

Setting up an NIS server

Setting up an NIS server involves:

1. Setting a domain name for NIS using **domainname**

2. Editing the *ypMakefile*, which identifies which databases to build and what sources to use in building them

3. Copying the *ypMakefile* to */var/yp/Makefile*

4. Running **make** from the */var/yp* directory, which builds the databases and initializes the server

5. Starting **ypserv**, the NIS server daemon.

Setting up an NIS client

Setting up an NIS client involves: Setting the domain name for NIS using **domain-name**, which should be the same name used by the NIS server; and running **ypbind**.

NIS user accounts

NIS networks have two kinds of user accounts: distributed and local. Distributed accounts must be administered from the master machine; they provide information that is uniform on each machine in an NIS domain. Changes made to distributed accounts are distributed via NIS maps. Local accounts are administered from the local computer; they provide account information unique to a specific machine. They are not affected by NIS maps, and changes made to local accounts do not affect NIS. When NIS is installed, preexisting accounts default to local accounts.

RPC and XDR

RPC (Remote Procedure Call) is the session protocol used by both NFS and NIS. It allows a host to make a procedure call that appears to be local, but is really executed remotely, on another machine on the network. RPC is implemented as a library of procedures, plus a network standard for ordering bytes and data structures called XDR (eXternal Data Representation).

CHAPTER 14

System and
Network Administration Commands

This chapter presents Linux system administration commands. See Chapter 13 for a description of their relationships to protocols and layers of network software. Other O'Reilly books cover related topics. *Essential System Administration*, Second Edition, by Æleen Frisch, describes how to use the local administration commands, while *TCP/IP Network Administration*, by Craig Hunt, and the *Linux Network Administrator's Guide*, by Olaf Kirch, explain the TCP/IP commands. Finally, NFS and NIS commands are covered in *Managing NFS and NIS* by Hal Stern.

Alphabetical Summary of Commands

adduser *user* Create the user *user*: define a new user ID and enter relevant information in */etc/passwd*. Consult */etc/adduser.conf* to determine appropriate user ID and group ID; create a home directory, and copy dotfiles into it from */etc/skel*; prompt user to set the password and finger information. Only a privileged user may run **adduser**.	**adduser**
agetty [*options*] *port baudrate* [*term*] The Linux version of **getty**. Set terminal type, modes, speed, and line discipline. **agetty** is invoked by **init**. It is the second process in the series **init-getty-login-shell**, which ultimately connects a user with the Linux system. **agetty** reads the user's login name and invokes the **login** command with the user's name as an argument. While reading the name, **agetty** attempts to adapt the system to the speed and type of device being used.	**agetty**
	→

agetty ←	You must specify a port, which **agetty** will search for in the /dev directory. You may use -, in which case **agetty** reads from standard input. You must also specify *baudrate*, which may be a comma-separated list of rates, through which **agetty** will step. Optionally, you may specify the *term*, which is used to override the TERM environment variable. ***Options*** -h Specify hardware, not software, flow control. -i Suppress printing of /etc/issue before printing the login prompt. -l *program* Specify the use of *program* instead of /bin/login. -m Attempt to guess the appropriate baud rate. -t *timeout* Specifies that **agetty** should exit if the **open** on the line succeeds and there is no response to the login prompt in *timeout* seconds. -L Do not require carrier detect: operate locally only. Use this when connecting terminals.
arp	**arp** [*options*] TCP/IP command. Clear, add to, or dump the kernel's ARP cache (/proc/net/arp). ***Options*** -v Verbose mode. -t *type* Search for *type* entries when examining the ARP cache. *type* must be **ether** (IEEE 802.3 10Mbps Ethernet) or **ax25** (AX.25 packet radio); **ether** is the default. -a [*hosts*] Display *hosts'* entries, or, if none are specified, all entries. -d *host* Remove *host*'s entry. -s *host hardware-address* Add the entry *host hardware-address*, where **ether** class addresses are 6 hexadecimal bytes, colon-separated. -f *file* Read entries from *file* and add them.
badblocks	**badblocks** [*options*] *device block–count* Search *device* for bad blocks. You must specify the number of blocks on the device (*block-count*).

Options

-b *blocksize*
: Expect *blocksize*-byte blocks.

-o *file*   Direct output to *file*.

-v   Verbose mode.

-w   Test by writing to each block and then read-
              ing back from it.

---

bootpd [*options*] [*configfile* [*dumpfile*]]

TCP/IP command. Internet Boot Protocol server. **bootpd** is normally run by */etc/inetd* by including the following line in the file */etc/inetd.conf*:

```
bootps dgram udp wait root /etc/bootpd bootpd
```

This causes **bootpd** to be started only when a boot request arrives. It may also be started in stand-alone mode, from the command line. Upon startup, **bootpd** first reads its configuration file, */etc/bootptab* (or the *configfile* listed on the command line), then begins listening for BOOTREQUEST packets.

bootpd looks in */etc/services* to find the port numbers it should use. Two entries are extracted: **bootps**—the **bootp** server listening port—and **bootpc**—the destination port used to reply to clients.

If **bootpd** is compiled with the –DDEBUG option, receipt of a SIGUSR1 signal causes it to dump its memory-resident database to the file */etc/bootpd.dump* or the command-line specified *dumpfile*.

Options

-c *directory*
: Force **bootpd** to work in *directory*.

-d *level*   Specify the debugging level. Omitting *level*
              will increment the level by 1.

-t *timeout*
: Specify a timeout value in minutes. A timeout
              value of zero means forever.

Configuration file
: The **bootpd** configuration file has a format in which two-
              character, case-sensitive tag symbols are used to repre-
              sent host parameters. These parameter declarations are
              separated by colons. The general format is:

```
hostname:tg=value:tg=value:tg=value
```

Sys Admin
Commands

→

bootpd
←
	where *hostname* is the actual name of a bootp client and *tg* is a tag symbol. The currently recognized tags are listed below.
	
	Tags
	
	    bf Bootfile
	    bs Bootfile size in 512-octet blocks
	    cs Cookie server address list
	    ds Domain name server address list
	    gw Gateway address list
	    ha Host hardware address
	    hd Bootfile home directory
	    hn Send hostname
	    ht Host hardware type (see Assigned Numbers RFC)
	    im Impress server address list
	    ip Host IP address
	    lg Log server address list
	    lp **lpr** server address list
	    ns IEN-116 name server address list
	    rl Resource location protocol server address list
	    sm Host subnet mask
	    tc Table continuation
	    to Time offset in seconds from UTC
	    ts Time server addresss list
	    vm Vendor magic cookie selector
	
	There is also a generic tag, **T***n*, where *n* is an RFC 1048 vendor field tag number. Generic data may be represented as either a stream of hexadecimal numbers or as a quoted string of ASCII characters.

bootpgw	**bootpgw** [*options*] *server* Internet Boot Protocol Gateway. Maintain a gateway that forwards **bootpd** requests to *server*. In addition to dealing with BOOTREPLY packets, also deal with BOOTREQUEST packets. **bootpgw** is normally run by */etc/inetd* by including the following line in the file */etc/inetd.conf*: ``` bootps dgram udp wait root /etc/bootpgw bootpgw ``` This causes **bootpgw** to be started only when a boot request arrives. **bootpgw** takes all the same options as **bootpd**, except –c.
bootptest	**bootptest** [*options*] *server* [*template*] TCP/IP command. Test *server*'s **bootpd** daemon by sending requests every second for ten seconds or until the server responds. Read options from the *template* file, if provided.

   -f *file*   Read the boot filename from *file*.

   -h   Identify client by hardware, not IP, address.

   -m *magic -number*

               Provide *magic-number* as the first word of the vendor options field.

---

cfdisk [*options*] [*device*]   **cfdisk**

Partition a hard disk. *device* may be */dev/hda* (default), */dev/hdb*, */dev/sda*, */dev/sdb*, */dev/sdc*, or */dev/sdd*. See also **fdisk**.

Options

   -a   Highlight the current partition with a cursor, not reverse video.

   -c *cylinders*

               Specify the number of cylinders.

   -h *heads* Specify the number of heads.

   -s *sectors*

               Specify the number of sectors per track.

   -z   Do not read the partition table; partition from scratch.

   -P *format*

               Display the partition table in *format*, which must be **r** (raw data), **s** (sector order), or **t** (raw format).

Commands

   up arrow, down arrow

               Move among partitions.

   b   Toggle partition's bootable flag.

   d   Delete partition (allow other partitions to use its space).

   g   Alter the disk's geometry. Prompt for what to change: cylinders, heads, or sectors (**c**, **h**, or **s**, respectively).

   h   Help.

   m   Attempt to ensure maximum usage of disk space in the partition.

   n   Create a new partition. Prompt for more information.

   p   Display the partition table.

   q   Quit without saving information.

   t   Prompt for a new filesystem type, and change to that type.

Sys Admin Commands

→

cfdisk ←	u	Change the partition size units, rotating from megabytes to sectors to cylinders and back.
	W	Save information. Note that this letter must be uppercase.

chroot

chroot *newroot* [*command*]

Change root directory for *command*, or, if none is specified, for a new copy of the user's shell. This command or shell is executed relative to the new root. The meaning of any initial / in pathnames is changed to *newroot* for a command and any of its children. In addition, the initial working directory is *newroot*. This command is restricted to privileged users.

clock

clock [*options*]

Set or read CMOS clock.

Options
You must specify only one of -a, -r, or -w.

-a   Set the system time in accordance with the CMOS clock.

-r   Print the current CMOS time.

-u   Specify universal time when reading or setting the clock. You must also specify another option.

-w   Set the CMOS clock in accordance with system time.

Files

/etc/adjtime

Store information for use in setting the CMOS clock: the correction in seconds per day, the last time the clock was used, and the part of a second that was left after the last adjustment.

cpio

cpio *flags* [*options*]

Copy file archives in from or out to tape or disk, or to another location on the local machine. Each of the three flags -i, -o, or -p accepts different options.

Function options

-i [*options*] [*patterns*]

Copy in (extract) files whose names match selected *patterns*. Each pattern can include filename metacharacters from the Bourne shell. (Patterns should be quoted or escaped so they are interpreted by **cpio**, not by the shell.) If no pattern is used, all files are copied in. During extraction, existing files are not overwritten by older versions in the archive (unless -u is specified).

-o [*options*]
Copy out a list of files whose names are given on the standard input.

-p [*options*] *directory*
Copy files to another directory on the same system. Destination pathnames are interpreted relative to the named *directory*.

Comparison of valid options

Options available to the -i, -o, and -p flags are shown respectively in the first, second, and third row below. (The – is omitted for clarity.)

```
i: 0a c         vABL VC HM O  F
o:    bcdf mnrtsuv B SVCEHMR IF
p: 0a  d lm     uv L V    R
```

Options

-0, --null
Expect list of filenames to be terminated with null, not newline. This allows files with a newline in their names to be included.

-a, --reset-access-time
Set access times of input files to now.

-A, --append
Append files to an existing archive, which must be a disk file. Specify this archive with -O or -F.

-b, --swap
Swap bytes and half-words.

-B   Block input or output using 5120 bytes per record (default is 512 bytes per record).

-c   Read or write header information as ASCII characters; useful when source and destination machines are of differing types.

-C *n*, --io-size=*n*
Like B, but block size can be any positive integer *n*.

-d, --make-directories
Create directories as needed.

-E *file*, --pattern-file=*file*
Extract filenames listed in *file* from the archives.

-f, --nonmatching
Reverse the sense of copying; copy all files *except* those that match *patterns*.

Sys Admin Commands

→

cpio	**-F, --file=***file*
←	Use *file* as archive, not **stdin** or **stdout**. *file* can exist on another machine, if given in the form *user@hostname:file*.

--force-local
Do not assume that *file* (provided by **-F**, **-I**, or **-O**) exists on remote machine, even if it contains an @.

-H *type*, **--format=***type*
Use *type* format. Default in copy-out is **bin**. Valid formats (all caps also accepted):

bin	Binary
odc	Old (POSIX.1) portable format
newc	New (SVR4) portable format
crc	New (SVR4) portable format with checksum added
tar	tar
ustar	POSIX.1 tar (also recognizes GNU tar archives)
hpbin	HP-UX's binary (obsolete)
hpodc	HP-UX's portable format

-I *file*
Read *file* as an input archive. May be on a remote machine (see **-F**).

-k Ignored. For backwards compatibility.

-l, --link
Link files instead of copying.

-L, --dereference
Follow symbolic links.

-m, --preserve-modification-time
Retain previous file modification time.

-M *msg*, **--message=***msg*
Print *msg* when switching media, as a prompt before switching to new media. Use variable **%d** in the message as a numeric ID for the next medium. **-M** is valid only with **-I** or **-O**.

-n, --numeric-uid-gid
When verbosely listing contents, show user ID and group ID numerically.

--no-preserve-owner
Make all copied files owned by yourself, instead of the owner of the original. Useful only if you are a privileged user.

-O *file*
  Direct the output to *file*. May be a file on another
  machine (see -F).

-r Rename files interactively.

-R [*user*][:.][*group*], --**owner** [*user*][:.][*group*]
  Reassign file ownership and group information to
  the user's login ID (privileged users only).

-s, --**swap-bytes**
  Swap bytes.

-S, --**swap-half-words**
  Swap half-words.

-t, --**list**
  Print a table of contents of the input (create no
  files). When used with the -v option, resembles
  output of **ls** -**l**.

-u, --**unconditional**
  Unconditional copy; old files can overwrite new
  ones.

-v Print a list of filenames.

-V, --**dot**
  Print a dot for each file read or written (this shows
  cpio at work without cluttering the screen).

Examples

Generate a list of old files using **find**; use list as input to
cpio:

```
find . -name "*.old" -print | cpio -ocBv\
   > /dev/rst8
```

Restore from a tape drive all files whose names contain
save (subdirectories are created if needed):

```
cpio -icdv "save" < /dev/rst8
```

Move a directory tree:

```
find . -depth -print | cpio -padm /mydir
```

cron

Normally started in a system startup file. Execute commands at scheduled times, as specified in users' files in
/var/cron/tabs. Each file shares its name with the user who
owns it. The files are controlled via the command **crontab**.

debugfs [[*option*] *device*]

Debug an **ext2** file system. *device* is the special file corresponding to the device containing the **ext2** file system (e.g.,
/dev/hda3).

$\rightarrow$

debugfs	
←	

Option

    -w   Open the filesystem read-write.

Commands

cat *file*   Dump the contents of an inode to standard output.

cd *directory*
                 Change the current working directory to *directory*.

chroot *directory*
                 Change the root directory to be the specified inode.

close   Close the currently open file system.

clri *file*   Clear the contents of the inode corresponding to *file*.

dump *file out_file*
                 Dump the contents of an inode to *out_file*.

expand_dir *directory*
                 Expand *directory*.

find_free_block [*goal*]
                 Find the first free block starting from *goal* and allocate it.

find_free_inode [*dir* [*mode*]]
                 Find a free inode and allocate it.

freeb *block*   Mark *block* as not allocated.

freei *file*   Free the inode corresponding to *file*.

help   Print a list of commands understood by **debugfs**.

icheck *block*
                 Do block-to-inode translation.

initialize *device blocksize*
                 Create an **ext2** file system on *device*.

kill_file *file*   Remove *file* and deallocate its blocks.

ln *source_file dest_file*
                 Create a link.

ls [*pathname*]
                 Emulate the **ls** command.

modify_inode *file*
                 Modify the contents of the inode corresponding to *file*.

mkdir *directory*
                 Make *directory*.

mknod *file* [p|[[c|b] *major minor*]]
                 Create a special device file.

ncheck *inode*
>   Do inode-to-name translation.

open [-w] *device*
>   Open a file system.

pwd
>   Print the current working directory.

quit
>   Quit **debugfs**.

rm *file*
>   Remove *file*.

rmdir *directory*
>   Remove *directory*.

setb *block*
>   Mark *block* as allocated.

seti *file*
>   Mark in use the inode corresponding to *file*.

show_super_stats
>   List the contents of the super block.

stat *file*
>   Dump the contents of the inode corresponding to *file*.

testb *block*
>   Test whether *block* is marked as allocated.

testi *file*
>   Test whether the inode correponding to *file* is marked as allocated.

unlink *file*
>   Remove a link.

write *source_file file*
>   Create a file in the filesystem named *file*, and copy the contents of *source_file* into the destination file.

debugfs

---

depmod [*options*] *modules*

depmod

Create a dependency file for the modules given on the command line. This dependency file can be used by **modprobe** to automatically load the relevant *modules*. The normal use of **depmod** is to include the line **/sbin/depmod –a** in one of the files in */etc/rc.d* so the correct module dependancies will be available after booting the system.

Options

-a
>   Create dependencies for all modules listed in */etc/conf.modules*.

-d
>   Debug mode. Show all commands being issued.

-e
>   Print a list of all unresoved symbols.

-v
>   Print a list of all processed modules.

Files

/etc/conf.modules
>   Information about modules: which ones depend on others, and which directories correspond to particular types of modules.

/sbin/insmod, /sbin/rmmod
>   Programs which **depmod** relies on.

Sys Admin Commands

dmesg	**dmesg** [*options*]
	
	Display the system control messages from the kernel ring buffer. This buffer stores all messages since the last system boot or the most recent ones, if the buffer has been filled.
	
	Options
	  -c Clear buffer after printing messages.
	  -n *level*
	           Set the level of system message that will display on console.

dnsdomainname	**dnsdomainname** TCP/IP command. Print the system's DNS domain name. See also **hostname**.
domainname	**domainname** [*name*] NFS/NIS command. Set or display name of current NIS domain. With no argument, **domainname** dislays the name of the current NIS domain. Only a privileged user can set the domain name by giving an argument; this is usually done in a startup script.
dumpe2fs	**dumpe2fs** *device* Print information about *device*'s superblock and blocks group.

e2fsck	**e2fsck** [*options*] *device*
	fsck.ext2 [*options*] *device*
	
	Similar to **fsck**, but specifically intended for Linux second extended filesystems. When checking a second extended filesystem, **fsck** calls this command.
	
	Options
	  -b *superblock*
	           Use *superblock* instead of default superblock.
	  -d Debugging mode.
	  -f Force checking, even if kernel has already marked the filesystem as valid. **e2fsck** will normally exit without checking if the system appears to be clean.
	  -1 *file* Consult *file* for a list of bad blocks, in addition to checking for others.
	  -n Ensure that no changes are made to the filesystem. When queried, answer "no."

-p	"Preen." Repair all bad blocks noninteractively.	**e2fsck**
-t	Display timing statistics.	
-v	Verbose.	
-y	When queried, answer "yes."	

-B *size*
    Expect to find the superblock at *size*; if it's not there, exit.

-F   Flush buffer caches before checking.

-L *file* Consult *file* for list of bad blocks instead of checking filesystem for them.

---

fdisk [*options*] [*device*]   **fdisk**

Maintain disk partitions via a menu. **fdisk** displays information about disk partitions, creates and deletes disk partitions, and changes the active partition. It is possible to assign a different operating system to each of the four partitions, though only one partition is active at any given time. You can also divide a physical partition into several logical partitions. The minimum recommended size for a Linux system partition is 40 megabytes. Normally, *device* will be */dev/hda, /dev/hdb, /dev/sda, /dev/sdb, /dev/hdc, /dev/hdd,* etc. See also **cfdisk**.

Options

-l   List partition tables and exit.

-s*partition*
    Display the size of *partition*, unless it is a DOS partition.

Commands

a   Toggle a bootable flag on current partition.

d   Delete current partition.

l   List all partition types.

m   Main menu.

n   Create a new partition; prompt for more information.

p   Print a list of all partitions, and information about each.

q   Quit; do not save.

t   Replace the type of the current partition.

u   Modify the display/entry units, which must be cylinders or sectors.

v   Verify: check for errors; display a summary of the amount of unallocated sectors.

w   Save changes; exit.

Sys Admin Commands

fingerd	**in.fingerd** [*option*] TCP/IP command. Remote user information server. **fingerd** provides a network interface to the **finger** program. It listens for TCP connections on the **finger** port, and, for each connection, reads a single input line, passes the line to **finger**, and copies the output of **finger** to the user on the client machine. **fingerd** is started by **inetd**, and must have an entry in **inetd**'s configuration file, */etc/inetd.conf*. **Option** -w Include additional information, such as uptime and the name of the operating system.
fsck	**fsck** [*options*] [*filesystem*] . . . Call the filesystem checker for the appropriate system type, to check and repair filesystems. If a filesystem is consistent, the number of files, number of blocks used, and number of blocks free are reported. If a filesystem is inconsistent, **fsck** prompts before each correction is attempted. **fsck**'s exit code can be interpreted as the sum of all of those conditions that apply:

1   Errors were found and corrected

2   Reboot suggested

4   Errors were found, but not corrected

8   **fsck** encountered an operational error

16   **fsck** was called incorrectly

128   A shared library error was detected

Options

--   Pass all subsequent options to filesystem-specific checker. All options that **fsck** doesn't recognize will also be passed.

-r   Interactive mode: prompt before making any repairs.

-s   Serial mode.

-t *fstype*
Specify the filesystem type. Do not check filesystems of any other type.

-A   Check all filesystems listed in */etc/fstab*.

-N   Suppress normal execution; just display what would be done.

-R   Meaningful only with -A: check all filesystems listed in */etc/fstab* except the root filesystem.

-T   Suppress printing of title.

-V   Verbose mode.

fsck.minix [*options*] *device*

Similar to **fsck**, but specifically intended for Linux MINIX filesystems.

Options

-l   List filesystems.

-r   Interactive mode: prompt before making any repairs.

-a   Automatic mode: repair without prompting.

-v   Verbose mode.

-s   Display information about superblocks.

-m   Enable MINIX-like "mode not cleared" warnings.

-f   Force checking, even if kernel has already marked the file system. **fsck.minix** will normally exit without checking if the system appears to be clean.

in.ftpd [*options*]

TCP/IP command. Internet File Transfer Protocol server. The server uses the TCP protocol and listens at the port specified in the **ftp** service specification. **ftpd** is started by **inetd**, and must have an entry in **inetd**'s configuration file, */etc/inetd.conf*.

Options

-d   Write debugging information to the syslog.

-l   Log each FTP session in the syslog.

-T*maxtimeout*
     Set maximum timeout period in seconds. Default limit is 2 hours.

-t*timeout*
     Set timeout period to *timeout* seconds.

fuser [*options*] [*files* | *filesystems*]

Identify processes that are using a file or filesystem. **fuser** outputs the process IDs of the processes that are using the *files* or local *filesystems*. Each process ID is followed by a letter code: **c** if process is using file as current directory, **e** if executable, **f** if an open file, **m** if a shared library, and **r** if the root directory. Any user with permission to read */dev/kmem* and */dev/mem* can use **fuser**, but only a privileged user can terminate another user's process. **fuser** does not work on remote (NFS) files.

If more than one group of files is specified, the options may be respecified for each additional group of files. A lone dash (–) cancels the options currently in force, and the new set of options applies to the next group of files.

→

fuser	*Options*	
←	-	Return all options to defaults.
	-signal	Send *signal* instead of SIGKILL.
	-a	Display information on all specified files, even if they are not being accessed by any processes.
	-k	Send SIGKILL signal to each process.
	-l	List signal names.
	-m	Expect *files* to exist on a mounted filesystem; include all files accessing that filesystem.
	-s	Silent.
	-u	User login name, in parentheses, also follows process ID.
	-v	Verbose.

gated

gated [*options*]

TCP/IP command. Gateway routing daemon. **gated** handles multiple routing protocols and replaces **routed** and any routing daemons that speak the Hello, EGP, or BGP routing protocols. **gated** currently handles the RIP, BGP, EGP, Hello, and OSPF routing protocols, and can be configured to perform all or any combination of the five.

Options

-c	Parse configuration file for syntax errors, then exit **gated**, leaving a dump file in */usr/tmp/gated_dump*.
-f *config_file*	Use alternate configuration file, *config_file*. Default is */etc/gated.conf*.
-n	Do not modify kernel's routing table.
-t [*trace_options*]	Start **gated** with the specified tracing options enabled. If no flags are specified, assume **general**. The trace flags are:

adv	Management of policy blocks
all	Includes **normal**, **policy**, **route**, **state**, **task**, and **timer**
general	Includes **normal** and **route**
iflist	The kernel interface list
normal	Normal protocols instances
parse	Lexical analyzer and parser
policy	Instances in which policy is applied to imported and exported routes
route	Any changes to routing table
state	State machine transitions

	symbols	Symbols read from kernel—note that they are read before the configuration file is parsed, so this option must be specified on the command line
	task	System tasks and interfaces
	timer	Timer usage
-C		Parse configuration file for errors and set exit code to indicate if there were any (1) or not (0); then exit.
-N		Do not daemonize.

gdc [*options*] *command*

TCP/IP command. Administer **gated**. Various commands start and stop the daemon, send signals to it, maintain the configuration files, and manage state and core dumps.

Options

- **-c** *size*   Specify maximum core dump size.
- **-f** *size*   Specify maximum file dump size.
- **-m** *size*   Specify maximum data segment size.
- **-n**   Suppress editing of the kernel forwarding table.
- **-q**   Quiet mode: suppress warnings and log errors to **syslogd** instead of standard error.
- **-s** *size*   Specify maximum stack size.
- **-t** *seconds*
  Wait *seconds* seconds (default 10) for **gated** to complete specified operations at start and stop time.

Commands

BACKOUT
  Restore */etc/gated.conf* from */etc/gated.conf–*, whether or not the latter exists.

backout   Restore */etc/gated.conf* from */etc/gated.conf–*, assuming the latter exists.

checkconf
  Report any syntax errors in */etc/gated.conf*.

checknew
  Report any syntax errors in */etc/gated.conf+*.

COREDUMP
  Force **gated** to core dump and exit.

createconf
  Create an empty */etc/gated.conf+* if one does not already exist, and set it to mode 664, owner **root**, group **gdmaint**.

→

Sys Admin
Commands

dump	Force **gated** to dump to */usr/tmp/gated_dump* and then continue normal operation.
interface	Reload interface configuration.
KILL	Terminate immediately (ungracefully).
modeconf	Set all configuration files to mode 664, owner **root**, group **gdmaint**.
newconf	Make sure that */etc/gated.conf+* exists and move it to */etc/gated.conf*. Save the old */etc/gated.conf* as */etc/gated.conf–*.
reconfig	Reload configuration file.
restart	Stop and restart **gated**.
rmcore	Remove any **gated** core files.
rmdmp	Remove any **gated** state dump files.
rmparse	Remove any **gated** files that report on parse errors. These are generated by the **gcd checkconf** and **gcd checknew** commands.
running	Exit with zero status if **gated** is running and non-zero if it is not.
start	Start **gated**, unless it is already running, in which case return an error.
stop	Stop **gated** as gracefully as possible.
term	Terminate gracefully.
toggletrace	Toggle tracing.

Files

/etc/gcd.conf+
> The test configuration file. Once you're satisfied that it works, you should run *gated newconf* to install it as */etc/gated.conf*.

/etc/gated.conf–
> A backup of the old configuration file.

/etc/gated.conf––
> A backup of the backup of the old configuration file.

/etc/gated.conf
> The actual configuration file.

/etc/gated.pid
> **gated**'s process ID.

/usr/tmp/gated_dump
> The state dump file.

/usr/tmp/gated_parse
> A list of the parse errors generated by reading the configuration file.

getty [*options*] *port* [*speed* [*term* [*lined*]]]

Set terminal type, modes, speed, and line discipline. Linux systems may use **agetty** instead, which uses a different syntax. **getty** is invoked by **init**. It is the second process in the series **init-getty-login-shell** which ultimately connects a user with the Linux system. **getty** reads the user's login name and invokes the **login** command with the user's name as an argument. While reading the name, **getty** attempts to adapt the system to the speed and type of device being used.

You must specify a *port* argument, which **getty** will use to attach itself to the device */dev/port*. **getty** will then scan the defaults file, usually */etc/default/getty*, for runtime values and parameters. These may also be specified, for the most part, on the command line, but the values in the defaults file take precedence. The *speed* argument is used to point to an entry in the file */etc/gettydefs*, which contains the initial baudrate, tty settings, and login prompt, and final speed and settings for the connection. The first entry in */etc/gettydefs* is the default. *term* specifies the type of terminal, with *lined* the optional line discipline to use.

Options

-c *file*   Check the *gettydefs* file. *file* is the name of the *gettydefs* file. Produces the files' values and reports parsing errors to standard output.

-d *file*   Use a different default file.

-h   Do not force a hangup on the port when initializing.

-r *delay*   Wait for single character from port, then wait *delay* seconds before proceeding.

-t *timeout*

             If no user name is accepted within *timeout* seconds, close connection.

-w *string*

             Wait for *string* characters from port before proceeding.

halt [*options*]

Insert a note in */var/log/wtmp*; if the system is in runlevel 0 or 6, stop all processes; otherwise, call **shutdown –nf**.

Options

-d   Suppress writing to */var/log/wtmp*.

-f   Call **halt** even when **shutdown –nf** would normally be called (i.e., force a call to **halt**, even when not in runlevel 0 or 6).

→

halt ←	-n Suppress normal call to **sync**. -w Suppress normal execution; simply write to */var/log/wtmp*.

host	**host** [*options*] *name* [*server*]
	
	TCP/IP command. Provide information about hosts and zones; convert between hostnames and IP addresses (*name* may be either). For more information, particularly about query types, see the Nutshell Handbook *DNS and BIND*, Second edition, by Paul Albitz and Cricket Liu.
	
	-a Same as -t ANY.
	
	-A With hosts, verify the authenticity of names and IP addresses. With zones, execute a reverse lookup for each address listed.
	
	-c *class*
	  Search only for *class* resource records. *class* may be IN, INTERNET, CS, CSNET, CH, CHAOS, HS, HESIOD, ANY, or *. By default, **host** searches for the IN class.
	
	-C Similar to -l, but tests responses to be sure they are authoritative, and reports if they are not.
	
	-d Debugging mode.
	
	-dd Extra debugging mode.
	
	-D Similar to -H, but includes duplicate hosts.
	
	-e Suppress listings for hosts that are not within the zone being listed, and for some glue records.
	
	-E Similar to -H, but includes extra-zone hosts (hosts in an undefined zone).
	
	-f *file* Print output to *filename* in addition to standard out.
	
	-F *file* Print normal output to *file* and extra resource record output to standard out.
	
	-G Similar to -H, but includes gateway hosts (hosts with multiple addresses).
	
	-H Interpret *name* as a zone. Display a list of all unique hostnames found within the *name* zone.
	
	-i Expect *name* to be a numeric address, and make a reverse lookup query.
	
	-I *chars*
	  Assume that *chars* are legal characters in domain names, in addition to the normal legal characters.
	
	-l *zone*
	  Do not require a *name* argument; display information for *zone*.

-L *level*
    Provide recursive zone listings for *level* levels of zones.

-m   Same as **-t MAILB**.

-o   Do not print resource record information to standard out.

-p   Query only a zone's primary nameserver in the case of a zone transfer.

-P *server*
    Query only *server* (which may be a comma-separated list) in the case of a zone transfer.

-q   Quiet. Do not print all normal warnings.

-r   Suppress nameserver recursion.

-R   Do not assume that *name* is fully qualified. If it doesn't exist as is, attempt to ascertain its full name.

-s *seconds*
    Time out if the nameserver does not reply in *seconds* seconds.

-S   Display statistics.

-t *type* Provide information only from *type* resource record field. You may specify **A**, **NS**, **PTR**, **ANY**, or *****.

-T   Include time-to-live values.

-u   Query using virtual circuits, not datagrams.

-v   Verbose mode. Provide information from all resource record fields.

-vv   Very verbose.

-w   Set the timeout period to infinity.

-Z   Display records in full zone file format.

---

icmpinfo [*options*]

TCP/IP command. Intercept and interpret ICMP packets. Print the address and name of the message's sender, the source port, the destination port, the sequence, and the packet size. By default, provide information only about packets that are behaving oddly.

Options

-k   Kill the **syslogd** process begun by **-l**.

-l   Record via **syslogd**. Only a privileged user may use this option.

-n   Use IP addresses instead of hostnames.

-p   Suppress decoding of port number: do not attempt to guess the name of the service that is listening at that port.

Sys Admin Commands

→

| icmpinfo ← | **-s** | Include IP address of interface that received the packet, in case there are several interfaces on the host machine. |
| | **-v** | Verbose. Include information about normal ICMP packets. You may also specify **-vv** and **-vvv** for extra verbosity. |

---

identd   **in.identd** [*options*] [*kernelfile* [*kmemfile*]]

TCP/IP command. Provide the name of the user whose process is running a specified TCP/IP connection. You may specify the kernel and its memory space.

Options

-a *ip_address*
: Bind to *ip_address*. Useful only with **-b**. By default, bind to the INADDR_ANY address.

-b
: Run standalone; not for use with **inetd**.

-d
: Allow debugging requests.

-g*gid*
: Attempt to run in the group *gid*. Useful only with **-b**.

-i
: Run as a daemon, one process per request.

-l
: Log via **syslogd**.

-m
: Allow multiple requests per session.

-n
: Return user IDs instead of user names.

-N
: Do not provide a user's name or user ID if the file *.noident* exists in the user's home directory.

-o
: When queried for the type of operating system, always return OTHER.

-p*port*
: Listen at *port* instead of the default, port 113.

-t*seconds*
: Exit if no new requests have been received before *seconds* seconds have passed. Note that, with **-i** or **-w**, the next new request will result in **identd** being restarted. Default is infinity (never exit).

-u*uid*
: Attempt to run as *uid*. Useful only with **-b**.

-V
: Print version and exit.

-w
: Run as a daemon, one process for all requests.

---

imapd   **imapd**

TCP/IP command. The Interactive Mail Access Protocol (IMAP) server daemon. **imapd** is invoked by **inetd** and listens on port 143 for requests from IMAP clients. IMAP allows mail programs to access remote mailboxes as if they were local. IMAP is a richer protocol than POP because it allows a client to retrieve message-level information from a server mailbox instead of the entire mailbox. IMAP can be used for online and offline reading. The popular Pine mail client contains support for IMAP.

imapd

---

ifconfig [*interface*]
ifconfig [*interface address_family parameters addresses*]

ifconfig

TCP/IP command. Assign an address to a network interface and/or configure network interface parameters. **ifconfig** is typically used at boot time to define the network address of each interface on a machine. It may be used at a later time to redefine an interface's address or other parameters. Without arguments, **ifconfig** displays the current configuration for a network interface. Used with a single *interface* argument, **ifconfig** displays that interface's current configuration.

Arguments

interface

> String of the form *name unit*, for example *en0*.

address_family

> Since an interface may receive transmissions in differing protocols, each of which may require separate naming schemes, you can specify the *address_family* to change the interpretation of the remaining parameters. You may specify **inet** (the default; for TCP/IP), **ax25** (AX.25 Packet Radio), **ddp** (Appletalk Phase 2), or **ipx** (Novell).

Parameters

> The following parameters may be set with **ifconfig**:
> **allmulti/-allmulti**
>
> > Enable/disable sending of incoming frames to the kernel's network layer.
>
> **arp/-arp**
>
> > Enable/disable use of the Address Resolution Protocol in mapping between network-level addresses and link-level addresses.
>
> **broadcast**
>
> > (**inet** only) Specify address to use to represent broadcasts to the network. Default is the address with a host part of all 1's, i.e., x.y.z.255 for a class C network.
>
> **debug/-debug**
>
> > Enable/disable driver-dependent debugging code.
>
> **dest_address**
>
> > Specify the address of the correspondent on the other end of a point-to-point link.

→

Sys Admin Commands

ifconfig
←

down
    Mark an interface "down" (unresponsive).

hw *class address*
    Set the interface's hardware class and address. *class* may be **ether** (Ethernet), **ax25** (AX.25 Packet Radio), or **ARCnet**.

irq *addr*
    Set the device's interrupt line.

metric *n*
    Set routing metric of the interface to *n*. Default is 0.

mtu *num*
    Set the interface's Maximum Transfer Unit (MTU).

multicast
    Set the multicast flag.

netmask *mask*
    (**inet** only) Specify how much of the address to reserve for subdividing networks into sub-networks. *mask* can be specified as a single hexadecimal number with a leading 0x, with a dot notation Internet address, or with a pseudo-network name listed in the network table */etc/networks*.

pointopoint/-pointopoint [*address*]
    Enable/disable point-to-point interfacing, so that the connection between the two machines is dedicated.

up   Mark an interface "up" (ready to send and receive).

trailers/-trailers
    Request/disable use of a "trailer" link-level encapsulation when sending.

address
    Either a hostname present in the hostname database (*/etc/hosts*), or an Internet address expressed in the Internet standard dot notation.

---

inetd

inetd [*option*] [*configuration_file*]

TCP/IP command. Internet services daemon. **inetd** listens on multiple ports for incoming connection requests. When it receives one, it spawns the appropriate server. When started, **inetd** reads its configuration information from either *configuration_file*, or from the default configuration file */etc/inetd.conf*. It then issues a call to **getservbyname**, creates a socket for each server, and binds each socket to the port for that server. It does a **listen** on all connection-based sockets, then waits, using **select** for a connection or datagram.

When a connection request is received on a listening socket, **inetd** does an **accept**, creating a new socket. It then forks, dups, and execs the appropriate server. The invoked server has I/O to **stdin**, **stdout**, and **stderr** done to the new socket, connecting the server to the client process.

When there is data waiting on a datagram socket, **inetd** forks, dups, and execs the appropriate server, passing it any server program arguments. A datagram server has I/O to **stdin**, **stdout**, and **stderr** done to the original socket. If the datagram socket is marked as **wait**, the invoked server must process the message before **inetd** considers the socket available for new connections. If the socket is marked **nowait**, **inetd** continues to process incoming messages on that port.

The following servers may be started by **inetd**: **bootpd**, **bootpgw**, **fingerd**, **ftpd**, **imapd**, **popd**, **rexecd**, **rlogind**, **rshd**, **talkd**, **telnetd**, and **tftpd**. Do not arrange for **inetd** to start **named**, **routed**, **rwhod**, **sendmail**, **listen**, or any NFS server.

inetd rereads its configuration file when it receives a hangup signal, SIGHUP. Services may be added, deleted, or modified when the configuration file is reread.

Option

-d   Turn on socket-level debugging and print debugging information to **stdout**.

Files

/etc/inetd.conf
        Default configuration file.
/var/run/inetd.pid
        inetd's process ID.

init [*option*] [*runlevel*]

Option

-t *seconds*
          When changing run levels, send SIGKILL *seconds* after SIGTERM. Default is 20.

→

init	**Files**
←	init is the first process run by any UNIX machine at boot time. It verifies the integrity of all filesystems and then creates other processes, using fork-and-exec, as specified by */etc/inittab*. Which processes may be run are controlled by *runlevel*. All process terminations are recorded in */var/run/utmp* and */var/log/wtmp*. When the run level changes, init sends SIGTERM and then, after 20 seconds, SIGKILL to all processes that cannot be run in the new run level.

Run levels

The current run level may be changed by **telinit**, which is often just a link to **init**. The default run levels vary from distribution to distribution, but these are standard:

0	Halt the system.
1, s, S	Single user mode.
6	Reboot the system.
q, Q	Reread */etc/inittab*.

Check the */etc/inittab* file for run levels on your system.

---

insmod

insmod [*options*] *file* [*symbol=value* ...]

Load the module *file* into the kernel, changing any symbols that are defined on the command line. If the module file is named *file.o* or *file.mod*, the module will be named *file*.

Options

-f	Force loading of module, even if some problems are encountered.
-m	Output a load map.
-o *name*	
	Name module *name* instead of attempting to name it from the object file's name.
-x	Do not export: do not add any external symbols from the module to the kernel's symbol table.

---

install

install [*options*] [*file*] *directories*

Used primarily in makefiles to update files. **install** copies files into user-specified directories. It will not overwrite a file. Similar to **cp**, but attempts to set permission modes, owner, and group.

Options

-d, --directory	
	Create any missing directories.

-g *group*, --group *group*
> Set group ID of new file to *group* (privileged users only).

-m *mode*, --mode *mode*
> Set permissions of new file to *mode* (octal or symbolic). By default, the mode is **0755**.

-o [*owner*], --owner [*owner*]
> Set ownership to *owner*, or, if unspecified, to root (privileged users only).

-s, --strip
> Strip symbol tables.

---

ipfw [*options*] *command*
ipfw [*options*] *action response protocol path*
ipfw [*options*] *action chain*

TCP/IP command. Control accounting and firewall facilities. You may specify the blocking, forwarding, or accounting of certain packets from certain destinations.

Options

-n   Never resolve IP addresses to domain names.

-v   Verbose. Print counters for packets and bytes.

Arguments

action   One of three kinds of actions: **entry, checking,** or **chain**. Entry and checking actions follow the second syntax shown above; chain actions follow the third. The specific actions are described below.

chain   Specifies the chain to perform the action upon. See "Chain actions" below.

path   Always in the form **from** *source* **to** *dest*. Both *source* and *dest* can be either domain names or IP addresses, and may include ports.

protocol
> One of **icmp, tcp, udp,** or **all**.

response
> One of three responses: **accept** (accept the packet), **deny** (ignore the packet and send no notification), or **reject** (refuse the packet, but send a "host unreachable" message back as notification).

Entry actions

a[dd]b[locking] *response protocol path*
> Add the specified *response protocol path* pattern to the list of patterns in the blocking firewall.

→

---

ipfw
←
	d[el]b[locking] *response protocol path*
	    Delete the specified *response protocol path* pattern from the list of patterns in the blocking firewall.
	
	a[dd]f[orwarding] *response protocol path*
	    Add the specified pattern to the list of patterns in the forwarding firewall.
	
	d[el]f[orwarding] *response protocol path*
	    Delete the specified pattern from the list of patterns in the forwarding firewall.
	
	a[dd]a[ccounting] *response protocol path*
	    Add the specified pattern to the list of patterns in the accounting chain.
	
	d[el]a[ccounting] *response protocol path*
	    Delete the specified pattern from the list of patterns in the accounting chain.
	
	Checking actions
	
	c[heck]b[locking] *response protocol path*
	    Perform check of the specified *response protocol path* pattern against the blocking firewall.
	
	c[heck]f[orwarding] *response protocol path*
	    Perform check of the specified pattern against the forwarding firewall.
	
	Chain actions
	
	flush [firewall|accounting], f [f|a]
	    Clear firewall, accounting, or both chains.
	
	list [forwarding|blocking|accounting], l [f|b|a]
	    Display forwarding, blocking, accounting, or all chains.
	
	zero [accounting], zero [a]
	    Clear all accounting chain counters.

ipfwadm	**ipfwadm -A|-B|-F** *command parameters* [*options*]
	
	Administer a firewall and its accounting rules. Three categories of commands exist: accounting, blocking firewall, and forwarding firewall.
	
	Command Categories
	
	    -A Accounting
	    -B Blocking firewall
	    -F Forwarding firewall
	
	Commands
	
	    You must specify exactly one command; it will be applied only to the specified list (accounting, blocking firewall, or forwarding firewall).

-a [accept|deny|reject]

　　Add the specified *parameters* to the specified list. If the list is the blocking or forwarding firewall, you must specify a policy, as well (**accept**, **deny**, or **reject**).

-d [accept|deny|reject]

　　Delete the specified *parameters* from the specified list. If the list is the blocking or forwarding firewall, you must specify a policy, as well (**accept**, **deny**, or **reject**).

-l　List all rules in the specified list.

-z　Clear all packet and byte counters in the specified list.

-f　Flush all rules from the specified list.

-p [accept|deny|reject]

　　Specify the list's default policy. Not applicable to -A operations.

-c　Report on a specific packet: would the specified firewall accept, deny, or reject it? Not applicable to -A operations.

Parameters

　　These may be used only in conjunction with -a, -d, or -c.

-P [tcp|udp|icmp|all]

　　Specify type of protocol to include in operations.

-S *address*[/*mask*] [*port* ...]

　　Specify source. *mask* is the network mask, for example 255.255.255.0.

-D *address*[/*mask*] [*port* ...]

　　Specify destination.

-I *address*

　　Send or receive packet by interface *address*.

Options

-b　Bidirectional mode: apply -a or -d commands to IP packets going in both directions.

-e　Extended: include interface address, rule options, and packet and byte counters, where applicable. Applies only to the -l command.

-n　Print all addresses and ports numerically.

-v　Verbose: include extra packet information. Applies only to the -a, -d, and -c commands.

-x　Expanded numbers: do not round numbers, and do not use **K** (1000) or **M** (1000K) to abbreviate.

-y　Match packets that have the SYN bit set but not the ACK bit. Applies only to the -a and -d commands.

Sys Admin Commands

kbdrate	**kbdrate** [*options*]
	
	Control the rate at which the keyboard repeats characters, as well as its delay time. Using this command without options sets a repeat rate of 10.9 characters per second; the default delay is 250 milliseconds. When Linux boots, however, it sets the keyboard rate to 30 characters per second.
	
	Options
	
	    -s Suppress printing of messages.
	
	    -r *rate* Specify the repeat rate, which must be one of the following numbers (all in characters per second): 2.0, 2.1, 2.3, 2.5, 2.7, 3.0, 3.3, 3.7, 4.0, 4.3, 4.6, 5.0, 5.5, 6.0, 6.7, 7.5, 8.0, 8.6, 9.2, 10.0, 10.9, 12.0, 13.3, 15.0, 16.0, 17.1, 18.5, 20.0, 21.8, 24.0, 26.7, or 30.0.
	
	    -d *delay*
	        Specify the delay, which must be one of the following (in milliseconds): 250mS, 500mS, 750mS, or 1000mS.

kerneld	**kerneld** **kerneld** automatically loads kernel modules when they are needed, thereby reducing kernel memory usage from unused loaded modules and replacing manual loading of modules with **modprobe** or **insmod**. If a module has not been used for more than one minute, **kerneld** automatically removes it. **kerneld** comes with the modules-utilities package and is set up during kernel configuration; its functionality is provided by interactions between that package and the kernel. **kerneld** is aware of most common types of modules. When more than one possible module can be used for a device (such as a network driver), **kerneld** uses the configuration file */etc/conf.modules*, which contains path information and aliases for all loadable modules, to determine the correct module choice. **kerneld** can also be used to implement dial-on-demand networking, such as SLIP or PPP connections. The network connection request can be processed by **kerneld** to load the proper modules and set up the connection to the server.
klogd	**klogd** [*options*] Control which kernel messages are displayed on the console; prioritize all messages, and log them through **syslogd**. On many operating systems, **syslogd** performs all the work

of **klogd**, but on Linux the features are separated. Kernel messages are gleaned from the */proc* filesystem and from system calls to **syslogd**. By default no messages appear on the console. Messages are sorted into 8 levels, 0–7, and the level number is prepended to each message.

Priority Levels

0   Emergency situation (**KERN_EMERG**).

1   A crucial error has occurred (**KERN_ALERT**).

2   A serious error has occurred (**KERN_CRIT**).

3   An error has occurred (**KERN_ERR**).

4   A warning message (**KERN_WARNING**).

5   The situation is normal, but should be checked (**KERN_NOTICE**).

6   Information only (**KERN_INFO**).

7   Debugging messages (**KERN_DEBUG**).

Options

-c *level*
: Print all messages of a higher priority (lower number) than *level* to the console.

-d   Debugging mode.

-f *file*   Print all messages to *file*; suppress normal logging.

-k *file*   Use *file* as source of kernel symbols.

-n   Avoid auto backgrounding. This is needed when **klogd** is started from **init**.

-o   One-shot mode. Prioritize and log all current messages, then immediately exit.

-s   Suppress reading of messages from the */proc* filesystem.

Files

/usr/include/linux/kernel.h, */usr/include/sys/syslog.h*
: Sources for definitions of each logging level.

/proc/kmsg
: A file examined by **klogd** for messages.

/var/run/klogd.pid
: **klogd**'s process ID.

---

ksysms [*options*]

Print a list of all exported kernel symbols (name, address, and defining module, if applicable).

Options

-a   Include symbols from unloaded modules.

→

ksysms ←	-h Suppress header message. -m Include starting address and size. Useful only for symbols in loaded modules. ***Files*** */proc/ksyms* Another source of the same information.

ldconfig	**ldconfig** [*options*] *directories*
	
	Examine the libraries in *directory*, */etc/ld.so.conf*, */usr/lib*, and */lib*; update links and cache where necessary. Usually run in startup files or after the installation of new shared libraries.
	
	Options
	-D Debug. Suppress all normal operations.
	
	-l Library mode. Expect libraries as arguments, not directories. Manually link specified libraries.
	
	-n Suppress examination of */usr/lib* and */lib* and reading of */etc/ld.so.conf*; do not cache.
	
	-N Do not cache; only link.
	
	-p Print all directories and candidate libraries in the cache. Expects no arguments.
	
	-v Verbose. Include version number, and announce each directory as it is scanned and links as they are created.
	
	-X Do not link; only rebuild cache.
	
	Files
	/lib/ld.so
	    Linker and loader.
	/etc/ld.so.conf
	    List of directories that contain libraries.
	/etc/ld.so.cache
	    List of the libraries found in those libraries mentioned in */etc/ld.so.conf*.

logger	**logger** [*options*] [*message* ...] TCP/IP command. Add entries to the system log (via **syslogd**). A message can be given on the command line, or standard input is logged. ***Options*** -f *file* Read *message* from *file*. -i Include the process ID of the **logger** process.

-p *pri* Enter message with the specified priority *pri*. Default is "user.notice".

-t *tag* Mark every line in the log with the specifed *tag*.

login [*name* | *option*]

Log in to the system. **login** asks for a username (*name* can be supplied on the command line), and password (if appropriate).

If successful, **login** updates accounting files, sets various environment variables, notifies users if they have mail, and executes startup shell files.

No user except **root** is able to log in when */etc/nologin* exists. That file will be displayed before the connection is terminated.

Root may connect only on a tty that is included in */etc/securetty*. If ~*/.hushlogin* exists, execute a quiet login. If */var/adm/lastlog* exists, print the time of the last login.

Options

-f   Suppress second login authentication.

-h *host* Specify name of remote host. Normally used by servers, not humans; may be used only by **root**.

-p   Preserve previous environment.

lpd [*option*] [*port*]

TCP/IP command. Line printer daemon. **lpd** is usually invoked at boot time from the *rc2* file. It makes a single pass through the printer configuration file (traditionally */etc/printcap*) to find out about the existing printers, and prints any files left after a crash. It then accepts requests to print files in a queue, transfer files to a spooling area, display a queue's status, or remove jobs from a queue. In each case, it forks a child process for each request, then continues to listen for subsequent requests. If *port* is specified, **lpd** listens on that port; otherwise, it uses **getservbyname** to ascertain the correct port.

The file *lock* in each spool directory prevents multiple daemons from becoming active simultaneously. After the daemon has set the lock, it scans the directory for files beginning wth **cf**. Lines in each **cf** file specify files to be printed, or nonprinting actions to be performed. Each line begins

→

lpd ←	with a key character, which specifies what to do with the remainder of the line. Key characters are:

C	classification—string to be used for the classification line on the burst page
c	**cifplot** file
f	formatted file—name of a file to print that is already formatted
g	graph file
l	formatted file, but suppress pagebreaks and printing of control characters
H	hostname—name of machine where **lpd** was invoked
J	jobname—string to be used for the jobname on the burst page
L	literal—this line contains identification information from the password file, and causes the banner page to be printed
M	mail—send mail to the specified user when the current print job completes
n	**ditroff** file
P	person—login name of person who invoked **lpd**
r	DVI file
T	pitle—string to be used as the title for **pr**
t	**troff** file
U	unlink—name of file to remove upon completion of printing

Option

-l   Enable logging of all valid requests.

Files

/etc/printcap Printer description file

/var/spool/*   Spool directories

/var/spool/*/minfree

Minimum free space to leave

/dev/lp*   Printer devices

/etc/hosts.equiv

Machine names allowed printer access

/etc/hosts.lpd Machine names allowed printer access, but not under same administrative control

---

lsmod

lsmod

List all loaded modules: their name, size (in 4k units), and, if appropriate, a list of referring modules.

Files

/proc/modules

Source of the same information.

makedbm [options] infile outfile

NFS/NIS command. Make NIS **dbm** file. **makedbm** takes *infile* and converts it to a pair of files in **ndbm** format, namely *outfile.pag* and *outfile.dir*. Each line of the input file is converted to a single **dbm** record. All characters up to the first TAB or SPACE form the key, and the rest of the line is the data. If line ends with **\&**, the data for that record is continued on to the next line. It is left for the NIS clients to interpret #; **makedbm** does not treat it as a comment character. *infile* can be -, in which case the standard input is read.

makedbm generates a special entry with the key **yp_last_modified**, which is the date of infile (or the current time, if infile is -).

Options

-b   Interdomain. Propagate a map to all servers using the interdomain name server **named**.

-d yp_domain_name
     Create a special entry with the key yp_domain_name.

-i yp_input_file
     Create a special entry with the key yp_input_file.

-l   Convert keys of the given map to lowercase.

-m yp_master_name
     Create a special entry with the key yp_master_name. If no master hostname is specified, yp_master_name is set to the local hostname.

-o yp_output_file
     Create a special entry with the key yp_output_name.

-s   Secure map. Accept connections from secure NIS networks only.

-u dbm filename
     Undo a dbm file—print out a **dbm** file, one entry per line, with a single space separating keys from values.

Example

It is easy to write shell scripts to convert standard files such as */etc/passwd* to the key value form used by **makedbm**. For example, the **awk** program:

```
BEGIN { FS =":";OFS = "\t";}
{ print $1, $0}
```

takes the */etc/passwd* file and converts it to a form that can be read by **makdbm** to make the NIS file *passwd.byname*. That is, the key is a username and the value is the remaining line in the */etc/passwd* file.

makemap	**makemap** [*options*] *type name*
	
	Transfer from standard input to **sendmail**'s database maps. Input should be formatted as:
	
	    key value
	
	You may comment lines with #, may substitute parameters with %n, and must escape literal % by entering it as %%. The *type* must be one of **dbm**, **btree**, or **hash**. The *name* is a filename to which **makemap** appends standard suffixes.
	
	Options
	
	  -**f** Suppress conversion of uppercase to lowercase.
	  -**N** Append a zero byte to each key.
	  -**o** Append to existing file instead of replacing it.
	  -**r** If some keys already exist, replace them. (By default, **makemap** will exit when encountering a duplicated key.)
	  -**v** Verbose mode.

mke2fs	**mke2fs** [*options*] *device* [*blocks*]
	mkfs.ext2 [*options*] *device* [*blocks*]
	
	Format *device* as a Linux second extended filesystem. You may specfy the number of blocks on the device, or allow **mke2fs** to guess.
	
	Options
	
	-**b** *block-size*
	    Specify block size in bytes.
	-**c** Scan *device* for bad blocks before execution.
	-**f** *fragment-size*
	    Specify fragment size in bytes.
	-**i** *bytes-per-inode*
	    Create an inode for each *bytes-per-inode* of space. *bytes-per-inode* must be 1024 or greater; it is 4096 by default.
	-**l** *filename*
	    Consult *filename* for a list of bad blocks.
	-**m** *percentage*
	    Reserve *percentage* percent of the blocks for use by privileged users.
	-**q** Quiet mode.
	-**v** Verbose mode.
	-**S** Write only superblock and group descriptors; suppress writing of inode table and block and inode bitmaps. Useful only when attempting to salvage damaged systems.

mkfs [*options*] [*fs–options*] *filesys* [*blocks*]

Construct a filesystem on a device (such as a hard disk partition). *filesys* is either the name of the device or the mount point. **mkfs** is actually a frontend that invokes the appropriate version of **mkfs** according to a filesystem type specified by the -t option. For example, a Linux second extended filesystem uses **mkfs.ext2** (which is the same as **mke2fs**); MS-DOS filesystems use **mkfs.msdos**. *fs-options* are options specific to the filesystem type. *blocks* is the size of the filesystem in 1024-byte blocks.

Options

-V Produce verbose output, including all commands executed to create the specific filesystem.

-t *fs-type*

Tells **mkfs** what type of filesystem to construct.

filesystem-specific options

These options must follow generic options and not be combined with them. Most filesystem builders support these three options:

-c Check for bad blocks on the device before building the filesystem.

-l *file* Read the file *file* for the list of bad blocks on the device.

-v Produce verbose ouput.

mkfs.minix [*options*] *device size*

Creates a MINIX filesystem. See **mkfs**.

mklost+found

Create a *lost+found* directory in the current working directory. Intended for Linux second extended filesystems.

mkswap [*option*] *device* [*size*]

Create swap space on *device*. You may specify its *size* in blocks; each block is a page of about 4K.

Option

-c Check for bad blocks before creating the swap space.

mkfs

| mkfs.minix |

| mklost+found |

| mkswap |

modprobe	**modprobe** [*options*] [*modules*]

With no options, attempt to load the specified module, as well as all modules on which it depends. If more than one module is specified, attempt to load further modules only if the previous module failed to load.

Options

-a   Load all listed modules, not just the first one.

-l [*pattern*]

List all existing modules. This option may be combined with -t to specify a type of module, or you may include a *pattern* to search for.

-r   Remove the specified modules, as well as the modules on which they depend.

-t *type* Load only a specific type of module. Consult */etc/conf.modules* for the directories in which all modules of that type reside.

Files

/etc/conf.modules

Information about modules: which ones depend on others, which directories correspond to particular types of modules.

/sbin/insmod, /sbin/rmmod, /sbin/depmod

Programs that **modprobe** relies on.

mount	**mount** [*options*] [*special–device*] [*directory*]

Mount a file structure. **mount** announces to the system that a removable file structure is present on *special-device*. The file structure is mounted on *directory*, which must already exist and should be empty; it then becomes the name of the root of the newly mounted file structure. If **mount** is invoked with no arguments, it displays the name of each mounted device, the directory on which it is mounted, whether the file structure is read-only, and the date it was mounted. Only a privileged user can use the **mount** command.

Options

-a   Mount all filesystems listed in */etc/fstab*. Note: this is the only option that cannot take a *special-device* or *node* argument.

-f   Fake mount. Go through the motions of checking the device and directory, but do not actually mount the filesystem.

-n   Do not record the mount in */etc/mtab*.

Note: this is the only option to **mount** that requires a *special-device* or *node* argument. Qualify the mount with one of the specified *options*:

async   Read input and output to the device asynchronously.

auto   Allow mounting with the –a option.

defaults   Use all options' default values (**async, auto, dev, exec, nouser, rw, suid**).

dev   Interpret any special devices that exist on the filesystem.

exec   Allow binaries to be executed.

noauto   Do not allow mounting via the –a option.

nodev   Do not interpret any special devices which exist on the filesystem.

noexec   Do not allow the execution of binaries on the filesystem.

nosuid   Do not acknowledge any **suid** or **sgid** bits.

nouser   Only privileged users will have access to the filesystem.

remount   Expect the filesystem to have already been mounted, and remount it.

ro   Allow read-only access to the filesystem.

rw   Allow read/write access to the filesystem.

suid   Acknowledge **suid** and **sgid** bits.

sync   Read input and output to the device synchronously.

user   Allow unprivileged users to mount the filesystem. Note that the defaults on such a system will be **nodev, noexec,** and **nosuid,** unless otherwise specified.

check=relaxed|normal|strict
Specify how strictly to regulate the integration of an MS-DOS filesystem when mounting it.

conv=binary|text|auto
Specify method by which to convert files on MS-DOS and ISO-9660 filesystems.

debug   Turn debugging on for MS-DOS and **ext2fs** filesystems.

errors=continue|remount|ro|panic
Specify action to take when encountering an error. **ext2fs** filesystems only.

→

mount ←	-v . Display mount information verbosely. -w Mount filesystem read/write.

Files

   /etc/fstab
> List of filesystems to be mounted and options to use when mounting them.

   /etc/mtab
> List of filesystems that are currently mounted, and the options with which they were mounted.

---

mountd

rpc.mountd [*options*]

NFS/NIS command. NFS mount request server. **mountd** reads the file */etc/exports* to determine which filesystems are available for mounting by which machines. It also provides information as to what filesystems are mounted by which clients. See also **nfsd**.

Options

  -d, --debug
> Debug mode. Output all debugging information via **syslogd**.

  -f *file*, **--exports-file** *file*
> Read the export permissions from *file* instead of */etc/exports*.

  -n, --allow-non-root
> Accept even those mount requests that enter via a non-reserved port.

  -p, --promiscuous
> Accept requests from any host that sends them.

  -r, --re-export
> Allow re-exportation of imported filesystems.

  -v, --version
> Print the version number.

Files

   /etc/exports
> Information about mount permissions.

---

named

named [*options*]

TCP/IP command. Internet domain name server. **named** is used by resolver libraries to provide access to the Internet distributed naming database. With no arguments, **named** reads */etc/named.boot* for any initial data and listens for queries on a privileged port. See RFC 1034 and RFC 1035 for more details.

There are several different **named** binaries available at different Linux archives, displaying various behaviors. If your version doesn't behave like the one described here, never fear—it should have come with documentation.

Options

-d *debuglevel*
> Print debugging information. *debuglevel* is a number indicating the level of messages printed.

-p *port* Use *port* as the port number. Default is 42.

[-b] *bootfile*
> File to use instead of *named.boot*. The -b is optional and allows you to specify a filename that begins with a leading dash.

Files

/etc/named.boot
> Read when **named** starts up.

netdate [*options*] [*protocol*] *hostname* . . .

TCP/IP command. Set the system time according to the time provided by one of the hosts in the list *hostname*. **netdate** tries to ascertain which host is the most reliable source. When run by an unprivileged user, **netdate** reports the current time, without attempting to set the system clock. You may specify the *protocol*—**udp** (the default) or **tcp**—once, or several times for various hosts.

Options

-l *time* The most reliable host is chosen from the list by sorting the hosts into groups based on the times they return when questioned. The first host from the largest group is then polled a second time. The differences between its time and the local host's time on each poll are recorded. These two differences are then compared. If the gap between them is greater than *time* (the default is five seconds), the host is rejected as inaccurate.

-v Display the groups into which hosts are sorted.

netstat [*options*]

TCP/IP command. Show network status. For all active sockets, print the protocol, the number of bytes waiting to be received, the number of bytes to be sent, the port number, the remote address and port, and the state of the socket.

→

Sys Admin Commands

netstat ←	**Options** -a Show the state of all sockets, not just active ones. -c Display information continuously, refreshing once every second. -i Include statistics for network devices. -n Show network addresses as numbers. -o Include additional information such as user name. -r Show routing tables. -t List only (and all) TCP sockets. -u List only UDP sockets. -v Print the version number and exit. -w List only raw sockets. -x List only UNIX domain sockets.
nfsd	**rpc.nfsd** [*options*] Daemon that starts the NFS server daemons that handle client filesystem requests. These daemons are user-level processes. The options are exactly the same as in **mountd**.
nslookup	**nslookup** [*−option* ...] [*host_to_find*	*−* [*server*]] TCP/IP command. Query Internet domain name servers. **nslookup** has two modes: interactive and noninteractive. Interactive mode allows the user to query name servers for information about various hosts and domains or to print a list of hosts in a domain. It is entered either when no arguments are given (default name server will be used), or when the first argument is a hyphen and the second argument is the hostname or Internet address of a name server. Noninteractive mode is used to print just the name and requested information for a host or domain. It is used when the name of the host to be looked up is given as the first argument. Any of the *keyword=value* pairs listed under the interactive **set** command can be used as an option on the command line by prefacing the keyword with a '−'. The optional second argument specifies a name server. **Options** All of the options under the **set** interactive command can be entered on the command line, with the syntax *−keyword*[*=value*]. ***Interactive commands*** **exit** Exit **nslookup**. **finger** [*name*] [>|>>*filename*] Connect with finger server on current host, optionally creating or appending to *filename*.

help, ?
    Print a brief summary of commands.

host [*server*]
    Look up information for *host* using the current default server or using *server* if specified.

ls -[ahd] *domain* [>|>>*filename*]
    List information available for *domain*, optionally creating or appending to *filename*. The -a option lists aliases of hosts in the domain. -h lists CPU and operating system information for the domain. -d lists all contents of a zone transfer.

lserver *domain*
    Change the default server to *domain*. Use the initial server to look up information about *domain*.

root Change default server to the server for the root of the domain name space.

server *domain*
    Change the default server to *domain*. Use the current default server to look up information about *domain*.

set *keyword*[=*value*]
    Change state information affecting the lookups. Valid keywords are:

   all   Print the current values of the frequently used options to **set**.

   class=*name*
       Set query class to IN (Internet), CHAOS, HESIOD, or ANY. Default is IN.

   domain=*name*
       Change default domain name to *name*.

   [no]debug
       Turn debugging mode on or off.

   [no]d2 Turn exhaustive debugging mode on or off.

   [no]defname
       Append default domain name to every lookup.

   [no]ignoretc
       Ignore truncate error.

   [no]recurse
       Tell name server to query or not query other servers if it does not have the information.

   [no]search
       With *defname*, search for each name in parent domains of current domain.

   [no]vc
       Always use a virtual circuit when sending requests to the server.

→

nslookup
←
	port=*port*
	    Connect to name server using *port*.
	querytype=*value*
	    See **type**=*value*.
	retry=*number*
	    Set number of retries to *number*.
	root=*host*
	    Change name of root server to *host*.
	srchlist=*domain*
	    Set search list to *domain*.
	timeout=*number*
	    Change time-out interval for waiting for a reply to *number* seconds.
	type=*value*
	    Change type of information returned from a query to one of:

A	Host's Internet address
ANY	Any available information
CNAME	Canonical name for an alias
HINFO	Host CPU and operating system type
MD	Mail destination
MG	Mail group member
MINFO	Mailbox or mail list information
MR	Mail rename domain name
MX	Mail exchanger
NS	Nameserver for the named zone
PTR	Host name or pointer to other information
SOA	Domain start-of-authority
TXT	Text information
UINFO	User information
WKS	Supported well-known services

view *filename*
    Sort and list output of previous **ls** command(s) with **more**.

pcnfsd	**/usr/sbin/rpc.pcnfsd** NFS/NIS command. NFS authentication and print request server. **pcnfsd** is an RPC server that supports ONC clients on PC systems. **pcnfsd** reads the configuration file */etc/pcnfsd.conf*, if present, then services RPC requests directed to program number 150001. This current release of the **pcnfsd** daemon (as of this printing) supports both version 1 and version 2 of the **pcnfsd** protocol. Requests ser-

viced by **pcnfsd** fall into three categories: authentication, printing, and other. Only the authentication and printing services have administrative significance.

Authentication

When **pcnfsd** receives a PCNFSD_AUTH or PCNFSD2_AUTH request, it will log in the user by validating the username and password, returning the corresponding user ID, group IDs, home directory, and umask. At this time, **pcnfsd** will also append a record to the *wtmp* database. If you do not want to record PC logins in this way, add the line:

```
wtmp off
```

to the */etc/pcnfsd.conf* file.

Printing

pcnfsd supports a printing model based on the use of NFS to transfer the actual print data from the client to the server. The client system issues a PCNFSD_PR_INIT or PCNFSD2_PR_INIT request, and the server returns the path to a spool directory that the client may use and that is exported by NFS. **pcnfsd** creates a subdirectory for each of its clients; the parent directory is normally */usr/spool/pcnfs* and the subdirectory is the hostname of the client system. If you want to use a different parent directory, add the line:

```
spooldir path
```

to the */etc/pcnfsd.conf* file. Once a client has mounted the spool directory and has transferred print data to a file in this directory, **pcnfsd** will issue a PCNFSD_PR_START or PCNFSD2_PR_START request. **pcnfsd** constructs a command based on the printing services of the server operating system and executes the command using the identity of the PC user. Every print request includes the name of the printer to be used. **pcnfsd** interprets a printer as either a destination serviced by the system print spooler or as a virtual printer. Virtual printers are defined by the following line in the */etc/pcnfsd.conf* file:

```
printer name alias-for command
```

where *name* is the name of the printer you want to define, *alias-for* is the name of a real printer that corresponds to this printer, and *command* is a command that will be executed whenever a file is printed on *name*.

Sys Admin Commands

pop2d	**in.pop2d**

Allow users to connect to port 109 and request the contents of their mailbox in */var/spool/mail*. **pop2d** requires a username and password before providing mail, and can serve individual messages. See also **pop3d**.

Commands

Each command must be entered on a separate line.

HELO Prompt for username and password.
FOLD Open */var/spool/mail/$USER*.
HOST Open */var/spool/pop/$USER*.
READ Read a message.
RETR Retrieve a message.
ACKS Save the last message retrieved and move to next message.
ACKD Delete the last message retrieved and move to next message.
NACK Save the last message retrieved and expect to resend it.
QUIT Exit. |
| pop3d | **in.pop3d**

pop3d is a more recent version of **pop2d**. It behaves similarly, but accepts a slightly different list of commands.

Commands

USER Prompt for name.
PASS Prompt for password.
STAT Display the number of messages in the mailbox and its total size.
LIST Display individual messages' sizes.
DELE Delete a message.
NOOP Perform a null operation.
LAST Print the number of the most recently received message that has been read.
RSET Reset: clear all deletion marks.
TOP Print the first part of a message.
QUIT Exit. |
| portmap | **rpc.portmap** [*option*]

NFS/NIS command. RPC program number to IP port mapper. **portmap** is a server that converts RPC program numbers to IP port numbers. It must be running in order to make RPC calls. When an RPC server is started, it tells **portmap** what port number it is listening to and what RPC program |

numbers it is prepared to serve. When a client wishes to make an RPC call to a given program number, it first contacts **portmap** on the server machine to determine the port number where RPC packets should be sent. **portmap** must be the first RPC server started.

Option

-d   Run **portmap** in debugging mode. Does not allow **portmap** to run as a daemon.

---

ping [*options*] *host*

Confirm that a remote host is online and responding. **ping** is intended for use in network testing, measurement, and management. Because of the load it can impose on the network, it is unwise to use **ping** during normal operations or from automated scripts.

Options

-c *count*
    Stop after sending (and receiving) *count* ECHO_RESPONSE packets.

-d   Set SO_DEBUG option on socket being used.

-f   Flood **ping**-output packets as fast as they come back, or 100 times per second, whichever is more. This can be very hard on a network and should be used with caution; only a privileged user may use this option.

-i *wait*
    Wait *wait* seconds between sending each packet. Default is to wait one second between each packet. This option is incompatible with the -f option.

-l *preload*
    Send *preload* number of packets as fast as possible before falling into normal mode of behavior.

-n   Numeric output only. No attempt will be made to look up symbolic names for host addresses.

-p *digits*
    Specify up to 16 pad bytes to fill out packet sent. This is useful for diagnosing data-dependent problems in a network. *digits* are in hex. For example, -p ff will cause the sent packet to be filled with all ones.

-q   Quiet output—nothing is displayed except the summary lines at startup time and when finished.

-r   Bypass the normal routing tables and send directly to a host on an attached network.

→

Sys Admin Commands

ping ←	**-s** *packetsize* 　　Specify number of data bytes to be sent. Default is 56, which translates into 64 ICMP data bytes when combined with the eight bytes of ICMP header data. **-v**　Verbose—list ICMP packets received other than ECHO_RESPONSE. **-R**　Set the IP record route option, which will store the route of the packet inside the IP header. The contents of the record route will be printed if the **-v** option is given, and will be set on return packets if the target host preserves the record route option across echoes, or the **-l** option is given.
powerd	**powerd** *device* Monitor the connection to an uninterruptible power supply, which the user must specify via *device*. When power goes low, signal **init** to run its **powerwait** and **powerfail** entries; when full power is restored, signal **init** to run its **powerokwait** entries.
pppd	**pppd** [*options*] [*tty*] [*speed*] PPP stands for the Point-to-Point Protocol; it allows datagram transmission over a serial connection. **pppd** attempts to configure *tty* for PPP (searching in */dev*), or, by default, the controlling terminal. You can also specify a baud rate of *speed*. ***Options*** **asyncmap** *map* 　　Specify which control characters cannot pass over the line. *map* should be a 32-bit hex number, where each bit represents a character to escape. For example, bit 00000001 represents the character 0x00; bit 80000000 represents the character 0x1f or _. You may specify multiple characters. **auth**　Require self-authentication by peers before allowing packets to move. **connect** *command* 　　Connect as specified by *command*, which may be a binary or shell command. **debug, -d** 　　Increment the debugging level. **defaultroute** 　　Add a new default route in which the peer is the gateway. When the connection shuts down, remove the route.

-detach
: Operate in the foreground. By default, **pppd** forks and operates in the background.

disconnect *command*
: Close the connection as specified by *command*, which may be a binary or shell command.

domain *d*
: Specify a domain name of *d*.

escape *character-list*
: Escape all characters in *character-list*, which should be a comma-separated list of hex numbers. You cannot escape 0x20–0x3f or 0x5e.

file *file* Consult *file* for options.

lock   Allow only **pppd** to access the device.

mru *bytes*
: Refuse packets of more than *bytes* bytes.

name *name*
: Specify a machine name for the local system.

netmask *mask*
: Specify netmask (for example, 255.255.255.0).

passive, -p
: Do not exit if peer does not respond to attempts to initiate a connection. Instead, wait for a valid packet from the peer.

silent   Send no packets until after receiving one.

[*local_IP_address*]:[*remote_IP_address*]
: Specify the local and/or remote interface IP addresses, as hostnames or numeric addresses.

Files

/var/run/pppn.pid
: **pppd**'s process ID.

/etc/ppp/ip-up
: Binary or script to be executed when the PPP link becomes active.

/etc/ppp/ip-down
: Binary or script to be executed when the PPP link goes down.

/etc/ppp/pap-secrets
: Contains usernames, passwords, and IP addresses for use in PAP authentication.

/etc/ppp/options
: System defaults. Options in this file are set *before* the command-line options.

Sys Admin
Commands

→

pppd ←	~/.ppprc The user's default options. These are read before command-line options, but after the system defaults. /etc/ppp/options.ttyname Name of the default serial port.
psupdate	**psupdate** [*mapfile*] Update the **psupdate** database (on some systems */boot/psupdate*, on others, */etc/psdatabase*), which contains information about the kernel image system map file. If no *mapfile* is specified, **psupdate** uses the default (either */usr/src/linux/vmlinux* or */usr/src/linux/tools/zSystem*, depending on the distribution).
ramsize	**ramsize** [*option*] [*image* [*size* [*offset*]]] If no options are specified, print usage information for the RAM disk. The pair of bytes at offset 504 in the kernel image normally specify the RAM size; with a kernel *image* argument, print the information found at that offset. To change that information, specify a new *size* (in kilobytes). You may also specify a different *offset*. Note that **rdev -r** is the same as **ramsize**. *Option* -o *offset* Same as specifying an *offset* as an argument.
rarp	**rarp** [*options*] Administer the Reverse Address Resolution Protocol (RARP) table (usually */proc/net/rarp*). *Options* -a [*hostname*] Show all entries. If *hostname* is specified, show only the entries relevant to *hostname*, which may be a list. -d *hostname* Remove the entries relevant to *hostname*, which may be a list. -s *hostname hw_addr* Add a new entry for *hostname*, with the hardware address *hw_addr*.

-t *type* Check only for *type* entries when consulting or changing the table. *type* my be **ether** (the default) or **ax25**.

-v   Verbose mode.

rdate [*option*]

TCP/IP command. Notify the time server that date has changed. If the local time server is a master, it will notify all of the slaves that the time has been changed. If the local time server is a slave, it will request that the master update the time.

Option

-p   Print the date; do not attempt to set it.

rdev [*options*] [*image* [*value* [*offset*]]]

If no arguments are specified, display a line, in */etc/mtab* syntax, that describes the root filesystem. Otherwise, change the values of the bytes in the kernel image that describe the RAM disk size (by default located at byte offset 504 in the kernel), VGA mode (default 506), and root device (default 508). You must specify the kernel *image* to change, and may specify a new *value* and a different *offset*.

Options

-o *offset*
          Same as specifying an *offset* as an argument.
-r   Behave like **ramsize**.
-s   Behave like **swapdev**.
-v   Behave like **vidmode**.
-R   Behave like **rootflags**.

rdist [*options*] [*names*]

Remote file distribution client program. **rdist** maintains identical copies of files over multiple hosts. It reads commands from a *distfile* to direct the updating of files and/or directories. *distfile* is specified with the -**f** option, the -**c** option, or -, in which case standard input is used.

Options

-a *num*
          Do not update filesystems with fewer than *num* bytes free.
-c *name* [*login@*]*host*[:*dest*]
          Interpret ([*login@*]*host*[:*dest*]) as a small *distfile*.

Sys Admin Commands

→

-d *var=value*
> Define *var* to have *value*. This option defines or overrides variable definitions in the *distfile*. Set the variable *var* to *value*.

-f *file*   Read input from *file* (by default, *distfile*). If *file* is -, read from standard input.

-l *options*
> Specify logging options on the local machine.

-m *machine*
> Update only *machine*. May be specified multiple times for multiple machines.

-n   Suppress normal execution. Instead, print the commands that would have been executed.

-o*options*
> Specify one or more *options*, which must be comma-separated.

> **chknfs**   Suppress operations on files that reside on NFS filesystems.

> **chkreadonly**
> > Check filesystem to be sure it is not read-only before attempting to perform updates.

> **chksym**   Do not update files that exist on the local host but are symbolic links on the remote host.

> **compare** Compare files; use this comparison as the criteria for determining which files should be updated, rather than using age.

> **follow**   Interpret symbolic links, copying the file to which the link points instead of creating a link on the remote machine.

> **ignlnks**   Ignore links that appear to be unresolvable.

> **nochkgroup**
> > Do not update a file's group ownership unless the entire file needs updating.

> **nochkmode**
> > Do not update file mode unless the entire file needs updating.

> **nochkowner**
> > Do not update file ownership unless the entire file needs updating.

> **nodescend**Suppress recursive descent into directories.

> **noexec**   Suppress **rdist** of executables that are in *a.out* format.

numchkgroup
> Check group ownership by group ID instead of by name.

numchkowner
> Check file ownership by user ID instead of by name.

quiet   Quiet mode; does not print commands as they execute.

remove Remove files that exist on the remote host but not the local host.

savetargets
> Save updated files in *name.old*.

verify   Print a list of all files on the remote machine that are out of date, but do not update them.

whole   Preserve directory structure by creating subdirectories on the remote machine. For example, if you **rdist** the file */foo/bar* into the directory */baz*, it would produce the file */baz/foo/bar*, instead of the default, */baz/bar*.

younger Do not update files that are younger than the master files.

-p *path*
> Specify the path to search for **rdistd** on the remote machine.

-t *seconds*
> Specify the timeout period (default 900 seconds) after which **rdist** will sever the connection if the remote server has not yet responded.

-A *num*
> Specify the minumum number of inodes that **rdist** requires.

-D   Debugging mode.

-F   Execute all commands sequentially, without forking.

-L *options*
> Specify logging options on the remote machine.

-M *num*
> Do not allow more than *num* child **rdist** processes to run simultaneously. Default is 4.

-P *path*
> Specify path to *rsh* on the local machine.

---

rdistd *options*

Start the **rdist** server. Note that you *must* specify the -S option, unless you are simply querying for version information with -V.

→

rdistd
←
	Options
	    -D Debugging mode.
	    -S Start the server.
	    -V Display the version number and exit immediately.

reboot

reboot [*options*]

Close out filesystems, shut down the system, then reboot the system. Because this command immediately stops all processes, it should be run only in single-user mode. If the system is not in run level 0 or 6, **reboot** calls **shutdown -nf**.

Options

-d   Suppress writing to */var/log/wtmp*.

-f   Call **reboot** even when **shutdown** would normally be called.

-n   Suppress normal call to **sync**.

-w   Suppress normal execution; simply write to */var/log/wtmp*.

rexecd

rexecd *command–line*

TCP/IP command. Server for the **rexec** routine, providing remote execution facilities with authentication based on usernames and passwords. **rexecd** is started by **inetd** and must have an entry in **inetd**'s configuration file, */etc/inetd.conf*. When **rexecd** receives a service request, the following protocol is initiated:

1. The server reads characters from the socket up to a null byte. The resulting string is interpreted as an ASCII number, base 10.

2. If the number received in step 1 is nonzero, it is interpreted as the port number of a secondary stream to be used for **stderr**. A second connection is then created to the specified port on the client's machine.

3. A null-terminated username of at most 16 characters is retrieved on the initial socket.

4. A null-terminated, unencrypted password of at most 16 characters is retrieved on the initial socket.

5. A null-terminated command to be passed to a shell is retrieved on the initial socket. The length of the command is limited by the upper bound on the size of the system's argument list.

6. **rexecd** then validates the user, as is done at login time, and, if the authentication was successful, changes to the user's home directory and establishes the user and group protections of the user.

7. A null byte is returned on the connection associated with **stderr** and the command line is passed to the normal login shell of the user. The shell inherits the network connections established by **rexecd**.

Diagnostics

`username too long`
Name is longer than 16 characters.

`password too long`
Password is longer than 16 characters.

`command too long`
Command passed exceeds the size of the argument list.

`Login incorrect`
No password file entry for the username exists.

`Password incorrect`
Wrong password was supplied.

`No remote directory`
chdir to home directory failed.

`Try again`
fork by server failed.

`<shellname>: . . .`
fork by server failed. User's login shell could not be started.

---

rlogind [*options*]

TCP/IP command. Server for the **rlogin** program, providing a remote login facility, with authentication based on privileged port numbers from trusted hosts. **rlogind** is invoked by **inetd** when a remote login connection is requested, and executes the following protocol:

- The server checks the client's source port. If the port is not in the range 0-1023, the server aborts the connection.

- The server checks the client's source address and requests the corresponding hostname. If the hostname cannot be determined, the dot-notation representation of the host address is used.

The login process propagates the client terminal's baud rate and terminal type, as found in the environment variable, TERM.

→

rlogind ←	*Options*
	-a Verify hostname.
	-1 Do not authenticate hosts via a nonroot *.rhosts* file.
	-n Suppress keep-alive messages.
rmail	**rmail** *user . . .*
	TCP/IP command. Handle remote mail received via **uucp**, collapsing From lines in the form generated by **mail** into a single line of the form return-path!sender and passing the processed mail onto **sendmail**. **rmail** is explicitly designed for use with **uucp** and **sendmail**.
rmmod	**rmmod** [*option*] *modules*
	Unload a module or list of modules from the kernel. This command is successful only if the specified modules are not in use and no other modules are dependent on them.
	Option
	-r Recursively remove stacked modules (all modules that use the specified module).
rootflags	**rootflags** [*option*] *image* [*flags* [*offset*]]
	Sets *flags* for a kernel *image*. If no arguments are specified, print *flags* for the kernel image. *flags* is a two byte integer located at offset 498 in a kernel *image*. Currently the only effect of *flags* is to mount the root filesystem in read-only mode if *flags* is non-zero. You may change *flags* by specifying the kernel *image* to change, the new *flags*, and the byte-offset at which to place the new information (the default is 498). Note that **rdev -R** is a synonym for **rootflags**. If LILO is used, **rootflags** is not needed. *flags* can be set from the LILO prompt during a boot.
	Option
	-o *offset*
	Same as specifying an *offset* as an argument.
route	**route** [*option*] [*command*]
	TCP/IP command. Manually manipulate the routing tables normally maintained by **routed**. **route** accepts two commands: **add**, to add a route, and **del**, to delete a route. The two commands have the following syntax:

add [-net | -host] *address* [gw *gateway*]
  [netmask *mask*] [mss *tcp-mss*] [dev *device*]
del *address*

address is treated as a plain route unless **-net** is specified or
address is found in */etc/networks*. **-host** can be used to specify that *address* is a plain route whether or not it is found in
/etc/networks. The keyword *default* means to use this route
for all requests if no other route is known. You can specify
the *gateway* through which to route packets headed for that
address, its *netmask*, TCP *mss*, and the *device* with which to
associate the route. Only a privileged user may modify the
routing tables.

If no command is specified, **route** prints the routing tables.

Option

  -n   Prevent attempts to print host and network
          names symbolically when reporting actions.

---

routed [*options*] [*logfile*]

TCP/IP command. Network routing daemon. **routed** is
invoked by a privileged user at boot time to manage the
Internet Routing Tables. The routing daemon uses a variant
of the Xerox NS Routing Information Protocol in maintaining up-to-date kernel routing-table entries. When **routed** is
started, it uses the SIOCGIFCONF ioctl to find those directly
connected interfaces configured into the system and marked
up. **routed** transmits a REQUEST packet on each interface,
then enters a loop, listening for REQUEST and RESPONSE
packets from other hosts. When a REQUEST packet is
received, **routed** formulates a reply based on the information maintained in its internal tables. The generated
RESPONSE packet contains a list of known routes. Any
RESPONSE packets received are used to update the Routing
Tables as appropriate.

When an update is applied, **routed** records the change in its
internal tables, updates the kernal Routing Table, and generates a RESPONSE packet reflecting these changes to all
directly connected hosts and networks.

Options

  -d   Debugging mode. Log additional information to
          the *logfile*.
  -g   Offer a route to the default destination.
  -q   Opposite of -s option.
  -s   Force **routed** to supply routing information,
          whether it is acting as an internetwork router or
          not.

$\rightarrow$

Sys Admin Commands

routed ←	-t Stop **routed** from going into background and releasing itself from the controlling terminal, so that interrupts from the keyboard will kill the process.

rpcinfo	**rpcinfo** [*options*] [*host*] [*program*] [*version*]
	
	NFS/NIS command. Report RPC information. *program* can be either a name or a number. If a *version* is specified, **rpcinfo** attempts to call that version of the specified *program*. Otherwise, it attempts to find all the registered version numbers for the specified *program* by calling version 0, and it attempts to call each registered version.
	
	Options
	
	-b *program version*
	    Make an RPC broadcast to the specified *program* and *version*, using UDP, and report all hosts that respond.
	
	-d *program version*
	    Delete the specified *version* of *program*'s registration. Can be executed only by the user who added the registration or a privileged user.
	
	-n *portnum*
	    Use *portnum* as the port number for the -t and -u options, instead of the port number given by the portmapper.
	
	-p [*host*]
	    Probe the portmapper on host and print a list of all registered RPC programs. If *host* is not specified, it defaults to the value returned by **hostname**.
	
	-t *host program* [*version*]
	    Make an RPC call to *program* on the specified *host*, using TCP, and report whether a response was received.
	
	-u *host program* [*version*]
	    Make an RPC call to *program* on the specified *host*, using UDP, and report whether a response was received.
	
	Examples
	
	To show all of the RPC services registered on the local machine, use:
	
	`$ rpcinfo -p`

To show all of the RPC services registered on the machine named **klaxon**, use:
 	
    $ **rpcinfo -p klaxon**
 	
To show all machines on the local net that are running the Network Information Service (NIS), use:
 	
    $ **rpcinfo -b ypserv** *version* | **uniq**
 	
where *version* is the current NIS version obtained from the results of the -**p** switch above.
	rpcinfo

rshd [*options*]

TCP/IP command. Remote shell server for programs such as **rcmd** and **rcp**, which need to execute a noninteractive shell on remote machines. **rshd** is started by **inetd**, and must have an entry in **inetd**'s configuration file, */etc/inetd.conf.*

All options are exactly the same as those in **rlogind**, except for –L, which is unique to **rshd**.

Option

 –L   Log all successful connections and failed attempts via **syslogd**.

rstat *host*

TCP/IP command. Summarize *host*'s system status: the current time, uptime, and load averages, the average number of jobs in the run queue. Queries the remote host's **rstat_svc** daemon.

run-parts [*options*] [*directory*]

Run, in lexical order, all scripts found in *directory*. Exclude scripts whose filename include nonalphanumeric characters (besides underscores and hyphens).

Options

 ––   Interpret all subsequent arguments as filenames, not options.
 ––**test** Print information listing which scripts would be run, but suppress actual execution of them.
 ––**umask**=*umask*
        Specify *umask*. The default is 022.

runlevel

Display the previous and current system runlevels.

rshd

rstat

run-parts

runlevel

Sys Admin Commands

ruptime	**ruptime** [*options*] TCP/IP command. Provide information on how long each machine on the local network has been up, and which users are logged in to each. If a machine has not reported in for 11 minutes, assume it is down. The listing is sorted by hostname. *Options* -a Include users who have been idle for more than one hour. -l Sort machines by load average. -r Reverse the normal sort order. -t Sort machines by uptime. -u Sort machines by the number of users logged in.
rusers	**rusers** [*options*] [*host*] TCP/IP command. List the users logged on to *host*, or to all local machines, in **who** format (hostname, user names). *Options* -a Include machines with no users logged in. -l Include more information: tty, date, time, idle time, remote host.
rwall	**rwall** *host* [*file*] TCP/IP command. Print a message to all users logged on to *host*. If *file* is specified, read the message from it; otherwise, read from standard input.
rwhod	**rwhod** TCP/IP command. System status server that maintains the database used by the **rwho** and **ruptime** programs. Its operation is predicated on the ability to broadcast messages on a network. As a producer of information, **rwhod** periodically queries the state of the system and constructs status messages, which are broadcast on a network. As a consumer of information, it listens for other **rwhod** servers' status messages, validates them, then records them in a collection of files located in the directory */var/spool/rwho*. Messages received by the **rwhod** server are discarded unless they originated at an **rwhod** server's port. Status messages are generated approximately once every three minutes.

script [*option*] [*file*]

Fork the current shell and make a typescript of a terminal session. The typescript is written to *file*. If no *file* is given, the typescript is saved in the file *typescript*. The script ends when the forked shell exits.

Option

-a   Append to *file* or *typescript* instead of overwriting the previous contents.

sendmail [*flags*] [*address* . . .]

sendmail is a mail router. It accepts mail from a user's mail program, interprets the mail address, rewrites the address into the proper form for the delivery program, and routes the mail to the correct delivery program.

Command-line flags

-b*x*   Set operation mode to *x*. Operation modes are:

     a   Run in ARPAnet mode.

     d   Run as a daemon.

     i   Initialize the alias database.

     m   Deliver mail (default).

     p   Print the mail queue.

     s   Speak SMTP on input side.

     t   Run in test mode.

     v   Verify addresses, do not collect or deliver.

-C*file*   Use configuration file *file*.

-d*level*   Set debugging level.

-F*name*

     Set full name of user to *name*.

-f*name*

     Sender's name is *name*.

-h*cnt*   Set hop count (number of times message has been processed by **sendmail**) to *cnt*.

-n   Do not alias or forward.

-o*x value*

     Set option *x* to value *value*. Options are described below.

-p*protocol*

     Receive messages via the *protocol* protocol.

-q[*time*]

     Process queued messages immediately, or at intervals indicated by *time* (for example, -q30m for every half hour).

-r*name*

     Obsolete form of -f.

Sys Admin Commands

→

-t   Read head for To:, Cc:, and Bcc: lines, and send to everyone on those lists.

-v   Verbose.

-X *file*   Log all traffic to *file*. Not to be used for normal logging.

Configuration options

The following options can be set with the -o flag on the command line, or the O line in the configuration file:

7   Format all incoming messages in seven bits.

a*min*   If the D option is set, wait *min* minutes for the *aliases* file to be rebuilt before returning an alias database out-of-date warning.

A*file*   Use alternate alias file.

b*minblocks/maxsize*

       Require at least *minblocks* to be free, and optionally, set the maximum message size to *maxsize*. If *maxsize* is omitted, the slash is optional.

B*char*   Set unquoted space replacement character.

c   On mailers that are considered "expensive" to connect to, don't initiate immediate connection.

C*num*   Checkpoint the queue when mailing to multiple recipients. **sendmail** will rewrite the list of recipients after after each group of *num* recipients have been processed.

d*x*   Set the delivery mode to *x*. Delivery modes are d for deferred delivery, i for interactive (synchronous) delivery, b for background (asynchronous) delivery, and q for queue only—i.e., deliver the next time the queue is run.

D   Try to automatically rebuild the alias database if necessary.

e*x*   Set error processing to mode *x*. Valid modes are m to mail back the error message, w to write back the error message, p to print the errors on the terminal (default), q to throw away error messages, and e to do special processing for the BerkNet.

E*text*   Set error message header. *text* is either text to add to an error message or the name of a file. A file name must include its full path and begin with a "/".

f   Save UNIX-style From: lines at the front of messages.

F*mode*   Set default file permissions for temporary files. If this option is missing, default permissions are 0644.

G	Compare local mail names to the GECOS section in the password file.
g *n*	Default group ID to use when calling mailers.
H*file*	SMTP help file.
h *num*	Allow a maximum of *num* hops per message.
i	Do not take dots on a line by themselves as a message terminator.
I *arg*	Use DNS lookups and tune them. Queue messages on connection refused. The *arg* arguments are identical to **resolver** flags without the RES_ prefix. Each flag can be preceded by a plus or minus to enable or disable the corresponding name server option. There must be a white space between the I and the first flag.
j	Use MIME format for error messages.
J*path*	Set an alternative *.forward* search path.
k*num*	Specify size of the connection cache.
K*time*	Timeout connections after *time*.
l	Do not ignore **Errors-To**: header.
L*n*	Specify log level.
m	Send to "me" (the sender) also if I am in an alias expansion.
M*Xvalue*	Define a macro's value in command line. Assign *value* to macro *X*.
n	When running **newaliases**, validate the right side of aliases.
o	If set, this message may have old-style headers. If not set, this message is guaranteed to have new-style headers (i.e., commas instead of spaces between addresses).
p*what,what, . . .*	Tune how private you want the SMTP daemon. The *what* arguments should be separated from one another by commas. The *what* arguments may be any of the following:

public	Make SMTP fully public (default).
needmailhelo	Require site to send HELO or ELHO to before sending mail.
needexpnhelo	Require site to send HELO or ELHO before answering an address expansion request.
needvrfyhelo	As above but for verification requests.

→

	noexpn	Deny all expansion requests.
	novrfy	Deny all verification requests.
	authwarnings	Insert special headers in mail messages advising recipients that the message may not be authentic.
	goaway	Set all of the above (except **public**).
	restrictmailq	Allow only users of the same group as the owner of the queue directory to examine the mail queue.
	restrictqrun	Limit queue processing to root and the owner of the queue directory.

P*user* Send copies of all failed mail to *user* (usually postmaster).

q*fact* Multiplier (factor) for high-load queueing.

Q*queuedir*
Select the directory in which to queue messages.

R Don't prune route addresses.

S*file* Save statistics in the named file.

s Always instantiate the queue file, even under circumstances where it is not strictly necessary.

T*time* Set the timeout on undelivered messages in the queue to the specified time.

t*stz, dtz*
Set name of the time zone.

U*database*
Consult the user database *database* for forwarding information.

u*N* Set default user ID for mailers.

v Run in verbose mode.

V*host* Fall-back MX host. *host* should be the fully qualified domain name of the fallback host.

w Use a record for an ambiguous MX.

x*load* Queues messages when load level is higher than *load*.

X*load* Refuse SMTP connections when load is higher than *load*.

y*factor*
Penalize large recipient lists by *factor*.

Y	Deliver each job that is run from the queue in a separate process. This helps limit the size of running processes on systems with very low amounts of memory.
z*factor*	Multiplier for priority increments. This determines how much weight to give to a messages's precedence header. **sendmail**'s default is 1800.
Z*inc*	Increment priority of items remaining in queue by *inc* after each job is processed. **sendmail** uses 90000 by default.

sendmail support files

/usr/lib/sendmail
> Binary of **sendmail**.

/usr/bin/newaliases
> Link to */usr/lib/sendmail*; causes the alias database to be rebuilt.

/usr/bin/mailq
> Prints a listing of the mail queue.

/etc/sendmail.cf
> Configuration file, in text form.

/etc/sendmail.hf
> SMTP help file.

/usr/lib/sendmail.st
> Statistics file. Doesn't need to be present.

/etc/aliases
> Alias file, in text form.

/etc/aliases.{pag,dir}
> Alias file in **dbm** format.

/var/spool/mqueue
> Directory in which the mail queue and temporary files reside.

/var/spool/mqueue/qf
> Control (queue) files for messages.

/var/spool/mqueue/df
> Data files.

/var/spool/mqueue/lf
> Lock files.

/var/spool/mqueue/tf
> Temporary versions of *qf* files, used during queue-file rebuild.

/var/spool/mqueue/nf
> Used when creating a unique ID.

/var/spool/mqueue/xf
> Transcript of current session.

Sys Admin Commands

showmount	**showmount** [*options*] [*host*]
	
	NFS/NIS command. List the clients that have mounted filesystems from *host*, if specified, or from the local host, if not.
	
	Options
	
	  -a, --all
	      Include client hostname and the name of the mounted directory.
	  -d, --directories
	      List mounted directories, not clients.
	  -e, --exports
	      List the directories that may be exported and the machines that are allowed to mount them.

shutdown	**shutdown** [*options*] *when* [*message*]
	
	Terminate all processing. *when* may be a specific time (in *hh*:*mm* format), a number of minutes to wait (in +*m* format), or **now**. A broadcast *message* notifies all users to log off the system. Processes are signalled with SIGTERM, to allow them to exit gracefully. */etc/init* is called to perform the actual shutdown, which consists of placing the system in runlevel 1. Only privileged users can execute the **shutdown** command. Broadcast messages, default or defined, are displayed at regular intervals during the grace period; the closer the shutdown time, the more frequent the message.
	
	Options
	
	  -c Cancel a shutdown that is in progress.
	  -f Reboot fast, by suppressing the normal call to **fsck** when rebooting.
	  -h Halt the system when shutdown is complete.
	  -k Print the warning message, but suppress actual shutdown.
	  -n Perform shutdown without a call to **init**.
	  -r Reboot the system when shutdown is complete.
	  -t *sec* Ensure a *sec*-second delay between killing processes and changing the runlevel.

slattach	**slattach** [*options*] [*tty*] TCP/IP command. Attach serial lines as network interfaces, thereby preparing them for use as point-to-point connections. Only a privileged user may attach or detach a network interface.

Options

- -c *command*
  Run *command* when the connection is severed.
- -d   Debugging mode.
- -e   Exit immediately after initializing the line.
- -h   Exit when the connection is severed.
- -l   Create UUCP style lockfile in */var/spool/uucp*.
- -L   Enable 3-wire operation.
- -m   Suppress initialization of the line to 8 bits raw mode.
- -n   Similar to **mesg n**.
- -p *protocol*
  Specify *protocol*, which may be **slip**, **adaptive**, **ppp**, or **kiss**.
- -q   Quiet mode, supress messages.
- -s *speed*
  Specify line speed.

---

swapdev [*option*] [*image* [*swapdevice* [*offset*]]]

If no arguments are given, display usage information about the swap device. If just the location of the kernel *image* is specified, print the information found there. To change that information, specify the new *swapdevice*. You may also specify the *offset* in the kernel image to change. Note that **rdev -s** is a synonym for **swapdev**.

Option

- -o *offset*
  Synonymous to specifying an *offset* as an argument.

---

swapon [*options*] *device*

Make *device* (which may be a space-separated list) available for swapping and paging.

Options

- -a   Consult */etc/fstab* for devices marked **sw**. Use those in place of the *device* argument.
- -p *priority*
  Specifies a *priority* for the swap area. Higher priority areas will be used up before lower priority areas are used.

Sys Admin Commands

swapoff	**swapoff** [*option*]	*device*
	Stop making *device* (which may be a space-separated list) availible for swapping and paging.
	Option
	-a Consult */etc/fstab* for devices marked **sw**. Use those in place of the *device* argument.
sync	**sync**
	Write filesystem buffers to disk. **sync** executes the **sync()** system call. If the system is to be stopped, **sync** must be called to ensure filesystem integrity. Note that **shutdown** automatically calls **sync** before shutting down the system. **sync** may take several seconds to complete, so the system should be told to **sleep** briefly if you are about to manually call **halt** or **reboot**. Note that **shutdown** is the preferred way to halt or reboot your system, since it takes care of **sync**-ing and other housekeeping for you.
syslogd	**syslogd**
	TCP/IP command. Log system messages into a set of files described by the configuration file */etc/syslog.conf.* Each message is one line. A message can contain a priority code, marked by a number in angle braces at the beginning of the line. Priorities are defined in *<sys/syslog.h>*. **syslogd** reads from an Internet domain socket specified in */etc/services.* To bring **syslogd** down, send it a terminate signal.
sysklogd	**sysklogd**
	sysklogd, the Linux program that provides **syslogd** functionality, behaves exacly like the BSD version of **syslogd**. The difference should be completely transparent to the user. However, **sysklogd** is coded very differently and supports a slightly extended syntax. It is invoked as **syslogd**. See also **klogd**.
	Options
	-d Turn on debugging.
	-f *configfile*
	Specify alternate configuration file.
	-h Forward messages from remote hosts to forwarding hosts.
	-l *hostlist*
	Specify hostnames that should be logged with just their hostname, not their fully qualified domain name. Multiple hosts should be separated with a colon (:).

-m *markinterval*
> Select number of minutes between mark messages.

-n   Avoid auto-backgrounding. This is needed when starting syslogd from **init**.

-p *socket*
> Send log to *socket* instead of /*dev*/*log*.

-r   Receive messages from the network using an internet domain socket with the **syslog** service.

-s *domainlist*
> Strip off domainnames specified in *domainlist* before logging. Multiple domain names should be separated by a colon (:).

---

systat [*options*] *host*

Get information about the network or system status of a remote host by querying its **netstat**, **systat**, or **daytime** service.

Options

-n, --netstat
> Specifically query the host's **netstat** service.

-p *port*, --**port** *port*
> Specify port to query.

-s, --systat
> Specifically query the host's **systat** service.

-t, --time
> Specifically query the host's **daytime** service.

---

talkd [*option*]

TCP/IP command. Remote user communication server. **talkd** notifies a user that somebody else wants to initiate a conversation. A **talk** client initiates a rendezvous by sending a CTL_MSG of type LOOK_UP to the server. This causes the server to search its invitation tables for an existing invitation for the client. If the lookup fails, the caller sends an ANNOUNCE message causing the server to broadcast an announcement on the callee's login ports requesting contact. When the callee responds, the local server responds with the rendezvous address, and a stream connection is established through which the conversation takes place.

Option

-d   Write debugging information to the **syslogd** log file.

tar

tar [*options*] [*tarfile*] [*other–files*]

Copy *files* to or restore *files* from an archive medium. If any *files* are directories, **tar** acts on the entire subtree. Options need not be preceded by - (though they may be). The exception to this rule is when you are using a long-style option (such as --**modification-time**). In that case, the exact syntax is:

tar --*long-option* -*function-options files*

For example: `tar --modification-time -xvf tar-file.tar`

Function options

You must use exactly one of these, and it must come before any other options.

-**c**, --**create**

> Create a new archive.

-**d**, --**compare**

> Compare the files stored in *tarfile* with *other-files*. Report any differences: missing files, different sizes, different file attributes (such as permissions or modification time).

-**r**, --**append**

> Append *other-files* to the end of an existing archive.

-**t**, --**list**

> Print the names of *other-files* if they are stored on the archive (if *other-files* are not specified, print names of all files).

-**u**, --**update**

> Add files if not in the archive or if modified.

-**x**, --**extract**, --**get**

> Extract *other-files* from an archive (if *other-files* are not specified, extract all files).

-**A**, --**catenate**, --**concatenate**

> Concatenate a second tar file on to the end of the first.

Options

n

> Select device *n*, where *n* is 0,...,9999. The default is found in */etc/default/tar*.

[*drive*][*density*]

> Set drive (0–7) and storage density (l, m, or h, corresponding to low, medium, or high).

--**atime-preserve**

> Preserve original access-time on extracted files.

-b, --block-size=n
> Set block size to $n \times 512$ bytes.

--checkpoint
> List directory names encountered.

--exclude=_file_
> Remove _file_ from any list of files.

-f _arch_, **--file=**_filename_
> Store files in or extract files from archive _arch_. Note that _filename_ may take the form _hostname:filename_.

--force-local
> Interpret filenames in the form _hostname:filename_ as local files.

-g, --listed-incremental
> Create new-style incremental backup.

-h, --dereference
> Dereference symbolic links.

-i, --ignore-zeros
> Ignore zero-sized blocks (i.e., _EOFs_).

--ignore-failed-read
> Ignore unreadable files to be archived. Default behavior is to exit when encountering these.

-k, --keep-old-files
> When extracting files, do not overwrite files with similar names. Instead, print an error message.

-l, --one-file-system
> Do not archive files from other file systems.

-m, --modification-time
> Do not restore file modification times; update them to the time of extraction.

--null Allow filenames to be null-terminated with **-T**. Override **-C**.

--old, --portability, --preserve
> Equivalent to invoking both the **-p** and **-s** options.

-p, --same-permissions, --preserve-permissions
> Keep ownership of extracted files same as that of original permissions.

--remove-files
> Remove originals after inclusion in archive.

--rsh-command=_command_
> Do not connect to remote host with **rsh**; instead, use _command_.

-s, --same-order, --preserve-order
> When extracting, sort filenames to correspond to the order in the archive.

$\rightarrow$

Sys Admin
Commands

--totals

> Print byte totals.

--use-compress-program=*program*

> Compress archived files with *program*, or uncompress extracted files with *program*.

-v, --verbose

> Verbose. Print filenames as they are added or extracted.

-w, --interactive

> Wait for user confirmation (y) before taking any actions.

-z, --gzip, --ungzip

> Compress files with **gzip** before archiving them, or uncompress them with **gunzip** before extracting them.

-C, --directory=*directory*

> **cd** to *directory* before beginning **tar** operation.

-F, --info-script, --new-volume-script=*script*

> Implies -M (multiple archive files). Run *script* at the end of each file.

-G, --incremental

> Create old-style incremental backup.

-K *file*, **--starting-file** *file*

> Begin **tar** operation at file *file* in archive.

-L, --tape-lgenth=*length*

> Write a maximum of *length* × 1024 bytes to each tape.

-M, --multi-volume

> Expect archive to multi-volume. With -c, create such an archive.

-N *date*, **--after-date** *date*

> Ignore files older than *date*.

-O, --to-stdout

> Print extracted files on standard out.

-P, --absolute-paths

> Do not remove initial slashes (/) from input filenames.

-R, --record-number

> Display archive's record number.

-S, --sparse

> Treat short file specially and more efficiently.

-T *filename*, **--files-from** *filename*

> Consult *filename* for files to extract or create.

-V *name*, **--label=***name*

> Name this volume *name*.

-W, --verify
> Check archive for corruption after creation.

-X *file*, --exclude *file*
> Consult *file* for list of files to exclude.

-Z, --compress, --uncompress
> Compress files with **compress** before archiving them, or uncompress them with **uncompress** before extracting them.

Examples

Create an archive of */bin* and */usr/bin* (**c**), show the command working (**v**), and store on the tape in */dev/rmt0*:

```
tar cvf /dev/rmt0 /bin /usr/bin
```

List the tape's contents in a format like **ls** **-l**:

```
tar tvf /dev/rmt0
```

Extract the */bin* directory:

```
tar xvf /dev/rmt0 /bin
```

Create an archive of the current directory and store it in a file *backup.tar*.

```
tar cvf - `find . -print` > backup.tar
```

(The – tells **tar** to store the archive on standard output, which is then redirected.)

tcpd

TCP/IP command. Monitor incoming TCP/IP requests (such as those for **telnet**, **ftp**, **finger**, **exec**, **rlogin**). Provide checking and logging services; then pass the request to the appropriate daemon.

tcpdchk [*options*]

TCP/IP command. Consult the TCP wrapper configuration (in */etc/hosts.allow* and */etc/hosts.deny*); display a list of all possible problems with it; attempt to suggest possible fixes.

Options

-a
> Include a list of rules; do not require an ALLOW keyword before allowing sites to access the local host.

-d
> Consult *./hosts.allow* and *./hosts.deny* instead of */etc/hosts.allow* and */etc/hosts.deny*.

$\rightarrow$

tcpdchk ←	**-i** *conf-file* Specify location of *inetd.conf* or *tlid.conf* file. These are files that **tcpdchk** automatically uses in its evaluation of TCP wrapper files. **-v** Verbose mode.

tcpdmatch

tcpdmatch [*options*] *daemon client*

TCP/IP command. Predict the TCP wrapper's response to a specific request. You must specify which *daemon* the request is made to (the syntax may be *daemon@host* for requests to remote machines) and the *client* from which the request originates (the syntax may be *user@client* for a specific user, or a wildcard). Consult */etc/hosts.allow* and */etc/hosts.deny* to determine the TCP wrapper's actions.

Options

-d   Consult *./hosts.allow* and *./hosts.deny* instead of */etc/hosts.allow* and */etc/hosts.deny*.

-i *conf-file*
        Specify location of *inetd.conf* or *tlid.conf* file. These are files that **tcpdmatch** automatically uses in its evaluation of TCP wrapper files.

telinit

telinit [*option*] [*runlevel*]

Signal **init** to change the system's runlevel. **telinit** is actually just a link to **init**, the grandparent of all processes.

Option

-t *seconds*
        Send SIGKILL *seconds* after SIGTERM. Default is 20.

Runlevels

The default runlevels vary from distribution to distribution, but these are standard:

0   Halt the system.

1, s, S Single user.

6   Reboot the system.

a, b, c Process only entries in */etc/inittab* that are marked with run level a, b, or c.

q, Q   Reread */etc/inittab*.

Check the */etc/inittab* file for runlevels on your system.

telnetd

telnetd [*options*]

TCP/IP command. TELNET protocol server. **telnetd** is invoked by the Internet server for requests to connect to the TELNET port (port 23 by default). **telnetd** allocates a pseudo-terminal device for a client, thereby creating a login process that has the slave side of the pseudo-terminal serving as **stdin**, **stdout**, and **stderr**. **telnetd** manipulates the master side of the pseudo-terminal by implementing the TELNET protocol and by passing characters between the remote client and the login process.

Options

 -debug [*port*]

   Start **telnetd** manually instead of through **inetd**. *port* may be specified as an alternate TCP port number on which to run **telnetd**.

-D *modifier*(s)

   Debugging mode. This allows **telnet** to print out debugging information to the connection, enabling the user to see what **telnet** is doing. Several modifiers are available for the debugging mode:

exercise	Has not been implemented yet.
netdata	Display data stream received by **telnetd**.
options	Print information about the negotiation of the TELNET options.
ptydata	Display data written to the pseudo-terminal device.
report	Print **options** information, as well as some additional information about what processing is going on.

tftpd [*homedir*]

TCP/IP command. Trivial File Transfer Protocol server. **tftpd** is normally started by **inetd** and operates at the port indicated in the **tftp** Internet service description in the */etc/inetd.conf* file. By default, the entry for **tftpd** in */etc/inetd.conf* is commented out; the comment character must be deleted to make **tfptd** operational. Before responding to a request, the server attempts to change its current directory to *homedir*; the default value is **tftpboot**.

traceroute [*options*] *host* [*packetsize*]

TCP/IP command. Trace route taken by packets to reach network host. **traceroute** attempts tracing by launching UDP probe packets with a small TTL (time to live), then listening for an ICMP "time exceeded" reply from a gateway. *host* is the destination hostname or the IP number of host to reach. *packetsize* is the packet size in bytes of the probe datagram. Default is 38 bytes.

→

traceroute	**Options**
←	

-d Turn on socket-level debugging.

-g *addr*

Enable the IP LSRR (Loose Source Record Route) option in addition to the TTL tests, to ask how someone at IP address *addr* can reach a particular target.

-l Include the time-to-live value for each packet received.

-m *max_ttl*

Set maximum time-to-live used in outgoing probe packets to *max-ttl* hops. Default is 30 hops.

-n Print hop addresses numerically rather than symbolically.

-p *port*

Set base UDP port number used for probe packets to *port*. Default is (decimal) 33434.

-q *n* Set number of probe packets for each time-to-live setting to the value *n*. Default is three.

-r Bypass normal routing tables and send directly to a host on an attached network.

-s *src_addr*

Use *src_addr* as the IP address that will serve as the source address in outgoing probe packets.

-t *tos* Set the type-of-service in probe packets to *tos* (default zero). The value must be a decimal integer in the range 0 to 255.

-v Verbose—received ICMP packets (other than TIME_EXCEEDED and PORT_UNREACHABLE) will be listed.

-w *wait*

Set time to wait for a response to an outgoing probe packet to *wait* seconds (default is 3 seconds).

---

tune2fs	**tune2fs** [*options*] *device*

Tune the parameters of a Linux second extended filesystem by adjusting various parameters. You must specify the *device* on which the filesystem resides; it must not be mounted read/write when you change its parameters.

Options

-c *mount-counts*

Specify the maximum number of mount counts between two checks on the filesystem.

-e *behavior*

> Specify the kernel's behavior when encountering errors. *behavior* must be one of:
>
> **continue**   Continue as usual.
>
> **remount-ro** Remount the offending filesystem in read-only mode.
>
> **panic**   Cause a kernel panic.

-g *group*

> Allow *group* (a group ID or name) to use reserved blocks.

-i *interval* [d|w|m]

> Specify the maximum interval between filesystem checks. Units may be in days (**d**), weeks (**w**), or months (**m**). If *interval* is 0, checking will not be time-dependent.

-l   Display a list of the superblock's contents.

-m *percentage*

> Specify the percentage of blocks that will be reserved for use by privileged users.

-r *num*

> Specify the number of blocks that will be reserved for use by privileged users.

-u *user*

> Allow *user* (a user ID or name) to use reserved blocks.

---

tunelp *device* [*options*]

Control a line printer's device parameters. Without options, print information about device(s).

Options

-a [on|off]

> Specify whether or not to abort if the printer encounters an error. By default, do not abort.

-c *n*   Retry device *n* times if it refuses a character. (Default is 250.) After exhausting *n*, sleep before retrying.

-i *irq*   Use *irq* for specified parallel port. Ignore -t and -c. If 0, restore noninterrupt driven (polling) action.

-o [on|off]

> Specify whether to abort if device is not online or is out of paper.

-q [on|off]

> Specify whether to print current IRQ setting.

-r   Reset port.

→

tunelp
←
	-s Display printer's current status.
	-t *time*
	        Specify a delay of *time* in jiffies to sleep before resending a refused character to the device. A jiffy is defined as either one tick of the system clock or one AC cycle time; it should be approximately 1/100 of a second.
	-w *time*
	        Specify a delay of *time* in jiffies to sleep before resending a strobe signal.
	-C [on|off]
	        Specify whether to be extremely careful in checking for printer error.

umount	**umount** [*options*] [*special–device/directory*] Unmount a filesystem. **umount** announces to the system that the removable file structure previously mounted on device *special-device* is to be removed. **umount** also works by specifying the directory. Any pending I/O for the filesystem is completed, and the file structure is flagged as clean. *Options* -a Unmount all filesystems that are listed in */etc/mtab*. -n Unmount, but do not record changes in */etc/mtab*. -t *type* Unmount only filesystems of type *type*.
update	**update** [idletasks] Flush all pending output to the display, wait for the server to process that output and handle any pending events, then flush again. **update** will repeat this process until there are no pending events or when-idle handlers remaining. If the **idletasks** keyword is specified, then no new events or errors are processed; only the when-idle handlers are.
vidmode	**vidmode** [*option*] *image* [*mode* [*offset*]] Sets the video mode for a kernel *image*. If no arguments are specified, print current *mode* value. *mode* is a one-byte value located at offset 506 in a kernel image. You may change the *mode* by specifying the kernel *image* to change, the new *mode*, and the byte-offset at which to place the new information (the default is 506). Note that **rdev** -v is a synonym for **vidmode**. If **LILO** is used, **vidmode** is not needed. The video mode can be set from the **LILO** prompt during a boot.

Modes

-3	Prompt
-2	Extended VGA
-1	Normal VGA
0	Same as entering 0 at the prompt
1	Same as entering 1 at the prompt
2	Same as entering 2 at the prompt
3	Same as entering 3 at the prompt
n	Same as entering n at the prompt

Option

-o *offset* Same as specifying an *offset* as an argument.

---

w [*options*] [*users*]

Print summaries of system usage, currently logged-in users, and what they are doing. **w** is essentially a combination of **uptime**, **who**, and **ps -a**. Display output for one user by specifying *user.*

Options

-h	Suppress headings and **uptime** information.
-i	Sort by idle time.
-n	Suppress translation of IP addresses to names.

Files

/var/run/utmp
   List of users currently logged on.

---

wall [*file*]

Write to all users. **wall** reads a message from the standard input until an end-of-file. It then sends this message to all users currently logged in, preceded by Broadcast Message from . . . . If *file* is specified, read input from that, rather from standard input.

---

ypbind [*options*]

NFS/NIS command. NIS binder process. **ypbind** is a daemon process typically activated at system startup time. Its function is to remember information that lets client processes on a single node communicate with some **ypserv** process. The information **ypbind** remembers is called a *binding*—the association of a domain name with the Internet address of the NIS server and the port on that host at which the **ypserv** process is listening for service requests. This information is cached in the file */var/yp/bindings/domainname.version.*

$\rightarrow$

ypbind	**Options**
←	**-ypset** May be used to change the binding. This option is very dangerous and should only be used for debugging the network from a remote machine.
	-ypsetme
	ypset requests may be issued from this machine only. Security is based on IP address checking, which can be defeated on networks where untrusted individuals may inject packets. This option is not recommended.

ypcat	**ypcat** [*options*] *mname*
	NFS/NIS command. Print values in an NIS database specified by *mname*, which may be either a mapname or a map nickname.
	Options
	-d *domain*
	Specify *domain* other than default domain.
	-k Display keys for maps in which values are null or key is not part of value.
	-t Do not translate *mname* to mapname.
	-x Display map nickname table listing the nicknames (*mnames*) known, and mapname associated with each nickname. Do not require a *mname* argument.

ypinit	**ypinit** [*options*]
	NFS/NIS command. Build and install an NIS database on an NIS server. **ypinit** can be used to set up a master or a slave server or slave copier. Only a privileged user can run **ypinit**.
	Options
	-c *master_name*
	Set up a slave copier database. *master_name* should be the hostname of an NIS server, either the master server for all the maps or a server on which the database is up-to-date and stable.
	-m Indicates that the local host is to be the NIS server.
	-s *master_name*
	Set up a slave server database. *master_name* should be the hostname of an NIS server, either the master server for all the maps or a server on which the database is up-to-date and stable.

ypmatch [options] key . . . mname

NFS/NIS command. Print value of one or more *keys* from an NIS map specified by *mname*. *mname* may be either a map-name or a map nickname.

Options

-d *domain*
Specify *domain* other than default domain.

-k Before printing value of a key, print key itself, fol-lowed by a colon (:).

-t Do not translate nickname to mapname.

-x Display map nickname table listing the nicknames (*mnames*) known, and mapname associated with each nickname. Do not require an *mname* argu-ment.

yppasswd [name]

NFS/NIS command. Change login password in network infor-mation service. **yppasswd** prompts for the old password, then for the new one. New passwords must be at least four characters long if a combination of upper- and lowercase characters are used, six characters long if monocase.

rpc.yppasswdd [option]

NFS/NIS command. Server for modifying the NIS password file. **yppasswdd** handles password change requests from **yppasswd**. It changes a password entry only if the password represented by **yppasswd** matches the encrypted password of that entry, and if the user ID and group ID match those in the server's */etc/passwd* file. Then it updates */etc/passwd* and the password maps on the local server.

Option

-s Support shadow password functions.

yppoll [options] mapname

NFS/NIS command. Determine version of NIS map at NIS server. **yppoll** asks a **ypserv** process for the order number and the hostname of the master NIS server for the named map.

Options

-h *host*
Ask the **ypserv** process at *host* about the map parameters. If *host* is not specified, the hostname of

→

yppoll ←	the NIS server for the local host (the one returned by **ypwhich**) is used. **-d** *domain* Use *domain* instead of the default domain.

yppush	**yppush** [*options*] *mapnames*
	
	NFS/NIS command. Force propagation of changed NIS map. **yppush** copies a new version of a NIS map, *mapname*, from the master NIS server to the slave NIS servers. It first constructs a list of NIS server hosts by reading the NIS map **ypservers** with the **-d** option's *domain* argument. Keys within this map are the ASCII names of the machines on which the NIS servers run. A "transfer map" request is sent to the NIS server at each host, along with the information needed by the transfer agent to call back the **yppush**. When the attempt has been completed and the transfer agent has sent **yppush** a status message, the results may be printed to **stdout**. Normally invoked by */var/yp/Makefile*.
	
	Options
	  -d *domain*
	    Specify a *domain*.
	  -v Verbose—print message when each server is called and for each response.

ypserv	**ypserv** [*options*]
	
	NFS/NIS command. NIS server process. **ypserv** is a daemon process typically activated at system startup time. It runs only on NIS server machines with a complete NIS database. Its primary function is to look up information in its local database of NIS maps. The operations performed by **ypserv** are defined for the implementor by the NIS protocol specification, and for the programmer by the header file *<rpcvc/yp_prot.h>*. Communication to and from **ypserv** is by means of RPC calls.
	
	Options
	  -d NIS service should go to the DNS for more host information.
	  -localonly
	    Indicates **ypserv** should not respond to outside requests.
	
	Files and directories
	  /var/yp/[domainname]/
	    Location of NIS databases.

/var/yp/Makefile
>   Makefile that is responsible for creating yp data-
>   bases.

ypserv

---

ypset [*options*] *server*

ypset

NFS/NIS command. Point **ypbind** at a particular server. **ypset**
tells **ypbind** to get NIS services for the specified domain
from the **ypserv** process running on *server. server* indicates
the NIS server to bind to and can be specified as a name or
an IP address.

Options

-d *domain*
>   Use *domain* instead of the default domain.

-h *host*
>   Set **ypbind**'s binding on *host*, instead of locally. *host*
>   can be specified as a name or an IP address.

---

ypwhich [*options*] [*host*]

ypwhich

NFS/NIS command. Return hostname of NIS server or map
master. Without arguments, **ypwhich** cites the NIS server for
the local machine. If *host* is specified, that machine is
queried to find out which NIS master it is using.

Options

-d *domain*
>   Use *domain* instead of the default domain.

-m *map*
>   Find master NIS server for a map. No host can be
>   specified with -**m**. *map* may be a mapname or a
>   nickname for a map.

-t *mapname*
>   Inhibit nickname translation.

-x Display map nickname table. Do not allow any
>   other options.

---

ypxfr [*options*] *mapname*

ypxfr

NFS/NIS command. Transfer an NIS map from the server to
the local host by making use of normal NIS services. **ypxfr**
creates a temporary map in the directory */etc/yp/domain*
(where *domain* is the default domain for the local host),
fills it by enumerating the map's entries, and fetches the
map parameters and loads them. If run interactively, **ypxfr**
writes its output to the terminal. However, if it is invoked
without a controlling terminal, and if the log file
/usr/admin/nislog exists, it appends all its output to that file.

→

ypxfr

←

Options

-b Preserve the resolver flag in the map during the transfer.

-C *tid prog ipadd port*

This option is only for use by **ypserv**. When **ypserv** invokes **ypxfr**, it specifies that **ypxfr** should call back a **yppush** process at the host with IP address *ipaddr*, registered as program number *prog*, listening on port *port*, and waiting for a response to transaction *tid*.

-c Do not send a "Clear current map" request to the local **ypserv** process.

-d *domain*

Specify a domain other than the default domain.

-f Force the transfer to occur even if the version at the master is older than the local version.

-h *host*

Get the map from *host*, regardless of what the map says the master is. If host is not specified, **ypxfr** asks the NIS service for the name of the master, and tries to get the map from there. *host* may be a name or an internet address in the form *h.h.h.h*.

-S Only use NIS servers running as **root** and using a reserved port.

-s *domain*

Specify a source *domain* from which to transfer a map that should be the same across domains (such as the *services.byname* map).

---

zdump

zdump [*options*] [*zones*]

Dump a list of all known time zones, or, if an argument is provided, a specific zone or list of zones. Include each zone's current time with its name.

Options

-c *year*

Specify a cutoff year to limit verbose output. Meaningful only with -**v**.

-v Verbose mode. Include additional information about each zone.

---

zic

zic [*options*] [*files*]

Create time conversion information files from the file or files specified. If the specified file is –, read information from standard input.

-d *directory*

　　Place the newly created files in *directory*. Default is
　　/usr/local/etc/zoneinfo.

-l *timezone*

　　Specify a *timezone* to use for local time. **zic** links
　　the zone information for *timezone* with the zone
　　localtime.

-p *timezone*

　　Set the default rules for handling POSIX-format envi-
　　ronment variables to the zone name specified by
　　timezone.

-s　Store time values only if they are the same when
　　signed as when unsigned.

-v　Verbose mode. Include extra error checking and
　　warnings.

-y *command*

　　Check year types with *command*. Default is **yearis-**
　　type.

-L *file*

　　Consult *file* for information about leap seconds.

The source file(s) for **zic** should be formatted as a sequence
of rule lines, zone lines, and link lines. An optional file
containing leap second rules can be specified on the command line. Rule lines describe how time should be calcu-
lated. They describe changes in time, daylight savings time,
war time, and any other changes that might affect a particular time zone. Zone lines specify which rules apply to a
given zone. Link lines link similar zones together. Leap
lines describe the exact time when leap seconds should be
added or subtracted. Each of these lines are made up of
fields. Fields are separated from one another by any number of white space characters. Comment lines are preceded
by a #. The fields used in each line are listed below.

Rule Line Fields

　　Rule *NAME FROM TO TYPE IN ON AT SAVE LETTERS*

　　NAME

　　　　Name this set of rules.

　　FROM

　　　　Specify the first year to which this rule applies. Gre-
　　　　gorian calendar dates are assumed. Instead of
　　　　specifying an actual year, you may specify *mini-*
　　　　mum or *maximum* for the minimum or maximum
　　　　year representable as an integer.

　　TO　Specify the last year to which this rule applies. Syn-
　　　　tax is the same as for the FROM field.

TYPE

Specify the type of year to which this rule should be applied. The wildcard - instructs that all years be included. Any given year's type will be checked with the command given with the -y option, or the default **yearistype** *year type*. An exit status of 0 is taken to mean the year is of the given type, an exit status of 1 means that it is not of the given type (see -y option).

IN Specify month in which this rule should be applied.

ON Specify day in which this rule should be applied. Whitespace is not allowed. For example:

1 The 1st

firstSun The first Sunday

Sun>=3 The first Sunday to occur before or on the 3rd

AT Specify the time after which the rule is in effect. For example, you may use **13**, **13:00**, or **13:00:00** for one o'clock pm. You may include one of several suffixes (without whitespace between):

s Local standard time.

u, g, z Universal time.

w Wall clock time (default).

SAVE

Add this amount of time to the local standard time. Formatted like AT, without suffixes.

LETTERS

Specify letter or letters to be used in time zone abbreviations (for example, S for EST). For no abbreviation, enter –.

Zone line fields

Zone *NAME GMTOFF RULES/SAVE FORMAT* [*UNTIL*]

NAME

Time zone name.

GMTOFF

The amount of hours by which this time zone differs from GMT. Formatted like AT. Negative times are subtracted from GMT; by default, times are added to it.

RULES/SAVE

Either the name of the rule to apply to this zone, or the amount of time to add to local standard time. To make the zone the same as local standard time, specify -.

How to format time zone abbreviations. Specify the variable part with %s.

UNTIL

Change the rule for the zone at this date. The next line must specify the new zone information, and therefore must omit the string "Zone" and the NAME field.

Link line fields

Link LINK-FROM LINK-TO

LINK-FROM

The name of the zone that is being linked.

LINK-TO

An alternate name for the zone which was specified as LINK-FROM.

Leap Line Fields

Leap *YEAR MONTH DAY HH:MM:SS CORR R/S*

YEAR MONTH DAY HH:MM:SS

Specify when the leap second happened.

CORR

Uses a "+" or a "-" to show whether the second was added or skipped.

R/S An abbreviation of Rolling or Stationary to describe whether the leap second should be applied to local wall clock time, or to GMT.

Sys Admin Commands

Index

text
  breaking lines, 46
  checking spelling, 61
  files (see files)
  whitespace (see whitespace)
TFTP (Trivial File Transfer Protocol),
    111
tftpd daemon, 397
time and date
  calendar, 14
  current, 27
  notifying server of change, 373
  scheduling command execution, 8
  setting system, 363
  time conversion files, 406
  time zones, 406
  uptime command, 116
  waiting for, 95
time command (csh/tcsh), 198
time variable (csh/tcsh), 172
tload command, 112
tolower command (gawk), 272
top command, 112
toupper command (gawk), 272
tr command, 113
traceroute command (TCP/IP), 397
transferring files, 48–53, 111
transposing text, Emacs commands
    for, 213
Trivial File Transfer Protocol (TFTP),
    111, 397
troubleshooting
  Emacs editor, 209
  TCP/IP, 319
true command, 114
tune2fs command, 398
tunelp command, 399

U

uid (see users)
ul command, 114
umask command (csh/tcsh), 199
umount command, 400
unabbreviate command (ex), 246
unalias command (csh/tcsh), 199
uncomplete command (tcsh), 199
uncompressing (see compression, file)
underscores/underlining, 114
undo command (ex), 246
undoing, Emacs commands for, 212
unexpand command, 115

unhash command (csh/tcsh), 199
uniq command, 115
UNIX, 2
unlimit command (csh/tcsh), 199
unloading modules, 378
unmap command (ex), 246
unmounting filesystems, 400
unset command (csh/tcsh), 199
unseten command (csh/tcsh), 183
unsettenv command (csh/tcsh), 199
update command, 400
UPS (Uninterruptible Power Supply),
    370
uptime command, 116
usernames, 71
users
  administration commands for, 313
  changing group identification of, 84
  creating, 323
  finger command, 45
  getting information about, 60, 118
  listing, 93, 116
  logging in, 71, 90
  NIS accounts, 322
  notifying of incoming mail, 14
  sending messages to, 382
  on specific host, listing, 382
  su command, 101
  talking to, 103, 391
  user ID, 119
  writing to, 93, 119, 401
users command, 116
/usr/lib/magic file, 40

V

v command (ex), 246
variables
  bash shell and, 138–141
  csh and tcsh, 166–174
  environment (see environment
      variables)
  gawk scripting language, 265–266
  shell (see shell variables)
verbose variable (csh/tcsh), 172
version command (ex), 247
version variable (csh/tcsh), 172
vi editor, 116, 225–238
  metacharacters for, 204
  setting up, 234–238
vi mode (csh/tcsh), 181
vidmode command, 400

About the Author

Jessica Perry Hekman lives in Somerville, Massachusetts, with rotating roommates, two gorgeous cats, and hundreds of books. She works for O'Reilly & Associates as an online developer; in the past, she has functioned for them as an assistant production editor, a system administrator, and a staff author. She graduated *magna cum laude* from Harvard University in 1995 with a concentration in the history and literature of the Middle Ages, specifically that of Wales and France. Her favorite color is green; her favorite author is Ursula K. LeGuin; and her hero is J. Michael Straczynski.

Colophon

Our look is the result of reader comments, our own experimentation, and feedback from distribution channels. Distinctive covers complement our distinctive approach to technical topics, breathing personality and life into potentially dry subjects.

The animal featured on the cover of *Linux in a Nutshell* is an Arabian horse. Known for its grace and intelligence, the Arabian is one of the oldest breeds of horse, with evidence of its existence dating back 5000 years. The Arabian was very instrumental as an ancestor to other popular breeds, most notably the Thoroughbred in the 17th and 18th centuries. Possibly one of the more characteristic horse breeds, the typical Arabian has large expressive eyes and nostrils, small ears, and a short, sturdy back. Its stamina suits it particularly well for endurance riding, where the breed dominates the sport. Its wonderful temperament makes the Arabian an all-around favorite riding horse in North America, though it also can be found in more specialized competitions such as dressage, jumping, and reining.

Edie Freedman designed the cover of this book, using a 19th-century engraving from the Dover Pictorial Archive. The cover layout was produced with Quark XPress 3.3, using the ITC Garamond font. Whenever possible, our books use RepKover™, a durable and flexible lay-flat binding. If the page count exceeds RepKover's limit, perfect binding is used.

The fonts used in the book are Garamond and Garamond book. Text was prepared using the troff text formatter. Figures were created by Chris Reilley in Macromedia Freehand 5.0 and Adobe Photoshop. This colophon was written by Nicole Gipson Arigo.

More Titles from O'Reilly

Linux

Linux in a Nutshell

By Jessica P. Hekman &
the Staff of O'Reilly & Associates
1st Edition January 1997
438 pages, ISBN 1-56592-167-4

Linux in a Nutshell covers the core commands available on common Linux distributions. This isn't a scaled-down quick reference of common commands, but a complete reference containing all user, programming, administration, and networking commands. Also documents a wide range of GNU tools.

Linux Multimedia Guide

By Jeff Tranter
1st Edition September 1996
386 pages, ISBN 1-56592-219-0

Linux is increasingly popular among computer enthusiasts of all types, and one of the applications where it is flourishing is multimedia. This book tells you how to program such popular devices as sound cards, CD-ROMs, and joysticks. It also describes the best free software packages that support manipulation of graphics, audio, and video and offers guidance on fitting the pieces together.

Running Linux, 2nd Edition

By Matt Welsh & Lar Kaufman
2nd Edition August 1996
650 pages, ISBN 1-56592-151-8

Linux is the most exciting development today in the UNIX world— and some would say in the world of the PC-compatible. A complete, UNIX-compatible operating system developed by volunteers on the Internet, Linux is distributed freely in electronic form and for low cost from many vendors. This second edition of Running Linux covers everything you need to understand, install, and start using your Linux system, including a comprehensive installation tutorial, complete information on system maintenance, tools for document development and programming, and guidelines for network and web site administration.

Linux Network Administrator's Guide

By Olaf Kirch
1st Edition January 1995
370 pages, ISBN 1-56592-087-2

One of the most successful books to come from the Linux Documentation Project is the Linux Network Administrator's Guide. It touches on all the essential networking software included with Linux, plus some hardware considerations. Topics include serial connections, UUCP, routing and DNS, mail and News, SLIP and PPP, NFS, and NIS.

Linux Device Drivers

By Alessandro Rubini
1st Edition November 1997 (est.)
300 pages (est.), ISBN 1-56592-292-1

Linux Device Drivers is for anyone who wants to support computer peripherals under the Linux operating system or who wants to develop new hardware and run it under Linux. This practical guide shows how to write a driver for a wide range of devices, revealing information previously passed by word-of-mouth or in cryptic source code comments.

You don't have to be a kernel hacker to understand and use this book; all you need is a knowledge of C and some background in UNIX system calls. It describes step-by-step how to write a driver for character devices, block devices, and network interfaces, illustrated with full-featured examples that show driver design issues, which you can compile and run without special hardware. For those curious about how an operating system does its job, this book provides insights into address spaces, asynchronous events, and I/O. The book is centered on version 2.0, but also covers 1.2.13 and experimental versions up to 2.1.44. Also discusses how to maximize portability among hardware platforms.

Developing Web Content

WebMaster in a Nutshell, Deluxe Edition

By O'Reilly & Associates, Inc.
1st Edition September 1997 (est.)
356 pages (est.), includes CD-ROM
ISBN 1-56592-305-7

The Deluxe Edition of *WebMaster in a Nutshell* is a complete library for web programmers. The main resource is the Web Developer's Library, a CD-ROM, containing the electronic text of five popular O'Reilly titles: *HTML: The Definitive Guide, 2nd Edition*; *JavaScript: The Definitive Guide, 2nd Edition*; *CGI Programming on the World Wide Web*; *Programming Perl, 2nd Edition*—the classic "camel book," written by Larry Wall (the inventor of Perl) with Tom Christiansen and Randal Schwartz; and *WebMaster in a Nutshell*. The Deluxe Edition also includes a printed copy of *WebMaster in a Nutshell*.

WebMaster in a Nutshell, Deluxe Edition, makes it easy to find the information you need with all of the convenience you'd expect from the Web. You'll have access to information webmasters and programmers use most for development—complete with global searching and a master index to all five volumes—all on a single CD-ROM. It's incredibly portable. Just slip it into your laptop case as you commute or take off on your next trip and you'll find everything at your fingertips with no books to carry.

The CD-ROM is readable on all hardware platforms. All files except Java code example files are in 8.3 file format and, therefore, are readable by older systems. A web browser that supports HTML 3.2 (such as Netscape 3.0 or Internet Explorer 3.0) is required to view the text. The browser must support Java if searching is desired.

The Web Developer's Library is also available by subscription on the World Wide Web. See http://www.ora.com/catalog/webrlw for details.

WebMaster in a Nutshell

By Stephen Spainhour &
Valerie Quercia
1st Edition October 1996
374 pages, ISBN 1-56592-229-8

Web content providers and administrators have many sources for information, both in print and online. *WebMaster in a Nutshell* puts it all together in one slim volume for easy desktop access. This quick reference covers HTML, CGI, JavaScript, Perl, HTTP, and server configuration.

HTML: The Definitive Guide, 2nd Edition

By Chuck Musciano & Bill Kennedy
2nd Edition May 1997
552 pages, ISBN 1-56592-235-2

This complete guide is chock full of examples, sample code, and practical, hands-on advice to help you create truly effective web pages and master advanced features. Learn how to insert images and other multimedia elements, create useful links and searchable documents, use Netscape extensions, design great forms, and lots more. The second edition covers the most up-to-date version of the HTML standard (HTML version 3.2), Netscape 4.0 and Internet Explorer 3.0, plus all the common extensions.

JavaScript: The Definitive Guide, 2nd Edition

By David Flanagan
2nd Edition January 1997
664 pages, ISBN 1-56592-234-4

This second edition of the definitive reference guide to JavaScript, the HTML extension that gives web pages programming-language capabilities, covers JavaScript as it is used in Netscape 3.0 and 2.0 and in Microsoft Internet Explorer 3.0. Learn how JavaScript really works (and when it doesn't). Use JavaScript to control web browser behavior, add dynamically created text to web pages, interact with users through HTML forms, and even control and interact with Java applets and Navigator plug-ins. By the author of the bestselling *Java in a Nutshell*.

O'REILLY™

TO ORDER: **800-998-9938** • **order@oreilly.com** • **http://www.oreilly.com/**
OUR PRODUCTS ARE AVAILABLE AT A BOOKSTORE OR SOFTWARE STORE NEAR YOU.
FOR INFORMATION: **800-998-9938** • **707-829-0515** • **info@oreilly.com**

Developing Web Content *continued*

GI Programming on the World Wide Web

By Shishir Gundavaram
1st Edition March 1996
450 pages, ISBN: 1-56592-168-2

This book offers a comprehensive explanation of CGI and related techniques for people who hold on to the dream of providing their own information servers on the Web. It starts at the beginning, explaining the value of CGI and how it works, then moves swiftly into the subtle details of programming.

Information Architecture for the World Wide Web

By Louis Rosenfeld & Peter Morville
1st Edition November 1997 (est.)
200 pages (est.), ISBN 1-56592-282-4

Information Architecture for the World Wide Web is about applying the principles of architecture and library science to web site design. With this book, you learn how to design web sites and intranets that support growth, management, and ease of use. This book is for webmasters, designers, and anyone else involved in building a web site.

Learning VBScript

By Paul Lomax
1st Edition July 1997
616 pages, includes CD-ROM
ISBN 1-56592-247-6

This definitive guide shows web developers how to take full advantage of client-side scripting with the VBScript language. In addition to basic language features, it covers the Internet Explorer object model and discusses techniques for client-side scripting, like adding ActiveX controls to a web page or validating data before sending it to the server. Includes CD-ROM with over 170 code samples.

Web Client Programming with Perl

By Clinton Wong
1st Edition March 1997
228 pages, ISBN 1-56592-214-X

Web Client Programming with Perl shows you how to extend scripting skills to the Web. This book teaches you the basics of how browsers communicate with servers and how to write your own customized web clients to automate common tasks. It is intended for those who are motivated to develop software that offers a more flexible and dynamic response than a standard web browser.

Building Your Own WebSite

By Susan B. Peck & Stephen Arrants
1st Edition July 1996
514 pages, ISBN 1-56592-232-8

This is a hands-on reference for Windows® 95 and Windows NT™ users who want to host a site on the Web or on a corporate intranet. This step-by-step guide will have you creating live web pages in minutes. You'll also learn how to connect your web to information in other Windows applications, such as word processing documents and databases. The book is packed with examples and tutorials on every aspect of web management, and it includes the highly acclaimed WebSite™ 1.1 server software on CD-ROM.

Designing for the Web: Getting Started in a New Medium

By Jennifer Niederst
with Edie Freedman
1st Edition April 1996
180 pages, ISBN 1-56592-165-8

Designing for the Web gives you the basics you need to hit the ground running. Although geared toward designers, it covers information and techniques useful to anyone who wants to put graphics online. It explains how to work with HTML documents from a designer's point of view, outlines special problems with presenting information online, and walks through incorporating images into web pages, with emphasis on resolution and improving efficiency.

How to stay in touch with O'Reilly

1. Visit Our Award-Winning Site

http://www.oreilly.com/

★"Top 100 Sites on the Web" —*PC Magazine*
★"Top 5% Web sites" —*Point Communications*
★"3-Star site" —*The McKinley Group*

Our web site contains a library of comprehensive product information (including book excerpts and tables of contents), downloadable software, background articles, interviews with technology leaders, links to relevant sites, book cover art, and more. File us in your Bookmarks or Hotlist!

2. Join Our Email Mailing Lists

New Product Releases

To receive automatic email with brief descriptions of all new O'Reilly products as they are released, send email to:
listproc@online.oreilly.com
Put the following information in the first line of your message (*not* in the Subject field):
subscribe oreilly-news "Your Name" of "Your Organization" (for example: subscribe oreilly-news Kris Webber of Fine Enterprises)

O'Reilly Events

If you'd also like us to send information about trade show events, special promotions, and other O'Reilly events, send email to:
listproc@online.oreilly.com
Put the following information in the first line of your message (*not* in the Subject field):
subscribe oreilly-events "Your Name" of "Your Organization"

3. Get Examples from Our Books via FTP

There are two ways to access an archive of example files from our books:

Regular FTP
- ftp to:
  ftp.oreilly.com
  (login: anonymous
  password: your email address)
- Point your web browser to:
  ftp://ftp.oreilly.com/

FTPMAIL
- Send an email message to:
  ftpmail@online.oreilly.com
  (Write "help" in the message body)

4. Visit Our Gopher Site
- Connect your gopher to:
  gopher.oreilly.com

- Point your web browser to:
  gopher://gopher.oreilly.com/

- Telnet to:
  gopher.oreilly.com
  login: gopher

5. Contact Us via Email

order@oreilly.com
To place a book or software order online. Good for North American and international customers.

subscriptions@oreilly.com
To place an order for any of our newsletters or periodicals.

books@oreilly.com
General questions about any of our books.

software@oreilly.com
For general questions and product information about our software. Check out O'Reilly Software Online at **http://software.oreilly.com/** for software and technical support information. Registered O'Reilly software users send your questions to:
website-support@oreilly.com

cs@oreilly.com
For answers to problems regarding your order or our products.

booktech@oreilly.com
For book content technical questions or corrections.

proposals@oreilly.com
To submit new book or software proposals to our editors and product managers.

international@oreilly.com
For information about our international distributors or translation queries. For a list of our distributors outside of North America check out:
http://www.oreilly.com/www/order/country.html

O'Reilly & Associates, Inc.
101 Morris Street, Sebastopol, CA 95472 USA
TEL   707-829-0515 or 800-998-9938
       (6am to 5pm PST)
FAX   707-829-0104

O'REILLY™

Titles from O'Reilly

Please note that upcoming titles are displayed in italic.

WEB PROGRAMMING
Apache: The Definitive Guide
Building Your Own Web
  Conferences
Building Your Own Website
Building Your Own Win-CGI
  Programs
CGI Programming for the World
  Wide Web
Designing for the Web
HTML: The Definitive Guide
JavaScript: The Definitive Guide,
  2nd Ed.
Learning Perl
Programming Perl, 2nd Ed.
Mastering Regular Expressions
WebMaster in a Nutshell
Web Security & Commerce
*Web Client Programming with
  Perl*
World Wide Web Journal

USING THE INTERNET
Smileys
The Future Does Not Compute
The Whole Internet User's Guide
  & Catalog
The Whole Internet for Win 95
Using Email Effectively
Bandits on the Information
  Superhighway

JAVA SERIES
Exploring Java
Java AWT Reference
Java Fundamental Classes
  Reference
Java in a Nutshell
Java Language Reference
Java Network Programming
Java Threads
Java Virtual Machine

SOFTWARE
WebSite™ 1.1
WebSite Professional™
Building Your Own Web
  Conferences
WebBoard™
PolyForm™
Statisphere™

SONGLINE GUIDES
NetActivism   NetResearch
Net Law   NetSuccess
NetLearning   NetTravel
Net Lessons

SYSTEM ADMINISTRATION
Building Internet Firewalls
Computer Crime: A Crimefighter's
  Handbook
Computer Security Basics
DNS and BIND, 2nd Ed.
Essential System Administration,
  2nd Ed.
Getting Connected: The Internet
  at 56K and Up
*Internet Server Administration
  with Windows NT*
Linux Network Administrator's
  Guide
Managing Internet Information
  Services
Managing NFS and NIS
Networking Personal Computers
  with TCP/IP
Practical UNIX & Internet
  Security. 2nd Ed.
PGP: Pretty Good Privacy
sendmail, 2nd Ed.
sendmail Desktop Reference
System Performance Tuning
TCP/IP Network Administration
termcap & terminfo
Using & Managing UUCP
Volume 8: X Window System
  Administrator's Guide
Web Security & Commerce

UNIX
Exploring Expect
Learning VBScript
Learning GNU Emacs, 2nd Ed.
Learning the bash Shell
Learning the Korn Shell
Learning the UNIX Operating
  System
Learning the vi Editor
Linux in a Nutshell
Making TeX Work
Linux Multimedia Guide
Running Linux, 2nd Ed.
SCO UNIX in a Nutshell
sed & awk, 2nd Edition
Tcl/Tk Tools
UNIX in a Nutshell: System V
  Edition
UNIX Power Tools
Using csh & tsch
When You Can't Find Your UNIX
  System Administrator
Writing GNU Emacs Extensions

WEB REVIEW STUDIO SERIES
Gif Animation Studio
Shockwave Studio

WINDOWS
Dictionary of PC Hardware and
  Data Communications Terms
Inside the Windows 95 Registry
Inside the Windows 95 File
  System
Windows Annoyances
*Windows NT File System
  Internals*
Windows NT in a Nutshell

PROGRAMMING
Advanced Oracle PL/SQL
  Programming
Applying RCS and SCCS
C++: The Core Language
Checking C Programs with lint
DCE Security Programming
Distributing Applications Across
  DCE & Windows NT
Encyclopedia of Graphics File
  Formats, 2nd Ed.
Guide to Writing DCE
  Applications
lex & yacc
Managing Projects with make
Mastering Oracle Power Objects
Oracle Design: The Definitive
  Guide
Oracle Performance Tuning, 2nd
  Ed.
Oracle PL/SQL Programming
Porting UNIX Software
POSIX Programmer's Guide
POSIX.4: Programming for the
  Real World
Power Programming with RPC
Practical C Programming
Practical C++ Programming
Programming Python
Programming with curses
Programming with GNU Software
Pthreads Programming
Software Portability with imake,
  2nd Ed.
Understanding DCE
Understanding Japanese
  Information Processing
UNIX Systems Programming for
  SVR4

BERKELEY 4.4 SOFTWARE
  DISTRIBUTION
4.4BSD System Manager's Manual
4.4BSD User's Reference Manual
4.4BSD User's Supplementary
  Documents
4.4BSD Programmer's Reference
  Manual
4.4BSD Programmer's
  Supplementary Documents
X Programming
Vol. 0: X Protocol Reference
  Manual
Vol. 1: Xlib Programming Manual
Vol. 2: Xlib Reference Manual
Vol. 3M: X Window System User's
  Guide, Motif Edition
Vol. 4M: X Toolkit Intrinsics
  Programming Manual, Motif
  Edition
Vol. 5: X Toolkit Intrinsics
  Reference Manual
Vol. 6A: Motif Programming
  Manual
Vol. 6B: Motif Reference Manual
Vol. 6C: Motif Tools
Vol. 8 : X Window System
  Administrator's Guide
Programmer's Supplement for
  Release 6
X User Tools
The X Window System in a
  Nutshell

CAREER & BUSINESS
Building a Successful Software
  Business
The Computer User's Survival
  Guide
Love Your Job!
Electronic Publishing on CD-ROM

TRAVEL
Travelers' Tales: Brazil
Travelers' Tales: Food
Travelers' Tales: France
Travelers' Tales: Gutsy Women
Travelers' Tales: India
Travelers' Tales: Mexico
Travelers' Tales: Paris
Travelers' Tales: San Francisco
Travelers' Tales: Spain
Travelers' Tales: Thailand
Travelers' Tales: A Woman's
  World

O'REILLY™

TO ORDER: **800-998-9938** • **order@oreilly.com** • **http://www.oreilly.com/**
OUR PRODUCTS ARE AVAILABLE AT A BOOKSTORE OR SOFTWARE STORE NEAR YOU.
FOR INFORMATION: **800-998-9938** • **707-829-0515** • **info@oreilly.com**

International Distributors

UK, Europe, Middle East and Northern Africa (except France, Germany, Switzerland, & Austria)

INQUIRIES
International Thomson Publishing Europe
Berkshire House
168-173 High Holborn
London WC1V 7AA, UK
Tel: 44-171-497-1422
Fax: 44-171-497-1426
Email: itpint@itps.co.uk

ORDERS
International Thomson Publishing Services, Ltd.
Cheriton House, North Way
Andover, Hampshire SP10 5BE,
United Kingdom
Tel: 44-264-342-832 (UK)
Tel: 44-264-342-806
  (outside UK)
Fax: 44-264-364418 (UK)
Fax: 44-264-342761 (outside UK)
UK & Eire orders:
itpuk@itps.co.uk
International orders:
itpint@itps.co.uk

France

Editions Eyrolles
61 bd Saint-Germain
75240 Paris Cedex 05
France
Fax: 33-01-44-41-11-44

FRENCH LANGUAGE BOOKS
All countries except Canada
Tel: 33-01-44-41-46-16
Email: geodif@eyrolles.com

ENGLISH LANGUAGE BOOKS
Tel: 33-01-44-41-11-87
Email: distribution@eyrolles.com

Australia

WoodsLane Pty. Ltd.
7/5 Vuko Place, Warriewood NSW 2102
P.O. Box 935,
Mona Vale NSW 2103
Australia
Tel: 61-2-9970-5111
Fax: 61-2-9970-5002
Email: info@woodslane.com.au

Germany, Switzerland, and Austria

INQUIRIES
O'Reilly Verlag
Balthasarstr. 81
D-50670 Köln
Germany
Tel: 49-221-97-31-60-0
Fax: 49-221-97-31-60-8
Email: anfragen@oreilly.de

ORDERS
International Thomson Publishing
Königswinterer Straße 418
53227 Bonn, Germany
Tel: 49-228-97024 0
Fax: 49-228-441342
Email: order@oreilly.de

Asia (except Japan & India)

INQUIRIES
International Thomson Publishing Asia
60 Albert Street #15-01
Albert Complex
Singapore 189969
Tel: 65-336-6411
Fax: 65-336-7411

ORDERS
Telephone: 65-336-6411
Fax: 65-334-1617
thomson@signet.com.sg

New Zealand

WoodsLane New Zealand Ltd.
21 Cooks Street (P.O. Box 575)
Wanganui, New Zealand
Tel: 64-6-347-6543
Fax: 64-6-345-4840
Email: info@woodslane.com.au

Japan

O'Reilly Japan, Inc.
Kiyoshige Building 2F
12-Banchi, Sanei-cho
Shinjuku-ku
Tokyo 160 Japan
Tel: 81-3-3356-5227
Fax: 81-3-3356-5261
Email: kenji@oreilly.com

India

Computer Bookshop (India) PVT. LTD.
190 Dr. D.N. Road, Fort
Bombay 400 001 India
Tel: 91-22-207-0989
Fax: 91-22-262-3551
Email:
cbsbom@giasbm01.vsnl.net.in

The Americas

O'Reilly & Associates, Inc.
101 Morris Street
Sebastopol, CA 95472 U.S.A.
Tel: 707-829-0515
Tel: 800-998-9938 (U.S. & Canada)
Fax: 707-829-0104
Email: order@oreilly.com

Southern Africa

International Thomson Publishing Southern Africa
Building 18, Constantia Park
138 Sixteenth Road
P.O. Box 2459
Halfway House, 1685 South Africa
Tel: 27-11-805-4819
Fax: 27-11-805-3648

O'REILLY™